CONTESTED SPACES OF NOBILITY
IN EARLY MODERN EUROPE

Contested Spaces of Nobility in Early Modern Europe

Edited by

MATTHEW P. ROMANIELLO
University of Hawai'i at Manoa, USA

CHARLES LIPP
University of West Georgia, USA

Routledge
Taylor & Francis Group

LONDON AND NEW YORK

First published 2011 by Ashgate Publishing

Published 2016 by Routledge
2 Park Square, Milton Park, Abingdon, Oxon OX14 4RN
711 Third Avenue, New York, NY 10017, USA

Routledge is an imprint of the Taylor & Francis Group, an informa business

Copyright © Matthew P. Romaniello and Charles Lipp 2011

Matthew P. Romaniello and Charles Lipp have asserted their right under the Copyright, Designs and Patents Act, 1988, to be identified as the editors of this work.

British Library Cataloguing in Publication Data
Contested spaces of nobility in early modern Europe.
   1. Nobility--Europe--History--16th century.
   2. Nobility--Europe--History--17th century.
   3. Nobility--Europe--History--18th century. 4. Europe--
Court and courtiers--History. 5. Europe--Social
conditions--16th century. 6. Europe--Social conditions--
17th century. 7. Europe--Social conditions--18th century.
   8. Europe--History--1517-1648. 9. Europe--History--
1648-1789.
   I. Romaniello, Matthew P. II. Lipp, Charles.
   305.5'22'094'0903-dc22

Library of Congress Cataloging-in-Publication Data
Romaniello, Matthew P.
   Contested spaces of nobility in early modern Europe / Matthew P. Romaniello and Charles Lipp.
      p. cm.
   Includes bibliographical references and index.
   ISBN 978-1-4094-0551-1 (hardcover) 1. Nobility--Europe-
-History. 2. Spatial behavior--Europe--History. 3. Self-protective behavior--Social aspects--Europe--
History. 4. Contests--Social aspects--Europe--History. 5. Power (Social sciences)--Europe--History.
6. Dominance (Psychology)--Europe--History. 7. Social change--Europe--History. 8. Europe--Social
conditions--16th century. 9. Europe--Social conditions--17th century. 10. Europe--Social conditions-
-18th century. I. Lipp, Charles. II. Title.
   HT653.E9R66 2010
   305.5'22094--dc22
                                                                                     2010033257

ISBN 978 1 4094 0551 1 (hbk)

Contents

List of Figures and Tables

Figures

Tables

Notes on Contributors

Erica Bastress-Dukehart is Associate Professor of History at Skidmore College in Saratoga Springs, New York. She is the author of *The Zimmern Chronicle: Nobility, Memory, and Self-Representation in Sixteenth-Century Germany* (2002), and is completing a monograph on family rivalries in Europe and the New World.

Grace E. Coolidge is Associate Professor of History at Grand Valley State University in Allendale, Michigan. She is the author of *Gender, Guardianship, and the Nobility in Early Modern Spain*, and has published articles in *The Journal of Family History* and *Sixteenth Century Journal*.

Sukanya Dasgupta is Reader in the Department of English of Loreto College of the University of Calcutta. She has published articles concerning both early modern English literature and Renaissance art and iconography, and co-edited *The Word and the World* (2008).

Ryan Gaston is a PhD candidate in History at the University of Kansas. He is currently completing his dissertation, titled "Kith and Kin: Family, Gender, and the Conservation of the Spanish Monarchy in the Early Seventeenth Century," which studies the relationship between gender, family, and the era's political reforms.

Susannah Humble Ferreira is Assistant Professor of History at the University of Guelph in Ontario. She has published articles in *Portuguese Studies Review* and *Itinerario*, and is completing her monograph on the royal court of Manuel I (1495–1521).

Elie Haddad is currently Chargé de recherches at the Centre de Recherches Historiques (CNRS/EHESS) in Paris. He is the author of *Fondation et ruine d'une "maison". Histoire sociale des comtes de Belin (1582–1706)* (2009) and of several articles, including a recent publication in *French Historical Studies*.

Charles Lipp is Assistant Professor of History at the University of West Georgia in Carrollton. He is the author of the forthcoming monograph, *A Portrait of Small-State Nobility: The Family de Mahuet of Lorraine, 1599–1737,* and several articles. He has begun working on a new project on alternative political realities in early modern Europe.

Jerzy Lukowski is Reader in Polish History at the University of Birmingham in the United Kingdom. He is the author of several books, including *Disorderly Liberty: The Political Culture of the Polish-Lithuanian Commonwealth in the Eighteenth Century* (2010), *The Eighteenth-Century European Nobility* (2003), *A Concise History of Poland* (2001) with W.H. Zawadski, and *The Partitions of Poland: 1772, 1793, 1795* (1999).

Mathieu Marraud is Ingénieur d'études at the Centre de Recherches Historiques (CNRS/EHESS) in Paris. He is the author of *La bourgeoisie parisienne aux XVIIe–XVIIIe siècles, de la Ville à l'Etat* (2008) and *La noblesse de Paris au XVIIIe siècle* (2000).

Matthew P. Romaniello is Assistant Professor of History at the University of Hawai'i at Mānoa. He is the co-editor of *Tobacco in Russian History and Culture* (2009), with Tricia Starks, and the author of several articles on the history of the Russian Empire. He is currently completing his monograph, *The Elusive Empire: Kazan' and the Creation of Russia, 1552–1671.*

Hamish Scott is Wardlaw Professor Emeritus of History at the University of St Andrews and an Honorary Senior Research Fellow at the University of Glasgow. He has published extensively on eighteenth-century international relations and government, and is currently writing a study of the aristocracy in Europe, c. 1350–1750.

M. Safa Saraçoğlu is Assistant Professor of History at Bloomsburg University of Pennsylvania. He is completing a study of Vidin in the late Ottoman Empire, and is the author of several articles, having published in *Ab Imperio* and in *Sociological Problems,* journal of the Institute of Sociology of the Bulgarian Academy of Sciences.

Cornelia Soldat is an independent scholar with affiliation to the University of Cologne, who has held lectureships at the University of Potsdam and the Freie Universität of Berlin. She is the author of *Urbild und Abbild. Untersuchungen zu*

Herrschaft und Weltbild in Altrussland, 11.–16. Jh. (2001) and several articles, including publications in *Russian History* and *Cahiers du Monde russe.*

Katherine L. Turner is Assistant Professor of Musicology and Ethnomusicology at Claflin University, South Carolina. She earned her PhD at the University of Texas at Austin with a dissertation entitled "The Musical Culture of La Concezione: Devotion, Politics and Elitism in Post-Tridentine Florence." Her new project concerns the musical educations of early modern women.

Acknowledgments

In the fall of 2005 we both began working at George Mason University in Fairfax, Virginia, as postdoctoral fellows in the Western Civilization Program. Over coffee one afternoon, we had the idea to propose a panel for the Sixteenth Century Society and Conference's annual meeting in Minneapolis in the fall of 2007—"Contested Spaces of the European Nobility." Based on the lively discussions in Minneapolis, we decided to expand this project, which became a series of panels at a subsequent conference. This volume emerged from those conversations.

We would like to thank our contributors, who span six countries and more time zones than can easily be counted. Your collegiality, enthusiasm, and support have made preparing this volume for publication a joyful experience. We must also thank Kathryn Edwards of the University of South Carolina, who accommodated our panels at the 2009 meeting of the Sixteenth Century Studies and Conference in Geneva, as well as the other conference organizers. The conference allowed the contributors an opportunity to share and discuss each other's work, greatly enriching the final product. Also, we thank Richard Ninness, who was a presenter on the original panel in Minneapolis, and his insights have continued to inform our discussions.

Finally, the illustrations that appear throughout the volume would not have been possible without the kind permission of the following institutions. We thank the Royal Collection of Her Majesty, Queen Elizabeth II, for permission to use the da Vinci image included in Chapter 3. Also, both the York Museums Trust and Fairfax House exerted considerable effort to track down the original copyright holder of the Daniel King woodcut printed in Chapter 10. As it turned out, the image was copyright free, but we appreciate the efforts put forth on our behalf. Finally, the photograph of Penshurst Place was taken from Wikimedia Commons. We appreciate the commitment of this website and its contributors to making such material available copyright free.

Chapter 1

The Spaces of Nobility

Matthew P. Romaniello and Charles Lipp

Considering the extent of their contemporary social dominance, the long-term scholarly neglect of the early modern nobility may appear surprising after several decades of revisionism.[1] Through the nineteenth and well into the twentieth century, the story of Europe's traditional social elite was believed to be one of inherent decline because of an inability to cope effectively with the emerging "modern world." Modern in this case was defined in a variety of ways, but above all in terms of economics, with the supposed rise of a commercial bourgeoisie and, most notably for this volume, in terms of politics, with the emergence of strong, centralized monarchies.[2] Noble failure, therefore, was connected to what Herbert Butterfield termed a "Whiggish conception" of Europe's history, a conception that saw the late fifteenth through the nineteenth centuries as a key period of progress, with all of that term's implications, from the medieval to the modern.[3]

Based on this teleological view, traditional scholarship tended to establish oppositions between old and new. For instance, the reigns of Louis XIV of France (r. 1643–1715; personal rule 1661–1715) Russia's Peter the Great (r. 1689–1725; personal rule 1696–1725) have long been portrayed as victories of the supposedly "progressive" centralized state over noble independence. Central to this process, it was argued, were courts, crucial spaces where monarchs eradicated the inherited medieval, and so, "backwards," social power of the nobles through the uses of patronage and the introduction of new customs and ceremonies.[4] One historian subscribing to this view wrote of Louis XIV's palace at Versailles that it was there that "the nobility were segregated and rendered

---

[1] For an overview of the historiography of the early modern European nobility, see Scott, this volume.

[2] For an example, see James D. Hardy, Jr, *Prologue to Modernity: Early Modern Europe* (New York: John Wiley & Sons, 1974).

[3] Herbert Butterfield, *The Whig Interpretation of History* (New York: W.W. Norton, 1965).

[4] For an influential example, see Norbert Elias, *The Court Society*, trans. Edmund Jephcott (New York: Pantheon Books, 1983).

impotent ... [Moreover,] [i]t was at Versailles that the nobility were concentrated and demoralized by idleness and gaming."[5] Another, in describing Petrine Russia, stated that "Peter's revolutionary changes were fraught with social implications ... Peter combined the boyars, the service nobility, and landed military aristocracy in the *dvoryanstvo*, or nobility, all of which owed service to the ruler."[6] These discussions of centralizing rulers and their courts have been linked closely to the scholarly debate concerning absolutism, a socio-political system traditionally defined as one where royal power freed from inherited medieval restraints coerced elites and other social groups to accept centralized monarchical power. The past two generations of scholarship have largely rejected the notion that Louis and Peter (or their counterparts) were "absolute" monarchs, as the term is ahistorical at the very least, contemporaries never having used the term, and problematic on multiple fronts, in particular as it obscures the many instances of cooperation between rulers and elites.[7]

At the same time, much new work has challenged the related notion of the decline of noble standing to the benefit of monarchical authority. Beginning with the work of social historians examining how the nobility functioned as an estate, a new vision of nobility emerged in which nobles were not only individual political actors but also members of families, whose goals were as much about dynastic prosperity as political authority or social privilege.[8] From the work of historians Lawrence Stone, Robert Forster, and Jean Meyer in the 1960s, scholars increasingly have stressed noble resilience in the face of the great transformations of the early modern period, and nobles' great ability to adapt to change.[9] William Beik and James Collins, for example, have demonstrated the cooperative relationship between Louis XIV, the traditional model of an

---

[5]   David Ogg, *Europe in the Seventeenth Century*, 8th edn (New York: Collier Books, 1962), 297, 299.

[6]   John B. Wolf, *The Emergence of the Great Powers, 1685–1715* (New York: Harper & Row, 1951), 161.

[7]   Nicholas Henshall, *The Myth of Absolutism: Change and Continuity in Early Modern European Monarchy* (New York: Longman, 1992); Hendrik Spruyt, *The Sovereign State and Its Competitors: An Analysis of Systems Change* (Princeton: Princeton University Press, 1994); and Fanny Cosandey and Robert Descimon, *L'absolutisme en France: Histoire et historiographie*, Series Points Histoire, L'Histoire en débats (Paris: Éditions du Seuil, 2002). See as well the introduction in James B. Collins, *The State in Early Modern France*, 2nd edn (Cambridge: Cambridge University Press, 2009).

[8]   David Warren Sabean, Simon Teuscher, and Jon Mathieu, eds, *Kinship in Europe: Approaches to Long-Term Development (1300–1900)* (New York: Berghahn Books, 2007), especially the opening chapter: David Warren Sabean and Simon Teuscher, "Kinship in Europe: A New Approach to Long-Term Development," 1–32.

[9]   For a discussion of this transformation, see Scott, this volume.

absolute monarch, and French nobles.[10] The revisionist approach to noble history was perhaps encapsulated best in Jonathan Dewald's *The European Nobility, 1400–1800,* which argued that the early modern period was not a time of progressive and universal noble decline, but rather a tumultuous era in which innovations in religion, politics, society, and economics provided opportunities to some if not all members of the elite for maintaining their traditional social place and privileges.[11] In regards to centralizing rulers, nobles, it has come to be seen, accomplished personal goals through negotiation with sovereigns rather than submitting before a monarch's "charismatic authority" or the growth of a centralizing state.[12] The older "absolutist" model of monarchical coercion has moved towards new concepts of political authority, emerging from a consensus between a monarch and his nobles as "composite monarchies" and fiscal-military states.[13] These revisionist models emphasize a sharing of power between rulers and nobles arising from both practical and ideological reasons. This idea of consensus has inspired an appreciation for the persistence of noble power in early modern Europe.[14] To put it simply, the scholarship of the early modern nobility has moved beyond an interest in the decline and failure of the nobles to confront change to the examination of adaptation and success.

In contrast to visions of deterioration or triumph, this volume's chapters demonstrate that the maintenance of the nobles' social position resulted from a complicated web of contestation, accommodation, and negotiation—nobles

---

[10]   William Beik, *Absolutism and Society in Seventeenth-Century France: State Power and Provincial Aristocracy in Languedoc* (Cambridge: Cambridge University Press, 1985); James B. Collins, *Classes, Estates, and Order in Early Modern Brittany* (Cambridge: Cambridge University Press, 1994).

[11]   Jonathan Dewald, *The European Nobility 1400–1800* (New York: Cambridge University Press, 1996). For other overviews, see the notes in Scott, this volume.

[12]   For an explanation of charismatic authority, see Clifford Geertz, "Centers, Kings, and Charisma: Reflections on the Symbolics of Power," *Culture and Its Creators: Essays in Honor of Edward Shils,* eds Joseph Ben-David and Terry Nichols Clark (Chicago: University of Chicago Press, 1977), 150–71.

[13]   H.G. Koenigsberger, "*Dominium Regale* or *Dominium Politicum et Regale,*" in his *Politicians and Virtuosi: Essays in Early Modern History* (London: Hambledon Press, 1986); John Brewer, *The Sinews of Power: War, Money and the English State, 1688–1783* (Cambridge, MA: Harvard University Press, 1988); J.H. Elliott, "A Europe of Composite Monarchies," *Past and Present,* 137 (1992), 48–71; and Jan Glete, *War and the State in Early Modern Europe: Spain, the Dutch Republic, and Sweden as Fiscal-Military States, 1500–1660* (New York: Routledge, 2002).

[14]   Today, noble power is seen as outlasting the early modern period and persisting through the nineteenth and into the twentieth century. For the classic statement of this view, see Arno Mayer, *The Persistence of the Old Regime: Europe to the Great War* (New York: Pantheon Books, 1981).

could rely not only on traditional mechanisms of authority but also new institutions, arguments, ideas, and privileges in order to claim a dominant space within a changing society. In short, it was the "contest" that allowed the nobles to claim continued legitimacy as social leaders and to pursue greater authority. The method that underlies this book as a whole is an innovative approach that views noble history as a series of "contested spaces," including those personal, physical, social, and political, among others. This methodology builds upon the theoretical work of scholars such as Henri Lefebvre and Edward Soja. Lefebvre proposed that space could be analyzed as an overlapping "conceptual triad": spatial practice, in which spaces are defined through physical production; representations of space, linked to the idea of producing order through knowledge and signs; and representational spaces, in which the symbols and significance of spaces may become detached from the physical reality.[15] Edward Soja offered a different assessment of space that also suggests a potential historical methodology. Soja classified traditional historical approaches to space as limited to two illusions. The "illusion of opaqueness" posited that space was permanently delineated, and the "illusion of transparency" countered with the idea that all concepts of space were ephemeral. Both of these are based on concepts of physical spaces. Soja usefully proposed a third framework, "one which recognizes spatiality as simultaneously a social product (or outcome) and shaping force (or medium) in social life."[16] Spaces, therefore, are not only the product of geography but also a method of delineating society, including the resulting interactions created by attempting to impose new definitions.

This volume reflects these approaches to analyzing space as a dynamic arena of society, politics, and physical environment. In doing so, it contributes to the revisionism of our understandings of the nobility, shifting their history from a narrative of victims of historical change to one of active participation in the great transformations of the early modern era. This does not mean, however, that the nobles always succeeded in their contests, but rather reveals the developments of the late-fifteenth through the nineteenth centuries as not being a linear, smooth, inevitable teleology of progress. Nobles' challenges and adaptations, this volume suggests, helped drive the process by which Europe became "modern." The early modern period confronted Europe's traditional social elite with a wide array of challenges in almost every space of life—political, religious, economic, intellectual, and social. Though success varied, all of these challenges, and all of these spaces, were contested.

---

[15]   Henri Lefebvre, *The Production of Space*, Donald Nicholson-Smith, trans. (Malden, MA: Blackwell, 1991), 33.

[16]   Edward W. Soja, *Postmodern Geographies: The Reassertion of Space in Critical Social Theory* (London: Verso, 1989), 7.

In addition, this volume continues the reevaluation of the early modern elite by adopting an explicitly interdisciplinary and transnational approach. Contributing scholars include historians, literary critics, and musicologists. Their different methodologies allow for a multifaceted exploration of the nobles' many contested spaces, ranging from explorations of the body, gender norms, courts, architecture, literature, law, education, and others. The chapters explore examples from across Europe. The central issue in this volume is the "spaces" of nobility, not particular national histories. Since John Hale argued for "Europe" as a common cultural place during the Renaissance, divisions of Europe have been revealed as later innovations rather than contemporary realities.[17] For example, Larry Wolff has shown persuasively that the division of Europe between "East" and "West" was born of the Enlightenment and overrode an earlier north/south separation of the continent that traced its origins back to the Roman Empire in the south and the "barbarians" of the north.[18] Even this divide was ephemeral, as exchanges of ideas and material goods between these two spheres—a "Mediterranean" and a "Baltic"—were common, even as each region had its own tensions and crises.

By taking a continent-wide perspective, the commonality of European experiences becomes clear. For example, when the seventeenth century witnessed a year of global crisis in 1648, it challenged political authorities in London, Paris, Naples, Istanbul, and Moscow.[19] This is not to argue that every area did not have a unique culture or identity, or that every political unit did not emerge autonomously with its own mechanisms of control, but instead to suggest that there was more than one avenue for understanding early modern Europe. Every region in Europe was both particular in its own right and connected to larger events. Social elites were as likely to adopt strategies to negotiate historical change from their counterparts across the continent as they were to arrive at their tactics independently.

Moreover, this volume contributes to an ongoing reexamination of the early modern understanding of "nobility." From traditional views of a universal unchanging definition, modern scholars have come to stress that the very meaning of nobility changed over the centuries. This volume shows that though new roles and new members of the nobility emerged, a similar set of obligations and rights distinguished an elite social group across the continent. Each society from Portugal to Russia managed to separate social ranks through

---

[17]   John Hale, *The Civilization of Europe in the Renaissance* (New York: Touchstone Books, 1993), 3–39.

[18]   Larry Wolff, *Inventing Eastern Europe: The Map of Civilization in the Mind of the Enlightenment* (Stanford, CA: Stanford University Press, 1994).

[19]   Geoffrey Parker, *Europe in Crisis, 1598–1648*, 2nd edn (Oxford: Blackwell, 2001).

legal precedents, property rights, or status and privilege, a separation frequently made public through sumptuary rights if not office-holding or political power. While individual groups with these privileges in Europe may not have been technically termed "noble," their common challenges as individuals, families, or even as an entire social order reveal a common European experience among these demarcated elites.

Whether "noble," "notable," "boiar," or "*slazchta*," this elevated social estate exploited any and all opportunities to preserve, or even increase, their social, economic, and political positions. Rather than viewing the great events of the early modern era such as the emergence of Renaissance science or the Reformation's religious upheaval as weakening the nobility's social position, this book argues strongly that they created opportunities for nobles to advance their standing. Neither the Enlightenment nor the rise of a market economy necessarily led to a world shorn of Europe's medieval inheritance; rather each movement simultaneously created a new set of terms and ideas that could be used by nobles to renegotiate and defend the traditions they valued, including their families and their privileges. By not viewing the Europe of the nineteenth and twentieth centuries as the inherent evolution of the continent's society, the chapters in this volume reconceptualize European history as a long process of social negotiation in a variety of different spaces—personal, social, geographic, and political—in which all parties could accomplish individual goals and agendas.

The transformation of the study of nobility is the subject of the opening historiographic chapter by Hamish Scott, "The Early Modern European Nobility and its Contested Historiographies, c. 1950–1980." While earlier political histories presumed the victory of the monarchy and the state, the rise of social history in the 1960s created a new framework for the analysis of the nobility. First and foremost, nobles were reconceived as social actors, and not necessarily political agents. As increasing numbers of historians have examined the possible roles and outcomes of noble involvement in historical events, rather than considering nobles the "losers" of historical evolution, the nobility has emerged as a dynamic group capable of pursuing their own interests. Scott argues that the work of Lawrence Stone in particular was crucial in transforming the debate about the early modern nobility, and thereby provided the tools for later historians to understand the continuing strength of the elite, a reality which is reflected in this volume's chapters.

New approaches to history, building on the developments discussed by Scott, created new avenues for examining the nobility and the spaces in which they challenged authority. In "Negotiating for Agnes' Womb," Erica Bastress-Dukehart examines one of the most intimate spaces—that of a noble woman's womb—to unpack the ways in which new innovations in science challenged traditional notions of inheritance and legitimacy. The center of her case study is the Margravine Agnes of Baden, Duchess of Schleswig-Holstein, who gave birth to fraternal twins as early as four-and-a-half months after conception. Though initially accepted as legitimate, the twins' parentage was challenged by family members hoping to displace their right to succession. This familial dispute occurred just as the Roman Catholic Church's ability to define legitimacy was being contested by recent scientific innovations. Arguing over one woman's womb, in fact, as Bastress-Dukehart argues, ultimately shaped the formation of political entities in northern Germany.

As Bastress-Dukehart draws upon new methods from the history of sexuality and science, Grace E. Coolidge examines the ways in which gender affected noble legitimacy and authority in "Contested Masculinity: Noblemen and Their Mistresses in Early Modern Spain." Coolidge reveals that a mistress created a charismatic authority of masculine power for Spanish noblemen. Masculinity became an essential virtue of noble privilege, though one ironically dependent upon women for validation. As a result, women, sometimes of lower classes, could access noble privilege. This symbiotic relationship oddly enhanced both parties through their illicit connections, which strongly contrasted with acceptable notions of noble virtue in other parts of early modern Europe. Though the outcomes of these contests undoubtedly remained linked to specific times and places, a lesson repeated throughout the chapters in this volume, Coolidge's chapter demonstrates the overall ability of nobles to use particular circumstances to protect their general position.

Gender also plays a great role in Katherine L. Turner's assessment of the new convent of La Concezione in sixteenth-century Florence, established by the ruling Medici family in an intentional attempt to create a noble space. As Turner shows in "*Il monastero nuovo*: The Cloistered Women of the Medici Court," any family which claimed a space for one of its daughters as a novitiate publicly declared their power and authority in Florentine society. Whereas Coolidge uncovers women actively exploiting their relationships with noblemen to claim privilege for themselves and their children, the cloistered daughters of Florentine society were more passive objects of noble strategy. This is not to imply that women won in one scenario and lost in another, but rather that family strategies could not rely upon one solution to all problems. As long as families as a whole prospered, any of its particular members could be exploited for the dynasty's general well-being.

Physical spaces of symbolic authority, as in Turner's work, were familiar sources of power and privilege throughout Europe. Imposing palaces like those of Louis XIV or Peter the Great might be the classic examples of symbolic authority, but nobles also could use physical space for similar purposes. In Cornelia Soldat's examination of burial practices of boiar families in Moscow, "Sepulchral Monuments as a Means of Communicating Social and Political Power of Nobles in Early Modern Russia," the most elite men in Russia continually challenged tsarist authority by physically positioning the family dead in highly important religious spaces. The tsar may have enjoyed a divine right to rule, but nobles demonstrated to society their right to share that divine connection. In Sukanya Dasgupta's chapter on country houses, "'Of polish'd pillars, or a roofe of gold': Authority and Affluence in the English Country House Poem," English nobles demonstrated their wealth and power through the construction of imposing private spaces. They did not build palaces, but thoughtfully challenged those structures as a demonstration of nobles' continuing influence. To any observer, these noble families also had access to wealth and power, and could easily dominate the English landscape as much as the monarch.

Despite the general approach of much current scholarship, this volume illustrates that the path for noble success was not smooth and, undoubtedly, nobles lost contestations as often as they won them. New innovations in law and the rising political authority of certain monarchs seemed to be difficult to engage successfully for the nobility. In Portugal, as Susannah Humble Ferreira observes in her chapter "Inventing the Courtier in Early Sixteenth-Century Portugal," the new Avis monarchy was sufficiently strong to break the authority of the traditional nobility. Many of their tools would be familiar to later monarchs— ostentatious new palaces and residences to display authority, increasing divisions and regulations of political authority, and general economic weakness, all of which could undermine the nobility. In some ways, nobles, like those in Soldat or Dasgupta's work, had success in using space to claim authority, but in this case the Portuguese nobility did not. However, when symbolic space was not available, physical space was, as at least one noble simply departed the country rather than lose his status. While Ferreira narrates an episode of noble failure, it still demonstrates that nobles were not necessarily limited as they struggled against monarchs seizing new authority and rights.

Innovations of the early modern era contributed to challenge noble privileges. In Ryan Gaston's chapter on royal investment in Spanish noble education in the early seventeenth century, "All the King's Men: Educational Reform and Nobility in Early Seventeenth-Century Spain," the nobility once again had to respond to growing monarchial authority and new restrictions upon their independence. Much like in Ferreira's exploration of Portugal, Gaston demonstrates that though the monarch could instruct, his mandate of noble behavior created as much opportunity to resist as to comply. As Gaston argues, the rise of an educated nobleman was a sign of "modernization" as the monarch worked with his nobles to forge a new identity. At the same time, nobles used education as a new tool for maintaining privilege, shifting this new space to their personal advantage. They could also reject the monarchy's efforts.

As the era created new tools for the nobles, it also generated opportunities for the monarchs. In Elie Haddad's analysis of the changes to French laws concerning ennoblement, "The Question of the Imprescriptibility of Nobility in Early Modern France," both monarch and nobility tested legal innovations to preserve their own conception of noble tradition. As the court added increasing restrictions on the right to claim the title of noble, nobles had to combat the new definitions targeted at removing their privileges and inheritance. As with Gaston's look at the Spanish nobility, the French nobles both rejected the changing idea of "noble" and yet found new ground for claiming their rights and privileges. Haddad emphasizes that while the idea of "noble" transformed, it was not necessarily a losing battle for the families involved. This is further made clear in Mathieu Marraud's discussion of noble strategies for surviving in the changing political and economic climate of seventeenth- and eighteenth-century France, "Nobility as a Social and Political Dialogue: The Parisian Example, 1650–1750." Placing the idea of a noble family at the forefront, Marraud uncovers familial strategies that involved pursuing careers outside of noble politics. The family could succeed in maintaining its rights, even if some of its members were not "noble" in the traditional sense. Rather than arguing that "modernization" ended the authority of the nobility, changing social and economic forces only created different opportunities. It was not the families or their elite position that were challenged, as much as the "traditional" concept of nobility shifted to fit the economic and social changes.

The nobility's ability to adapt to these new challenges proves to be another recurrent theme in this book, and yet the nobles' social position was ultimately eroded by the late eighteenth and nineteenth centuries. Two populations sitting in precarious positions reveal this process—Polish nobles during the era of the Partitions, and Ottoman nobles living on the exposed Balkan frontier. In Jerzy Lukowski's chapter, "Challenging the Status Quo: Attempts to Modernize the Polish Nobility in the Later Eighteenth Century," Enlightenment political ideology became a tool of the Polish *slazchta* to challenge the unraveling of their state. As their political privilege had defined the unique political culture of Poland's distinctive elective monarchy, some nobles attempted to exploit innovative political notions to revitalize their role in society and defeat outside military and political pressures. Among these measures were educational reforms reminiscent of those discussed by Ryan Gaston. While the *slazchta* were not successful in preventing the partitions of Poland, it was not for lack of understanding the changing nature of political theory in the "modern" era. In his chapter, "Resilient Notables: Looking at the Transformation of the Ottoman

Empire from the Local Level," M. Safa Saraçoglu uncovers similar problems facing the traditional elites of the Ottoman frontier provinces, as the modern era did not end their political importance but rather it created opportunities for new families to rise to prominence at the expense of formerly entrenched notables. In both the provinces and in the capital, the modern era did not remove elite families' pursuit of prominence, status, or authority, but it did shift the argument into new spaces of negotiation.

The early modern nobility were more successful in their confrontation with change than was long believed by scholars. In fact, the early modern elite displayed many supposed modern values. They were adaptable, innovative, and self-interested. They adapted to new circumstances to protect and increase their traditional social place and opposed strongly all challenges to their dominance. This does not mean that the nobles were always successful, but rather that they fought an endless series of contests in a variety of spaces, contests which they won as often as they lost. The nobility exploited Renaissance science and education, disruptions caused by war and religious strife, changing political ideas and concepts, the growth of a market economy, and the evolution of centralized states in order to maintain their lineage, reputation, and position. If a monarch could claim charismatic authority with signs and symbols of power, so too could the nobles. Personal, geographic, ceremonial, political, and social spaces were all contested, and each arena provided multifaceted opportunities to preserve their familial status. In crucial ways, the shared nature of these contests and spaces helped create a European-wide culture of nobility.

The contested spaces of the early modern European nobility, therefore, challenge Whiggish notions of modernity. This volume suggests that nobles were quite capable of using seemingly modern methods to protect things apparently medieval, and so the dichotomy between tradition and modernity long held by scholars should be rejected. There was no one solution to maintain inherited privileges; likewise there were multiple means for defending against challenges. As will be seen in the following chapters, the Europe that followed the early modern era was not an inevitable outcome of "progress," but rather the outcome was produced by the particular contest itself. Seen in this light, the development of European history was not linear, but a variable and dynamic product of multiple actors working together and apart, pursuing individual goals and desires, and ultimately producing something greater than any could have imagined.

Chapter 2

The Early Modern European Nobility and its Contested Historiographies, c. 1950–1980

Hamish Scott

One striking feature of recent historical scholarship has been an ever increasing and ubiquitous interest in Europe's nobilities, from the Roman Empire to the present day. This has been particularly evident for early modern history, broadly the period from the mid-fifteenth century to the French Revolution of 1789, where the topic has flourished quite spectacularly after prolonged earlier neglect.[1] Since the mid-1970s, noblemen and noblewomen have moved

[1]   Earlier versions of this chapter were given as papers at the University of Glasgow, the Institute for Advanced Study in Princeton, Emory University, the University of Chicago and the University of Oxford, and I am indebted to these audiences for helpful criticism, which has done much to improve the argument. It was largely written at the Institute for Advanced Study in Princeton during 2008–09, and I thank the Andrew Mellon Foundation for financial support during that year. Earlier drafts have been read by Keith M. Brown, Peter Brown, David Cannadine, Regina Grafe, T.K. Rabb, Adam Sisman, and the editors of this volume, and I am very grateful for their generous and constructive advice. Lyndal Roper made some characteristically acute suggestions at an Oxford seminar, and I am indebted to her for these.

In what follows the titles cited are illustrative of the argument advanced, and no attempt is made to provide anything approaching a full bibliography. There are now two overlapping syntheses by Ronald G. Asch, *Nobilities in Transition 1550–1700: Courtiers and Rebels in Britain and Europe* (London: Edward Arnold, 2003) and *Europäischer Adel in der Frühen Neuzeit* (Cologne: Böhlau, 2008), which together constitute the best available introduction, and have full bibliographies of recent scholarship. The pioneering anglophone synthesis by Jonathan Dewald, *The European Nobility 1400–1800* (Cambridge: Cambridge University Press, 1996), retains its value, while *The European Nobilities in the Seventeenth and Eighteenth Centuries*, ed. H.M. Scott, 2 vols (London: Longman, 1995; 2nd expanded edition, Basingstoke: Palgrave, 2007), contains detailed national essays which together constitute a comprehensive survey of Europe's social elite. Considerations of space have prevented specific attention being given to German-language scholarship, which has followed a distinctive if broadly comparable trajectory.

from near-invisibility to center stage, from a situation where they were all but ignored to one where scholarly interest has reached such proportions that there is a considerable risk of exaggerating their historical role and importance. An identical, though marginally earlier, process of rediscovery has been under way in the historiography of both medieval Europe and the world of Late Antiquity, while more recently it has extended into the nineteenth and twentieth centuries.[2] Interest in all historical topics and epochs is cyclical, with phases of neglect interspersed with bouts of intensive study. But the growing interest has been a consequence of far more positive, and also more enduring, developments than the carousel of academic fashion.

With hindsight it can be dated to the third quarter of the twentieth century—the decades between the 1950s and the 1970s—when overlapping developments within the wider historical profession and in the study of early modern history itself merged to renew interest in the nobility. The present chapter explores this development, primarily in anglophone and Western European historical scholarship, and aims to explain both the current interest, evident in the chapters assembled in this volume, and the distinctive approach which became established in many national historiographies at that time and continues until the present day. Two overlapping dimensions will be emphasized: an important shift in the study of history, and the impact of influential books by two noted historians, Lawrence Stone and Jean Meyer, which shaped subsequent research.

The Wider Historiographical Context

The first and, in many ways, most fundamental factor has been a significant widening of the range of subjects studied by historians. The key transformations in Western historiography over the past four or five decades have been the decline of traditional political history and the advent of what can broadly be described as "social history," beginning with demography and the family and going on to include gender and what would now be styled "cultural history" in

---

[2]   Scholarly investigation of the medieval elite is surveyed by Timothy Reuter, "The Medieval Nobility in Twentieth-Century Historiography," in *Companion to Historiography*, ed. Michael Bentley (London: Routledge, 1997), 177–202, while for its predecessor see Peter Brown, "The Study of Elites in Late Antiquity," *Arethusa*, 33 (2000), 321–46, introducing an informative special issue devoted to "Elites in Late Antiquity." No comparable comprehensive survey appears to exist for the late-modern period, but German-language scholarship is valuably surveyed by William D. Godsey, Jr, "Nobles and Modernity," *German History*, 20 (2002), 504–21.

the widest sense.[3] This is such a well-known development that it can be briefly surveyed, though its impact upon the study of noblemen and noblewomen was to be crucial, providing the essential broader context. The surviving records for the nobility and especially its leading families are, of course, almost always much better than for other groups within society, and this has encouraged social historians of all kinds to exploit sources and evidence from noble lineages for their research and particularly for the quantitative studies which were so important during the period before social history rapidly gave way to cultural history around 1980. Some of the pioneering work on demography, for example, examined the English aristocracy and the French *ducs et pairs*, while more recently historians of marriage, family life, gender relations, and cultural trends have exploited the relatively abundant surviving records left by leading families, in the process immeasurably benefiting historians interested in the narrower subject of nobility.[4] The far greater survival and availability of such sources has been one important reason why French and Italian scholars in particular have produced such major studies of particular noble lineages or groups within the nobility during this last generation. The development of social and cultural history, however, came chronologically slightly later and strengthened an increasing interest in nobilities; it certainly reinforced but did not create it.

There were several more general reasons why the subject revived so notably. Three additional and much less specific developments—all lying far beyond the study of sixteenth- to eighteenth-century Europe—can briefly be suggested. The first was a notable change in approaches to the history of the state and specifically to its early modern variant, that of absolute monarchy, with the adoption of a much broader approach to government and governance.[5] Institutional approaches have been less and less favored, as the limitations of a purely Weberian framework for any period before the twentieth century came to be acknowledged, while in their place scholars have recognized that people were more important than formal bureaucratic structures and procedures.

---

    [3]   An illuminating introduction is provided by William H. Sewell, Jr., "The Political Unconscious of Social and Cultural History, or, Confessions of a Former Quantitative Historian," in his *Logics of History: Social Theory and Social Transformation* (Chicago: University of Chicago Press, 2005), 22–80.

    [4]   See Bastress-Dukehart, Coolidge, Marraud, and Turner, this volume.

    [5]   In many ways this was a response to Perry Anderson, *Lineages of the Absolutist State* (London: NLB, 1974); for subsequent scholarship see in particular Wolfgang Reinhard, *Geschichte der Staatsgewalt: eine vergleichende Verfassungsgeschichte Europas von den Anfängen bis zur Gegenwart* (Munich: Beck, 1999). Part III of this remarkable work examines relations between nobilities and monarchies; cf. the collaborative volume in the series sponsored by the European Science Foundation on "The Origins of the Modern State in Europe" and edited by Reinhard, *Power Elites and State Building* (Oxford: Clarendon Press, 1996).

This involved directing far more attention to the social and political elite, now seen not as the victim of absolute monarchy as it had earlier been, but as both agent and beneficiary of strengthened royal authority.[6] The central role played by Europe's nobilities in supporting monarchy has been revealed by the past generation's scholarship, further strengthening the growing interest in the topic. It has been reinforced by a parallel expansion of research on the monarchical court, viewed as the key "point of contact" between rulers and their nobilities. Here the belated English translation of Norbert Elias's *The Court Society*, which appeared in the early 1980s, was an important catalyst, though its arguments have not stood up well to detailed scrutiny.[7] The important links—both historiographical and historical—between the elaboration of court society and the development is well brought out by Susannah Humble Ferreira in a detailed study of early sixteenth-century Portugal.[8]

Interest has also been strengthened by the importance now attributed to the nobility during the nineteenth and even twentieth centuries. The impact of an influential work by Arno J. Mayer, *The Persistence of the Old Regime*, with its central thesis that noble power was alive and well until the generation between the 1880s and World War I, was enormous.[9] It focused and pushed forward work by English, French, German, and Italian scholars, which was already making clear the enduring importance of the traditional elite down to 1914 and, in some measure, beyond.[10] Given the continuing role and demonstrable importance of

---

[6]   This has been particularly evident in studies of seventeenth-century France: see especially William Beik, *Absolutism and Society in Seventeenth-Century France: State Power and Provincial Aristocracy in Languedoc* (Cambridge: Cambridge University Press, 1985) and the comments in his notable review essay, "The Absolutism of Louis XIV as Social Collaboration," *Past and Present*, 188 (2005), 195–224; James Collins, *Classes, Estates, and Orders in Early Modern Brittany* (Cambridge: Cambridge University Press, 1994); and, more generally, the same author's *The State in Early Modern France* (Cambridge: Cambridge University Press, 1995).

[7]   Norbert Elias, *The Court Society* (New York: Pantheon Books, 1983). Two valuable collections which introduce this detailed scholarship are Ronald G. Asch and Adolf M. Birke, eds, *Princes, Patronage and the Nobility: The Court at the Beginning of the Modern Age, c.1450–1650* (Oxford: Oxford University Press, 1991), and John Adamson, ed., *The Princely Courts of Europe 1550–1700* (London: Weidenfeld & Nicolson, 1999), while Romaniello and Lipp's chapter in this volume provides a fuller account of the importance of court studies.

[8]   See Humble Ferreira, this volume.

[9]   *The Persistence of the Old Regime: Europe to the Great War* (New York: Pantheon Books, 1981), which was translated into French, German, and Italian.

[10]   For some examples of this, see David Cannadine, *The Decline and Fall of the British Aristocracy* (New Haven, Conn.: Yale University Press, 1990); *Aspects of Aristocracy: Grandeur and Decline in Modern Britain* (New Haven, Conn.: Yale University Press, 1994);

the aristocracy after 1800, how could historians of the early modern period and especially the eighteenth century pretend that the nobility was a declining group, far less neglect it altogether?

A willingness to learn from the social sciences has been important, though it proved to have drawbacks as well. The existence of a corpus of social science literature devoted to both state building and elites encouraged historians to exploit these writings.[11] From around 1900 social scientists, reacting against a Marxist—or at least *marxisant*—emphasis on production and class, had begun to develop distinctive theories of elites, and this had flourished during the first half of the twentieth century. The process began with the Italian writers Gaetano Mosca and Vilfredo Pateto—and also Antonio Gramsci—continued with Karl Mannheim in the 1930s, and concluded with the American political scientist C. Wright Mills in mid-century. During the 1950s and 1960s, however, elites became less fashionable in social science circles, exactly at the moment that historians were turning to their writings to illuminate their own work. One consequence was that the literature upon which they drew was in some cases already out of date or rapidly becoming so, though since the 1980s the use of Michael Mann's large-scale *Sources of Social Power* has been a significant improvement.[12] But the awareness of social science theory has overall been a very positive development in the historiography of nobility, raising new questions and suggesting fresh approaches. An outstanding example of such interaction has been the work of the French historical anthropologist, Gérard Delille, in his studies of early modern Naples and more recently of the wider Mediterranean

Suzanne Fiette, *La noblesse française des Lumières à la Belle Époque* (Paris: Perrin, 1997); Claude-Isabelle Brelot, *La noblesse réinventée: nobles de Franche-Comté de 1814 à 1870*, 2 vols (Paris: Belles-Lettres, 1992); Heinz Reif, *Adel im 19. und 20. Jahrhundert* (Munich: Oldenbourg, 1999), which contains abundant bibliographical guidance; William D. Godsey, Jr., "Quarterings and Kinship: The Social Composition of the Habsburg Aristocracy in the Dualist Era," *Journal of Modern History*, 71 (1999), 56–104; A. Moroni, *Antica gente e subiti guadagni: Patrimoni aristocratici fiorentini nell'800* (Florence: Olschki, 1997); an excellent synthesis of the first wave of this research is Dominic Lieven, *The Aristocracy in Europe 1815– 1914* (Basingstoke: Macmillan, 1992), which is usefully updated by Ellis Wasson, *Aristocracy and the Modern World* (Basingstoke: Palgrave, 2006).

[11]   See for example Peter-Michael Hahn's notable study of the Junkers of Brandenburg as a "Power Elite," in the sense made fashionable by C. Wright Mills in his *Struktur und Funktion des brandenburgischen Adels im 16. Jahrhundert* (Berlin: Colloquium-Verlag, 1979).

[12]   *The Sources of Social Power*, vol. 1: *A History of Power from the Beginning to A.D. 1760* (Cambridge: Cambridge University Press, 1986).

region, which have much to say about noble family structures and inheritance practices.[13]

Early Beginnings and the Notion of Noble Decline

The rapidly growing interest also had more specific origins. The publication of family correspondence and narratives, and even some influential academic studies, goes back at least to the nineteenth century. Books, articles, and other relevant materials, such as noble genealogies, armorials, handbooks of heraldry, and the like, had long been published in profusion. Many were sponsored by noble families themselves, and while their quality can be uneven, they often contain material and especially correspondence of enduring importance.[14] Aristocratic lineages encouraged studies of their own past, particularly during the second half of the nineteenth century, as a way of unifying and legitimating their role in the present and inspiring current and future generations to emulate the Great Deeds of their ancestors, whether these had been real or imaginary. The continuing importance of lineage and House was deliberately fostered through a study of the past, as a means by which the nineteenth-century nobility could reinvent itself at a period when many of the traditional foundations of its privileged status were being undermined.

A wide variety of media was employed to encourage an enduring sense of family and history—buildings, furniture, portraits, libraries, and archives—though the most important were family histories, genealogies, and armorials.[15] It was these kinds of production that Jean Meyer had in view when he sighed that the problem about being a historian of nobility was not too few studies, but too many of the wrong type and of mediocre quality.[16] Such publications

---

[13]   *Famille et propriété dans le Royaume de Naples, XVe–XIXe siècle* (Rome: École Française de Rome and Paris: Éditions de l'ÉHESS, 1985); *Le maire et le prieur: pouvoir central et pouvoir local en Méditerranée occidentale (XVe–XVIIIe siècle)* (Rome: École Française de Rome and Paris: Éditions de l'ÉHESS, 2003).

[14]   Outstanding examples of the genre are Jacob von Falke, *Geschichte des Fürstlichen Hauses Liechtenstein*, 3 vols (Vienna: Braumüller, 1868–82); Henri d'Orléans, duc d'Aumale, *Histoire des princes de Condé pendant les XVIe et XVIIe siècles*, 7 vols (Paris: Calmann-Lèvy, 1885–96); Karl Fürst von Schwarzenberg, *Geschichte der reichsständischen Hauses Schwarzenberg* (Neustadt an der Aisch: Degener, 1963).

[15]   See in particular Brelot, *La noblesse réinventée*, I, 15; and II, 797–806. This continued well into the twentieth century: see Eric Mension-Rigau, *Aristocrates et grands bourgeois: éducation, traditions, valeurs* (Paris: Plon, 1994), especially chapters 1–3.

[16]   Jean Meyer, *La noblesse Bretonne au XVIIIe siècle*, 2 vols (Paris: SEVPEN, 1966), I, xxi.

continue until the present day: the Liechtenstein have been particularly energetic in encouraging study of their own past, while there has recently been a three-volume work devoted to the Campbell earls of Argyll, a prominent Scottish and British noble lineage, written, like many such narratives, by a member of the family whose achievements and endurance it celebrates.[17] Publications such as these remain an important resource for any historian of nobility, though they are not the focus of this chapter.

A handful of more academic studies had even been published before the mid-twentieth century, but most were one-dimensional, being overwhelmingly political in approach and biographical in focus.[18] They were the products of a conceptual framework which assumed that by the early modern centuries, if not earlier, nobles were in decline: politically they had lost out to the absolutist state, the emergence of which was viewed as the central development, while economically and even socially they were being eclipsed by a rising middle class who benefited from Europe's commercial expansion and specifically from the advent of capitalism. This was especially true on its Western and Protestant periphery, where the spectacular success of the Dutch Republic exemplified a non-aristocratic and so more "modern" form of social and political organization.

This narrative had been particularly influential within France. It went back at least as far as Alexis de Tocqueville, who in his celebrated *L'Ancien Régime et la Révolution* (1856) had presented French history from the eleventh century to his own day as a story of continuing noble decline, particularly evident during the decades which preceded the Revolution of 1789, and of the parallel rise of a commercial middle class.[19] Some authors went even further and portrayed an alliance between the crown and the middle class directed against the nobility, which brought about its decline. In this way the nobility had been written out of France's history during the nineteenth century, and its eclipse was confirmed by the modernizing narratives embraced by twentieth-century scholarship. Variations on this development are to be found within many national historiographies. In Italian-language scholarship, for example, the nobility has often appeared in the

---

[17] See especially Volker Press and Dietmar Willoweit, eds, *Liechtenstein: Fürstliches Haus und Staatliche Ordnung* (Munich: Oldenbourg, 1987) and Evelin Oberhammer, ed., *Der ganzen Welt ein Lob und Spiegel: Das Fürstenhaus Liechtenstein in der frühen Neuzeit* (Vienna: Verlag für Geschichte und Politik, 1990); Alastair Campbell of Airds, *A History of Clan Campbell*, 3 vols (Edinburgh: Edinburgh University Press, 2000–04).

[18] Two good examples were G. d'Avenel, *La noblesse française sous Richelieu* (Paris: Colin, 1901) and E. Schwenke, *Friedrich der Grosse und der Adel* (Burg: Hopfer, 1911).

[19] See Jonathan Dewald's stimulating recent study, *Lost Worlds: The Emergence of French Social History, 1815–1970* (University Park: Pennsylvania State University Press, 2006), 165 and *passim*.

guise of agents of foreign rule over parts of the peninsula and so an obstacle to the emergence of a national state before the nineteenth century.

It contributed in a second, more indirect way to the historiographical neglect of the nobility. Theories of modernization—though not the concept itself—were formulated primarily during the 1950s and 1960s. This was almost contemporaneous with both a revival of interest in nobility as a subject and with the invention of "early modern history," which occurred during the third quarter of the twentieth century both as a descriptive term to describe the centuries between the sixteenth and the eighteenth and as a label for a distinct epoch with its own distinctive characteristics.[20] The notion of "*frühe Neuzeit*" as a specific historical period, beginning after the Renaissance and finishing in the later eighteenth century, seems to have been articulated for the first time by a German historical philosopher, Wilhelm Kamlah, in 1957. It was taken up by Reinhart Koselleck in his studies of chronology and historical time, and first became established in German-language scholarship during the 1960s and 1970s, and then was adopted far more widely, particularly in anglophone scholarship.

The notion of "early modernity" initially incorporated assumptions drawn from modernization theory and even Marxist historiography about the inevitability of progress towards Industrial Society and its corollary, the Modern State, and in this way strengthened an established Grand Narrative. There was no place for the nobility within such a framework, and this reinforced the prevailing negative view. Nobles, in other words, were cast as the inevitable "losers" in an intellectual tradition which long carried all before it, in which the two great "winners" appeared to be the commercial bourgeoisie and the monarchical state. Here there was an important intersection with the separate, though compatible, traditions of social history which evolved in the United States, France, and Britain during the 1960s and 1970s. Each, in its different way, sought to explain the preconditions of subsequent modernization and therefore "worked outwards and upwards from the process of social production in its specific setting."[21] In time a recognition of the real and important continuities

---

[20] For what follows see Johannes Burkhardt, "Frühe Neuzeit," in *Fischer Lexikon Geschichte*, ed. Richard van Dülmen (Frankfurt-am-Main: Fischer Verlag, 1990), 364–85; Wolfgang Reinhard, "The Idea of Early Modern History," in *Companion to Historiography*, 281–92; Jack A. Goldstone, "The Problem of the 'Early Modern' World," *Journal of the Economic and Social History of the Orient*, 41 (1998), 249–84; the special issue of *Daedalus*, 127:3 (1998), devoted to "Early Modernities"; Randolph Starn, "The Early Modern Muddle," *Journal of Early Modern History*, 6 (2002), 296–307; and the "Introduction" to Lynn A. Struve, ed., *The Qing Formation in World Historical Time* (Cambridge, Mass.: Harvard East Asian Monographs, 2004), 1–54, esp. 31–46.

[21] E.J. Hobsbawm writing in 1971, quoted by Sewell, "Political Unconscious," 39.

within early modern history would develop, and this would contribute to the growing interest in nobility, which exemplified exactly that persistence and survival. Initially, however, the impact of the construction of early modernity had confirmed the neglect of the traditional elite.

Pre-History: The 1920s to the 1950s

There had in fact been a few influential scholarly studies before the second half of the twentieth century, though these were usually of individual noblemen and particular families, rather than the wider nobility. Between the 1920s and 1950s a series of individual publications had appeared which, with the benefit of hindsight, were clearly important and contributed to the subsequent renewal of interest. Their impact at the time, however, was slight, and they took place almost entirely in isolation and were not sustained. In this they reflected the academic world of the first half of the twentieth century, with a relatively small number of individual researchers who had limited contacts with their fellow scholars and where there were relatively few graduate students.

The first, and also the best known, was in eighteenth-century British history. Sir Lewis Namier, who made his career in England but had been brought up in former Polish Galicia (by then part of the Austro-Hungarian empire) in a minor landowning family at a period when noble power was still very real, had written with an unusual degree of sympathy and even admiration about the mid-Hanoverian landholding caste in his *The Structure of Politics at the Accession of George III*, published in 1929.[22] This adopted a novel structural approach, rather than the established narrative or biographical format. Namier long dreamed of producing a wide-ranging prosopographical study of England's political and social elite, and successfully launched the collaborative and multivolume "History of Parliament" as the vehicle for this, backed by considerable public funding. Yet he was unable to focus his own energies sufficiently to ensure the completion of even his own volumes during his lifetime. He was diverted into contemporary politics, crusading against appeasement and on behalf of the cause of political Zionism, and also into the study of nineteenth-century European

---

[22]   London: MacMillan. For Namier, see Lucy S. Sutherland, "Sir Lewis Namier 1888–1960," *Proceedings of the British Academy*, 48 (1962), 371–85; Linda Colley, *Namier* (London: Weidenfeld & Nicolson, 1989); Lady Julia Namier, *Lewis Namier: A Biography* (Oxford: Oxford University Press, 1971).

history. His projected biographical study of the mid-eighteenth-century English political elite would remain unfinished at his death.[23]

The second initiative was no more successful. In the mid-1930s the great French historian Marc Bloch attempted to launch a comparative and chronologically wide-ranging enquiry into Europe's nobilities, in the consciously innovatory journal which he had founded jointly with Lucien Febvre in 1929: *Annales d'histoire économique et sociale*.[24] This was part of a series of "Enquêtes" (directed enquiries) launched by the journal during these years, which were characterized by a concern both with the past history and the present state of their subject. Banking and agricultural crises had been examined by earlier investigations. Bloch, who was already working towards his celebrated study of "Feudal Society," which was to be published in 1939–40 and would include an important and influential examination of the *noblesse*, was acutely conscious of the scholarly neglect of the French and European elites.[25] Though he evidently shared the established view that France's nobility underwent a long-term decline, he recognized the need for a wide-ranging comparative study. Bloch had intended, from the very foundation of the journal, to sponsor such an enquiry, along with a parallel investigation into the bourgeoisie.[26] In 1935 he began a review by declaring unambiguously that "the history of the French nobility remains an almost blank page" and he sought to utilize both his own wide-ranging contacts within and beyond France and the pages of the new journal to remedy this neglect.[27]

His co-editor, Lucien Febvre, though initially supportive, came to be patently skeptical about the value of such an *Enquête*. Febvre's own thesis had contained a dismissive and even hostile portrait of the nobility of the Franche-Comté, portrayed—in keeping with established orthodoxy—as inevitably losing out to

---

[23]   It was to be completed by his most important collaborator. L.B. Namier and John Brooke, eds, *History of Parliament: The House of Commons 1754–1790*, 3 vols (London: Her Majesty's Stationery Office, 1964).

[24]   The wider context is provided by André Burguière, *The Annales School: An Intellectual History* (2006; English translation, Ithaca: Cornell University Press, 2009), esp. chapter 4, and Carol Fink, *Marc Bloch: A Life in History* (Cambridge: Cambridge University Press, 1989), esp. chapter 7; there is also much of interest in the second volume of Bertrand Müller, ed., *Marc Bloch, Lucien Febvre et les 'Annales d'histoire économique et sociale': Correspondance*, 3 vols (Paris: Fayard, 1994–2003).

[25]   *La société féodale*, 2 vols (Paris: Albin Michel, 1939–40). The main exception to this generalization was the classic work of Paul Guilhiermoz, *Essai sur l'origine de la noblesse en France au moyen âge* (Paris: Picard, 1902).

[26]   Müller, ed., *Marc Bloch, Lucien Febvre*, I, 203, 212, 249.

[27]   Marc Bloch, "Anoblissements et Anoblis," *Revue de Synthèse*, 9 (1935), 155–8, at 155.

a rising middle class.[28] In any case he had his own, more immediate, priorities during the mid-1930s and, as a result, Bloch provided momentum.[29] But finding contributors proved time-consuming and extremely difficult, in itself evidence of the lack of interest among professional historians.[30] The "directed enquiry" was launched in 1936 with a prospectus written by Bloch himself and an article by the Comte Guy de Courtin de Neufbourg, a respected semi-professional scholar as well as a nobleman who was married to a Zamoyska.[31] The Zamoyski were one of the most important aristocratic lineages of Poland-Lithuania and thus a living reminder of the world that had been lost, as of course was Courtin de Neufbourg himself. In the course of the next three years a further nine articles of decidedly uneven quality were published, on topics ranging from Ancient Greece to the twentieth century. These included a notable short study by Bloch himself of France's nobility through the ages, and a substantial investigation by his graduate student, Robert Boutruche, of the noble society of the late medieval *Bordelais*.[32] But the investigation as a whole primarily confirmed the low level of scholarly interest and had little enduring impact. Bloch himself—as is well known—joined the Resistance during World War II, was captured and executed in 1944. When the *Annales* was relaunched by Febvre after the conclusion of peace, it had an even more pronounced center-left political outlook, which—as will be seen—was for long hostile to any study of the nobility.

A year or two later, in 1939, the Austrian scholar Otto Brunner published *Land und Herrschaft*, a difficult, complex, and highly innovative examination of the Austrian territories between the fourteenth and sixteenth centuries,

---

[28] *Philippe II et la Franche-Comté: La crise de 1567, ses origins et ses consequences—Étude d'histoire politique, religieuse et sociale* (Paris: Champion, 1912); see Dewald, *Lost Worlds*, 179.

[29] See in particular Müller, ed., *Marc Bloch, Lucien Febvre*, II, 407.

[30] Ibid., II, 155, 205, 209, 227, 289, 304–5, for glimpses of the problems which he encountered. Interestingly enough, Namier—on the advice of Eileen Power—was vetoed as a potential author for an article on the modern English nobility, eventually contributed by one of her colleagues at the London School of Economics, T.H. Marshall (1893–1981), who became a distinguished sociologist. Ibid., II, 306.

[31] *Annales d'histoire économique et sociale*, 8 (1936), 238–42; 243–55. Bloch affectionately described Neufbourg as a "bonhomme pittoresque!": Müller, ed., *Marc Bloch, Lucien Febvre*, II, 227.

[32] "Sur le passé de la noblesse française, quelques jalons de recherches," *Annales d'histoire économique et sociale*, 8 (1936), 366–78; "Aux origins d'une crise nobiliaire: Donations pieuses et pratiques successorales en Bordelais du XIIIe au XVIe siècle," *Annales d'histoire sociale*, 1 (1939), 161–78, 257–77. [The journal was temporarily renamed at that point.]

which remains fundamental to any serious study of the pre-modern nobility.[33] It was predicated upon a critique of traditional constitutional and legal history as it had evolved during the nineteenth century and the reification of the state which this had encouraged. Instead Brunner located the individual nobleman and the extended family over which he presided—the "household lordship" (*Hausherrschaft*)—at the very heart of the world of "Old Europe" (*Alteuropa*).[34] Social, economic, legal, and political developments should be viewed, he contended, both from this and from the perspective of the local community of the *Land* or province, and not from that of an imagined monarchical and centralizing state, which he demonstrated to be an invention of later scholarship. The *Land* community was as much, if not more, the source of law as the edicts of rulers.

The change of perspective involved was fundamental, and underlined the nobility's quite central role in pre-modern European history. Though individual dimensions of Brunner's arguments have been the target of significant criticisms, above all his discussion of the feud, his wider insights remain fundamental. But the impact of *Land und Herrschaft* has been muted, due primarily to its author's undoubted Nazi sympathies which led to his removal from his professorship at Vienna University at the end of the Second World War, and for half a century after 1945 his work was beyond the pale. This neglect was strengthened by the noted development of social history after the 1960s. The contours of this increasingly new subject made his authoritarian view of society and its construction from above appear more and more outdated. In a significant phrase Fernand Braudel once criticized and rejected what he styled Brunner's "structural and conservative social history" in favor of "a liberal, flexible, evolutionist sort of

---

[33]   Otto Brunner, *Land und Herrschaft: Grundfragen der territorialen Verfassungsgeschichte Südostdeutschlands im Mittelalter* (Baden bei Wien: Veröffentlichungen des Instituts für Geschichtsforschung und Archivwissenschaft in Wien, vol. 1, 1939). There is a remarkable English translation, based upon the fourth edition (1959) of the immensely complex German text, by Howard Kaminsky and James Van Horn Melton, *Land and Lordship: Structures of Governance in Medieval Austria* (Philadelphia: University of Pennsylvania Press, 1992); the "Translators' Introduction" (xii–lxi) to this is the best guide to Brunner and his impact. Though written from a less sympathetic perspective, Peter N. Miller, "Nazis and Neo-stoics: Otto Brunner and Gerhard Oestreich before and after the Second World War," *Past and Present*, 176 (2002), 144–86, is interesting on the wider context.

[34]   Especially in a series of essays conveniently assembled in *Neue Wege der Verfassungs- und Sozialgeschichte* (Göttingen: Vandenhoeck & Ruprecht, 1968); this was a second, expanded edition of a collection which had initially been published in 1956 under a slightly different title.

history."[35] Brunner himself was rehabilitated, teaching first at Cologne and then at Hamburg, and publishing a second major book on a noble theme: an elegiac, widely praised, and much more accessible study of a seventeenth-century Lower Austrian nobleman, Wolf Helmhard von Hohberg (1612–88).[36] His earlier study was less fortunate. Though a defective Italian translation appeared in 1983[37] and a notable English version a decade later, *Land und Herrschaft* has been rather neglected by historians of the nobility.

Indeed, before the 1960s, if there was a field of European history where the social elite was both subjected to intensive study and integrated into an overall explanation of political change, it was Ancient History. The publication of Sir Ronald Syme's *The Roman Revolution* in 1939, building upon the work of the German prosopographers, brought the nobility of the Roman world much more clearly into focus and, like Namier, came to exert an influence far beyond its own specialist field.[38] Quite unlike Namier, however, Syme integrated his structural analysis of families and careers into a remarkable and persuasive narrative of political events, and this contributed to its immense influence both within and far beyond the study of the Ancient World.

The writings of both Syme and Namier clearly influenced the Oxford medievalist K.B. McFarlane, who single-handedly revived interest in the fifteenth-century English nobility in a series of lectures and seminal articles from around 1940 onwards. His achievement was to be nothing less than to create the subject of England's late medieval nobility, which he constructed from the abundant published materials for English local and family history.[39] Exactly like Brunner, McFarlane's starting point was his profound dissatisfaction with

---

[35]   Fernand Braudel, "On a Concept of Social History", in his *On History* (1969; English translation, Chicago: University of Chicago Press, 1980), 120–31, at 122. [This essay first appeared in *Annales ESC* in 1959 and was a review of the first edition of Brunner's collected essays, cited above, n. 33.]

[36]   *Adeliges Landleben und europäischer Geist* (Salzburg: O. Müller, 1949). He was also one of the founding editors (along with Werner Conze and Reinhart Koselleck) of the celebrated *Geschichtliche Grundbegriffe*.

[37]   *Terra e Potere: Strutture pre-statuali e pre-moderne nella costituzionale dell' Austria medievale* (Milan: Arcana Imperii, 3, 1983). An Italian translation of Brunner's study of Helmhard von Hohberg had been published in 1972, 11 years earlier.

[38]   Oxford: Clarendon Press. See the illuminating biographical memoir by G.W. Bowersock, "Ronald Syme, 1903–1989," *Proceedings of the British Academy*, 84 (1993), 536–63. Interestingly enough, Syme always denied that he had read Namier's *Structure of Politics* until after the completion of *The Roman Revolution*. Bowersock, "Ronald Syme," 554–5.

[39]   These dominate McFarlane's personal library, which is preserved substantially intact at Magdalen College, Oxford, where he taught for four decades. I am indebted to the Archivist and Librarian, Robin Darwall-Smith, for facilitating my visit.

traditional constitutional history and especially the continuing and—as he saw it—baleful influence of its founding father in England, the nineteenth-century historian and Oxford Regius Professor, Bishop William Stubbs. McFarlane began a pioneering series of studies of the nobility particularly during the fifteenth century: his aim, as he wrote in 1944, was "to do justice to that much maligned class the medieval English barons."[40] But the scale of the task—together with his own perfectionism, his notable dedication to undergraduate teaching, and the less pressured academic environment of that era—ensured that he published only essays and gave lectures on noble themes during his lifetime. The majority of his most important contributions would remain unpublished until after his death in 1966.[41]

Foundations: The 1960s and Early 1970s

In the previous year McFarlane had written a paper for the Congress of Historical Sciences which met in Vienna, though—characteristically—he refused to attend, due to an acrimonious dispute about the numerous errors which the printed version in the conference proceedings contained. This Congress both reflected and further strengthened growing scholarly interest.[42] The 1950s and even more the early 1960s had seen a groundswell of interest in all periods and

---

[40]   K.B. McFarlane, *Letters to Friends 1940–1966*, ed. G.L. Harriss (Oxford: Magdalen College, 1997), 12. This also reprints Karl Leyser's biographical memoir of McFarlane (ix–xxviii), which first appeared in *Proceedings of the British Academy*, 62 (1976), 485–506.

[41]   The most important was *The Nobility of Later Medieval England: The Ford Lectures for 1953 and Related Studies* (Oxford: Oxford University Press, 1973). J.P. Cooper's "Introduction" to this volume (vii–xxxvii) is the most incisive discussion of McFarlane's scholarship. On his influence, see *The McFarlane Legacy: Studies in Late Medieval Politics and* Society, eds R.H. Britnell and A.J. Pollard (Stroud: Allen Sutton Publishing, 1995), especially the penetrating essay by Christine Carpenter, "Political and Constitutional History: Before and After McFarlane," 175–206. (I am very grateful to Professor Carpenter for sending me a copy of her article.) Andrew Hegarty, "The Tutorial Takeover 1928–1968," in *Magdalen College Oxford—A History*, ed. L. W.B. Brockliss (Oxford, 2008), 567–744, underlines McFarlane's immersion in all aspects of College life; cf. ibid, 621, for an explicit assertion of its importance.

[42]   The papers and discussions are published in *International Congress of Historical Sciences*. See Hans L. Mikoletzky, ed., *Rapports*, 5 vols (Vienna: Verlag F. Berger, 1965), I, 271–387, and V, 145–84. Essential context is provided by Karl Dietrich Erdmann, *Towards a Global Community of Historians: The International Historical Congresses and the International Committee of Historical Sciences 1898–2000* (1987; expanded English translation, New York and Oxford: Berg, 2005).

many countries. The study of the eighteenth-century nobility had been advanced by a notable collection of national essays by British scholars which originated in a series of seminars at the University of Oxford, while another Oxford historian, H.J. Habakkuk, was opening up the subject of the post-1650 landed elite in England.[43] The Oxford in which Lawrence Stone researched *Crisis of the Aristocracy* was the focal point for anglophone studies of nobility in all periods with Habakkuk, McFarlane, Syme, and their graduate students. The university also retained something of its established aristocratic social ethos.[44]

Elsewhere increasing interest was also evident. In 1962 the distinguished Belgian medievalist Léopold Genicot, who had published a substantial study of the nobility of the region around Namur in the southern Netherlands, and his French counterpart Georges Duby both noted the early beginnings of scholarly interest and called for more research on the medieval *noblesse*.[45] This opened a quarter-century during which the study of the medieval nobility came of age.[46] Within the field of early modern French history American scholars played a leading role. Franklin L. Ford published a notable study of the eighteenth-century *noblesse* in 1953, emphasizing the fault lines which divided *robe* and sword and the ways in which the former merged with and, to a certain extent, came to predominate within the latter. Robert Forster contributed a methodologically innovative exploration of the nobility in Toulouse and the surrounding region in 1960, while four years later another American, J. Russell Major, persuasively

---

[43] Albert Goodwin, ed., *The European Nobility in the Eighteenth Century* (London: A. & C. Black, 1953); the publications of H.J. Habakkuk are conveniently listed in F.M.L. Thompson, ed., *Landowners, Capitalists and Entrepreneurs: Essays for Sir John Habakkuk* (Oxford: Clarendon Press, 1994), xi–xiii. See also Thompson's illuminating biographical memoir, "Hrothgar John Habakkuk (1915–2002)," *Proceedings of the British Academy*, 124 (2004), 91–114.

[44] This is well captured by the recent biography of the legendary Warden of Stone's own college, Wadham: Leslie Mitchell, *Maurice Bowra: A Life* (Oxford: Oxford University Press, 2009), esp. chapters 7 and 9.

[45] Léopold Genicot, "La noblesse au Moyen Âge dans l'ancienne 'Francie'," *Annales ESC*, 17 (1962), 1–22; Léopold Genicot, *L'Économie rurale namuroise au bas Moyen Âge*, II: *Les hommes. La Noblesse* (Louvain: Bureau du recueil, Collège Érasme, 1960); Georges Duby, "Une Enquête à poursuivre: la noblesse dans la France médiévale," *Revue Historique*, 226 (1961), 1–22.

[46] Léopold Genicot, "Recent Research on the Medieval Nobility," first published in 1975 and available in English translation in Timothy Reuter, ed., *The Medieval Nobility* (Amsterdam: North Holland, 1979), 17–36, and Reuter's more recent "The Medieval Nobility," provide surveys and bibliography; Werner Hechberger, *Adel, Ministerialität und Rittertum im Mittelalter* (Munich: Oldenbourg, 2004) surveys the development of German-language scholarship (see especially chapter 2) and provides an extensive bibliography of recent publications.

challenged the established and widely prevailing interpretation which portrayed a feudal aristocracy being eclipsed by a rising bourgeoisie.[47] The early 1960s were even more important for the Italian nobilities, with the publication of four major studies between 1962 and 1965.[48] Everywhere, it seemed, nobility was coming into fashion. Social history was rapidly becoming established, while it was assumed that a knowledge of the make-up of the governing caste in all periods, its families and their careers, would deepen understanding of political events.

The choice of the "ruling classes" (*classes dirigeantes*) from Antiquity to the nineteenth century as one of the International Congress's "major themes" both reflected and significantly strengthened this interest. The discussions in Vienna were tinged by political controversy, since the 1960s were the heyday of the Cold War, and there were clashes between historians, often from the West, who objected to the use of the term "class" to describe any social group before the nineteenth century and those, often from the East, who criticized the study of any social group other than the peasantry and its successor in the vanguard of history, the industrial proletariat. Nevertheless, the International Congress in 1965 stimulated interest, and many participants would sponsor or carry out research into the nobility. It was the first of three contemporaneous events which significantly increased scholarly interest.

The other two were the near-simultaneous—though quite unconnected—publication of major books which transformed scholarship in the field, in the process creating a social history of the nobility which has proved influential and enduring. In 1965 the Oxford historian Lawrence Stone, who by then had migrated to Princeton University, produced his celebrated study of the English peerage, *The Crisis of the Aristocracy 1558–1641*, while the very next year, the French scholar Jean Meyer published his great thesis on the nobility of

---

[47]   Franklin L. Ford, *Robe and Sword: The Regrouping of the French Aristocracy after Louis XIV* (Cambridge, Mass.: Harvard University Press, 1953); Robert Forster, *The Nobility of Toulouse in the Eighteenth Century: A Social and Economic Study* (Baltimore, MD: Johns Hopkins University Press, 1960); J. Russell Major, "The Crown and the Aristocracy in Renaissance France," *American Historical Review*, 69 (1964), 631–45.

[48]   Franco Angiolini, "Les noblesses italiennes à l'époque moderne: approches et interprétations," *Revue d'histoire moderne et contemporaine*, 45 (1988), 66–87, at 69. The titles in question were James C. Davis, *The Decline of the Venetian Nobility as a Ruling Class* (Baltimore, MD: Johns Hopkins University Press, 1962); S.J. Woolf, *Studi sulla nobiltà piemontese nell'epoca dell'assolutismo* (Turin: Memorie dell'Accademia delle Scienze di Torino, 1963); A. Ventura, *Nobiltà e popolo nella società veneta del '400 e '500* (Bari: Laterza, 1964); and M. Berengo, *Nobili e mercanti nella Lucca del Cinquecento* (Turin: Einaudi, 1965).

Brittany during the long eighteenth century.[49] These two studies were each, in their own ways, quite seminal. Though written in isolation, there was a striking degree of overlap between them. In addition to asserting the nobility's central importance, they established a range of topics and a distinctive approach which future historians followed. Despite their real similarities, however, these studies had strikingly different origins. Meyer's book, based on the exceptionally rich Breton evidence, was a regional monograph of the kind which French historians at that period wrote as their *doctorat d'état*, which was the essential preliminary to an academic career, and it seems to have been undertaken at the suggestion of Henri Fréville, who had written on the intendancy in Brittany, though the author himself was quick to claim Marc Bloch as its spiritual father.[50] By contrast Stone's book was rooted in—and to a significant extent colored by—an acrimonious controversy among Oxford historians during the later 1940s and 1950s over the social origins of England's mid-seventeenth-century Civil Wars and Revolution.[51] He himself had participated in this "Storm over the Gentry," as it became known, and had suffered exceptionally severe criticism over an attempt in one of his early articles to demonstrate the financial plight of the peerage during the later sixteenth century.[52] His principal scourger was Hugh Trevor-Roper, his own former tutor and subsequently Oxford's Regius Professor of Modern History.[53]

A connection between contemporary developments and scholarly fashion was evident. Historians have themselves been influenced by the cultural trends of the second half of the twentieth century, which in many countries have been inimical to aristocracy, and this helped to encourage interest in noble power in the past. There has clearly been a link—though its exact nature is elusive—between the decline of Europe's traditional landed class and the revival of scholarly interest in its forerunner. The continental European nobility lost much of its political and social power, together with a large part of its extensive landholding,

---

[49]   Lawrence Stone, *The Crisis of the Aristocracy 1558–1641* (Oxford: Clarendon Press, 1965); Jean Meyer, *La noblesse Bretonne au XVIIIe siècle*, 2 vols (Paris: SEVPEN, 1966).

[50]   Meyer, *Noblesse bretonne*, I, xi, xvii.

[51]   Essential context is provided by David Cannadine, "Historians in 'The Liberal Hour': Lawrence Stone and J.H. Plumb Re-Visited," *Historical Research*, 75 (2002), 316–54.

[52]   Lawrence Stone, "The Anatomy of the Elizabethan Aristocracy," *Economic History Review*, 18 (1948), 1–53; see also H.R. Trevor-Roper, "The Elizabethan Aristocracy: An Anatomy Anatomised," *Economic History Review*, 2nd series, 3 (1950–51), 279–98; Lawrence Stone, "The Elizabethan Aristocracy: A Restatement," *Economic History Review*, 2nd series, 4 (1951–52), 302–21.

[53]   Richard Davenport-Hines, ed., *Letters from Oxford: Hugh Trevor-Roper to Bernard Berenson* (London: Weidenfeld & Nicolson, 2006), 130–2; cf. ibid., 281, 287.

between—very approximately—the 1880s and 1945. An identical development occurred a generation later in England, where the final demise of the landed classes only took place after the Second World War. Stone's extensive research on aristocratic papers was possible because these were becoming available in great quantities due to the financial plight of many of England's leading families and the consequent depositing of their muniments in local Record Offices.[54] He would subsequently write that an "Englishman ... does not have to read Pareto to learn about the dominance of elites," and he acknowledged that his major work on the Elizabethan and early Stuart aristocracy "was researched at a time when that class was in full financial crisis and when great country houses were being abandoned and allowed to tumble down by the score."[55] Indeed, he had begun research (he subsequently wrote) with the "assumption that the English aristocracy in that period was the epitome of an incompetent, frivolous and decadent ruling class about to be set aside by a rising bourgeoisie," only to find this destroyed by the detailed evidence he found.[56] The established Grand Narrative was overthrown by his own extensive researches, in a way which would become familiar to many historians of nobility.

Three particular sources of Stone's highly novel approach can be identified. In the first place he was far more open than most British or American scholars of that period to the approach of the *Annales* school, which was increasingly dominant in France. Married to the daughter of a leading French medieval historian, Robert Fawtier, he frequently attended conferences there.[57] Stone was also an avid reader both of the journal *Annales: Économies, Sociétés, Civilisations (ESC)*—as it had been renamed on its relaunch after 1945—and of its English counterpart, *Past and Present*, the editorial board of which he had joined in 1958, as well as the *Economic History Review*. Though his concern to explain historical change in terms of short-term events as well as *structures* and *conjonctures* set him apart from the *Annales'* approach, the debt of *Crisis of the Aristocracy* to French scholarship was clear and acknowledged.[58] Its concern with demography, social

---

[54]　See "Lawrence Stone—as seen by himself," in *The First Modern Society: Essays in English History in Honour of Lawrence Stone*, eds A.L. Beier, David Cannadine, and James Rosenheim (Cambridge: Cambridge University Press, 1989), 575–95, at 586; cf. Stone, *Crisis of the Aristocracy*, 2, on the "archive revolution" in England after 1945 which made serious study of the peerage possible for the first time. Some 30 such collections were consulted in the writing of *Crisis of the Aristocracy*, xvii.

[55]　"Lawrence Stone—as seen by himself," 586, 594.

[56]　Ibid., 585.

[57]　Davenport-Hines, *Letters from Oxford*, 130–31.

[58]　Stone, *Crisis of the Aristocracy*, 3. His subsequent and notably judicious assessment of *Annaliste* scholarship is to be found in "The Past and the Present," reprinted in *The Past and*

and economic factors, marriage, and the aristocracy's distinctive culture and *mentalité* was partly rooted in his knowledge of the work of *Annales'* historians, as was its structural and analytical framework and its desire to quantify.

A further intellectual debt was evident: to Max Weber, whom Stone discovered and began to read in the mid-1950s, by which point substantial extracts from his writings were available in English translation.[59] Weber's distinction between wealth and status, and his emphasis on examining both side by side with elite power as the dominant triad, reinforced an emphasis which had taken shape during Stone's extended exploration of family archives. A third influence upon him is also the most elusive and remains problematical: that of his Oxford colleague, K.B. McFarlane. The two men do not seem to have been on good terms, which was far from uncommon in the Oxford of the 1950s, while the "Introduction" to *Crisis of the Aristocracy* contained what appears to be an oblique and slighting reference to the latter's scholarship, or at least his non-publication.[60] In the mid-1950s, however, Stone had been among the "majority of dons" attending McFarlane's History Faculty lectures on "English Seignorial Administration and its Records, 1290–1536"; he was in Oxford when the latter gave the "Ford Lectures" on the late medieval English nobility in 1953 (though his attendance cannot be established), while his own major book contains numerous echoes of themes first introduced by McFarlane's lectures and articles.[61]

A final, more immediate origin of Stone's large-scale investigations, which extended over some 15 years, was an attempt to prove his detractors wrong and so vindicate both himself and his mentor, R.H. Tawney, whom he had first got to know during the Second World War.[62] Though in the course of research and

---

the Present Revisited (London: Routledge and Kegan Paul, 1987), 74–96.

[59]   "Lawrence Stone—as seen by himself," 585. The Weber primer was probably *From Max Weber: Essays in Sociology*, trans. and eds H.H. Gerth and C. Wright Mills, which had first been published in 1946 (New York: Oxford University Press).

[60]   Stone, *Crisis of the Aristocracy*, 7: "Even if recent attempts to modify the traditional picture of the late medieval nobility ultimately prove to be well founded ..."; cf. McFarlane, *Letters to Friends*, 142. The full text of seven lectures on "English Seignorial Administration," which were highly original in approach for the period at which they were given and anticipate some of the themes of *Crisis of the Aristocracy*, is preserved in the McFarlane papers, Magdalen College, Oxford, GPD/26/II/36. I am grateful to the President and Fellows of the College for permitting me to examine these papers.

[61]   McFarlane, *Letters to Friends*, 101, 103. It should be added that it also diverged in significant ways: to give only the most striking example, whereas McFarlane diminished the extent of noble violence in the fifteenth century, Stone emphasized how violent some peers remained 100 years later.

[62]   See especially *Crisis of the Aristocracy*, 6.

writing Stone retreated significantly from some of his earlier claims, the specific origins of his study in the "Storm over the Gentry" ensured that the "crisis" part of his title and his material on the peerage's financial predicament monopolized attention and criticism in the Anglophone scholarly world when the book was published.[63] This restricted perspective was strengthened by the appearance, eight years later, of an overlapping volume containing a series of case studies of individual families and their finances.[64]

With hindsight these three events—one International Congress and two books—can be recognized as moments at which the scholarly study of the early modern nobility came of age. In the short-term, however, Stone's book initially appeared to have a much more negative impact, launching a scholarly debate about a "Crisis of the Nobility" which flourished during the later 1960s and 1970s and was predicated upon the established view that the traditional elite was a spent force. There had been a debate in *Past and Present* during the 1950s and 1960s about a supposed "General Crisis of the seventeenth century," variously portrayed as the birth pangs of capitalism, as a consequence of the alienation of the "country" against the swollen royal courts of the period, and as the product of the incessant fiscal demands of monarchical states almost permanently at war.[65] Building both on this debate and on Stone's book, and embracing their central metaphor, a full-blown "crisis of the European nobility" was pronounced by the French scholar François Billaçois in 1976, by which point

---

[63]   E.g. G.E. Aylmer, "The Crisis of the Aristocracy 1558–1641," *Past and Present*, 32 (1965), 113–25; D.C. Coleman, "The 'Gentry' Controversy and the Aristocracy in Crisis, 1558–1641," *History*, 51 (1966), 165–78; [J.P. Cooper], "Back to the Sources," *The Times Literary Supplement*, 7 April 1966, reprinted in *TLS 5: Essays and Reviews from the Times Literary Supplement, 1966* (London: Oxford University Press, 1967), 84–98 [At that period all *TLS* reviews appeared anonymously; Cooper's authorship is confirmed by McFarlane, *Letters to Friends*, 239]; J.H. Hexter, "Lawrence Stone and the English Aristocracy," *Journal of British Studies*, 8 (1969), 22–78.

[64]   Lawrence Stone, *Family and Fortune: Studies in Aristocratic Finance in the Sixteenth and Seventeenth Centuries* (Oxford: Clarendon Press, 1973).

[65]   The key essays were collected in T.S. Aston, ed., *Crisis in Europe, 1560–1660* (New York: Basic Books, 1965) and valuably updated by the contributions to Geoffrey Parker and Lesley M. Smith, eds, *The General Crisis of the Seventeenth Century* (London: Routledge & Kegan Paul, 1985; 2nd enlarged edn, London: Routledge, 1997). See more recently Philip Benedict and Myron P. Gutmann, eds, *Early Modern Europe: From Crisis to Stability* (Newark: University of Delaware Press, 2005); *American Historical Review*, 113 (2008), 1031–99, a forum devoted to "The General Crisis of the Seventeenth Century Revisited," and especially Jonathan Dewald's incisive examination of the debate's historiographical origins, "Crisis, Chronology and the Shape of European Social History," 1031–52; and the more recent special issue of the *Journal of Interdisciplinary History*, 40:2 (2009), devoted to "The Crisis of the Seventeenth Century: Interdisciplinary Perspectives."

it had already been applied to Denmark, Castile, Sicily, France, and Muscovy; it would subsequently be applied to Bohemia and may have been canvased even more widely.[66] Significantly, in the very same year Guy Chaussinand-Nogaret published his influential study of the eighteenth-century French *noblesse*, with its strongly etched portrait of a traditional elite which was internally divided and reduced to near-impotence by the eve of the French Revolution.[67]

This "crisis" debate was predicated upon assumptions concerning the seventeenth-century origins of modernity, whether these lay in nascent capitalism or the protean modern state. It incorporated and developed established ideas about continuing noble decline during the early modern centuries, and had three overlapping elements: political, ideological, and economic. Politically nobles were believed to be losing out to absolute monarchy, while their traditional military function—that of "warrior-elite," the traditional basis of their claim to special status—was undermined by near-simultaneous developments in warfare. These were primarily the emergence of standing armies, the enlarged role of infantry, and the advent of gunpowder weapons, which were the central elements in what has been styled the "Military Revolution." This was also integral to the second strand in the "noble crisis": an ideological challenge to the nobility's traditional preeminence, rooted in Renaissance ideas of honor and virtue, rather than the claims of birth, ancestry, and function as the basis of exalted social standing put forward by noble propagandists. It was taking place, moreover, at exactly the point at which the nobility's established claim to be the military caste, the "men on horseback" and so the dominant group within society, was becoming increasingly difficult to sustain.

Thirdly and most importantly, many noble families were believed to have experienced real economic difficulties which fatally weakened them. The idea of an economic "crisis" of the English peerage which contributed to the political breakdown of the early 1640s had been central to Stone's arguments, and became the principal target of his critics. In the wider European context it has stood up rather better than the ideological or political strands, though whether the undoubted economic problems merit the overused description "crisis" is more

---

[66] François Billaçois, "La crise de la noblesse européenne (1550–1650): Une mise au point," *Revue d'histoire moderne et contemporaine*, 23 (1976), 258–77; five years earlier, Henry Kamen had argued in a similar if more nuanced vein in his *The Iron Century: Social Change in Europe, 1550–1660* (London: Weidenfeld & Nicolson, 1971), 129–65. A faint Italian echo of Billaçois's arguments appeared the next year: Oscar Di Simplicio, "La crisi della nobiltà," *Studi Storici*, 18 (1977), 201–16.

[67] *La noblesse française au XVIIIe siècle* (Paris: Hachette, 1976). An English translation was published a decade later: *The French Nobility in the Eighteenth Century: From Feudalism to Enlightenment* (Cambridge: Cambridge University Press, 1985).

problematic, particularly since the nobility seems to have fared distinctly better than other social groups. These difficulties were the product, very broadly, of two linked developments. The sixteenth-century Price Revolution had created problems for individuals and families whose income, above all rents from long-term leases which could not easily be increased, could not keep up with rapidly rising prices. When the period of expansion ended around 1600 (and the chronology varied not merely from country to country but from region to region), nobles found it difficult to keep their heads above water during a period of falling prices, unstable markets, and general economic slow-down. A second development increased pressure upon their finances at exactly this period, as family expenditures were forced up by what has come to be styled "conspicuous consumption": the nobility began to build expensive country residences and town palaces, and generally to bear the costs of a more opulent lifestyle which centered on the burgeoning royal courts.

The impact of such economic problems has been most persuasively explored by the Danish historian E. Ladewig Petersen,[68] and is clearly particularly valid where poorer nobles were concerned, though some better-off lineages also experienced real difficulties at this time. One obvious index appeared to be the spiraling level of debt which many families were shouldering: borrowing and credit had featured prominently in Stone's pages. Yet while individual families undoubtedly experienced real periods of difficulty, increasing indebtedness should not be seen as an index of problems, far less decline, and the argument for a generalized economic "crisis," like the wider thesis, remains unproven.

The real importance of the "crisis" theory was the way it directed attention to nobility as a subject and further stimulated research exactly at the moment when social history was undergoing a "meteoric rise," and the resulting research began to appear in print from the later 1970s.[69] Within France, Meyer's great work was widely influential and shaped the next generation's burgeoning scholarship. By contrast Stone's was effectively ignored there until Billaçois's article: this was a period when French historians took far less account of anglophone publications than they would do subsequently. In any case until relatively recently the *Annales* school was unsympathetic to any study of the nobility.[70] It ignored the insights

---

[68]   See his *The Crisis of the Danish Nobility 1580–1660* (Odense: Universitetsforlag, 1967).

[69]   Sewell, "Political Unconscious," 22. Two review articles provide a particularly helpful introduction to this first wave of scholarship: Carlo Capra, "La nobiltà europea prima della Rivoluzione," *Studi Storici*, 18 (1977), 117–38; and K.G. Faber, "Mitteleuropäischer Adel im Wandel der Neuzeit," *Geschichte und Gesellschaft*, 7 (1981), 276–96.

[70]   See, e.g., Fernand Braudel's comments in a review first published in 1959: "On a Concept of Social History," 125.

of Marc Bloch, accepted and perpetuated a century and a half of neglect of the *noblesse*, and reinforced this by a center-left political outlook and a conviction that only the peasantry and the commercial middle class merited attention. This approach was epitomized by Pierre Goubert's renowned study of rural society in the Beauvaisis during the seventeenth century, which portrayed a regional nobility in full decline, condemned by economic failure to sell its lands to successful merchants.[71]

The historiographical emergence of nobility during the 1960s and 1970s left few traces in the pages of *Annales ESC*.[72] *Crisis of the Aristocracy* was not reviewed by either it or the *Revue d'histoire moderne et contemporaine*, while the only apparent mention in France's other leading historical periodical, the *Revue historique*, was a discussion of its key arguments in the course of a retrospective survey of recent scholarship on Tudor England contributed by an English scholar.[73] The fate of Stone's French counterpart was even more striking. At this period Jean Meyer was a frequent contributor to *Annales ESC*, but not even this secured him a review of the *Noblesse bretonne*, which was ignored by the journal. Though Stone and Meyer were both examining topics—demography, society, economy, *mentalités*—at the very heart of the *Annaliste* approach, their focus condemned them to oblivion. These considerations make the ignoring of *Crisis of the Aristocracy* in France more comprehensible.[74] Stone's admiration for *Annaliste* historical scholarship was not reciprocated and only one of his many

---

[71]   Pierre Goubert, *Beauvais et le Beauvaisis de 1600 à 1730*, 2 vols (Paris: SEVPEN, 1960), I, 187, 206–21 and *passim*. Goubert, it is only fair to add, subsequently came to adopt a more positive view of the *noblesse*: see especially [with Daniel Roche], *Les Français et l'Ancien Régime: La société et l'état*, 2 vols (Paris: Colin, 1984), I, 115–50. Another emblematic work of French scholarship, Pierre Deyon, *Amiens: Capitale provinciale—étude sur la société urbaine au XVIIe siècle* (Paris and The Hague: Mouton, 1967), gave equally little space to the nobility and its role, devoting one unsympathetic chapter (265–92) in a text of almost 500 pages.

[72]   Several exceptions can be noted: Frédéric Mauro, "La noblesse toulousaine au XVIII siècle," *Annales ESC*, 16 (1961), 1012–6, reviewing Forster's monograph on Toulouse, cited above, n. 47; Genicot's 1962 article, cited above, n. 45; and a French version of E. Ladewig Petersen's study of the Danish nobility, cited above, n. 68, ibid., 23 (1968), 1237–61. But Mauro, as he acknowledged, had known Robert Forster when he was researching in France, while Petersen's arguments exactly fitted the established Grand Narrative of inevitable noble decline due to economic weakness.

[73]   Helen Miller, "Bulletin historique: L'Angleterre au XVIe siècle," *Revue historique*, 241 (1969), 381–408, at 393–6.

[74]   It may have been reinforced by a recollection of the earlier "Storm over the Gentry," during which *Annales* had abandoned plans at a very late stage to publish a French translation (sponsored by Fawtier) of Stone's "Anatomy of the Elizabethan Aristocracy," when Trevor-Roper's critique appeared: Davenport-Hines, *Letters from Oxford*, 132.

books was ever to be translated into French: his short study of the *Causes of the English Revolution, 1529–1642*.[75] It is revealing that when his subsequent study of the English peerage, *An Open Elite?*, appeared he was careful to publish an immediate French summary of the principal conclusions in *Annales ESC*.[76]

In sharp contrast, two leading Italian historical periodicals published long, acute, and admiring reviews within four years of the book's publication.[77] Stone's impact was much greater elsewhere, facilitated by translations into Italian (1972) and Spanish (1976).[78] In this way, teachers and their increasing number of doctoral students began to examine individual nobilities through the eyes of Stone and Meyer, whose books guided a new generation. Though written in isolation, their approaches and the major themes which emerged were remarkably similar. Together, they set out a programmatic agenda, which subsequent historians adopted. The topics to be examined included: What was noble status and how was it acquired? How was it transmitted? What do we know about noble demography? The structure of noble families and the importance of the wider lineage? Marriage and inheritance? Landholding? Income, expenditure and the role of credit? Attitudes to violence and dueling? Court and office-holding? Education? Cultural activities of all kinds? Detailed research, however, had the opposite effect anticipated: what began as an enquiry which, it was assumed, would write its obituary, in the event achieved the reverse. It made clear that the nobility was not merely alive but flourishing and actually gaining in social, economic, and political power. The "crisis" metaphor was shown to be not only simplistic in the extreme, but actually untenable. Instead, an emphasis on resilience and adaptability to changing circumstances became the overarching theme, and this has persisted until the present day. The key word became, and remains, "consolidation" rather than "crisis."

---

[75] Lawrence Stone, *Les causes de la révolution anglaise 1529–1642* (Paris: Flammarion, 1974).

[76] "L'Angleterre de 1540 à 1880: Pays de noblesse ouverte?" *Annales ESC*, 40 (1985), 71–94, summarizing Lawrence Stone and Jeanne C. Fawtier Stone, *An Open Elite? England 1540–1880* (Oxford: Clarendon Press, 1984).

[77] By Vittorio Gabrieli: *Rivista Storica Italiana*, 79 (1967), 260–76, in which *Crisis of the Aristocracy* was reviewed along with two titles by Christopher Hill: see especially 260–67; S.J. Woolf, "La trasformazione dell'aristocrazia e la rivoluzione inglese," *Studi Storici*, 10 (1969), 309–34. These no doubt paved the way for the Italian translation which appeared in 1972: see below, n. 78.

[78] The Italian translation was of the entire text (Turin: Einaudi, 1972); the Spanish version (Madrid: Revista de Occidente, 1976) of an abridged paperback edition, less than half of the original text but with the identical title, which Stone had produced two years after the book's initial publication (Oxford: Oxford University Press, 1967).

Establishing the Subject

During the 1970s and the 1980s academic historians, and especially doctoral students, fully embraced nobility, which was now viewed largely in collective terms. The overriding importance of the group, rather than the individual upon whom historians had traditionally focused, which was rooted in Marxism and emblematic of the new social history, characterized this wave of publications and has continued until the present day. By this point the nature of research was also changing, and this too influenced the way in which the subject was to develop. A world where a small number of scholars worked in near isolation was giving way to the graduate seminars and PhD factories of the later-twentieth century. In Britain until the 1950s and 1960s, graduate training was all but unknown and even the completion of a doctorate by no means essential. Stone recalled how, when he graduated in 1946, he did not embark upon PhD research, which "was still something that a graduate of Oxford or Cambridge felt to be beneath his dignity—a peculiar academic *rite de passage* that foreigners went in for, like Germans, or French, or Americans."[79] Both the vast expansion of the academic profession during the twentieth century and the changed nature of the graduate education and doctoral supervision it provided were to be important for the growth of interest in the early modern nobility.

A series of large-scale publications began to appear during the 1970s. In France the first three were Jean-Pierre Labatut's study of the *ducs et pairs*, Arlette Jouanna's examination of changing ideas of nobility, and Jean-Marie Constant's exploration of the nobility of the Beauce.[80] Significantly, all three scholars were to spend their careers in provincial French universities and were not appointed to a prized chair in Paris, which only Meyer among all the French historians of the nobility appears to have secured with his appointment at the Sorbonne. This underlines the extent to which France's historical establishment long remained antipathetic to nobility as a topic of research. The more substantial, second-level doctorates in some continental European countries, especially France and

---

[79] "Lawrence Stone—as seen by himself," 581. Instead he began working on the subject on which he would publish his second book: *An Elizabethan: Sir Horatio Palavicino* (Oxford: Clarendon Press, 1956). Stone's first book had been a study of *Sculpture in Britain: The Middle Ages* (Harmondsworth: Pelican Books, 1955; 2nd revised edn, London: Penguin Books, 1972), which he had been contracted to write while still an undergraduate.

[80] Jean-Pierre Labatut, *Les ducs-et-pairs de France au XVIIe siècle: Étude sociale* (Paris: Presses Universitaires de France, 1972); Arlette Jouanna, *L'idée de race en France au XVIe siècle et au début de XVII siècle*, 3 vols (Lille: Université Lille III, 1976; republished in 2 vols, Montpellier: Université Paul Valéry, 1981); Jean-Marie Constant, *Nobles et paysans en Beauce au XVI et XVIIe siècles*, 2 vols (Lille: Université Lille III, 1981).

Germany, and the more generous time available for their completion, together with the subsidized publication of academic monographs, were especially suited to the kind of large-scale and multigenerational study of a particular region's nobility—a single family or a strata within the nobility which were needed and which, over the next few decades, would transform knowledge of the early modern nobility across Europe.[81]

One partial exception was England, despite its central role in the initial revival. Important books were published, but they were rather fewer in number.[82] By contrast, in the United States numerous significant contributions have been made during recent decades, particularly in the fields of Russian and French history. American scholars have produced notable studies of the boiars of early modern Russia.[83] Sixteenth- and seventeenth-century France and its nobilities inspired a series of important theses and books sponsored by J. Russell Major at Emory University.[84] Its eighteenth-century successors have been the subject of important doctoral work at the University of Michigan supervised by David D.

---

[81]   These included Janine Fayard, *Les members du conseil de Castile à l'époque moderne (1621–1746)* (Geneva: Droz, 1979); Marie-Claude Gerbet, *La noblesse dans le royaume de Castille: Étude sur les structures sociales en Estrémadure (1454–1516)* (Paris: Publications de la Sorbonne, 1979); Jean Nicolas, *La Savoie au 18e siècle: Noblesse et bourgeosie*, 2 vols (Paris: Maloine, 1979); Calixte Hudemann-Simon, *La noblesse Luxembourgeoise au XVIIIe siècle* (Paris: Publications de la Sorbonne, 1985); Ignacio Atienza Hernández, *Aristocracia, poder y riqueza en la España moderna: La Casa de Osuna siglos XV–XIX* (Madrid: Siglo Veintiuno, 1987); S. Aragón Mateos, *La nobleza extremeña en el siglo XVIII* (Mérida: Consejo Ciudadano de la Biblioteca Pública Municipal Juan Pablo Forner, 1990).

[82]   The principal contributions have been: John Cannon, *Aristocratic Century: The Peerage of Eighteenth-Century England* (Cambridge: Cambridge University Press, 1984), J.V. Beckett, *The Aristocracy in England, 1660–1914* (Oxford: Blackwell, 1986), and H.J. Habakkuk, *Marriage, Debt and the Estates System: English Landownership, 1650–1950* (Oxford: Oxford University Press, 1994), together with the two books by David Cannadine cited above, n. 10.

[83]   This was launched by the writings of Gustav Alef, collected in *Rulers and Nobles in Fifteenth-Century Muscovy* (London: Variorum, 1983). In addition, see Robert O. Crummey, *Aristocrats and Servitors: The Boyar Elite in Russia 1613–1689* (Princeton, NJ: Princeton University Press, 1983); Nancy Shields Kollmann, *Kinship and Politics: The Making of the Muscovite Political System, 1345–1547* (Stanford, CA: Stanford University Press, 1987); Nancy Shields Kollmann, *By Honor Bound: State and Society in Early Modern Russia* (Ithaca, NY: Cornell University Press, 1999); Valerie Kivelson, *Autocracy in the Provinces: The Muscovite Gentry and Political Culture in the Seventeenth Century* (Stanford, CA: Stanford University Press, 1996); and Marshall T. Poe, *The Russian Elite in the Seventeenth Century*, 2 vols (Helsinki: Suomalainen Tiedeakatemia, 2004).

[84]   These can be approached through the *Festschrift* in his honor. See Mack P. Holt, ed., *Society and Institutions in Early Modern France* (Athens: University of Georgia Press, 1991).

Bien, which has yielded a series of significant monographs.[85] The contribution of Jonathan Dewald has been particularly notable, with three major and contrasting studies of the early modern *noblesse*.[86]

On the European continent abundant research has been and continues to be published. In France, the regional monograph has been preeminent, accompanied by an emphasis upon continuities and the enduring importance of traditions.[87] The study of the nobility has also flourished in Italy and Spain during recent decades. In Italian academic circles a revival of interest had been evident from the early 1960s, and drew upon an older tradition of studying urban patriciates which evolved into landed nobilities during the early modern centuries.[88] An important conference in 1977 focused research.[89] By the 1980s the study of the peninsula's diverse noble societies was securely established, once again encouraged by growing international interest, and generating studies of noble identity as well as of individual families and regions.[90] An identical pattern

---

[85]   The work of some of his students is conveniently assembled in Robert M. Schwartz and Robert A. Schneider, eds, *Tocqueville and Beyond: Essays on the Old Regime in Honor of David D. Bien* (Newark: University of Delaware Press, 2003).

[86]   Jonathan Dewald, *The Formation of a Provincial Nobility: The Magistrates of the Parlement of Rouen 1499–1610* (Princeton, NJ: Princeton University Press, 1980); *Pont-St-Pierre, 1398–1789: Lordship, Community and Capitalism in Early Modern France* (Berkeley and Los Angeles: University of California Press, 1987); *Aristocratic Experience and the Origins of Modern Culture: France, 1570–1715* (Berkeley and Los Angeles: University of California Press, 1993).

[87]   E.g. Michel Nassiet, *Noblesse et pauvreté: La petite noblesse en Bretagne, XVe–XVIIIe siècle* (Bannalec: Société d'Histoire et d'Archéologie de Bretagne, 1993); Laurent Bourquin, *Noblesse seconde et Pouvoir en Champagne aux XVIe et XVIIe siècles* (Paris: Publications de la Sorbonne, 1994). Bourquin's later manual, *La noblesse dans la France moderne* (Paris: Belin, 2002), contains a full bibliography of the last generation's scholarship, which can also be sampled in the notable collection of essays edited by Josette Pontet, Michel Figeac, and Marie Boisson, *La noblesse de la fin du XVIe au début du XXe siècle: un modèle social?* 2 vols (Anglet: Atlantica, 2002).

[88]   Cf. above, p. 34.

[89]   *Patriziati e aristocrazie nobiliari: Ceti dominanti e organizzazione del potere nell'Italia centro-settentrionale dal XVI al XVIII secolo*, eds Cesare Mozzarelli and P. Schiera (Trento: Istituto storico Italo-germanico in Trento, 1978).

[90]   E.g. Claudio Donati, *L'idea di Nobiltà in Italia: Secoli XIV–XVIII* (Rome: Laterza, 1988); Maria Antonietta Visceglia, *Territorio, feudo e potere locale: Terra d'Otranto tra Medio Evo ed Età moderna* (Naples: Guida, 1988), a regional study which gives (part II) considerable attention to the area's nobilities, and the essays collected in the same author's *Il bisogno di eternità: I comportamenti aristocratici a Napoli in età moderna* (Naples: Guida, 1988). Visceglia also edited an influential collection of essays: *Signori, patrizi, cavalieri nell'età moderna* (Rome: Laterza, 1992). Her introduction (v–xxxiii) surveys the development of

was evident in Spain, where modern scholarly interest can be traced back to the 1960s and early 1970s, but was significantly boosted by awareness of growing international interest.[91] In both countries translations, which were themselves becoming much more common, played an important part. Stone's *Crisis of the Aristocracy* appeared in Italian in 1972 and in Spanish four years later, and his *The Family, Sex and Marriage 1500–1800*—which may have been even more influential[92]—was translated in (respectively) 1983 and 1989, while Brunner's *Land und Herrschaft* appeared in Italian in 1983. Stone's writings encouraged a focus upon finances and marital arrangements, which has been to the fore in Italian and Spanish scholarship. The generation which came to maturity in post-Franco Spain was influenced by the *Annales* and therefore notably sympathetic to the emphasis upon the financial and economic foundations of noble power championed by *Crisis of the Aristocracy*.[93]

In these varied ways interest in the nobilities of early modern Europe has grown remarkably. While wider developments within the historical profession have contributed to this renaissance, the impact of individuals and their publications has been even greater, during what may prove to be the twilight of individual scholarship. The move to collaborative projects characteristic of recent developments in humanities research in Europe in particular carries with it the risk that the impact of individual breakthroughs in the study of a particular topic will be reduced. The central figure and arguably the hero was

---

Italian scholarship, especially during the 1980s, while additional bibliographical guidance is provided by Angiolini, "Noblesses."

[91]   Enrique Soria Mesa, *La nobleza en la España moderna: Cambio y continuidad* (Madrid: Marcial Pons, 2007), 23–37, sketches the development of Spanish scholarship and provides bibliographical guidance. Interest had initially been stimulated by the writings of Antonio Domínguez Ortiz, above all his *La clases privilegiadas en la España del Antiguo Régimen* (Madrid: Ediciones ISTMO, 1973; an earlier version had appeared a decade earlier) and *Sociedad y Estado en el siglo XVIII español* (Barcelona: Ariel, 1976).

[92]   London: Weidenfeld and Nicolson, 1977; abridged edn, Harmondsworth: Penguin Books, 1979; Italian translation, Turin: Einaudi, 1983; Spanish translation, Madrid: Fondo de Cultura Economica, 1989. For its influence, see Visceglia, *Bisogno di Eternità*, 79, 101, 103, 105, 135, 167; cf. Angiolini, "Noblesses," 80.

[93]   E.g. Atienza Hernández, *Aristocracia, poder y riqueza*, 5, 7 and n., 17, 35 and n., 225n., for Stone's impact in Spanish academic circles. The emphasis upon aristocratic finances which dominates this study owed much to his approach, and became characteristic of Spanish-language scholarship: see, e.g., the important collection of essays edited by Carmen Iglesias, *Nobleza y Sociedad en la España Moderna*, 2 vols (Oviedo: Nobel, 1996–97). See also Bartolomé Yun Casalilla, "La 'Crisis de la Aristocracia' en España e Inglaterra: Una Visión Comparativa," reprinted in his *La Gestión del Poder: Corona y economías aristocráticas en Castilla (siglos XVI–XVIII)* (Madrid: Akal Ediciones, 2002), 247–75.

Lawrence Stone: something which would have been difficult to predict amidst the cautious and even critical response to *Crisis of the Aristocracy* in anglophone scholarly circles and its simultaneous neglect in France, then in the forefront of historical research in the Western world. By around 1980 nobility as a subject was becoming part of the historiographical mainstream, and the tide of publications has strengthened until the present day and shows no sign of ebbing.

Chapter 3

Negotiating for Agnes' Womb

Erica Bastress-Dukehart

> Unto the woman he said, I will greatly multiply thy sorrow and thy conception; in
> sorrow thou shalt bring forth children; and thy desire shall be to thy husband, and
> he shall rule over thee.
>
> Genesis 3:16

Ever since God decreed in the Garden of Eden that women would suffer the pain
of childbirth as penance for Eve's offering of the apple to Adam, the womb has
been a contested space.[1] Ancient Greek and early Christian natural philosophers
thought the empty womb a malevolent organ that rampaged throughout a
woman's body, causing her illness and, perhaps more perplexing, ill humor.[2]
Plato wrote in *Timaeus* that "there is the matrix or so-called womb in women,
which is an indwelling animal desirous of childbearing; and whenever this
comes to be fruitless long beyond its due season, it grows difficult and irritable;
and wandering everywhere throughout the body, it blocks up the breathing-
passages, and, not by allowing breathing, throws one into the most extreme

---

[1]   For a recent feminist discussion of Genesis and Eve's role in the fall, see Helen
Schüngel-Straumann, "Eva, die Frau am Anfang," in *Geschlechterstreit am Begin der
Europäischen Moderne: Die Querelle des Femmes*, eds Gisela Engel, Friederike Hassauer, Brita
Rang, and Heide Wunder (Königstein/Taunus: Ulrike Helmer Verlag, 2004), 28–37.

[2]   The study of humors in classical and medieval medicine and their affect on generation
is well known and documented and beyond the scope of this article. For the suffocation
of the womb, see Edward Jordan, *A Briefe Discourse of a Disease Called the Suffocation of
the Mother* (London, 1603); G.S. Rousseau, "A Strange Pathology: Hysteria in the Early
Modern World, 1500–1800," in *Hysteria Beyond Freud* (Berkeley: University of California
Press, 1993), 91–221. The best current discussions are David C. Lindberg, *The Beginnings of
Western Science: The European Scientific Tradition in Philosophical, Religious, and Institutional
Context, Prehistory to A.D. 1450* (Chicago: University of Chicago Press, 2008); Nancy G.
Siraisi, *Medieval and Early Renaissance Medicine: An Introduction to Knowledge and Practice*
(Chicago: University of Chicago Press, 1990); and Joan Cadden, *Meanings of Sex Difference
in the Middle Ages: Medicine, Science, and Culture* (Cambridge: Cambridge University Press,
1994).

frustrations."[3] By the Middle Ages, the uterus was better understood than it had been in Plato's day, but only marginally.[4] It continued to wander with evil intent when unfulfilled, and, even though eyewitness accounts of autopsies noted that it was a single space, the prevailing opinion remained that it was multivalent.[5] Still largely a puzzle as to its passions, its dislikes, its cycles, and its productivity, the medieval uterus was massaged, assuaged, wooed, coddled, and even coerced into accepting its duty. Once it did, and a uterus became a womb, the mystery of its character only deepened as its significance increased.[6] For the nobility of late-medieval and early modern Europe, the uterus represented promise, but the womb symbolized everything noble families stood for: it was the cradle of far more than a fetus. It was the harbinger of family honor, the living room of lineal continuity; the pregnant womb nurtured familial immortality. "The power of life and death," writes Barbara Duden, "was embodied above all by women in their capacity as 'vessels of life and death,' for this power was grounded in the ambiguity of their womb."[7]

It is the ambiguity about which Duden writes that guides the following chapter. Among the more general questions that this piece asks, perhaps the most fundamental are: what did fifteenth-century men and women understand about conception, gestation, and birth? And what were the most pressing issues they faced as they contemplated the mysteries of the womb? More specifically, this chapter applies these questions to the all-important problem of inheritance as it concerned noble families in fifteenth-century Europe.

---

[3]   Plato, *Timaeus*, trans. Peter Kalkavage (Newburyport, MA: Focus Classical Library, 2001), 129.

[4]   Danielle Jacquart and Claude Thomasset write "Plato had seen women as nothing but womb: in the Middle Ages, she was still a creature who had something incomprehensible about her." Danielle Jacquart and Claude Thomasset, *Sexuality and Medicine in the Middle Ages* (Princeton: Princeton University Press, 1988), 67.

[5]   Fridolf Kudlein, "The Seven Cells of the Uterus: The Doctrine and Its Roots," *Bulletin of the History of Medicine*, 39 (1965), 415–23; Katherine Crawford, *European Sexualities 1400–1800* (Cambridge: Cambridge University Press, 2007), 101; Jacquart and Thomasset, *Sexuality and Medicine*, 18, 34–35.

[6]   Monica H. Green, ed. and trans., *The Trotula* (Philadelphia: University of Pennsylvania, 2002), 65–112.

[7]   Barbara Duden, *The Woman beneath the Skin: A Doctor's Patients in Eighteenth-Century Germany*, trans. Thomas Dunlap (Cambridge, MA: Harvard University Press, 1991), 8. It was not until the beginning of the seventeenth century that ideas about the uterus, which according to Plato had its own will and a sense of smell, became a much more benevolent organ. Ian Maclean, *The Renaissance Notion of Woman: A Study in the Fortunes of Scholasticism and Medical Science in European Intellectual Life* (Cambridge: Cambridge University Press, 1980), 33.

At its heart, this chapter explores the case study of Margravine Agnes of Baden, Duchess of Schleswig-Holstein and the questions that arose at the birth of her fraternal twins. Born in 1432, Agnes' children immediately came under suspicion when they arrived early—perhaps as early as four-and-a-half months after conception—raising serious concerns within Agnes' natal family and with her in-laws regarding their paternity and legitimacy. The discussions that followed the twins' birth not only cast aspersions on Agnes' character but also transformed her womb into the locus for biological, religious, and political debates over inheritance in late-medieval and early modern Germany.

There is little doubt that the most pressing concern of the early modern nobility was inheritance.[8] In most European countries the future of an aristocratic lineage depended on the birth of at least one son, and the legal issues surrounding the devolution of lands, properties, and goods hinged, in theory, on this child's legitimacy. In countries where primogeniture was the rule, the determination of paternity was a central matter for families, legal courts, religious councils, kings, emperors, and medical experts when an heir's legitimacy came under scrutiny. In her chapter in this volume, "Contested Masculinity: Noblemen and their Mistresses in Early Modern Spain," Grace Coolidge argues that "the proper management of wealth, estates, and family members and the smooth transition of patriarchal power between generations were also important elements of noble masculinity." Coolidge makes an important case for how and why Spanish noblemen went to extraordinary lengths to legitimize their bastard sons, because the "ultimate proof of a nobleman's masculinity was, of course, a son."[9] The same was true for Italy, where Katharine Park notes that early modern Italian nobles and patricians "understood family membership primarily in terms of blood relationships defined by biological descent through the male line."[10]

---

[8]　Karl-Heinz Spiess, *Familie und Verwandtschaft im deutschen Hochadel des Spätmittelalters, 13. bis Anfang des 16. Jahrhunderts* (Stuttgart: Franz Steiner, 1993); Heide Wunder, ed., *Dynastie und Herrschaftssicherung in der Frühen Neuzeit: Geschlechter und Geschlecht* (Berlin: Duncker & Humblot, 2002); Beatrix Bastl, *Tugend, Liebe, Ehre: Die adelige Frau in der Frühen Neuzeit* (Vienna: Böhlau Verlag, 2000); Hans Medick and David Warren Sabean, *Interest and Emotion: Essays on the Study of Family and Kinship* (Cambridge: Cambridge University Press, 1984). For the most recent studies, see Stefan Brakensiek, Michael Stolleis and Heide Wunder, *Generationengerechtigkeit? Normen und Praxis im Erb- und Ehegüterrecht 1500–1850*, Zeitschrift für historische Forschung, 37 (Berlin: Duncker & Humblot, 2006). Susan Broomhall, "Corresponding Affections: Emotional Exchange Among Siblings in the Nassau Family," *Journal of Family History*, 34 (2009), 143–65.

[9]　See Coolidge, this volume.

[10]　Katharine Park, *Secrets of Women: Gender, Generation, and the Origins of Human Dissection* (New York: Zone Books, 2006), 25–6.

Unfortunately for those most interested in determining paternity, the emphasis on male blood continuity required knowing what was at the time unknowable. The early modern womb held many secrets, one of them being the sex and paternity of the fetus. This made the desire to assure families that the child was of their blood difficult, if not impossible. "Men could never know for certain if their children were in fact their own," Park writes; "paternity, constructed this way, was fragile, dependent on the sexual fidelity of women, whose untrustworthiness was the stuff of a thousand fables, jokes, and songs."[11] For some families, this collision between the desire to know on the one hand and a clear understanding of the realities of conception, gestation, birth, and the female body on the other was "unnerving." For other families, overlooking the possible betrayal of the mother to "see" the resemblance between father and son was sometimes deemed socially and politically prudent. Rather than bring shame on the family, or risk losing valuable lands because of a dearth of legitimate male heirs, there were many noble bastards in late-medieval Europe who took on the qualities and physical characteristics of their "fathers" in order to ensure familial continuity, even if it was not through paternal blood.[12]

In Germany, as in Spain and Italy, inheritance was a primary concern for aristocratic families, the courts, and the Holy Roman Empire. Unlike Spain and Italy, however, partible inheritance rather than primogeniture was a more common form of cross-generational property transfer in the fifteenth and sixteenth centuries. This division of properties made the dispersal of lands and material goods more complicated than in other countries.[13] Aristocratic sons in Germany divided lands, titles, and immovable goods with their brothers; daughters inherited moveable goods, rents, and mortgages as part of their dowries. While all sons were "considered to have equal rights," physical qualities

---

[11]   Ibid.

[12]   Claude Thomasset, "The Nature of Woman," in *A History of Women in the West: Silences of the Middle Ages*, vol. II, eds Christiane Klapisch-Zuber, Georges Duby, and Michelle Perrot, trans. Arthur Goldhammer (Cambridge, MA: Belknap Press of Harvard University Press, 1992), 43–69, here 60. Katherine Crawford argues that in "areas of late marriage, the law often compensated for paternal uncertainty. All children born during a marriage were regarded as the husband's. Only extreme exceptions such as years at sea during which children were born to the wife could challenge the legal presumption of paternity." Crawford, *European Sexualities*, 25. As the following chapter shows, this "presumption of paternity" was not always the case in fifteenth-century Germany.

[13]   Among the few countries where partible inheritance was the norm was Russia. Valerie A. Kivelson, "The Effects of Partible Inheritance: Gentry Families and the State in Muscovy," *The Russian Review*, 53 (1994), 197–212.

and character were taken into consideration when dividing properties.[14] If a single son was chosen to be the primary heir of a noble estate, he was not necessarily the eldest. Second, third, and younger sons could become heads of households if their older brothers were deemed inadequate or unsuitable. What this meant for disputes over a child's legitimacy in Germany was that paternity could be called into question not only by suspicious husbands but also by brothers or even brothers-in-law who were competing for titles, properties, and the rights to the privileges afforded heads of households.[15] These contests were apparently so common in the fifteenth century that legal and medical language combined with complicated formulas were developed to set the parameters for debates over generation and gestation as they applied to paternity cases and inheritance laws.

It was also in Germany at precisely the same time that texts about and images of the womb in all of its stages began to appear.[16] At the heart of Germany's legal machinations, medical discourses, and images was the seemingly impenetrable enigma: the womb—"the dark, inaccessible place where the child's tie with its father was created, its sex determined, its body shaped."[17] It was in this space where the potential of an aristocratic son's future and his family's legacy was either ensured or doomed. The womb held the secrets of generation. It also controlled what ancient and medieval medical experts considered to be the voracious sexual appetites of women.[18] Because of the latter, the nobility mistrusted the womb as profoundly as they depended on it for survival.

---

[14]   Karl-Heinz Spiess, "Lordship, Kinship, and Inheritance Among the German High Nobility in the Middle Ages and Early Modern Period," in *Kinship in Europe: Approaches to Long-Term Development 1300–1900*, eds David Warren Sabean, Simon Teuscher, and Jon Mathieu (New York: Berghahn Books, 2007), 57–75, here 59. For more on inheritance strategies in southwest Germany, see Judith J. Hurwich, *Noble Strategies: Marriage and Sexuality in the Zimmern Chronicle* (Kirksville, MO: Truman State University Press, 2006); Erica Bastress-Dukehart, *The Zimmern Chronicle: Nobility, Memory, and Self-Preservation in Sixteenth-Century Germany* (Aldershot: Ashgate, 2002).

[15]   Spiess, "Lordship, Kinship, and Inheritance," 57; Erica Bastress-Dukehart, "Sibling Conflict within Early Modern German Noble Families," *Journal of Family History*, 33 (2008), 61–80.

[16]   Park, *Secrets of Women*, 27.

[17]   Ibid.

[18]   Joan Cadden writes "From the Hippocratic writers—and no doubt the popular conceptions represented by Plato—came the womb-centered version, according to which females (still likely to be cool and weak) were subject to the erratic influence of a powerful and active organ that affected health and disposition and was the repository of a formidable sexual appetite." Cadden, *Meanings of Sex Difference*, 26.

Part of the reason for the conflicting and often conflicted emotional and social responses to the vexing problem of the womb was that the fifteenth century was a liminal period for reproductive and scientific knowledge in Europe. Reliance on Aristotle's theories of gestation, an "experience that was already universalized," continued to hold a privileged place at the universities and among late-medieval scholastic educators, but the competing theories of Galen and Hippocrates were now also being tested.[19] In general terms, medical understanding of reproduction, gestation, embryology, and birth in fifteenth-century Germany depended on the medieval scholastics' interpretations of the ancient theories of generation, combined with the writings of the early Italian humanists.[20] Aristotle believed that the childbearing woman provided only the location and the nourishment for reproduction. The father's semen supplied the form, movement, and direction of the fetus' growth.[21] Thus, according to those who followed Aristotle's logic of generation, the father was the only true parent, making the determination of paternity for familial and dynastic continuity all

----

[19]   O. Temkin, *Galenism: Rise and Decline of a Medical Philosophy* (Ithaca, NY: Cornell University Press, 1973); Peter Dear, *Revolutionizing the Sciences: European Knowledge and its Ambitions, 1500–1700* (Princeton, NJ: Princeton University Press, 2001), 6; Jeffrey R. Wigelsworth, *Science and Technology in Medieval European Life* (London: Greenwood Press, 2006), 108–9; David C. Lindberg, *The Beginnings of Western Science: The European Scientific Tradition in Philosophical, Religious, and Institutional Context, Prehistory to A.D. 1450* (Chicago: University of Chicago Press, 2008). See also Christine R. Johnson, *The German Discovery of the World: Renaissance Encounters with the Strange and Marvelous* (Charlottesville: University of Virginia Press, 2008). Allen G. Debus, *Man and Nature in the Renaissance* (Cambridge: Cambridge University Press, 1978). For women and medicine in early modern France, see Susan Broomhall, *Women's Medical Work in Early Modern France* (Manchester: Manchester University Press, 2004).

[20]   Ian Maclean writes "The subject of woman as seen by physiologists, anatomists and physicians is complex and multifaceted, because of its contiguity (and coincidence) with spermatology, hysterology, the science of the humours and theories of physical change. It is also very closely related to embryology, which exercises a deep influence on medical discussions about woman, and even determines to some degree the series of problems considered by medieval and Renaissance writers." Maclean, *The Renaissance Notion of Woman*, 28.

[21]   Alcuin Blamires, ed., *Woman Defamed and Woman Defended: An Anthology of Medieval Texts* (Oxford: Oxford University Press, 1992), 39; Maryanne Cline Horowitz, "The 'Science' of Embryology Before the Discovery of the Ovum," in *Connecting Spheres: Women in the Western World, 1500 to the Present*, eds Marilyn J. Boxer and Jean H. Quataert (Oxford: Oxford University Press, 1987), 86–94. See also Galen, *On the Anatomy of the Uterus*, trans. Charles Mayo Goss, *Anatomical Record*, 144:2 (1962), 77–83; Park, *Secrets of Women*; Crawford, *European Sexualities*; and Maclean, *The Renaissance Notion of Woman*.

the more important.[22] Thomas Aquinas adopted Aristotelian logic in the late-thirteenth century when he applied natural philosophy to filial obligation. "It is the father who ought to be loved more than the mother," the medieval philosopher wrote in his *Summa Theologica*, "for one's father and mother are loved as principles in our natural origin. But the father, as the active partner, is a principle in a higher way than the mother, who supplies the passive or material element. And so, speaking *per se*, the father should be loved more."[23] For early humanists and followers of Galen's and Hippocrates' theories of generation, the woman played a more active role in procreation. As Joan Cadden has argued, Galen "incorporated the Hippocratic notion that the fetal environment influences the development of the child. Enter, therefore, the uterus." Despite Galen's conviction that the uterus was an active participant in generation, the woman's role remained subordinate to the man's.[24]

In more specific terms, however, European noble families were apparently less concerned with the centrality of the biological details of generation for their own sake, and more interested in how and if natural science could aid in determining the social, economic, and political considerations surrounding a son's legitimacy. The issue, in its most essential form, was political: if the biological arguments could further a noble family's cause for proving or disproving a son's right to inherit, then the science of Aristotle, Hippocrates, and Galen became essential considerations. Lawyers defending a noble family's rights found these theories of generation useful as evidence in legal disputes. It appears that scientific knowledge of the womb had the potential to protect the nobility *qua* nobility, and thus the role this elite group played in the larger good of the early modern European social order. It was, for example, Aristotle's theory of generation combined with Aquinas' admonitions regarding filial duty that supported the tradition of a son and heir remaining with his paternal family if his father died and his mother remarried. Excluding women from inheriting fiefs was also a matter for debate. Medieval scholars provided myriad reasons why daughters could not succeed their fathers as principal heirs, many of which had as much to do with women's inferior physical characteristics and weaknesses as they did with the perception that they were deceitful and lacked good judgment.[25] Nevertheless, all who wrote about women and procreation had to acknowledge—often grudgingly—that

---

[22] Aristotle, *Generation of Animals*, ed. and trans. A. L. Peck (Cambridge, MA: Harvard University Press, 1953), I, xvii–xviii. To answer the problem of how men could generate girl children, Aristotle argued that female babies were failed males. Cadden, *Meanings of Sex Difference*, 133.

[23] Thomas Aquinas, *Summa Theologica*, article 10.

[24] Cadden, *Meanings of Sex Difference*, 35.

[25] Maclean, *Renaissance Notion of Woman*, 74.

women were the instruments of procreation. They bore the sons and heirs of the aristocracy. Thus how to determine an heir's legitimacy, how to legally assure that he inherited his father's estates, or, conversely, how to assure that he did not if his legitimacy were contested were questions at the heart of the debates over women, reproduction, and theories of generation and gestation.

All of the considerations and theories about women, all of the doubts and emotional arguments regarding generation and inheritance that arose in early modern Europe were manifest in the case of Agnes, the Margravine of Baden, Duchess of Schleswig-Holstein and her "seven-month twins."

When Agnes arrived as the new bride to the Duke of Schleswig-Holstein in the far northern reaches of Germany in 1432, she was reportedly already visibly pregnant, invoking in her new subjects and her husband's family a mixture of joyful anticipation and deep misgivings.[26] Agnes' condition first gave rise to the hopes that her child would ensure the continuity of the house of Schauenburg and protect the empire's interests in the north. Her new husband, Duke Gerhard, and her brother-in-law, Duke Adolf, were the last of the House of Schauenburg dynasty. But the anticipatory murmurs developed into ugly rumors and gossip as word spread that she had not only brought the child with her from Baden, but had in fact "brought" it with her into the marriage. In her first few months in Gottorf, Agnes did not fare well. Her letters to her brother Jakob recount her growing unhappiness with his choice for her husband. Duke Gerhard, she complained, was frail and sickly, and Adolf was proving less than welcoming.[27] Nor did it help that in her first weeks in the north she was publicly outspoken in her antipathy for her new home and its inhabitants. So public, indeed, that her in-laws reported her unpleasant behavior to her brother. Thus, when she gave birth to suspiciously healthy fraternal twins—a girl and a boy—seven months after the wedding, the whispers regarding their paternity grew louder and more

---

[26]   It is unclear whether Gerhard went south to collect his bride, or whether she traveled north alone. Paul Herrmann, ed., *Zimmerische Chronik*, 4 vols (Meersburg am Bodensee: F.W. Hendel Verlag, 1932), I, 180.

[27]   For more on Agnes and her relationship with her brother, see Heinrich Witte, "Margravine Agnes von Baden, Herzogin von Schleswig," *Zeitschrift für die Geschichte des Oberrheins*, 17 (1902), 503–30. For public and private correspondence and the *Echtheitserklärung* and *Gutachten*, Heinrich Witte, ed., *Regesten der Markgrafen von Baden und Hachberg 1050–1515*, vol. 3, 1431–53 (Innsbruck: Verlag der Wagner'schen Universitäts-Buchhandlung, 1907); Peter Hirschfeld, *Markgräfin Agnes von Baden: Gemahlin Herzog Gerhards VII. von Schleswig* (Neumünster: Karl Wachholtz Verlag, 1957). Hirschfeld has included full texts of documents that pertain to Agnes and her troubles in the appendix to his biography of the Margravine; see Bastress-Dukehart, "Sibling Conflict."

insistent: who was this promiscuous interloper from the south, people wondered, and who was the father of these children?[28]

Gerhard's insistence that the twins were his and that his wife had been a virgin the night of the wedding at first apparently only fueled the rumors. Agnes remained uncharacteristically silent on the subject. Although she had written frantically to her brother regarding her financial concerns, she never referred to her pregnancy.[29] It was her brother-in-law and not Agnes who informed the surprised Baden family that she had been delivered of healthy children. For her detractors, of whom by this time Agnes had garnered many, her silence was indicative of how they perceived her personality: she was deceptive, secretive, and these "seven-month twins," the issue of her equally secretive and deceptive womb, meant trouble for the House of Schauenburg dynasty.

"The children were no bigger than a hand span," wrote Hermann Korner in his *Chronica Novella* from Lübeck in 1433, "and their early birth delivered into the hearts of the enemies of both families the cause for scandal and the opportunity for the most hateful slander."[30] As rumors of the twins' parentage spread, the crux of the problem was twofold: first was the exoneration of Jakob for having assured the dukes of Shleswig-Holstein that he had delivered his sister to them as a virgin. The second, equally pressing problem was how to insure the legitimacy of the boy for the House of Schauenburg. To both ends, the dukes of Schleswig-Holstein, along with Jakob, initiated an investigation and explanation for the twins' premature birth in order to legitimize the son in the eyes of the law, the church, and, perhaps most important, their aristocratic peers.

In February of 1433, two months following the twins' birth, Adolf, Gerhard, and Jakob turned to expert witnesses to establish the twins' legitimacy through a public declaration (*Echtheitserklärung*). The primary issue that needed to be addressed was the length of Agnes' pregnancy. While medical experts and laymen alike understood from Aristotle and other natural philosophers that nine months was a normal gestation period, it is clear that they also recognized that a child could survive if born earlier. Hippocrates wrote extensively on the viability of premature babies, but twins presented a more difficult challenge for the lawyers and doctors. Few multiple births ended successfully in the fifteenth

---

[28] Hirschfeld, *Markgräfin Agnes*, 93. The sources fail to illuminate many aspects of the birth of the twins. As Hirschfeld laments in his biography of Agnes, "Über die Geburt der Zwillinge am 16. Januar 1433, dies wegen seiner Vorzeitigkeit zentrale Ereignis, aus dem alle die traurigen Verwicklungen erwuchsen, fehlen urkundliche Belege. Wir wissen nichts Authentisches, weder über die Taufe noch über die Vornamen der Kinder." Ibid., 92

[29] Ibid., 93.

[30] Hermann Korner, *Die Chronica Novella des Hermann Korner* (Göttingen: J. Schwalm, 1895), 522–30; Hirschfeld, *Markgräfin Agnes*, 93.

century, and even fewer survived if they were born premature. The fact that these twins were small, as Korner noted in his chronicle, helped Agnes' cause. That they were healthy, however, did not.

In order to explain the early birth, Gerhard once again insisted, this time before witnesses, that his wife was a virgin when they consummated the marriage in June of 1432. To reinforce his claim, he asked the women who bathed with Agnes on her wedding night to testify under oath that she had been a virgin. Even the maid who changed the couple's bedsheets was called to testify that on the morning following the consummation (*Beischlafen*) there was blood on the linens. Noblewomen from Lübeck and Gottdorp then testified that they had attended the birth and it had "taken place with God and honor." They also supported Agnes by telling their own tales of childbirth. Many of them, they claimed, "as well as many other women," had given birth after a short gestation period, some even shorter than seven months, and the children had lived for many years and "some were even still alive." Finally, the medical experts offered their opinions. The midwives and doctors who attended the birth testified not to any medical theories regarding gestation, but to how the timing could be explained by the fact that Agnes had fallen the day previous to the birth "doing herself harm" (*sich we getan*). The implication was that her fall had induced labor. Had she not stumbled on the stairs, they suggested, the twins would have likely gone to full term.[31]

Throughout the entire ordeal, Agnes remained silent. She was not asked to testify on her own behalf, nor was there an indication that her brother interrogated her to elicit a confession about her alleged infidelity. In the end, it appears that her word had little or no value. What mattered for the declaration of legitimacy was the condition of her uterus before, during, and after the wedding and resultant birth. For those most concerned with this issue, Agnes was "mere fertility."[32] The evidence that Agnes' uterus itself provided was far more conclusive according to the *Echtheitserklärung* than any explanation Agnes herself could have supplied. Thus, other witnesses, in particular the women who had bathed with Agnes the night before the wedding, demonstrated what they understood about pregnancy and gestation when they noted that Agnes' body did not appear pregnant, that in fact she appeared to be a virgin during the bath. The maid who cleaned the sheets the following morning while the "couple was at church" testified that the bloodstains on the bedclothes proved that Agnes had lost her virginity the night before. From purifying bath to bedding to church,

---

[31]   Ibid., 223–4. Echtheitserklärung der Bischöfe Nikolaus von Schleswig und Johannes von Lübeck für die Zwillinge, 1433 Februar 4. Also see *Die Chronica Novella des Hermann Korner*, 522.

[32]   Jacquart and Thomasset, *Sexuality and Medicine*, 67.

Agnes' uterus had been carefully protected and monitored by family, friends, and even strangers. As a result, her brother Jakob was, with this *Echtheitserklärung*, exonerated from blame. It gave evidence that he had handed his sister to her new husband sexually pure and fertile. The Schauenburg dukes were also exonerated with this public declaration. Agnes' womb and the twins it produced were cleared of any deception.

The matter should have ended with the publication of the *Echtheitserklärung*. Gerhard and Agnes' son should have become the heir to the duchy of Schleswig-Holstein. Through a combination of social support, political authority, expert medical knowledge, and eyewitness accounts, the legitimacy of the male twin should have been assured, the rumors put to rest. "In that moment," writes Hirschfeld, "hardly anyone in Schleswig-Holstein dared to doubt publicly the innocence of the duchess Agnes."[33] But, when Gerhard died shortly after the signing of the *Echtheitserklärung*, the issue of the "seven-month twins" reemerged.

This time it was Adolf who began proceedings to deny Agnes' son his paternity and inheritance. Without Gerhard to defend the children, Adolf no longer felt compelled to accept the boy as his heir. In a letter to Agnes' brother Jakob, dated July 1434, Adolf accused Agnes of causing her husband's death. As with the *Echtheitserklärung*, he depended on medical expertise to make his claim: he wrote that Agnes had, "against the advice of the medical doctors in Lübeck and Hamburg," taken her deathly ill husband out of Schleswig-Holstein.[34] He then argued that he could no longer overlook the fact that the twins were illegitimate. They could not be Gerhard's issue, he wrote, because Gerhard and Agnes had actually consummated their marriage in September of 1432, not the previous June, as Gerhard and others had claimed in the *Echtheitserklärung*. This meant that the twins were born four and a half months after the wedding night, not seven.[35] Gerhard challenges Jakob to make a case for the legitimacy of the children born after such a short gestation. And he rebukes Agnes for having betrayed the trust of her deceased husband. It is unclear from the correspondence or following documentation how Adolf came to this conclusion, but the implications were clear: seven-month twins might survive outside the womb, but four and a half months was far too short a period for gestation and the birth of viable children. To support his contention, Adolf included a lengthy legal testimonial (*Gutachten*) written and signed by Gregory of Heimburg, Doctor of Law and

---

[33]   Hirschfeld, *Markgräfin Agnes*, 105.

[34]   Herzog Adolf VIII. Von Schleswig an Markgraf Jakob, 1434 Juli. Segeberg. Reg. M. Bad. 5452. Agnes does not say why she took her husband out of the northern duchy, but Adolf intimated that it was for nefarious reasons.

[35]   Ibid.

the General Curate of Mainz, and ten other doctors of law. This testimonial, unlike the *Echtheitserklärung* before it, combined the laws of inheritance with scientific knowledge regarding generation, gestation, and birth to deny Agnes' son any rights to the Schauenburg estate. Because seven months was generally recognized by medical experts in the late Middle Ages as the minimum length of time for a child to gestate and expect to survive outside of the womb, these legal experts turned to the law of *Septimo Mense*, which states that the birth of a child who had gestated for under seven months could not be considered legitimate for purposes of inheritance.[36]

"In this legal case," reads the *Gutachten*, "the confusion is over whether the child can be designated according to canon or civil law as the legal heir of the dead Gerhard, and, indeed to that end, the legal decision will decide whether he will inherit his father's estate."[37] But, in conjunction with canon and civil law, Gregory of Heimburg and his ten legal councilors based their decision on the determination of "medical doctors and natural scientists" (*Ärzte und Naturforscher*), who argued that any birth under seven months of gestation could not be considered legitimate.[38] That this law was meant to decide issues of inheritance is clear from the complicated formula they used to determine paternity. "The entire strength of this question goes back to the law of *Septimo Mense*," Heimburg wrote, and because the law was "scientific" it was considered appropriate to use it to decide legitimacy. The law states that "no fully formed fetus can be born under six months." To apply this calculation, Heimburg argued that the law of *Septimo Mense* meant that "if a woman remarried within the mourning year for her first husband and gave birth to a child 11 months after his death but less than seven months after her remarriage, then it is clear that the child is not the issue of either man." Although there were doctors who were willing to testify that "a child could survive after only five or six months' gestation," Heimburg was determined to follow the law, which supported his argument that babies born under seven months were not viable, "and not the frivolous assertions of some medical doctors ... who take liberties with the opinion of the authority of

---

[36]   Hirschfeld, *Markgräfin Agnes*, 184. There was something else going on here as well. This decision ignored the earlier eyewitness accounts from those who had bathed with Agnes that helped her make her case. Now, in this second decision, the court ignored the women's testimony. This decision was indicative of Adolf's authority in Schleswig-Holstein, as well as the growing marginalization of women when it came to medical matters.

[37]   *Gutachten von Gregor Heimburg und zehn weiteren Juristen über die Frage der Erbberechtigung bei Frühgeburten*, (Basle?, 1434).

[38]   Ibid. Hippocrates actually argued that a seven-month premature baby was more likely to be viable than an eight-month child. Lana Thompson, *The Wandering Womb: A Cultural History of Outrageous Beliefs about Women* (Amherst, MA: Prometheus Books, 1999), 35.

Hippocrates in his book on the nature of the child. And Hippocrates wrote," Heimburg continues, "that a fetus could only survive outside the womb after seven months, although the rule was certainly nine months."[39]

Adolf argued before this tribunal that "in early September, Gerhard finalized the marriage with Agnes, and at that time they had their first sexual relations with one another. On the sixteenth of the following January, Agnes gave birth to a living and healthy child, who is now over a year old and remains in good health. Between this birth and the first sexual encounter," Adolf pointed out, "lay only four and one half months."[40] As a result of this calculation, Heimburg had little choice but to decree that the twins were not born seven months after the consummation of the marriage. With this new information, he concluded that Agnes must have had a sexual relationship before her marriage, which meant that the twins could not have been Gerhard's.

For Adolf, despite the fact that he was the last male of the House of Schauenburg lineage, and that with this decision the duchy would likely go to his sister's son, the potential heir to Denmark, his ire was directed at the deception of Agnes' womb. Nothing else mattered than assuring that this child born of that unknowable space would not inherit. Whether Agnes could keep her morning gift and widow's pension, over which they had argued for two years, was apparently now irrelevant, overshadowed by the larger question of the boy's paternity.[41] Nor did it help Agnes' cause that she refused to be party to a new marriage arrangement made by Adolf and Jakob as they attempted to salvage the situation. Rather than agree to marry another man of her brother's choosing, Agnes announced that she had arranged for her own marriage to Hans von Höwen, a knight from Straßburg, who was beneath her in social status. As Jakob had no intention of allowing her to marry a man of her own choosing, Agnes' determination to chart her own future made matters significantly worse.[42]

Unfortunately for Agnes and her family, they could not turn to any biological argument to defend their position that the boy should be the heir to the House of Schauenburg inheritance. Where the natural philosophers could support Adolf's claim, they had little to offer fifteenth-century noblewomen when it came to a contested inheritance of a son. Although Hippocrates and Galen suggested that women's wombs were more than mere vessels for a growing fetus because both the father and the mother produced seeds, they also theorized that the mother's seed was in fact weaker than the father's, making it only capable

---

[39]   All above quotes in this paragraph are from the *Gutachten von Gregor Heimburg und zehn weiteren Juristen über die Frage der Erbberechtigung bei Frühgeburten.*

[40]   Ibid. Adolf never again mentions the daughter.

[41]   Hirschfeld, *Markgräfin Agnes*, 184.

[42]   Bastress-Dukehart, "Sibling Conflict," 67.

of generating females. The thirteenth-century philosopher and theologian Albertus Magnus, like Aristotle, argued that the father's sperm determined the sex of the child, and because reproduction in this period meant quite literally reproducing one's characteristics in offspring, then the child would naturally be a boy. However, if the father's sperm was weak or lacked the required heat to create a son, or, as Galen and Hippocrates argued, if the woman's sperm was stronger than the man's, then the child would be female.[43] Even if one combined Galen's and Hippocrates' theories that gave the mother a more active role in generation with Aristotle's, which gave full parenthood to the father, the ancient natural philosophy writ large failed to help a woman who insisted on her son's legitimacy if her husband or his family questioned it. Because, according to all of the ancient theories, she had no role in the generation of a son, if a family rejected a male child of questionable paternity, there was little the mother's family could do to contradict the finding.[44] Hippocrates', Aristotle's, and Galen's theories of female generation—or the lack thereof—combined with the scholastics' and humanists' arguments regarding filial duty to the father effectively justified the paternal family's conclusions. Agnes could have demanded custody of her daughter, but because of Germany's laws of partible inheritance, where a daughter might inherit if she had no male relatives, it is unlikely that she would have won the argument.[45] It is not a surprise then that Adolf made no offer to return the daughter to her mother. In the end it did not seem to matter; Agnes apparently had no interest in either child once it was clear that they could not inherit. Even before the publication of the *Gutachten*, Agnes had abandoned the twins in Gottorf and returned to Baden.

As the negotiations over Agnes' womb played out across Germany, there were broader movements gathering force throughout Europe that challenged the medieval ways of knowing. New discoveries of the inner workings of the body proliferated as autopsies of both men and women became increasingly common.[46] Aristotle, Galen, and Hippocrates and the early scholastics had understood nature and the body largely through theory and contemplation. Medieval physicians

---

[43]   Cadden, *Meanings of Sex Difference*, 133; Galen, *On Semen*, ed. Phillip de Lacy (Berlin: Akademic Verlag, 1992), 94–5; Maclean, *The Renaissance Notion of Woman*, 36–7.

[44]   Hippocrates, *On Intercourse and Pregnancy: An English Translation of On Semen and On the Development of the Child*, trans. Tage U.H. Ellinger (New York: Henry Schuman, 1952); Cadden, *Meanings of Sex Difference*, 91–2. See also Park, *Secrets of Women*, 141–2.

[45]   This was, in the fifteenth century, still a point of contention. Aristocratic daughters were expected to renounce their hereditary entitlements in exchange for their dowries. While this was true in theory, it often did not work in practice. Bastress-Dukehart, "Sibling Conflict"; Spiess, "Lordship, Kinship, and Inheritance," 67.

[46]   Park, *Secrets of Women*, 141; Siraisi, *Medieval and Early Renaissance Medicine*, 88–9.

who had access to human cadavers wherein they discovered conflicting evidence often ignored it as they clung to the ancient theories. Others reiterated earlier findings rather than doing their own research. Yet, more and more often the late fifteenth- and early sixteenth-century medical experts were experiencing the natural world as something that, if not entirely controllable, was at the very least observable, open to experiment, and thus potentially comprehensible. Allen Debus writes that "characteristic of the period was a growing reliance on observation and a gradual move toward our understanding of experiment as a carefully planned—and repeatable—test of theory."[47] Humanists commenting on Aristotle's works questioned the natural philosopher's conclusions and the medieval dependence on them. As Renaissance doctors rejected Aristotle's findings, they adopted Galen's and Hippocrates' theories of generation. "It is the last for whom the greatest respect is shown," writes Ian Maclean. "Where [Hippocrates'] texts are thought to be erroneous, interpolation is invoked; Aristotle is sometimes described as his vulgar plagiarist."[48] Where Aristotelian tradition did still dominate, heated debates took place at the universities and medical schools among natural philosophers over theories that conflicted with eyewitness accounts. Medical experts published their findings, in particular case histories not unlike Agnes', in order to highlight various diseases and medical procedures and their legal implications.[49] In fact, as late as the nineteenth century, one historian published Gregory of Heimburg's *Gutachten* regarding Agnes' twins as a theoretical case that tested fifteenth-century inheritance laws in Germany.[50] As doctors and surgeons literally peered into the bowels of the human body and dissected uteruses in search of answers to its mysteries, they precipitated the messy, halting process of developing a new epistemology that would, within the century, become the science of the Renaissance.

As the process continued, as science became a standard by which to measure legal contests, did the European nobility keep a close eye on the changes in scientific knowledge? In law as in science, did judges, magistrates, courts, and legal experts continue to depend on the ancient theories of the inner workings of the body? Did they include scientific observations to support the nobility's laws of inheritance as they did in Agnes' case? It is well documented that between the fifteenth and the seventeenth centuries judges used "scientific evidence"

---

[47] Debus, *Man and Nature*, 7–8. Debus notes that Western medieval scholars did not have ready access to Galen's anatomical works until after the thirteenth century. When this was discovered in the fifteenth century, "a determined effort was soon underway to prepare them for publication in both Greek and Latin." Ibid., 57, quote from 59.

[48] Maclean, *The Renaissance Notion of Woman*, 28.

[49] Ibid.

[50] Hirschfeld, *Markgräfin Agnes*, 184.

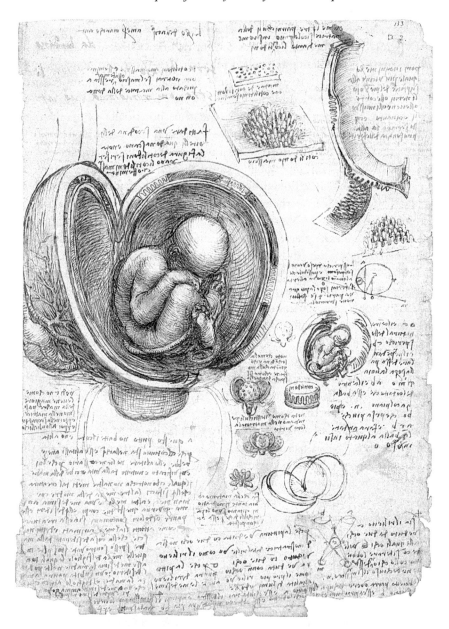

Figure 3.1   Leonardo da Vinci, "The Babe in the Womb"

Source: The Royal Collection © 2008, Her Majesty Queen Elizabeth II.

to accuse women of witchcraft and infanticide.[51] According to Ian Maclean, in Italy, the medieval school of law "sought to create a coherent framework for legal discourse by juxtaposing legal texts and by drawing justification and elucidation from theological, medical, and ethical writings."[52] In Bologna, the law school demanded anatomical studies and post-mortem examinations as part of legal evidence as early as the fourteenth century.[53] There are even records indicating that kings, queens, and emperors had to consider scientific evidence. In Elizabethan England, for example, the queen "had the authority to rescind any license or overturn any decision made by her church, her City of London, her College of Physicians, or her Barber-Surgeons' Company."[54] The Holy Roman Emperor, Sigismund, attempted but failed to intervene in the House of Schauenburg case in his efforts to save Schleswig-Holstein from falling into the hands of the Danish king. It appears that he was forced to acquiesce to the legal findings of Heimburg and to his use of the law of *Septimo Mense* in his decision.

There are other questions specific to Agnes' case about which the sources are frustratingly silent. Was Agnes' "fall" the day before she went into labor her attempt to miscarry the twins? In accusations of infanticide in early modern Germany and Italy it is recorded that women often "fell" in their efforts to abort their fetuses rather than admit to their babies' illegitimacy.[55] Was this also true for Agnes? What was Agnes' emotional and mental state throughout this ordeal? That she does not defend herself or the paternity of the twins led to much speculation. A century later the Zimmern chroniclers were quick to accuse her of infidelity while simultaneously sympathizing with her predicament.[56] And, perhaps the most bewildering question that the sources do not answer: How did Adolf determine that the marriage was not consummated until September? He offers no evidence for this revised date; he contradicts his brother's sworn testimony recorded in the *Echtheitserklärung* as well as the eyewitnesses'

---

[51] Alison Rowlands, "Midwifery, Fraud and Gender," in *Gender in Early Modern German History*, ed. Ulinka Rublack (Cambridge: Cambridge University Press, 2002), 73–4.

[52] Maclean, *Renaissance Notion of Woman*, 69.

[53] Debus, *Man and Nature*, 57.

[54] Deborah E. Harkness, *The Jewel House: Elizabethan London and the Scientific Revolution* (New Haven: Yale University Press, 2007), 69.

[55] For infanticide in Germany see Ulinka Rublack, *The Crimes of Women in Early Modern Germany* (Oxford: Oxford University Press, 2001). For Italy see Suzanne Magnanini, *Fairy-Tale Science: Monstrous Generation in the Tales of Straparola and Basile* (Toronto: University of Toronto Press, 2008).

[56] Herrmann, ed., *Zimmerische Chronik*, I, 180.

accounts. Why did Heimburg and the other legal experts accept Adolf's claim? Because there is apparently no definitive evidence, one might only note that the decision to accept Adolf's new date for consummation makes clear the level of his animosity toward his sister-in-law, and the political influence and authority he enjoyed in the Holy Roman Empire. That he was able to hold the emperor at arm's length as he denied Agnes and her son rights to inherit confirms once again that aristocratic family politics continued to triumph over imperial and religious intervention in early modern Germany.[57]

Scientific knowledge and Germany's partible inheritance laws together helped to make the case against Agnes. They made fitting partners: fifteenth-century science was methodologically flawed and contradictory, making it a contested space in its own right.[58] Germany's complicated laws of partible inheritance were not yet codified: the devolution of property was as often decided by emotions and sibling jealousies as it was by legal precepts. Partible inheritance led to legal ambiguities and family conflicts in the same way that incompatible scientific theories and "evidence" led to questionable conclusions regarding human generation.

Unlike the womb of today, which can be implanted with in-vitro fertilized, test-tube nurtured, genetically altered eggs, the fifteenth-century womb only gave up its secrets at the birth of the child, and perhaps not even then. No sonogram could determine sex, no DNA test paternity. In the case of the Baden dynasty, the mystery that remained following the birth of Agnes' twins destroyed its relationship with the duchy of Schleswig-Holstein, and with it a future attachment to the northern empire. With that loss, the fate of the twins was sealed: the daughter, whose name we never learn, died of neglect and starvation just after her first birthday; the son drowned under mysterious circumstances while on a fishing trip at the age of two. Both had been abandoned by their mother, whose continued silence ultimately cost her her own freedom. As she refused to divulge the paternity of the twins who had inhabited one contested space for four and a half, seven, or nine months, Agnes found herself ultimately confined to another. Her brother, still aggrieved at the loss of her morning gift and inheritance and by her perceived sexual infidelity, angered by her attempts

---

57   Bastress-Dukehart, "Sibling Conflict." Adolf died childless on 4 December 1459. His estate went to his nephew, Christian I, King of Denmark, the son of Adolf's sister. Christian promised to keep Schleswig-Holstein together, and he accepted the inheritance as the Duke of Schleswig-Holstein, not as the King of Denmark. Hirschfeld, *Markgräfin Agnes*, 204.

58   Crawford, *European Sexualities*, 101.

to secretly negotiate a second marriage—all of which reflected so badly on the Baden dynasty—imprisoned her for the remainder of her life.[59]

If Agnes' womb was a locus of conflict for the houses of Baden and Schauenberg, the womb in general is also where different modes of historical inquiry converge. Its study tells us a great deal about family and gender history; it reveals how, as a political space, the womb must be taken into account in issues of inheritance, birthright, and property ownership. Studies such as these can offer new insight into the nobility's struggle for continuity and survival. As Hamish Scott notes in his historiographical chapter in this volume, "historians of marriage, family life, gender relations, and cultural trends have exploited the relatively abundant surviving records left by elite families, in the process immeasurably benefiting historians interested in the narrower subject of nobility."[60] More work needs to be done on this subject, but Scott's acknowledgment of methodologies available to historians for the study of family records is certainly the case for the sources left by the Baden dynasty. They tell the long, complicated, and sad tale of conflict that arose as a result of Agnes' twins.

The womb has also, of course, inspired centuries of scientific inquiry. From the theories of the ancient philosophers to medieval Christian interpretations, from the Renaissance to the scientific revolution and the Enlightenment, scientific studies of the womb have led to new ways of thinking about the human body, sexuality, reproduction, and gestation in pre-modern Europe. At no point, however, regardless of era or knowledge, has the womb ever ceased to be a contested space.

---

[59]   Bastress-Dukehart, "Sibling Conflict." Despite attempts by the Holy Roman Emperor and the Council of Basel to free her, Agnes spent 37 years under house arrest at the Baden family castle of Alt-Eberstein.

[60]   See Scott, this volume.

Chapter 4

Contested Masculinity: Noblemen and their Mistresses in Early Modern Spain

Grace E. Coolidge

Masculinity was an important, if confusing, concept in early modern Spanish social and cultural life. In the fifteenth and sixteenth centuries, Spanish noblemen were expected to perform masculine roles that enhanced their power, wealth, and status, thus benefiting their families. The nature of these theoretical roles was debated by contemporaries, and masculinity was often difficult to achieve. In practice, noble masculinity was both a flexible concept and a contested space. Far from being static, an individual's masculine reputation could be challenged, damaged, repaired, and rewritten. This flexibility was closely intertwined with male sexuality. Studying the lives of women who had extramarital relationships with noblemen in the early modern period opens a window into how noblemen actually performed or managed their masculinity. I argue that although masculinity was the trait that separated men from the dangers of effeminacy and the flaws that contemporaries associated with women, the successful performance of a masculine role among the nobility in early modern Spain often depended heavily on the presence and cooperation of women.[1]

---

[1]   Earlier versions of this chapter were presented at the Great Lakes History Conference at Grand Valley State University in 2008 and at the Sixteenth Century Studies Conference in Geneva, Switzerland, in 2009. I am grateful to participants at both these events for their helpful suggestions, and I would especially like to thank Jodi Bilinkoff and Scott Taylor for their constructive comments.
    Various scholars have analyzed some of the ways that gender could be performed in early modern Spain. Scott Taylor, looking at honor, which was a crucial part of early modern Spanish masculinity, argues that honor was a tool "used equally by men and women to manage relations with their neighbors and maintain their place in the community." Scott K. Taylor, *Honor and Violence in Golden Age Spain* (New Haven and London: Yale University Press, 2008), 7. Abigail Dyer argues that seduced women used the law to transform themselves into honorable, marriageable female partners. Abigail Dyer, "Seduction by Promise of Marriage: Law, Sex, and Culture in Seventeenth-Century Spain," *Sixteenth Century Journal*, 34 (2003), 439–55. For a more theoretical analysis of gender as a performance, see Judith Butler,

While some Spanish noblemen had casual affairs with women of lower social status than their own, others practiced an unofficial form of polygamy that could enhance their masculinity, meet their sexual and emotional needs outside the restrictions of an arranged marriage, and often provide them with alternative families. Practiced over generations, this tradition of having alternate families amounted to a family strategy that protected the nobility's ability to pass their titles and property on to their own children, even if those children were illegitimate.[2] The extramarital affairs of Spanish noblemen paradoxically provided them with options that could bolster and repair their masculine images while simultaneously threatening their control over their masculinity. On the one hand, mistresses and their offspring could demonstrate noblemen's sexual potency and heterosexuality, provide male heirs, and strengthen their hold on wealth and power. On the other hand, mistresses and their offspring could also disrupt marriage, threaten the smooth transfer of power between generations, lead to questions about noblemen's ability to control their sexuality and their families, and challenge accepted church doctrine. Mistresses, and the alternative families they produced, could make the noble family a contested space if they claimed legitimacy or formal inheritance rights. The contradictory role of the mistress suggests that in practice noble masculinity was a flexible, and perhaps fragile, concept that varied through time and over a man's lifetime, could be used to enhance family inheritance strategies, and could be repaired or rewritten if necessary.

This study is based on documents pertaining to the lives of 38 women who had extramarital relationships with 30 noblemen from six of the highest ranking families (the dukes of Infantado, Frías, Arcos, Gandía, and Medina de Ríoseco, and the count-dukes of Benavente) in fifteenth- and sixteenth-century Spain. These noblemen were politically and economically powerful, and they represented families that had dominated and would continue to dominate the political and social structure of the time period. Their family records are collected

---

"Performative Acts and Gender Constitution: An Essay in Phenomenology and Feminist Theory," *Theatre Journal*, 40 (1988), 519–31.

 [2] Marraud and Soldat in this volume also provide compelling examples of noble family strategies. See also Ann Crabb, *The Strozzi of Florence: Widowhood and Family Solidarity in the Renaissance* (Ann Arbor: University of Michigan Press, 2000); Barbara J. Harris, *English Aristocratic Women, 1450–1550: Marriage and Family, Property and Careers* (Oxford: Oxford University Press, 2002); Judith J. Hurwich, *Noble Strategies: Marriage and Sexuality in the* Zimmern Chronicle (Kirksville, MO: Truman State University Press, 2006); Charles T. Lipp, "Power and Politics in Early Modern Lorraine: Jean-Francois de Mahuet and the Grand Prévoté de Saint-Dié," *French Historical Studies*, 26 (2003), 31–53; Jonathan Spangler, "Benefit or Burden? The Balancing Act of Widows in French Princely Houses," *Proceedings of the Western Society for French History*, 31 (2003), 65–83.

in the Sección Nobleza of the Archivo Historico Nacional, which is housed in Toledo. I have used wills, the records of civil court cases concerning inheritance rights, entails (*mayorazgos*), letters, genealogies, records proving purity of blood (*limpieza de sangre*), and civil and papal legitimations to reconstruct these relationships.

Recent scholarship on early modern Spanish masculinity has emphasized both its flexible and changing nature and the importance of sexuality in understanding how it functioned. Elizabeth Lehfeldt argues that the seventeenth century saw a crisis in perceptions of masculinity in Spain which coincided with fear about the nation's decline. After Ferdinand and Isabella had begun to create Spain by unifying the various distinct regions of the Iberian Peninsula in the late fifteenth century, Spain enjoyed an empire and an influence (both cultural and political) that dominated Europe. When that balance of power began to shift, contemporaries (and generations of later historians) worried about Spain's perceived decline and felt compelled to explain Spain's loss of international dominance.[3] Seventeenth-century commentators struggled to articulate a "systematic and coherent model of noble manhood that could be realistically embodied by seventeenth-century men," and in the process they rewrote the life stories of earlier generations of noblemen to meet their new expectations, leaving out troublesome elements such as extramarital affairs or political scandals that conflicted with the new definition.[4] Part of the problem that seventeenth-century commentators faced in trying to define noble masculinity was that earlier generations of Spanish men did not have a "systematic and coherent model" of masculinity either. Instead, masculinity in fifteenth- and sixteenth-century Spain (part of the time period idealized by later commentators) was flexible rather than systematic, making it arguably easier to achieve.

Seventeenth-century commentators asserted that noblemen could demonstrate their masculinity through virtuous Christianity, moderation in behavior and lifestyles that would allow them to control and administer their households and estates, sexual restraint and chastity, wealth that was derived from productive sources (not loans or mortgages), restraint in dress, and demonstrable military skills and service.[5] The importance of lifestyles and behavior that would allow noblemen to successfully control and administer their households, families, and estates and the glory that surrounded military activities were elements of earlier definitions of masculinity also. However, before the seventeenth-century emphasis on moderation in lifestyles, dress, and sexuality,

---

[3] J.H. Elliott, *Imperial Spain, 1469–1716* (London: Penguin Books, 2002), 13.

[4] Elizabeth A. Lehfeldt, "Ideal Men: Masculinity and Decline in Seventeenth-Century Spain," *Renaissance Quarterly*, 61 (2008), 470, 472, 475.

[5] Ibid., 476–85.

earlier generations of noblemen had more flexibility, especially in their sexual behavior, than their seventeenth-century descendants. In fact, they developed multiple ways to achieve masculinity that often embraced extramarital sexuality precisely because it could demonstrate sexual potency and heterosexuality. In practice (and not yet burdened by the impending sense of decline that hindered their descendants) fifteenth- and sixteenth-century noblemen who were members of a dominant class at the height of its power had crafted creative and practical ways to be masculine that allowed them to make mistakes, to overcome family scandals, and to adapt to changing circumstances.

Male sexuality and its performance was an important, public, and sometimes burdensome aspect of early modern masculinity. Edward Behrend-Martínez argues that "[m]ale authority, even male honor, was contingent on male sexual potency." Women who accused their husbands of impotence in the Basque region of Spain argued "that they were sexually unfit and not true men."[6] The pressure to produce a public image of successful sexuality pushed noblemen to develop alternate ways to achieve this goal. Although officially "marital sex maintained society" and "sex outside marriage could bring social chaos," in reality the situation was much more fluid.[7] Christian Berco argues that even male homosexual behavior "formed part of the encompassing structure of masculine identity and sociability," a rational outcome of a society that valued male virility.[8] The seventeenth-century *arbitristas* were handicapped by their need to reject this flexibility in favor of a more rigid morality that would counterbalance Spain's perceived decline.[9] They were also influenced by the Council of Trent and changing ideas about sexuality, male chastity, and the role of marriage. Extramarital sexuality could help or hinder noblemen in pursuit of a public masculine identity, but before the seventeenth-century emphasis on male chastity and moderation,[10] earlier generations of nobility were able to maintain adulterous affairs without damage to their masculinity as long as those affairs did not interrupt the inheritance process.[11] Being a devout Christian was easier in a time period that crafted ambiguity into its very law codes.

---

[6]   Edward Behrend-Martínez, *Unfit for Marriage: Impotent Spouses on Trial in the Basque Region of Spain, 1650–1750* (Reno: University of Nevada Press, 2007), xii, 4.

[7]   Ibid., x.

[8]   Christian Berco, *Sexual Hierarchies, Public Status: Men, Sodomy, and Society in Spain's Golden Age* (Toronto: University of Toronto Press, 2007), 39–40.

[9]   The *arbitristas* were writers who directly addressed and tried to solve issues presented by Spain's seventeenth-century troubles. See Lehfeldt, "Ideal Men," 465.

[10]   Ibid., 478.

[11]   The small number of case studies used as the basis of this chapter prevents any conclusive statements about the number of extramarital affairs being carried on by the

Both the Catholic Church and Spanish law codes such as the *Siete Partidas* officially endorsed the institution of marriage as the only acceptable venue in which to have sexual relations or to produce children. The *Siete Partidas* sums this up, stating "The Holy Church forbids Christians to keep concubines, because they live with them in mortal sin" and remarking that "although the Holy Church does not consider, or accept" illegitimate children, still "it happens that men beget them."[12] The fact that "men beget them" interested the law more than the church's disapproval, and the *Siete Partidas* goes on to devote three laws to concubinage and nine to illegitimate children and their legal rights. In early modern Spain, if there was no legal impediment to their parents' marriage, illegitimate children were known as *hijos naturales* and had some legal rights of inheritance if they were acknowledged by their father. If the parents of *hijos naturales* subsequently married, then these children were automatically legitimated. On the other hand, if their parents were legally unable to marry at the time of their birth (because they were married to someone else or bound by religious vows) illegitimate children were known as *hijos bastardos*.[13] It was more difficult for *hijos bastardos* to claim any legal rights to inherit, but in practice both married men and priests often claimed and passed on property to their illegitimate children.

This ambivalent attitude towards extramarital affairs and illegitimate children was shared by the nobility. Before the resolutions of the Council of Trent took effect at the end of the sixteenth century, marriage laws in early modern Spain were both changing and flexible; and even after Trent it took a long time for the new, stricter codes governing legal marriage to take effect. It could be very difficult for even a well-educated layperson to negotiate the complex marriage laws correctly, and this difficulty made it much easier for people who wished to bypass the law altogether. Renato Barahona notes that "when engaging in

---

nobility in general in this time period. However, it is striking that in the Seccion Nobleza of the Archivo Historico Nacional, I was able to locate 19 mistresses in the fifteenth century, 19 mistresses in the sixteenth century, three mistresses in the seventeenth century, one in the eighteenth, and two in the nineteenth. I do not know if noblemen actually had fewer extramarital affairs after 1600, if they were simply more discreet about their affairs (and thus less likely to legitimize their children) after 1600, or if this is an anomaly of the collection. However, I suspect that the Council of Trent, coupled with the changing social mores that Lehfeldt explores, probably had an effect either on the number of affairs or at least on their publicity.

[12]   Robert I. Burns, SJ, ed., *Las Siete Partidas*, vol. 4, *Family, Commerce, and the Sea: The Worlds of Women and Merchants* (Philadelphia: University of Pennsylvania Press, 2001), partida 4, title 14, 950 and title 15, 952.

[13]   Ann Twinam, *Public Lives, Private Secrets: Gender, Honor, Sexuality, and Illegitimacy in Colonial Spanish America* (Stanford: Stanford University Press, 1999), 128.

significant sexual relationships, individuals often skirted ecclesiastical tenets and codes of conduct in various ways."[14] While the nobility continued to arrange, invest in, and value marriage as the most appropriate way to beget children and pass on property, they also accepted sexuality that occurred outside of the bonds of marriage.

This was especially true for men. While the ambivalent attitudes toward extramarital sexuality in early modern Spain allowed even women a degree of flexibility with regards to chastity and honor,[15] the extramarital affairs of men were widely accepted. It was not unusual for noblemen across Europe to father illegitimate children,[16] and Spanish noblemen in the fifteenth and sixteenth centuries often had mistresses before and during their marriages. In addition, Spanish noblemen who became clerics sometimes had affairs and produced illegitimate offspring. The fact that under Spanish law there were various different categories of illegitimate children demonstrates a degree of legal and social acceptance for children born outside of marriage.[17] More than just being overlooked, mistresses and illegitimate children could be beneficial to noblemen for a variety of reasons, and it was often in a nobleman's best interests to recognize and support his illegitimate children.

In early modern Spain, marriage was a symbol of adulthood for both men and women among the nobility. When marriage was not possible for economic or social reasons, younger sons or members of the minor nobility could find their masculinity in question because they were not in a position to demonstrate their

---

[14]   Renato Barahona, *Sex Crimes, Honour, and the Law in Early Modern Spain: Vizcaya, 1528–1735* (Toronto: University of Toronto Press, 2003), xx.

[15]   For more information on attitudes towards women's chastity and honor in relation to their sexuality in early modern Spain, see Allyson Poska, "Elusive Virtue: Rethinking the Role of Female Chastity in Early Modern Spain," *Journal of Early Modern History*, 8:1–2 (2004), 135–46; Abigail Dyer, "Seduction by Promise of Marriage: Law, Sex, and Culture in Seventeenth-Century Spain," *Sixteenth Century Journal*, 34 (2003), 439–55; Barahona, *Sex Crimes*; Grace E. Coolidge "'A Vile and Abject Woman': Noble Mistresses, Legal Power, and the Family in Early Modern Spain," *The Journal of Family History*, 32 (2007), 195–214. For an analysis of these issues in colonial Latin America, see Twinam, *Public Lives, Private Secrets*.

[16]   For illegitimacy among other European nobilities, see Jane Fair Bestor, "Bastardy and Legitimacy in the Formation of a Regional State in Italy: The Estense Succession," *Comparative Studies in Society and History*, 38 (1996), 549–85; Thomas Kuehn, *Illegitimacy in Renaissance Florence* (Ann Arbor: University of Michigan Press, 2002); Helen S. Ettlinger, "Visibilis et Invisibilis: The Mistress in Italian Renaissance Court Society," *Renaissance Quarterly*, 47 (1994), 770–92; Hurwich, *Noble Strategies*.

[17]   The existence of categories of illegitimacy is found in some other European countries. For example, it exists in Italian and French law but is not true of English law. Kuehn, *Illegitimacy*, 33.

sexual potency. A charge of impotence could be fatal to a nobleman's political career because, as Edward Behrend-Martínez states, "a loss of sexual power ... was directly connected to the loss of political power and status."[18] According to Behrend-Martínez, a good example of this is Enrique IV, "the impotent" King of Castile (and brother of the future Queen Isabel) whose failure to provide a male heir or to control his wife's extramarital affairs linked his sexual failures to his "political weakness and the war of succession that followed his reign."[19]

In an example of the flexibility of fifteenth- and sixteenth-century masculinity, extramarital affairs, especially if they resulted in male offspring, could resolve the dilemma of young men unable to marry but needing to demonstrate their sexual potency, at least temporarily. In the winter of 1516–17, Juan de Velasco, a young nobleman from the ducal house of Frías, seduced Ana de Galves, who then gave birth to their son, Baltasar. Juan de Velasco formally acknowledged his paternity, giving Ana a dowry of 200 ducats (*ducados*), which enabled her to marry "a very honorable *hidalgo*."[20] A *hidalgo* was a minor noble who retained the status of a tax-exempt layman but usually did not have a title. Since Ana's family is not described as *hidalgo*, the implication in the documents is that this dowry was larger than one she might have had without Juan de Velasco's assistance, and thus allowed her to marry above her social status and enhance her own family's social standing.

While it is hard to uncover Ana's side of the story, a chance memory recorded in Baltasar's later attempt to prove his relationship to Juan de Velasco gives us a vivid insight into what Juan gained from his affair with Ana. Court life, which involved subjection to the king and an increasingly frivolous lifestyle based on conspicuous consumption, was "portrayed as decadent, and thus threatening to masculinity" by the seventeenth century.[21] Juan was a courtier, a role which combined with his unmarried status to challenge his masculinity even in the early sixteenth century. In the winter of 1516/17, Luis de Herrera, the inquisitive servant of Cardinal Francisco Ximenez, wondered why Juan was spending so much time in the town of Bayona when the court was in Madrid. He asked various residents of Bayona, who obligingly informed him that "the cause was the daughter of the host where [don Juan] was staying who was very well dressed."[22] Luis de Herrera permitted himself to doubt this because, he claimed,

---

[18]   Edward Behrend-Martínez, "Female Sexual Potency in a Spanish Church Court, 1673–1735," *Law and History Review*, 24 (2006), 297.

[19]   Ibid.

[20]   "un hidalgo mui honrrado," Archivo Historical Nacional [hereafter AHN], Sección Nobleza, Frías, legajo 606, no. 26.

[21]   Lehfeldt, "Ideal Men," 471.

[22]   AHN, Nobleza, Frias, legajo 606, no. 26.

"el senor don Juan had in court a reputation for being castrated."[23] The *hidalgo* he mentioned this to "said to me, 'look, the one you call castrated left the daughter of the host pregnant.'"[24]

The result of this pregnancy was Baltasar de Velasco, whom one witness "saw cared for in the said house where the said maiden was" and heard referred to as "Velasquito."[25] In the vicious world of court rumors, where courtiers like Luis de Herrera could openly speculate on another man's virility, the presence of Ana and her son served to restore Juan de Velasco's damaged prestige and affirm his masculinity.[26] By giving his son his name, Juan de Velasco did not need to marry his son's mother to reap the benefits of having a son, benefits which included losing his reputation for being castrated. Years later, after Juan was dead, Baltasar was able to collect the accounts of five witnesses who were all prepared to swear under oath that Juan had been his father. The publicity surrounding this affair was part of Juan's performance of masculinity. The presence of his mistress had helped him repair a damaged masculine reputation without the expense and difficulty of marriage, a burden that he perhaps could not afford at that time.

In addition to sexual potency, the proper management of wealth, estates, and family members and the smooth transmission of patriarchal power between generations were also important elements of noble masculinity. Membership in a noble lineage was an important part of a nobleman's successful performance of masculinity, and the successful transfer of property between generations was what kept lineages alive.[27] Noblemen were seen as stewards of their estates, with an obligation, as the Marquis of Cenete expressed in his will in the late sixteenth century, to "dispose of what is theirs to their own advantage and that of their family and discharge their own conscience and leave order and clarity in their

---

[23]   "yo ponia duda en ello porque el Señor Don Juan le tenian en la Corte en reputacion de Capon." Ibid.

[24]   "me dijo mira el capon que decia, que dejó preñada la hija del Huesped." Ibid.

[25]   Ibid.

[26]   Jonathan Dewald argues that there was a dark side to European court life, which required nobles to exercise self control and conceal their inner thoughts for fear of misrepresentation. Jonathan Dewald, *The European Nobility, 1400–1800* (Cambridge: Cambridge University Press, 1996), 127–8. See also David Starkey, "The Court: Castiglione's Ideal and Tudor Reality," *Journal of the Warburg and Courtauld Institutes*, 45 (1982), 232–9.

[27]   This emphasis on lineage meant that the nobility developed increasingly complex rituals about death and the transfer of property. The establishment of *mayorazgos* (the Castilian form of entail), guardianships, increasingly elaborate funeral rituals, and the building of funeral chapels and monuments all illustrate the importance of the moment when property was transferred. For more on these rituals in Spain, see Carlos M.N. Eire, *From Madrid to Purgatory: The Art and Craft of Dying in Sixteenth-Century Spain* (Cambridge: Cambridge University Press, 1995). For a comparative perspective, see Soldat, this volume.

property."[28] While multiple mistresses and illegitimate children could publicly affirm a nobleman's virility and even provide back-up heirs who could sustain the family strategy, they could also threaten loss of control when it came to disposing of his property.

The third Duke of Infantado (1461–1531) had at least three mistresses over the course of his lifetime, but only the last one disrupted his family and his ability to manage his property. His first recorded affair happened before his marriage and resulted in the birth of a son in 1489. This son, who was publicly acknowledged and supported by the duke, later became archdeacon of the regions of Gaudalajara and Talavera in Castile.[29] This affair clearly enhanced the unmarried duke's masculinity, proving his virility by giving him a son, but not challenging the orderly transmission of property. The duke married María Pimentel, daughter of the counts of Benavente, in 1491 and although the couple's first child died only days after his birth, they went on to have at least five more children.[30] The smooth transition of the Infantado estate was secured by the presence of the young fourth duke, Iñigo, and his healthy younger brother, Rodrigo.

These healthy, legitimate children meant that some degree of extramarital freedom was available to the third duke, who proceeded to have at least six more illegitimate children. He acknowledged and supported all of them, marrying off one illegitimate son and three illegitimate daughters and placing two other illegitimate children into religious careers.[31] None of this appears to have publicly disrupted his family life or his ability to manage his property. In fact, his masculinity was probably enhanced by his ability to provide marriages and careers for so many offspring. The third Duke of Infantado was clearly virile, wealthy, and powerful, and he was able to manage his family and his estate.

However, after his wife's death in the early sixteenth century, when the third duke became infatuated with his daughter's maid, María Maldonada, his legitimate adult children were disgusted and tried to intervene. The duke responded by marrying the maid, permitting her to use the title of duchess, and bestowing many of his worldly goods (especially jewelry) on her. However, the

---

[28]   AHN, Nobleza, Osuna, legajo 1763, no. 15.2.

[29]   Cristina Arteaga y Falguera, *La Casa del Infantado, cabeza de los Mendoza*, vol. I (Madrid: Duque del Infantado, 1940), 286.

[30]   AHN, Nobleza, Osuna, legajo 1773, no. 13 and 26 for the marriage; also Francisco Layna Serrano, *Historia de Guadalajar y sus Mendozas en los siglos XV y XVI*, vol. II (Madrid: Aldus, S.A., 1942), 126 for the death of their first son.

[31]   Layna Serrano, *Guadalajara*, vol. III, p. 141; AHN, Nobleza, Osuna, legajo 1776, no. 23; Diego Gutiérrez Coronel, *Historia Genealógica de la Casa de Mendoza*, vol. 2, ed. Ángel González de Palencia (Madrid: CSIC and Ayuntamiento de Cuenca, 1946), 236.

duke "did not consummate the marriage due to his many illnesses, weakness, and age."[32] Clearly, this was not a relationship or a marriage that enhanced the duke's masculinity, but he clung stubbornly to his new wife even when his children left the ducal palace in protest.

In addition to making the duke the laughing-stock of his contemporaries, this relationship complicated the duke's ability to hand on his property to his heirs. After the duke's death, his son and heir had to sue María to regain the property she had taken with her when she left the palace to marry the *regidor* Francisco de Santisteban in Valladolid. Although the new duke officially won the lawsuit, María remained a wealthy woman and continued to use the title of duchess throughout her long life, much to the disgust of the new duke and his siblings.[33] If noble masculinity was a performance that varied over time, the third Duke of Infantado had a very successful run until he met María Maldonada. He had successfully managed to have a wife and at least two mistresses, to support all the children of these liaisons in ways that were appropriate to their stations in life, and none of the previous affairs or their offspring had disrupted his ability to fulfill his family responsibilities and hand on the estate of Infantado to his son. He was the image of a powerful, masculine, and virile nobleman until old age caught up with him and he was perceived to have made a fool of himself over a woman who was both very much his junior and his social inferior. Even so, he might have managed to carry it off if he had not married María Maldonada. Marriage gave mistresses legal rights that threatened male control over them.

Noblemen often sidestepped the dangers of marrying their mistresses and thus investing them with the legal powers and rights of a wife by simply legitimizing their offspring. In Spain, as in other parts of early modern Europe, legitimation was a complicated legal strategy. Thomas Kuehn describes legitimation in Renaissance Italy as a "social and legal paradox" that "was carefully managed and maintained," adding "creative manufacture, maintenance, and management of such ambiguities was one of the hallmarks of life in a Renaissance city-state, if not of all societies."[34] Like masculinity, legitimacy could be finessed. The monarchs

---

[32]   Ibid., 117.

[33]   Ibid., 118–20. For more on the complications of remarriage, see Giulia Calvi, "Reconstructing the Family: Widowhood and Remarriage in Tuscany in the Early Modern Period," in *Marriage in Italy, 1300–1650*, eds Trevor Dean and K.J.P. Lowe (Cambridge: Cambridge University Press, 1998); Barbara Diefendorf, "Widowhood and Remarriage in Sixteenth-Century Paris," *Journal of Family History*, 7 (1982), 379–95; Lyndan Warner, "Widows, Widowers and the Problem of 'Second Marriages' in Sixteenth-Century France," in *Widowhood in Medieval and Early Modern Europe*, eds S. Cavallo and L. Warner (New York: Pearson Education Limited, 1999).

[34]   Kuehn, *Illegitimacy*, ix.

of Spain could use their royal power to set aside the law in a process that evolved from "individual exceptions for favored subjects" in the fifteenth century to a bureaucratic process by the eighteenth century.[35] In addition, the Pope could waive the church law and dispense legitimacy to his to faithful Catholic subjects. For example, Alvaro de Luna, a powerful fifteenth-century nobleman and the ill-fated advisor to King Juan II of Castile, was legitimated three times, twice by the king and once by Pope Eugenio IV in 1445.[36]

The nobility used this legal strategy throughout the early modern period. *Hijos naturales* (born to parents who could have married) were the easiest to legitimate. If their parents married, they were automatically legitimated. However, the fifteenth- and sixteenth-century nobility managed to legitimate even children whose parents never married or were bound by religious vows. The first Duke of Gandía, who was the son of Pope Alexander VI, was legitimated in 1481.[37] On a slightly less exalted level, Inés and Juana, daughters of Abbot Diego de Zuñiga and Isabel de Mercado, were also successfully legitimated in the mid-sixteenth century, although the abbot claimed that his daughters had been conceived before he took religious vows.[38]

The ultimate proof of a nobleman's masculinity was, of course, a son. A legitimate son simultaneously proved a man's sexual potency, symbolized the success of his marriage, and made "order and clarity" possible in the transfer of his property. It was the presence of two healthy legitimate sons that enabled the third duke to successfully maintain a masculine image that was uncomplicated by his illegitimate children. When a nobleman did not have a legitimate son, his masculine image suffered. A mistress had the potential to provide a son, but her son's success as an heir could be complicated by his own illegitimacy and by his mother's social status.

Even when a mistress could provide a son, if her social status was low it could compromise a nobleman's ability to successfully transfer his property, and thus undermine his masculinity. In the mid-sixteenth century, a minor nobleman named Pedro Maça had a wife, four legitimate children, a mistress named Esperanza Cascant, and an illegitimate son, Juan. Clearly his virility was not in doubt, but death cheated him of his ability to pass on his property in an orderly way when his wife and all four of his children predeceased him. Pedro persuaded the king to legitimate his son Juan, but unfortunately Juan's

---

[35]   Twinam, *Public Lives*, 35. Spanish monarchs could also create and abolish entails, dispense citizenship, grant nobility, and even change racial status in the Spanish colonies. Ibid., 43.

[36]   Gutiérrez Coronel, *Historia Genealógica*, 61.

[37]   AHN, Nobleza, Osuna, carpeta 121, document 22.

[38]   AHN, Nobleza, Frías, legajo 892, no. 26–8.

mother was the daughter of a laborer. After his death, Pedro's family contested the legitimation and the transfer of property by alleging (among other things) that Esperanza Cascant was a "vile and abject woman" who had polluted the Maça family blood lines. The result was a lawsuit that dominated the lives of the next three generations of the Maça family and destroyed much of the value of Pedro's inheritance.[39] Far from saving his masculine reputation, the presence of Pedro's mistress had destroyed any success he might have had in passing on his property.

In contrast, mistresses of higher social status who produced male children could enhance the masculinity of noblemen who were compromised by the lack of a legitimate male heir. The difficulty of ending a marriage, combined with the immense pressure to produce a male heir, helped create what was almost a system of polygamy among Spanish noblemen, many of whom had a wife and several mistresses.[40] The first Duke of Infantado, born in 1417, had three recorded mistresses. His brother Pedro (a cardinal) had two mistresses. The duke's sons, Juan and García, each had a mistress, and his grandson the third duke had three mistresses and at least eight illegitimate children.[41] The practice of having long-term mistresses and recognizing and supporting their offspring could create dynasties (a very masculine thing to do). The dukes of Medina de Ríoseco were descended from the *infante* (prince) Fadrique Enrique y Guzmán and his mistress, while the dukes of Gandía were descended from Pope Alexander VI and his mistress.[42]

The fifteenth-century counts of Arcos are good examples of the benefits of this unofficial form of polygamy. Two generations of the family lacked a legitimate male heir and turned to illegitimate descendants to keep the title and estate together. The second Count of Arcos, Juan Ponce de León, was married to his niece, Sancha, but their marriage did not produce any children. Juan, however, had left nobody in any doubt about his own virility. He had at least three mistresses and about 26 illegitimate children. One of his mistresses seems

[39]   AHN, Osuna, legajo 642, no. 11a.

[40]   Behrend-Martínez argues for the use of annulments as de facto divorce in early modern Spain, but the process was still complicated, expensive, and difficult. Behrend-Martínez, *Unfit for Marriage*, 1–3.

[41]   AHN, Osuna, legajo 1762, no. 8.1; legajo 1763, no. 2–3; legajo 1832; legajo 1976; legajo 1761, no. 5; legajo 1969, nos 2 and 13; legajo 1966, nos 25 and 30; legajo 1967, nos 7 and 8; legajo 1968, no. 1; legajo 3202; legajo 3402; Layna Serrano, *Guadalajara*, vol. II, 221, 223; Arteaga y Falguera, *La Casa del Infantado*, vol. I, 173, 179, 286, 294.

[42]   AHN, Nobleza, Osuna, carpeta 5, no. 38; legajo 932, no. 15; Michael Mallett, *The Borgias: The Rise and Fall of a Renaissance Dynasty* (New York: Barnes and Noble, 1969), 101–2.

to have been a maid or lady-in-waiting in his household since he commended her in his will "for the seventeen years she has served me here in my house and been with me and worked with these my children."[43] Another mistress is mentioned by name in his will, but she does not carry any noble title. After his wife's death, Rodrigo married his third mistress, the noblewoman Leonor Nuñez. In 1448 he obtained a royal decree to legitimize their children.[44] This marriage and legitimation provided him with a son, a legal heir, and the ability to transfer his property to another male member of his lineage. His eldest surviving son, Rodrigo Ponce de León, inherited the title and became the third Count of Arcos.

The third Count of Arcos (1443–92) again depended on a mistress with some social status to save a troubled dynasty and allow him to fulfill his masculine responsibilities by passing on the estate and title to his own descendants. The count, Rodrigo Ponce de León, had no legitimate children from either of his two marriages, but he did have three illegitimate daughters with his mistress Inés de la Fuente (thereby establishing his sexual potency). Like Juan de Velasco's lover Ana, Inés is described as "the daughter of a *hidalgo* from Marchena."[45] Rodrigo used the presence of Inés and her offspring to repair his masculine image and create a legitimate male heir. He legitimated his eldest daughter, Francisca, and stipulated in his will that his title should pass to her son. He then arranged for her to marry a distant cousin, Luis Ponce de León, the lord of Villagracia. Their son, Rodrigo, inherited the title at a very young age and became the first Duke of Arcos.[46] A list of the titled males in the house of Arcos shows the title passing from Rodrigo, the third Count of Arcos, directly to Rodrigo, the first Duke of Arcos, with no public mention of either Inés or Francisca.

Juan's and Rodrigo's solution to their lack of legitimate male heirs highlights the importance of women in providing a properly masculine image. In early modern Spain, passing on one's power and property smoothly to a properly recognized male heir was an important component of masculinity. Often, the only way that could actually happen was if the man in question had a network of women that he could trust and rely on. The women in the Arcos family played a vital role in this transfer of power. When Juan's wife could not give him children (with 26 illegitimate children, it seems clear that the lack of legitimate children can be blamed on her), he turned to his mistress's womb to provide

---

[43] AHN, Nobleza, Osuna, legajo 118, no. 9d.

[44] AHN, Nobleza, Osuna, legajo 121, no. 13ñ; legajo 3476, no. 16; legajo 4165.

[45] AHN, Nobleza, Osuna, legajo 1619, no. 10.

[46] David Garcia Hernàn, *Los Grandes de España en la epoca de Felipe II: Los Duques de Arcos* (Madrid: Editorial de la Universidad Complutense de Madrid, 1993), 336.

a male heir, whom he then was able to legitimate.[47] When Juan's son and heir, Rodrigo, lacked a male heir, he was even more creative. As he arranged for his title to pass to his grandson (who had been born from a legitimate marriage), he recognized that his young grandson would need a guardian. He chose his second wife, Beatriz Pacheco, to be the guardian of his grandson. Whatever Beatriz Pacheco thought of being asked to take over the guardianship of her husband's illegitimate grandson, she did her job well. By 1500, she had arranged Rodrigo's marriage to her own niece, Isabel Pacheco, and was ready to formally recognize his maturity by releasing control of her husband's property to Rodrigo. Beatriz had effectively run the entire Arcos estate for eight years, and had probably helped to raise and train her husband's grandson, and perhaps also her niece, during that same time period. Rodrigo's wife and his mistress had formed an unlikely partnership that prevented the disruption of power and property that the Spanish nobility dreaded, and preserved Rodrigo's reputation as a man who could govern his estates well. Having illegitimate children "in waiting" was a noble family strategy that could work to preserve noble titles and retain a family's status, wealth, and power.

On the other hand, too much social status could empower a mistress to the point where she became disruptive, which meant that a family strategy involving mistresses and their potential children risked making the noble family a contested site. In another example of sexual virility that was not coupled with the competent transfer of goods, Diego Hurtado de Mendoza had two wives, six legitimate children, and a mistress who was his first cousin and the daughter of the powerful nobleman, Pedro López de Ayala. Diego left his mistress as an executor of his will and this legal power, combined with her own wealth and social standing, enabled her to retain her possession of the family palace and all the moveable goods that went with it after Diego's death in 1404. Diego's widow, who was also the guardian of his heir, was forced to appeal to the monarch to get her husband's mistress to relinquish her son's property and complete the transfer of power and goods between generations.[48] In this case, the presence of a mistress disrupted the transfer of property between generations and tarnished a nobleman's reputation for being able to control his family and estates.

Property was not the only thing that noblemen struggled to transmit to their sons. Masculinity was also transmitted between generations, since a nobleman derived so much of his identity and status from his connection to his family and lineage. The person and identity of a mistress could be an important factor in the

---

[47]   For the importance of women's wombs in providing legitimate heirs and saving dynasties, see Bastress-Dukehart in this volume.

[48]   Helen Nader, *The Mendoza Family in the Spanish Renaissance 1350 to 1550* (New Brunswick, NJ: Rutgers University Press, 1979), 44.

masculinity of her sons and grandsons. When a nobleman married, his marriage was arranged. Whatever implications this might have for the couple's future happiness, it was an important part of their children's identity, since the families of the marriage partners were carefully scrutinized to make sure that their lineage was impeccable. This ability to make a socially approved and expensive marriage was, in itself, a marker of status, nobility, and thus masculinity. Stanley Chojnacki argues that increasingly strict marriage regulations in Renaissance Venice also regulated masculinity by increasing the importance of legal marriage in the transmission of nobility. In Venice, men who could not marry for economic or family reasons found their extramarital options increasingly stigmatized until "the women with whom they consorted, and the illegitimate offspring of their unions were officially represented as polluting threats to the nobility's most sacred traditions."[49] Fifteenth- and sixteenth-century Spanish society was more flexible. It did not regulate marriage as strictly as Venice and did not automatically stigmatize illegitimate offspring. Men like the Count of Arcos were able to establish their illegitimate offspring as noble and socially acceptable. However, illegitimacy could create risks and challenges that might threaten a man's masculinity.

In the late sixteenth century, Pedro de Velasco found himself struggling to maintain a properly masculine and noble reputation in an era which was becoming increasingly concerned with purity of blood and legitimate birth and working toward the more restricted definition of masculinity that dominated the seventeenth century.[50] Pedro's problems stemmed from the fact that he was the illegitimate son of an illegitimate son of the third Duke of Frías (who was also named Pedro). In 1535, when Pedro the third Duke of Frías married Juliana Angela de Velasco y Aragón, there was no question about the equality of rank and privilege possessed by the couple. Pedro was the third Duke of Frías and Juliana was his first cousin, the daughter of the first Duke of Frías.[51] Unfortunately, this carefully arranged marriage did not produce the desired result. The couple had no children, and the title passed to the third duke's brother. The third Duke of Frías did have descendents, however. He had three sons by two different mistresses. Years later, in 1585, his grandson, Pedro de Velasco, a gentleman of the royal household, found himself required to demonstrate in public that he did not have ancestors who were Jews, Moors, or *Conversos* (Jews who had converted to Christianity) "or any other bad race" but were all noble and of

49   Stanley Chojnacki, *Women and Men in Renaissance Venice: Twelve Essays on Patrician Society* (Baltimore, MD: Johns Hopkins University Press, 2000), 67.

50   See Lehfeldt, *Ideal Men*.

51   AHN, Nobleza, Frías, legajo 606, no. 1.

clean blood.[52] The fact that the direct descendant of a Duke of Frías (a grandee of the realm and one of the most powerful noblemen in sixteenth-century Castile) would ever have to articulate in public that his blood was clean is startling, but times were changing.

Pedro's problem stemmed from his grandmother. His grandfather's lineage was known and his nobility public, but his grandmother did not carry the same assurance, and the fact that his father was illegitimate counted against him. The connection between illegitimacy and pure blood (*limpieza de sangre*) had grown stronger over the course of the fifteenth century. In 1414 Pope Benedict XIII had linked the two, and by 1430 the constitution of the College of Naples demanded that medical doctors have no "excommunicated or infamous" ancestors and be of legitimate birth. Illegitimates were increasingly asked to prove their *limpieza*.[53] Pedro was fortunate that he could name his grandmother and verify her social status.

Pedro de Velasco had to prove his nobility by demonstrating that his grandmother was of pure blood and could have contracted a legitimate and noble marriage. The document that Pedro presented emphasizes the importance of publicity when demonstrating social standing. Pedro's grandmother was Isabel de Barreda. Pedro was able to gather nine witnesses (eight men and one woman) who were all older than 40. They testified that while they knew Pedro and his family well, they were not related to Pedro and did not owe him anything. They all affirmed that the Barreda family was publicly accepted as both noble and of pure blood. One witness put the importance of public reputation into words, stating "the principal old and ancient men of the said city [Palencia]" knew Isabel and her family and that it was "very public and notorious that Isabel de Barreda and her parents and grandparents were *hijosdalgos*" who "possessed reputation" and had no trace of Jewish or Moorish blood.[54] This status enhanced the probability that she was of pure blood, but was not high enough to make her a potential bride for the Duke of Frías. Instead, the witnesses stated that it was also public knowledge that Isabel had had a son with Pedro Fernández de Velasco, the third Duke of Frías, and that both Isabel and the constable had publicly acknowledged their son.[55]

---

[52]   AHN, Nobleza, Frías, legajo 614, no. 7. Pedro does not seem to have been asked about his mother. Perhaps her family and lineage were better known, or perhaps he dealt with her in other documents, but this particular incident centers on his grandmother's identity.

[53]   Twinam, *Public Lives*, 45. See Twinam p. 45, note 52 for a more complete discussion about discrimination against illegitimates.

[54]   AHN, Nobleza, Frías, legajo 614, no. 7.

[55]   Ibid.

The importance of a public understanding of reputation and of the nature of a couple's relationship is underscored by another case, a lawsuit brought before the courts in 1572 in which Cristobál de Colón attempted to gather witnesses to prove that his parents actually were married. In this case, the judge decided against Cristobál because of the public reputation of the case. "Note," the judge said, "that here the book calls them [the parents] single and not married ... and the names and titles of the nobility of his parents are silenced, and the godmother is a woman of low connections and of bad qualities [so that] the notorious qualities that the witnesses gave this marriage are mostly contradicted by this baptism." Summing up his objections, the judge added "there is nothing more like bad faith than to hide and conceal a name."[56] Cristobál's parents had courted secrecy by withholding their names and titles (which signified lineage) from his baptismal record and by choosing a godmother who was not publicly connected with their families. Secrecy was a sign of guilt in early modern Spain, and while Cristobál's case was complicated by the decrees of the Council of Trent, earlier generations of the nobility could hope to overcome some of the stigma of illegitimacy by courting publicity.

Isabel de Barreda's identity and her relationship to her son and grandson also had to be proved by a collection of reliable witnesses because she was not an acceptable bride for a Duke of Frías. Her lack of a marriage license could potentially compromise her grandson's career (and thus damage his masculinity). However, Pedro de Velasco could compensate for his grandmother's irregular status by affirming her family's public reputation. This could have been a risky move, since it affirmed Pedro's purity of blood, but it also emphasized that both he and his father were illegitimate. Pedro, however, must have thought that his approach (which involved finding a notary and tracking down nine witnesses as well as raking up the circumstances of his father's birth) could succeed. Pedro's story reveals both the fragility and the flexibility of masculinity. Masculinity could be damaged by the behavior of previous generations, it could be transmitted or compromised by female family members, and it could be repaired by a careful appeal to the public knowledge of one's family status and reputation. In the fifteenth and sixteenth centuries, legitimations often paved the way for men to publicly affirm their masculinity. Alvaro de Luna was legitimized by King Juan II of Castile in 1423 when Luna was 33 years old. Twenty-two years later, both the king and Pope Eugenio IV legitimated Luna again so that he could enter the Order of Santiago, an accomplishment that affirmed his social standing and prestige, thus enhancing his masculinity.[57]

---

[56] AHN, Nobleza, Osuna, carta 4, doc. 2.

[57] Gutiérrez Coronel, *Historia Genealógica*, 61.

Another segment of the male population who might have trouble demonstrating their masculinity were members of the church whose vocation demanded celibacy. Illegitimate children of the clergy were technically categorized as *sacrilegos* and carried the heaviest stigma of all illegitimate children.[58] They should have been the hardest to legitimate and the most socially shunned. Nevertheless, of the 30 men in this study who fathered illegitimate children, four of them were members of the church. Pope Alexander VI, the Archbishop of Zaragoza, Cardinal Mendoza, and the Abbot of Santillana all broke their vows of celibacy to have relatively public affairs with women of significant social status.[59] Pope Alexander VI is, of course, notorious for his illegitimate children, and while his success as a Pope can be questioned, he did successfully found the dynasty of the dukes of Gandía. If masculinity was a complicated affair for laymen in the fifteenth and sixteenth centuries, it must have been even more difficult for the higher-ranking clergy, many of whom were noble and actively participated in the noble culture that demanded a sexualized masculinity as a prerequisite for power.

One man who brilliantly managed to balance the demands of a career that required celibacy with the need to project a masculine image was Cardinal Pedro Gonzalez de Mendoza, son of the Marquis of Santillana and brother of the first Duke of Infantado. Pedro Gonzalez de Mendoza rose rapidly in his chosen career, from Bishop of Sigüenza and Abbot of Valladolid to Archbishop of Toledo and Seville, and finally became a cardinal.[60] He was a key player in the success of Isabella of Castile's bid for power in the fifteenth century, fought for her in the civil war that ensued, and was a powerful member of her government.[61] His wealth, political power, and military prowess were well established. In addition to these elements of masculinity, the cardinal was able to prove his sexual potency by fathering three sons by two different noblewomen.[62] He went on to further demonstrate his masculinity by successfully passing his wealth and status on to his sons. He obtained royal and papal legitimations for all three of his sons, finessing their legal status as children of an ordained Catholic clergyman

---

[58]   Twinam, *Public Lives*, 128.

[59]   Layna Serrano, *Guadalajara*, vol. I, 170, 179; vol. II, 223; vol. III, 139–41; AHN, Osuna, legajo 1976.

[60]   Gutiérrez Coronel, *Historia Genealógica*, 373.

[61]   Peggy Liss, *Isabel the Queen: Life and Times* (Philadelphia: University of Pennsylvania Press, 2004), 89, 203.

[62]   Gutiérrez Coronel, *Historia Genealógica*, 379 and AHN, Nobleza, Osuna, legajo 1858, no. 7.

by focusing on the unmarried status of their mothers.[63] In addition, he formed entails for them that they could inherit and pass down to their own children. In 1478 Queen Isabella I of Castile gave him permission to form entails that his sons could inherit "as if they were legitimate and of legitimate marriage," and in 1488 he received a Papal Bull allowing him to provide for his sons from his *bienes libres*, property that belonged to him personally and was not entailed or connected to his offices in the church.[64] By the time he died, the cardinal was able to leave a formal, public will that left his belongings to the church because he had already provided for all three of his sons outside of his will. One of his sons became the Marquis of Cenete, another the Count of Melito and both were patriarchs in their own right, starting two more important, noble, and titled families. The fact that the cardinal had two extramarital families does not seem to have hampered his spectacular career in the Catholic Church in any way, suggesting that proved masculinity was an important factor in retaining power in early modern Spain. A man as publicly masculine as Cardinal Mendoza apparently could be as creative as he needed to be in interpreting what it meant to be a devout Christian.

Was it possible for a nobleman to be too masculine? Masculinity was an ambiguous and dangerous performance in the fifteenth and sixteenth centuries. Cardinal Mendoza is an example of a brilliant success and although other noblemen managed more commonplace successes by using the presences of mistresses and illegitimate children to adjust their reputations and craft successful inheritance strategies, being a noble male was a dangerous job. The case of Alvaro de Luna, a powerful nobleman and the Castilian royal favorite under Juan II, highlights the difficult nature of noble masculinity in a time of tensions between nobles and between the nobility and the crown. Born in 1390, Alvaro de Luna was himself illegitimate. Provided with a nobleman's education, he was sent to court at the age of 18 to serve as a page to the young Juan II.[65] He contracted two marriages with high-ranking noblewomen. His first marriage produced no children, but he had two legitimate children with his second wife, Juana Pimentel, the daughter of the second Count of Benavente, whose status and rank greatly enhanced his own. Luna also had two illegitimate children with Margarita Manuel, the daughter of the Count of Montealegre. He provided

---

63   AHN, Nobleza, Osuna, legajo 1762, no. 15 and 1858, no. 7; Gutiérrez Coronel, *Historia Genealógica*, 379.

64   "que sean legítimos y de legitimo matrimonio," AHN, Nobleza, Osuna, legajo 1858, no. 7 and legajo 1760, no. 1.

65   Isabel Beceiro Pita and Ricardo Córdoba de Llave, *Parentesco, Poder, y Mentalidad: La Nobleza Castellana, Siglos XII–XV* (Madrid: Consejo Superior de Investigaciones Cientificas, 1990), 117–8; Liss, *Isabel the Queen*, 105.

handsomely for both of his illegitimate children, founding entails for them and enabling them to make good marriages.[66]

Luna rose quickly to the height of power, becoming King Juan II's most trusted favorite and advisor. Juan appointed him constable of Castile and, according to Peggy Liss, "largely left all governance in his hands."[67] J.H. Elliott describes him as "virtual master of the country from 1420 to 1453,"[68] and Liss notes that he acted "like a king in the name of the king and himself became the wealthiest and most powerful of lords, an effective (if avaricious) administrator who established a governing apparatus dedicated to centralizing power."[69] In addition to becoming the effective ruler of Castile for a time, Luna was also the arbiter of the masculinity of two generations of Castilian monarchs. He roused resentment in Juan II by attempting to restrict his access to his second wife's bed. Juan II had Luna executed in 1453, but the king's masculine reputation was permanently damaged, since his own death in 1454 was attributed by contemporaries to immoderate indulgence in the pleasures of love.[70] Luna was also credited with introducing Juan's son, Enrique IV of Castile, to homosexual activities, an accusation which in this case did not enhance Enrique's virility but instead allowed his enemies to link the king's name with accusations of both sodomy and impotency.[71] For the king's critics, his reign would provide a contrast to the much more effective rule of his half-sister Isabel, who possessed, according to Peggy Liss, "moral certitude, decisiveness, ambition, mental acuity, political savvy, piety, prudence, and a firm sense of both royal prerogative and royal obligation," a very masculine set of qualities. Isabel and her chroniclers exploited her predecessor's weaknesses to challenge his masculine reputation.[72]

Alvaro de Luna's execution at the order of the king who had given him his power illustrates the dangerous role that noblemen occupied. Luna demonstrates most of the characteristics of fifteenth- and sixteenth-century masculinity quite effectively. He was sexually potent, with two legitimate and two illegitimate children. While the existence of his two illegitimate children challenged church doctrine, Luna demonstrated masculine control of his family by leaving them each an entail that enabled them to marry and prosper at a social level appropriate to their rank and status. Luna accumulated great wealth and more power than almost any other nobleman of the time period. His military prowess is boasted

---

66   Gutiérrez Coronel, *Historia Genealógica*, 61–5.

67   Liss, *Isabel the Queen*, 105.

68   Elliott, *Imperial Spain*, 18.

69   Liss, *Isabel the Queen*, 105.

70   Ibid., 11

71   Ibid., 28.

72   Ibid., 24; Berco, *Sexual Hierarchies*, 19.

about by contemporary biographers and genealogists, and his Christianity must have been sufficiently devout to fit in well with that of his peers. Up to this point, his life and career illustrate both the public nature of a masculine performance and the flexibility that allowed pre-seventeenth-century noblemen to be both devout Christians and adulterers without apparent conflicts or problems.

However, Luna's brutal execution undid much of his masculine success. Noble masculinity was, by its very nature, competitive. Someone had to lose, and Alvaro de Luna had plenty of enemies, including the powerful Iñigo López de Mendoza, the Marquis of Santillana, father of Cardinal Mendoza.[73] His political power failed and his ability to hand his property on to his legitimate heir was severely curtailed. It was at this moment that the importance of women in holding together a masculine reputation becomes evident in Luna's life. In this case it was not Luna's mistress but his wife, Juana Pimentel, who became an important part of his defense. Juana had already enhanced Luna's masculinity by providing him with her own rank and status and a male heir. When Luna was arrested, Juana actively supported their eldest son in very public attempts to defend him. After his death, she reached a bargain with the king that enabled her son to inherit. Alvaro de Luna's execution launched his widow on a complicated, public, violent, and ultimately successful career in her own right. She controlled much of his land, dominated their son until his death in 1456, fought for her grandchildren's rights, and became wealthy and powerful in her own right.[74] Alvaro de Luna died by violence, but his execution diminished but did not destroy his reputation for masculinity, in large part through the posthumous efforts of his widow.

Masculinity in fifteenth- and sixteenth-century Spain was a flexible concept that was also a performance. It could sometimes be repaired when damaged, but the attempt was risky and did not always work. Masculinity was an important part of a nobleman's political, social, and financial success, but it was also ambiguous and could be difficult to achieve. Ironically, although masculinity was the trait that separated men from the dangers of effeminacy and the flaws that contemporaries associated with women, the successful performance of a masculine role among the nobility in early modern Spain often depended heavily on the presence and cooperation of women. Many of the public aspects of successful male sexuality, such as demonstrating heterosexuality, proving virility, and producing a son and heir, required women. In addition, the successful

---

[73] Liss, *Isabel the Queen*, 107.

[74] See Christian Berco, "Juana Pimentel, The Mendoza Family, and the Crown," in *Power and Gender in Renaissance Spain: Eight Women of the Mendoza Family, 1450–1650*, ed. Helen Nader (Chicago and Urbana: University of Illinois Press, 2004), especially 30–31.

functioning of the inheritance system depended on women. Women provided the children who could inherit, but they could also take active roles as guardians and widows.

In early modern Spain, the nobility defined themselves in relation to their families and their lineage. They did this because it gave them greater flexibility and more options in a difficult world that often challenged their power and prestige. If a man could draw on an entire family, he had more resources to protect his masculinity or compensate for his own mortality. Using the family in this way, however, violated prescriptive gender norms by making the noble family a publicly contested space and thrusting its female members into the world of public images and public business. Spanish women were supposed to be chaste, silent, enclosed, and submissive, but most Spanish noblemen did not try to impose obedience or enclosure on women of their own rank and status. Spanish noblewomen were economically and politically skilled and they worked hard (and often publicly) to preserve, protect, and extend their families' rights and powers.

The policy of a flexible patriarchy that depended heavily on the abilities and activities of women is one that characterizes the nobility across early modern Europe. In Renaissance Italy, Tudor England, the early modern Netherlands, and early modern France women managed noble property, were executors for wills, took guardianship of their children, managed family finances when husbands were in exile or away at war, and advised their adult male children.[75] Across Europe, noblewomen played an important role in sustaining a successful public image for noble lineages. In a more passive role, women's bodies provided noble heirs. When Agnes, Duchess of Schleswig-Holstein delivered seven-month twins, a woman's body became the center of medical and political debates and an ugly controversy about inheritance in fifteenth-century Germany.[76] Spanish culture and law gave women concrete rights and powers that some of their

---

[75]   For examples of active noblewomen across Europe, see Chojnacki, *Women and Men in Renaissance Venice*; Ann Crabb, *The Strozzi of Florence: Widowhood and Family Solidarity in the Renaissance* (Ann Arbor: University of Michigan Press, 2000); Barbara J. Harris, *English Aristocratic Women, 1450–1550: Marriage and Family, Property and Careers* (Oxford: Oxford University Press, 2002); Sherrin Marshall Wyntjes, "Survivors and Status: Widowhood and Family in the Early Modern Netherlands," *Journal of Family History*, 7 (1982), 396–406; Robert J. Kalas, "The Noble Widow's Place in the Patriarchal Household: The Life and Career of Jeanne de Gontault," *The Sixteenth Century Journal*, 24 (1993), 519–39.

[76]   See Bastress-Dukehart, this volume.

European sisters lacked,[77] but the presence and activities of women were a vital part of the contested spaces of the nobility across early modern Europe.

The mistresses of Spanish noblemen are a more ambiguous group. They did not automatically have the same rank and status as noble wives, and their rights and powers varied accordingly. However, the Spanish noble tradition of turning to women for help in preserving their families and reputations allowed Spanish noblemen to use even women who were connected to them through extramarital affairs as allies in the fight to preserve their masculine, public image. Many fifteenth- and sixteenth-century noblemen used their extramarital affairs to repair masculinity that had been damaged by loss of reputation, an inability to marry, or the lack of a legitimate male heir. This was risky, but it could be quite effective. Mistresses and their offspring could bolster a man's masculinity by demonstrating his sexual potency and providing him with male heirs. Mistresses could also threaten masculinity by implying loss of financial and sexual control and disrupting the smooth transfer of property between generations. The sons of extramarital liaisons might find their own masculinity questioned by the presence of earlier generations of mistresses whose social and racial status was suspect. However, noblemen in fifteenth- and sixteenth-century Spain were both resourceful and practical.

Before the more anxious morality of the seventeenth century and the Counter-Reformation's increased control of sexuality, Spanish noblemen actively used their assets to repair the holes in their masculinity. They manipulated the law to legitimize their illegitimate children and enlisted public opinion to proclaim the pure-blood status of their extramarital partners. They survived challenges to their masculinity by exploiting its flexibility and rearranging the elements that made up their public performance of it. This practicality prompted them to use women in their efforts to prop up their masculine reputations, and also occasionally to empower women whom they trusted to help them safeguard their masculinity and thus the family's reputation. Whether they helped or hindered, it is clear that the contested space of noble masculinity was also occupied by women who, in their capacity as mistresses, widows, daughters, and guardians, often joined in the nobility's project of creating the masculinity and honor that would enhance family power and prestige.

---

[77]   For the legal status of women in early modern Spain, see Grace E. Coolidge, *Gender, Guardianship, and the Nobility in Early Modern Spain* (Farnham: Ashgate, 2010); Helen Nader, ed., *Power and Gender in Renaissance Spain: Eight Women of the Mendoza Family, 1450–1650* (Urbana and Chicago: University of Illinois Press, 2004); Allyson Poska, *Women and Authority in Early Modern Spain: The Peasants of Galicia* (Oxford: Oxford University Press, 2005).

Chapter 5

Inventing the Courtier
in Early Sixteenth-Century Portugal

Susannah Humble Ferreira

In early modern Europe, the royal court was easily identified as a contested space, teeming with elites who jockeyed for position and vied for patronage. Although the term "courtier" stretched back to the thirteenth century, the caste of men and women who came to fit this description in the sixteenth century had only recently been formed. Two factors ushered the debut of the new courtier, and indeed a new court culture. The first was an emphasis on learning that accompanied the burgeoning humanist movement. The second was a generalized economic recovery that began in many European kingdoms around the turn of the sixteenth century. In Portugal, such recovery was marked with a sudden enrichment, as the crown came to control the European spice trade. Within two decades, the environs, the size, and the rhythms of the Portuguese royal court were dramatically transformed.

The growth of the court accompanied political centralization. The strategy used by King Manuel I (1495–1521), of filling vacant household positions with men and women whose social connections could help him govern the kingdom, was nothing new.[1] Historians K.B. MacFarlane, J. Russell Major, and others have established that medieval and early modern rulers governed through the manipulation of clientage networks—networks which largely emanated from the royal household.[2] What changed at the beginning of the sixteenth century,

---

[1] For important recent works on European royal courts see: Jeroen Duindam, *Vienna and Versailles: The Courts of Europe's Dynastic Rivals, 1550–1780* (Cambridge: Cambridge University Press, 2003); Rita Costa Gomes, *The Making of A Court Society: Kings and Nobles in Late-Medieval Portugal* (Cambridge: Cambridge University Press, 2003); Malcolm Vale, *The Princely Court: Medieval Courts and Culture in North-West Europe* (Oxford: Oxford University Press, 2001); John Adamson, ed., *The Princely Courts of Europe 1500–1750* (London: Weidenfeld & Nicolson, 1999).

[2] J. Russell Major, *Representative Institutions in Renaissance France, 1442–1559* (Madison: University of Wisconsin Press, 1960) and *Representative Government in Early Modern France* (New Haven: Yale University Press, 1980), 175–6; K.B. McFarlane, *The*

at least within Portugal, was that household size was no longer limited by the financial constraints as in the past. In part, this chapter seeks to show how Manuel I was able to exercise political patronage on an unprecedented scale and create a court culture that promoted deference to the king. As an alternative to the strategy described by Ryan Gaston, whereby Philip IV and his ministers competed against family interests for the allegiance of the Spanish nobility, this chapter posits that Manuel I aimed to co-opt familial and local allegiances in an attempt to centralize power.[3] It also maintains that the elites who ambitiously solicited household appointments for themselves and family members were seldom puppets of the crown.

Baldassare Castiglione's *The Book of the Courtier* (1528), the widely read handbook of courtly behavior, holds an important place in Renaissance literature as an articulation of new codes of conduct among elites as well as the new socio-cultural problems that they faced.[4] The courtier to whom it was dedicated was Portuguese: Dom Miguel da Silva, the Bishop of Viseu. Born around 1480, Dom Miguel spent many of his formative years at the courts of kings João II (1481–95) and Manuel I. By 1514, the year in which he was named Portuguese ambassador to Rome (and the year in which he first met Castiglione), he would have already been a politician of great skill. By 1528, when *Book of the Courtier* went to press, he held the reputation of a renowned humanist, a generous patron, a skillful diplomat and a nobleman of enormous political influence: the embodiment of Castiglione's perfect courtier. In 1540, when amidst a power struggle between Pope Paul III and Portugal's King João III (1521–47), he defied his king and defected to Rome in order to secure the post of cardinal, he showed the degree to which courtiers could retain personal agendas while in the service of a strong centralizing monarchy.[5]

Nobility of Later Medieval England: The Ford Lectures for 1953 and Related Studies, eds J.R. Highfield and G.L. Harriss (Oxford: Clarendon Press, 1973). See also Sharon Kettering, *Patrons, Brokers and Clients in Seventeenth-Century France* (New York: Oxford University Press, 1986).

[3]   See Gaston, this volume.

[4]   Baldassare Castiglione, *The Book of the Courtier: The Singleton Translation*, ed. Daniel Javitch (New York: W.W. Norton & Co., 2002); Peter Burke, *The Fortunes of the Courtier* (University Park: Pennsylvania State University Press, 1995), 27.

[5]   See Sylvie Deswarte, *Il "Perfetto Cortegiano"* (Rome: Bulzoni Editore, 1989); Uberto Motta, *Castiglione e il mito di Urbino: studi sull'elaborazione del "Cortegiano"* (Milan: Vita e Pensiero, 2003).

Financial Footings

While the courts of Pope Leo X (1513–21) and João III were the backdrops for the dramas of his political life, it was the court of Manuel I that shaped Dom Miguel da Silva's diplomatic career and honed his skills. Manuel I, dubbed "the Fortunate," had been born seventh in line to the Portuguese throne. Yet according to his own propaganda, divine providence had made him king following the early deaths of his father, four brothers, the crown prince, and finally his cousin, João II. Fortune had smiled on his reign when Vasco da Gama, building on the achievements of ·others, navigated the sea route to India that ushered wealth to Portugal from the commercial spice trade.

The Portuguese dynasty known as the House of Avis had, since the early fifteenth century, played an important role in overseas expansion. During the reign of the first Avis king, João I (1385–1433), the invasion of Ceuta (1415) marked Portugal's foray into North Africa. Further voyages of exploration were sponsored by Prince Henry the Navigator during the reigns of his successors Duarte I (1433–38) and Afonso V (1438–81). However, the profits of these raiding and trading expeditions were inconsequential from the crown's standpoint because the costs of defending Portuguese outposts in North Africa far outweighed the profits. Rather, the North African captaincies were retained as training grounds for young nobles and the primary importance of Portugal's overseas possessions, prior to the 1490s, was cultural rather than economic. Through much of the fifteenth century, the Portuguese crown remained impoverished, to the extent that when João II came to the throne in 1481, he had complained that he had been left nothing but the kingdom's roads.

As elsewhere in Europe, the Portuguese crown had suffered at the hands of the economic crisis of the fourteenth and fifteenth centuries—its impact on the royal household being severe. The operation of the royal household in these years relied on the proceeds of crown rents and taxation which were greatly reduced.[6] Although periods of growth and cultural florescence did occur at the courts of Duarte I and Afonso V, the associated costs were paid by mechanisms of credit (such as tallies) and borne by the communities which housed the court. Thus, throughout the fifteenth century, the size of the royal household was regularly checked by the vehement complaints of local representatives at the sessions of the *Cortes*.[7]

---

[6] João Cordeiro Pereira, *Para a história das Alfândegas em Portugal no início do Século XVI* (Lisbon: Universidade Nova de Lisboa, 1983), 22–6.

[7] António Joaquim Dias Dinis, ed., *Monumenta Henricina*, vol. 1 (Coimbra: Commissão Executiva do V Centenário da Morte do Infante D. Henrique, 1974), 280; João José Alves Dias, ed., *Cortes Portuguesas: Reinado de D. Manuel, Cortes de 1498* (Lisbon: Centro de Estudos Históricos, Universidade Nova de Lisboa, 2002), 179; "Livro Vermelho do

By the late 1480s the financial position of the Portuguese crown had somewhat improved as trade in slaves, gold, and sugar now supplemented the king's income. However, it was not until the middle of the reign of Manuel I that overseas revenues overtook domestic revenues. When Vasco da Gama returned to Portugal from India in the summer of 1499, the new king and his councilors immediately grasped the commercial implications of the voyage. Commercial treaties, first with the King of Cochin and later with others, fixed prices for the purchase of pepper and other spices in India. In 1508, a contract drawn up with the Mendes-Affaitadi syndicate fixed the price of sale and secured, for the Portuguese crown, a regular buyer. Between 1505 and 1515, the quantity of pepper and spices quadrupled those amounts imported by Venetian merchants, signaling the establishment of an effective royal monopoly on the European spice trade.[8]

Even before these profits began to sail in, the Portuguese crown attempted to reorganize its financial administration and facilitate the flow of cash into the coffers of the household treasury. One of the major problems that had been faced by treasurers of the royal household was the manner in which crown revenues had been collected prior to the sixteenth century. Rents and taxes, collected in local tax districts called *almoxarifados*, had often been preassigned and collected at source by the king's local creditors and clients. Such a practice significantly reduced the income (both in cash and in kind) that reached the central coffers and increased the potential for corruption. A series of reforms to the kingdom's fiscal machinery (culminating in the reforms of the *Fazenda* in 1516) streamlined the process by which domestic revenues moved from the local communities to the court.[9] As a consequence crown revenues from the *almoxarifados*, nearly doubled between 1506 and 1518.[10]

Overseas profits were even more effectively channeled into the household through the creation of the *Casa da Índia*, and the impact that Portugal's new-found wealth had on the court was both immediate and profound. In 1501, when Manuel I ordered the construction of a sumptuous new palace adjacent

---

Senhor Rey D. Affonso V," in *Collecção de Livros Ineditos de História Portugueza dos reinados de D. João I, D. Duarte, D. Affonso V e D. João II*, ed. José Correia de Serra, vol. 3 (Lisbon: The Academia, 1793), 477; and Armindo da Sousa, *As Cortes Medievais Portuguesas, 1385–1490* (Lisbon: Porto Instituto Nacional de Investigação Científica, Centro de História da Universidade do Porto, 1990), 363, 384.

[8]   Donald Lach, *Asia in the Making of Europe*, vol. 1 (Chicago: University of Chicago Press, 1965), 119; Vitorino Magalhães Godinho, *Ensaios. II. Sobre História de Portugal* (Lisbon: Sá da Costa, 1978), 251.

[9]   Virginia Rau, *A Casa dos Contos* (Coimbra: Faculdade de Letras, 1951), 62–7.

[10]   Vitorino Magalhães Godinho, "Finanças públicas e estrutura do estado", vol. 3, *Dicionário de História de Portugal*, ed. Joel Serrão (Lisbon: Iniciativas Editoriais, 1979), 32–3.

to the Lisbon harbor, he reserved the ground floor for the accounting house, then known as the *Casa da Índia, Guiné and Mina* (later renamed the *Casa da Índia*).[11] When the carracks from India came into port, they were immediately boarded by the *Casa da Índia's* officials. Goods were then impounded in crown warehouses, subjected to a thorough inspection and audit, and any duties were then paid in kind.[12] Spices, gemstones, gold, silver, and luxury textiles owed to the crown could then be used immediately to enhance the environs of the court and to subsidize the king's courtiers.

Because the royal household was a permeable institution whose numbers were always in flux, it is difficult to assess the extent and chronology of its growth with complete certainty. Still it is clear that the profits from both the *Casa da Índia* and the increased revenues from the *almoxarifados* underwrote the expansion of the royal court during the reign of Manuel I. According to the extant rolls of the household, or *listas das moradores*, the number of *cavaleiros fidalgos* more than doubled between 1484 and 1518. The number of royal councilors appears to have doubled between 1484 and 1512 and then tripled by 1518.[13] Other data also suggests that the size of the court may have begun to increase around 1510, when overseas revenues began to make their mark. For example it appears that the number of porters of the chamber (*porteiros da camara*) nearly doubled between 1509 and 1513.[14] Also in 1507, the king lifted past restrictions on the number of *monteiros* and *mocos de monte* who served in the stable.[15] Quittance records further reveal that in 1518, 70 percent of revenues used to pay for the *moradias* or living allowances of *fidalgos* of the household came from the *Casa da Índia*.[16] This vast sum, of 18 million *reis*, represented nearly a fifth of annual revenues of the *Casa da Índia*.[17]

Center of Patronage

The expansion of the court during the reign of Manuel I made it a vehicle of upward social mobility for many elites, and Dom Miguel da Silva was no

---

[11]   Nuno Senos, *O Paço da Ribeira* (Lisbon: Editorial Notícias, 2002), 18.

[12]   Anthony Disney, *A History of Portugal and the Portuguese Empire*, vol. 2 (New York: Cambridge University Press, 2009), 150–1.

[13]   Arquivo Nacional Torre do Tombo (hereafter ANTT), *Núcleo Antigo*, no. 924.

[14]   Ibid., nos. 837–59.

[15]   ANTT, *Chançelarias de D. Manuel*, liv. 38, f. 58v.

[16]   Anselmo Braamcamp Freire, "Cartas de quitação del Rei D. Manuel," *Archivo Historico Portuguez*, 2 (1904), 159.

[17]   Godinho, "Finanças públicas e estrutura do estado," 33.

different. Dom Miguel was the second son of Dom Diogo da Silva e Meneses, a celebrated knight connected to the entourage of Manuel I's father. By 1487, Dom Diogo was in service at court as both councilor to João II and tutor to the future Manuel I, by then a crown ward. It is probable, given his age and social rank, that Dom Miguel would have then come to court as a *moço fidalgo*, and have been educated alongside other social elites. The process of *criação*, as it was termed, was meant to foster enduring bonds of loyalty among young nobles, royal children, and the crown. It is likely that Dom Miguel would have remained at court until the mid-1490s when he left Portugal to pursue a formal education at the universities of Paris and Bologna.

In 1502, when Dom Miguel da Silva returned to the Portuguese royal court to take up the position of *escrivão da puridade*, or keeper of the royal seal, to Manuel I's eldest son, he came back to a new king and a new political climate. Even before overseas revenues made their impact on crown finance, the king was able to use his personal wealth from the Duchy of Viseu to transform the royal household into a center of patronage. During his reign, several important officers of the royal household were elevated to the high nobility, one of whom was Dom Miguel's father. At the time of his accession, Manuel I had named his former tutor as his *escrivão da puridade*, and in 1498 he elevated him to the honor of Count of Portalegre. In part these promotions came as a reward for the service and loyalty that Dom Diogo da Silva e Meneses had demonstrated toward Manuel I in his youth. But Dom Diogo had also long held the title of Senhor de Celorico and his family had been extremely influential in the region of Beira and Alto-Alentejo for generations.[18] By appointing him to the royal household, Manuel I may well have been attempting to co-opt Dom Diogo's support and gain a better foothold in this area. The elevation to Count of Portalegre would then have been of mutual benefit to both Dom Diogo and to Manuel I, enhancing the influence of both in these regions.

Dom Diogo da Silva e Meneses was not the only recipient of this type of political patronage. In 1499, the *Mordomo Mor*, or chief steward of the household, Dom João de Meneses, was elevated to the honor of Count of Tarouca in 1499, extending his influence in the Beira Region. Dom Martinho de Castelo-Branco, councilor and *Vedor da Fazenda*, became the Count of Vila Nova de Portimão in about 1504, thereby increasing the king's foothold in the Algarve. Dom Francisco de Portugal, who was elevated to the title of Count of Vimioso in 1515 and appointed *Vedor da Fazenda* in the following year, fostered a stronger connection between the crown and the remote region of Trás-as-Montes. In

---

[18]   Anselmo Braamcamp Freire, *Brasões da Sala de Sintra*, vol. 3 (Lisbon: Imprensa Nacional, 1996), 349–50.

addition to these men, four other members of the titled nobility came to hold important and lucrative positions at court: the Counts of Redondo and Feira became members of the council; the Baron of Alvito served as another *Vedor da Fazenda*; and Dom Francisco Coutinho, Count of Marialva and Loulé, was the *Meirinho-Mor*, or bailiff of the court. These important officers of the royal household did not simply forget about their estates in the kingdom; rather it was in their best interests to actively monitor the political and physical condition of their lands.[19]

There is evidence that Manuel I attempted to manipulate patronage networks at other levels of service in the royal household. Links between the royal court to the rest of the kingdom were forged by plural appointments, where an individual might be named to both a position within the household and to a regional office. At the highest levels of service were the many *cavaleiros do conselho*, who also served the king as his *alcaides*. The role of the *alcaides* was to govern castles and their surrounding area. In times of war they were responsible for enlisting the help of villagers from the surrounding areas, and as such had to be men of local importance. The military nature of the office also meant that many office-holders came from noble families. But, above all, given the fact that many castles were located in vulnerable areas along the Luso-Castilian frontier, it was imperative that *alcaides* be loyal to the crown. When appointed to positions at court, the king's councilors accepted and appointed deputies to fulfill their duties while they exerted influence from afar.

At a lower level, many of the royal household's grooms of the stable, or *moços de estrebaria*, functioned as notaries in local areas. One example was Cristivão Goncalves, who in 1502 was already serving as a *moço da estrebaria*, and who was then appointed to the position of *tabelião* of Évora.[20] Duarte Afonso and Diogo Mendes de Silva are two of many other examples.[21] According to the sixteenth-century anecdotes, *moços da estrebaria* were ideal candidates for these local posts as *Ditos Portuguesas*, often serving as the king's messengers.[22] The plural appointment in this case allowed the crown to more easily exercise its will around the kingdom. Thus, in addition to enhancing his image as a generous

[19]   See for example a story about the Baron of Alvito who travelled back to Alvito to survey his estates. Ditto no. 628 in Josè Hermano Saraiva, ed., *Ditos Portugueses Dignos de Memòria* (Lisbon: Publicaçoes Europa-América, 1997), 225.

[20]   26 November 1502, appointment of Cristivão Goncalves, ANTT, *Chançelarias de D. Manuel*, liv. 2, f. 59.

[21]   16 December 1503, appointment of Duarte Afonso, ANTT, *Chançelarias de D. Manuel*, liv.35, f. 59v; and 12 October 1511, appointment of Diogo Mendes de Silva, ANTT, *Chançelarias de D. Manuel*, liv. 8, f. 102.

[22]   Saraiva, *Ditos Portugueses*, no. 21.

and magnanimous monarch, political patronage helped Manuel I to centralize his power.

The increase in the numbers of *fidalgos* at court during the reign of Manuel I undoubtedly affected the culture of the court. In the mid-fifteenth century, when their numbers were fewer, the service provided by *fidalgos* would have been much more concrete: *cavaleiros do conselho* would have actively counseled the king on matters of great importance; *cavaleiros fidalgos* would have offered him protection and military support and served as his companions; and *moços fidalgos* would have served as the companions of the royal children. While the *Ditos Portuguesas* suggest that the king did have opportunities to interact with his *fidalgos*, the growth in numbers precludes the possibility of an intimate relationship with all *cavaleiros fidalgos* or of regular consultation with all those men who bore the title of royal councilor. According to the chronicler Damião de Góis, the king habitually consulted with only a few councilors of his inner circle. Moreover, the creation of the royal guard in 1490 meant that *fidalgos* were no longer responsible for protecting the king; in fact the recruitment of more guards and *porteiros* served to restrict access to the king's person. Correspondingly, the royal apartments at the palace of Sintra were moved, in around 1510, from the center of the palace to a peripheral wing, presumably to limit access.

The royal household had always operated, to a certain extent, as a center of royal patronage. However at the turn of the sixteenth century, the wealth of the crown meant that the king's generosity touched a much greater number of his subjects. The anecdotes contained in the *Ditos Portuguesas* point to an environment where the king and his high-ranking servants were constantly being lobbied for favors, or *mercês*. That there was this expectation at court and that it was being met by Manuel I's magnanimity is evidenced by the extent of *mercês* and gifts documented in the Manueline chanceries. Favors were, of course, not only granted in cash and in kind by the king to his servants but also by his high-ranking officers. Thus Dom Luís de Meneses, while a *moço fidalgo*, granted 10,000 *reis* to a *moço da capela* who had solicited the sum.[23] Similarly Martim Vaz do Casal lobbied his brother, who served as *Meirinho da Corte*, to secure the appointment of two of his sons to the position of *moço da camara*.[24]

By 1514, when Dom Miguel da Silva left the court for Rome, the *fidalgos* of the royal household had become a caste of courtiers. Very few of the 400 who received *moradias* performed concrete functions within the household. Instead their task was to act as a liaison between the court and their communities— writing letters, exercising influence, and soliciting favors. The political functions

---

[23]   Ibid., no. 61.

[24]   Ibid., no. 30.

of these new courtiers were all but invisible to the observer. And as the number of courtiers increased after 1510, competition for the king's ear increased, lending credence to accusations that had stretched back to the thirteenth century—that men and women at court were little but sycophants and social parasites.

Majesty

The inflation of the royal household and accrued crown wealth also transformed its physical environs in the early sixteenth century. Changes to the royal itinerary prompted the investment in the spaces that the court occupied on a regular basis. In the fifteenth century, growth had been stanched by limitations of accommodation and supply. *Moradores*, or residents, who accompanied the peripatetic household, claimed the right to both food and lodging, and although suppliers and innkeepers had the right to fair compensation, often they did not. Even as late as 1498, bitter complaints were voiced in the *Cortes* about the burden which the court placed on the communities that housed it, and the crown was pressured to keep a modest household.[25]

The vast increase in the size of the royal household was accompanied by a shift in the royal itinerary, after about 1508, whereby the court began to orbit around the three largest municipalities of south central Portugal: Lisbon, Santarém, and Évora.[26] These communities were much better equipped to lodge courtiers and supplying provisions than smaller communities. Already in the fifteenth century, royal hostels, or *estaus*, had cropped up in the main squares of Lisbon and Évora in an attempt to reduce the burdens imposed by house-to-house billeting.[27] In addition, the expulsion of the Jews, which took place in Portugal in 1497, subsequently saw the disbanding of the *judiarias*. These ghettos were often located in close proximity to the royal palace and could be

---

[25] António Joaquim Dias Dinis, ed., *Monumenta Henricina*, vol. 1 (Coimbra: Commissão Executiva do V Centenário da Morte do Infante D. Henrique, 1974), 280; João José Alves Dias, ed., *Cortes Portuguesas: Reinado de D. Manuel, Cortes de 1498* (Lisbon: Centro de Estudos Históricos, Universidade Nova de Lisboa, 2002), 179; "Livro Vermelho do Senhor Rey D. Affonso V," in *Collecção de Livros Ineditos de História Portugueza dos reinados de D. João I, D. Duarte, D. Affonso V e D. João II*, ed. José Correia de Serra, vol. 3 (Lisbon: The Academia, 1793), 477; and Armindo da Sousa, *As Cortes Medievais Portuguesas, 1385–1490* (Lisbon: Porto Instituto Nacional de Investigação Científica, Centro de História da Universidade do Porto, 1990), 363, 384.

[26] See João Paulo Oliveira e Costa, *D. Manuel I, 1469–1521: um principe do renascimento* (Rio de Mouro: Circulo de Leitores, 2005), 124–6.

[27] Augusto Soares d'Avezedo Barbosa de Pinho Leal, *Portugal, Antigo e Moderno*, 12 vols (Lisbon: Mattos Moreira, 1873–1890), vol. 4, 125.

sizeable: it seems that more than 600 houses comprised the *judiaria* of Évora.[28] In Lisbon, many houses of the *judiaria* came to be owned and improved by nobles and *fidalgos* of the court.[29] The crown too saw it fit to provide residences for prominent household servants and officers. Manuel I granted a house, a small farm, and stables in Évora to his *Mordomo Mor* as well as houses in Santarém and Lisbon to two of his *Vedores da Fazenda*.[30]

A more permanent attachment to Lisbon (and nearby Sintra), to Santarém and the adjacent hunting lodge in Almerim, and to Évora led the crown to invest more heavily in the palaces in these places. In 1502, when Dom Miguel da Silva began his service as *escrivão da puridade do Principe*, he would have arrived at a court that had already outgrown its traditional accommodations in Lisbon and that was divided between the hilltop palace of São Jorge and the palace of Santos down on the river.[31] By this time the king had already commissioned the construction of the expansive Ribeira Palace that, with its connection to the administration of the *Casa da Índia*, would secure Lisbon more firmly as the kingdom's capital. Millions of *reis* were also spent on the palace at Sintra, which was only a few hours from Lisbon by horse and a favorite residence of Portuguese kings during the hot summer months. And in 1510 a whole new wing of royal apartments was added to the complex.[32] In Évora, where the royal household had traditionally housed itself in a Franciscan convent, Manuel I spent in excess of 5 million *reis* between 1503 and 1507 on the construction of a new church and convent, a move which allowed the court to annex the old buildings. Later the king ordered the construction of a new palace, of which only the porticos of the Gallery of Ladies now exists.[33]

Early sixteenth-century buildings, constructed in the style now known as Manueline gothic, were extremely elaborate and featured ornate lacework and iconography carved into the stone. Apart from one of the wings at Sintra, no Manueline palace has survived. Yet it is evident that those which existed would have been impressive. According to chronicler Damião de Góis, Ribeira Palace

---

[28]   Braamcamp Freire, "Cartas de quitação," 472.

[29]   Leal, *Portugal, Antigo e Moderno*, vol. 4, 140–41.

[30]   ANTT, *Chancelaria de D. Manuel*, liv. 6, f. 102; liv. 26, f. 43v; *Leitura Nova, Estramadura*, liv. 2, f. 79.

[31]   Senos, *O Paço da Ribeira*, 53.

[32]   Braamcamp Freire, "Cartas de quitação," 350; José Custódio Vieira da Silva, *The National Palace, Sintra* (Lisbon: Ministério da Cultura, Instituto Português do Património Arquitectónico, 2002), 219.

[33]   Braamcamp Freire, "Cartas de quitação," 276, 360.

was considered to be both large and sumptuous for the period.[34] And Afonso de Albuquerque wrote the king from Goa that there was "more gold in Malacca than in the palace at Sintra."[35] Impressive examples of buildings that have survived are the Hieronymite Monastery, *Mosteiro dos Jerónimos*, begun in 1502 on the banks of the Tagus estuary, and the adjacent Torre de Belem. Although neither of these buildings served as a royal palace, both were only a short ride from the Ribeira Palace and can be viewed as an extension of the Manueline court. Their purpose was to make an impression on the merchants, diplomats, and others as they entered Lisbon. Motifs in these buildings, and others built in the Manueline style, included the armillary sphere and the cross of the Order of Christ. The armillary sphere was Manuel I's heraldic device, which represented the cosmos, pictorially stating the king's involvement in overseas expansion. The cross of the Military Order of Christ served as a reminder that Manuel I was the head of this order, and that the conquests made in his name were part of a religious crusade approved by the papacy. Courtiers and officers, such as Dom Miguel da Silva, were thus constantly surrounded by these and other symbols that conveyed the king's power and celebrated his achievements overseas and the divine legitimacy of his rule.[36]

In congruence with their exteriors, palace interiors also became more opulent in the early sixteenth century. Inventories suggest that Manuel I commissioned many elaborate tapestries, from the famous workshops of the Low Countries, to adorn the walls of his palaces, many of which depicted scenes relating to conquests of North Africa and the Portuguese expansion into Africa. Painters and sculptors were also commissioned to decorate the churches and chapels of the court with scenes that combined traditional biblical themes with statements of Manueline imperialism. One recurring theme was Manuel I depicted as one of the Magi, a motif that both underlined the king's suzerainty over the Orient and conveyed the holiness of his mission there.[37] In the famous *Sala dos Brasões* in the palace of Sintra, which was almost certainly the seat of the court of appeals known as the *Casa do Suplicação*, Manuel I's paramount judicial role was expressed on the ornamented ceiling which dates to 1517 or 1518. In the center is the king's coat of arms, surrounded by those of six of his children. Below these, on the vaulted ceiling, were 72 coats of arms of noble families painted

---

[34]   Damião de Góis, *Descrição da Cidade de Lisboa* (Lisbon: Livros Horizonte, 1988), 61.

[35]   Silva, *The National Palace*, 95.

[36]   See the in-depth study on the projection of Manueline power, by Ana Maria Alves, *Iconologia do Poder Real no Período Manuelino* (Lisbon: Imprensa Nacional, 1985).

[37]   Ibid., 47.

according to social rank.[38] The decorated ceiling communicated the role that both the king and his nobility played in the dispensation of justice, but, at the same time, situated them in a strict hierarchical order under the king.

By the reign of Manuel I, the court was on its way to becoming a permanent spectacle. The use of royal trains and canopies had been at one time reserved only for important festivals, but now came to be used almost on a regular basis to distinguish the king from his *fidalgos*.[39] In addition Manuel I's fondness for music meant that he was almost always accompanied by musicians and, according to both chroniclers Damião de Góis and Garcia de Resende, encouraged both playing and dancing while he dined.[40] Portugal's overseas commercial involvement ensured a greater availability of luxury textiles during the reign and the king's own clothing was extremely lavish: heavily ornamented with gold and jewels in an attempt to set him apart from the other members of his court.[41] Suits of luxury cloth were also provided to household servants and *fidalgos* according to rank, and in 1512 the clothing of councilor António de Azevedo cost more than twice that of Sebastião da Fonseca, knight and *servidor do toalha*.[42] The arrival of greater quantities of luxury cloth, such as silk, taffeta, damask, and velvet, meant that the many increments of social status could be expressed more visually at the court than ever before.

Emphasis on Learning

While the culture of the Portuguese court was undoubtedly affected by the increase of wealth, it was also colored by a new emphasis placed on learning. Part of this emphasis originated from the humanist education offered to royal children. A humanist presence had been felt at the Portuguese court during the reign of Afonso V, when the scholars Justo Baldino and Mateus Pisano (son of Christine de Pisan) had been in residence. When Dom Miguel da Silva began his education at the court of João II as a *moço fidalgo* he would likely have been exposed to the influence of the Italian scholar Cataldo Sículo, who had been

---

[38]   Braamcamp Freire, *Brasões da Sala de Sintra*, vol. 1, 23.

[39]   Alves, *Iconologia*, 66.

[40]   Damião de Góis, *Crónica do felicíssimo rei D. Manuel*, vol. 4 (Coimbra: Universidade de Coimbra, 1949–55), 224. Garcia de Resende, *Crónica de D. João II e Miscelânea* (Lisbon: Imprensa Nacional-Casa da Moeda, 1991), 362–3.

[41]   Alves, *Iconologia*, 80–81.

[42]   "António de Azevedo," ANTT, *Núcleo Antigo*, no. 924, f. 132; "Sebastiao da Fonseca," *Chançelarias de D. Manuel*, liv. 25, f. 86v.

appointed as tutor to the crown prince, Príncipe Dom Afonso, in 1485.[43] Under Manuel I, the emphasis placed upon a humanist and classical education became even stronger and according to the chronicler Francisco de Andrade, João III, who began his education at age four (in 1506), was among the first generation of Portuguese nobles to learn Greek.[44]

During the reign of Manuel I, the general growth in the population of the court meant that more elites were being affected by the spread of humanism and other types of learning. It had long been common for young nobles and other social elites to enter the royal household at about age seven, to begin their training and education. These *moços fidalgos* began this period of service, or *criação*, alongside royal children, in part to learn skills such as hunting and riding as well as to receive an education, and in part to foster ties of political affinity.[45] Between 1484 and 1518, the number of *moços fidalgos* increased fourfold, from just over 50 to more than 200, meaning that a much greater number of social elites were being touched by humanist teachings. As numbers increased, the education of *moços fidalgos* came to be carried out in schools attached to the nearby University of Lisbon. The increasing importance of academic education is evidenced by the royal ordinance of 1500, requiring *moços fidalgos* to provide proof of their satisfactory progress and attendance at lessons in order to receive their *moradia*.[46] The education of a greater number of *moços* was almost certainly aided by the arrival in Lisbon of the printing presses of Valentim Fernandes (1495) and João Pedro de Cremona (1501), who associated themselves with the Manueline court. Among the first works that they printed were Pastrana's *Gramatica* and the Catechism, whose cover was engraved not only with the heraldic device of the king but also the Master of Grammar for the court.[47]

By the turn of the sixteenth century, education was widely seen as opening up avenues of social mobility for *moços fidalgos* and others which could lead to appointments in the royal household as well as in the ecclesiastical administration. During the upheavals of the 1480s, João II relied heavily on legal scholars, or *letrados*, to help him prosecute members of the nobility who had taken part in two major conspiracies against him in 1483 and 1484. Manuel I also understood

---

[43] Américo da Costa Ramalho, *Estudos sobre a epoca da Renascimento* (Coimbra: Faculdade de Letras, 1969), 93.

[44] Francisco de Andrade, *Chronica del Rei D. João III*, ed. M. Lopes de Almeida (Porto: Lello & Irmão, 1976), 5–6.

[45] Rita Costa Gomes, *The Making of A Court Society: Kings and Nobles in Late Medieval Portugal* (Cambridge: Cambridge University Press, 2003), 205–8, 231.

[46] ANTT, *Gaveta* 2, maço 4, no. 32.

[47] António Joaquim Anselmo, *Bibliografia das Obras Impressas no Século XVI* (Lisbon: Biblioteca Nacional, 1926), 160.

the advantages of staffing his council and household with university graduates, as the legal and administrative reforms that he undertook were only effective so far as they were enforced. Admittedly Dom Miguel da Silva's appointment to the position of *escrivão da puridade* of the *principe* in 1502 probably had less to do with his academic credentials and more to do with the fact that his father was *escrivão da puridade* of the king (his brother João was appointed as *Mordomo Mor* of the prince's household on the same day). But, given that many important positions were passed from father to son, the king also viewed the appointment as an opportunity to groom a young scholar from a family of proven loyalty for an important position within his own household. Such appointments encouraged other elites, such as Dom João de Meneses, Count of Tarouca, to encourage their younger sons to pursue a university education.[48] The crown too came to invest directly in the education of young nobles. Manuel I sponsored a number of scholars, who, like Dom Miguel da Silva, chose to study at the University of Paris, and at one point even tried to purchase the college of Sainte-Barbe.[49] He further invested in the University of Lisbon by undertaking extensive repairs and founding the College of São Tomé in 1517.[50] Although an interest in humanist thought and in formal learning had long been present at the Portuguese court, the growth in the number of *moços* being educated there and the stronger link between education and appointment fostered during the reign of Manuel I led to a transformation in court culture that helped to create the persona of the Renaissance courtier.

The transformation of the household, at one time militaristic and male dominated, was almost certainly affected by the increased presence of women. In the fifteenth century, the presence of women was restricted to a handful of ladies who attended the queen, a few female servants, as well as, perhaps, local prostitutes. Concern over the size of the household meant that many *moradores* were discouraged from bringing their families to court. However by 1516, most lower-ranking servants were allowed to marry and received stipends that allowed them to maintain a family at court. By 1518, a number of ladies, or *damas*, received *moradias* in their own right.[51] The importance of women to the culture of the Renaissance court was perhaps best expressed by Castiglione, who claimed:

---

48   Goís, *Crónica de D. Manuel*, vol. 4, 210–11.

49   A.H. Oliveira Marques, *Portugal na Crise dos Séculos XIV e XV* (Lisbon: Editorial Presença, 1987), 468–70.

50   Leal, *Portugal Antigo e Moderno*, vol. 4, 160.

51   British Library, *Additional Manuscripts*, no. 20958.

> There is no court, however great, that can possess adornment or splendour or gaiety without the presence of women, and no courtier, no matter how graceful or pleasing or bold, who can ever perform gallant deeds of chivalry unless inspired by the loving and delightful company of women ...[52]

The effect of women on the culture of the court may be best evidenced by the *Cancioneiro Geral* (1516). Preserved as a collection of works attributed to prominent *fidalgos* from the Portuguese royal court, the poems of the *Cancioneiro Geral* were meant to be sung and served as after-dinner entertainment, accompanied by kettle drums, sackbuts, trumpets, flutes, tambors, minstrels, and voice.[53] The subjects of the various poems differ: some, like the elegy of Dom João de Meneses, recounted the tragic death of João II's son, the Principe Dom Afonso, who fell from his horse in Santarém. Others were mocking, such as the poem which recalled an ostentatious hat donned by Dom Lopo de Sousa when he returned from the Castilian court. But a number were almost certainly influenced by the presence of real women at the Portuguese court and drew on the theme of courtly love. Although its antecedents lay in the Gallego-Portuguese tradition of twelfth- and thirteenth-century troubadour poetry, the depth, creativity, and nature of the court satire set the poems of the *Cancioneiro Geral* apart from earlier works. Classical and humanist forms that had been part of the education of Dom Miguel da Silva's generation undoubtedly enriched the poetry that they composed.

Conclusion

The turn of the sixteenth century marked a period when royal households and courts grew in dimensions and complexities. By 1520, the world of the court had changed beyond recognition in Portugal; the sharp roll-backs and austere conditions of the fifteenth-century royal household contrasted starkly with the majesty and opulence of the Manueline court. No doubt fifteenth-century kings were aware of the political advantage to be had in maintaining a large household of well-connected elites. However, the economic conditions and the paucity of crown resources during the reigns of Duarte I, Afonso V, and, to a certain extent, João II, prevented them from doing so.

Across Europe the economic recovery of the sixteenth century allowed monarchs not only to exercise political patronage on a much larger scale but also

---

[52]   Castiglione, *Book of the Courtier*, 210.

[53]   Aida Fernanda Dias, "A Temática," vol. 5, *Cancioneiro Geral de Garcia de Resende* (Lisbon: Imprensa Nacional-Casa da Moeda, 1998), 24.

to invest in more permanent spaces to house their expanding courts. In Portugal, where the economic rebound was marked by rapid enrichment, the impact on the royal court was more dramatic. As the court grew, its movements came to be restricted to larger urban areas. In turn, a more regularized itinerary prompted a greater investment in permanent buildings, resulting in new palaces in Lisbon and Évora and significant renovations undertaken at the palace of Sintra. In the new wings of these palaces access to the king could be limited and interactions were better controlled.

Increased wealth allowed the crown to appoint a greater number of social elites to household positions. More than 400 *fidalgos* came to reside at the court on a more or less permanent basis and were accompanied by servants and, increasingly, their families. Few of them occupied positions that had a concrete functional role at court. But these *fidalgos* had a political purpose, to act as a liaison between the court and local communities. The king expected his *fidalgos* to extend his political will; kinsmen and local communities expected them to lobby the crown in their interests. Thus this group of *fidalgos* now became a class of courtiers who competed with one another for resources. Political success at court required enhanced skills in negotiation and diplomacy. To stand out, courtiers required all abilities: linguistic, rhetorical, athletic, musical as well as, perhaps, the wit, nonchalance, and beauty that epitomized Castiglione's courtier.

Few courtiers in the early sixteenth century soared to the same heights as Dom Miguel da Silva. As a younger son of one of Manuel I's household men, and a "new" court noble, he could have expected a comfortable position at court, modest pensions, and several local offices placed in his gift. But in sending Dom Miguel to Leo X's Rome in 1514, Manuel I was attempting to put his best face forward. As a graduate of Paris and Bologna, Dom Miguel would have been endowed with both humanist and scholastic training. As the son of one of the king's most trusted servants, he was well connected and ostensibly trustworthy. Since his father's elevation to the title Count of Portalegre in 1498, he was considered a member of the high nobility. In his mid-30s, Dom Miguel had over a decade of experience negotiating relationships in the changing and competitive environment of the Portuguese court, his judgment and speech honed by the important role that he had played there. Able to insert himself into the intellectual circle of the Pope, Dom Miguel da Silva began his political ascent.

In selecting Dom Miguel da Silva as ambassador to Rome, Manuel I may have been trying to forge an enduring tie between the Holy See and the Portuguese court. As the *escrivão da puridade* to the 12-year-old prince, the king might have expected from Dom Miguel the sort of lifelong loyalty to the future João III that household service was supposed to foster. But like many courtiers, including Castiglione himself, Dom Miguel was an ambitious animal. Tumultuous from the onset of the reign, the relationship between João III and the Bishop of Viseu ended when Dom Miguel da Silva cut his sovereign off at the knees, in order to secure his nomination as cardinal.[54]

---

[54] Braamcamp Freire, *Brasões da Sala de Sintra*, vol. 2, 25–6.

Chapter 6

Sepulchral Monuments as a Means of Communicating Social and Political Power of Nobles in Early Modern Russia

Cornelia Soldat

In the community of early Slavic scholars, the assumption has prevailed for some time that in the early modern period relations between the tsar and his nobles were founded on a consensus between equal partners, the tsar being *primus inter pares*, first among equals, rather than the autocratic ruler that was described by Western observers. This assumption brought with it new research on the social relations of Russian nobles as well as on the relationship between the tsar and his nobles and the discourse of autocracy.

Following Edward Keenan's pathbreaking essay on Muscovite folkways,[1] Nancy Kollmann has shown that nobles had a hereditary right to be promoted to the court ranks of *okol'nichii* and, above that, boiar (nobleman), when the family had relationships within these ranks or came to them by marriage.[2] Marriage ties were thus carefully chosen in order to maintain a balance in court ranks, a choice that in the middle of the sixteenth century extended to commemoration practice.[3] Sergei Bogatyrev has explained that the decisions in politics were made in consensus between the tsar and his boiars.[4] Anna Choroshkevich pointed out a case when the boiars even wrote letters instead of the tsar in order to maintain

---

[1]   Edward L. Keenan, "Muscovite Political Folkways," *The Russian Review*, 45 (1986), 115–81.

[2]   Nancy Shields Kollmann, *Kinship and Politics: The Making of the Muscovite Political System, 1345–1547* (Stanford, CA: Stanford University Press, 1987).

[3]   Russell E. Martin, "Political Folkways and Praying for the Dead in Muscovy: Reconsidering Edward Keenan's 'Slight' Against the Church," *Canadian Slavonic Papers*, 48 (1996), 269–89; Russell E. Martin, "Gifts for the Dead: Kinship and Commemoration in Muscovy (The Case of the Mstislavskii Princes)," *Russian History/Histoire Russe*, 26 (1999), 171–202.

[4]   Sergei N. Bogatyrev, *The Sovereign and His Counsellors: Ritualised Consultations in Muscovite Political Culture, 1350s–1570s* (Helsinki: Sarja Humaniora, 2000).

a peace that was favorable for the land.[5] Hartmut Rüß showed that in pre-Petrine Russia the tsar and nobles moved within a social network of "lords" and "servitors," the tsar being *primus inter pares* in this network[6]—a thesis that has been supported by André Berelowitch.[7]

This research shows us a social network of a ruling elite that was carefully composed of family ties, guaranteeing participation in the political power of the state as well as in economic success. Outwardly this group represented itself as a hierarchy with the tsar at the top, surrounded first by the most powerful boiars—usually descended from families with marriage ties to the ruling dynasty—then by lesser boiars from families with weaker ties. At court, one was normally promoted through the ranks of *okol'nichii* to boiar at a certain age when the right lay within the family. Members of lesser families served as court officials (*d'iaki*), a cognate of the word "deacon," and had the possibility of being promoted to high counselors.

The tsar ruled in conjunction with a council of boiars, the logic of whose composition has not yet been made entirely clear.[8] Be that as it may, the political communication presented an almighty tsar as an image of Christ whose rule was implicitly equated with the rule of God on Earth.[9] In continuation of my research of this discourse, and reading about the social bonds within the Muscovite ruling elite, I have focused on the self-conceptualization of the nobility—the image they had of themselves and their position in the country's rule—and the way this image was projected within their circle and opposite the tsar.[10] Given the notorious lack of sources and ego-documents in Muscovy, there are no known

---

[5]   Anna L. Choroshkevich, "Die Bojarenduma und der Zar in den fünfziger Jahren des 16. Jahrhunderts," in *Zwischen Christianisierung und Europäisierung: Beiträge zur Geschichte Osteuropas in Mittelalter und früher Neuzeit: Festschrift für Peter Nitsche*, eds Eckhard Hübner, Ekkehard Klug, and Jan Kusber (Stuttgart: Geburtstag, 1998), 129–36.

[6]   Hartmut Rüß, *Herren und Diener. Die soziale und politische Mentalität des russischen Adels, 9.–17. Jahrhundert* (Cologne: Beiträge zur Geschichte Osteuropas, 1994).

[7]   André Berelowitch, *La hiérarchie des égaux. La noblesse russe d'Ancien Régime (XVIe–XVIIe siècles)* (Paris: Seuil, 2001).

[8]   Aleksandr Filiushkin has recently challenged the existence of a privy council in Muscovy. Aleksandr I. Filushkin, *Istoriia odnoi mistifikatsii. Ivan Groznyi i "Izbrannaia rada"* (Moscow: VGU, 1998).

[9]   Cornelia Soldat, *Urbild und Abbild. Untersuchungen zu Herrschaft und Weltbild in Altrussland, 11.–16. Jh.*, Slavistische Studien, 402 (Munich: Otto Sagner, 2001).

[10]   See, e.g., Cornelia Soldat, "Von der Freiheit eines Ratgebers im frühneuzeitlichen Russland, Klaus Zernack zum 75. Geburtstag," *Zeitschrift für Ostmitteleuropakunde*, 57 (2008), 23–33; Cornelia Soldat, "The Limits of Muscovite Autocracy: Relations between Grand Prince and Boyars on the Basis of Iosif Volotskii's Prosvetitel'," *Cahiers du Monde russe*, 46:1–2 (2005), 265–76; Cornelia Soldat, "Herrschaft, Familie und Selbstverständnis in der

written sources for this topic, and the research has had to be stretched to the analysis of actions and symbolical communication.

One source for this symbolical communication are the burial places of noble families that appeared after the coronation of Grand Prince Ivan IV ("the Terrible") as Tsar in 1547. An analysis of these spaces for family burial, usually being in a sacred space, a church, will show that they were linked to popular symbols of power in early modern Muscovy, being at the same time an affirmation of the system as it existed and a challenge to the assumption of autocratic power from the side of the tsar himself.

In this chapter I shall discuss the relationship between nobles and tsar in sixteenth-century Russia. With this purpose in mind I will first give a brief insight into the governmental, social, and economic situation of sixteenth-century Russia (or Muscovy as it was then called), then discuss the question of an autocratic government versus a government based on consensus and the question of resistance of nobles to the tsar. I then will discuss the spaces of communication, and of symbolic communication, that were open to nobles in that time. A more detailed discussion of a sepulchral monument of the sixteenth-century noble Vorotynskii family as a case study will follow, arguing that sepulchral monuments marked the family burial places of nobles in imitation of the ruling dynasty's burial church in Archangel Cathedral in the Kremlin. While the pious moment of the burial *ad sanctos* is not denied, and which took place in the West as well, in the current study there will be a different focus on the burial places of the upper echelon of Muscovy. They will be interpreted in relation to royal representation, state ideology, and Jewish, Byzantine, and Russian royal traditions, especially in regard to the Archangel Michael. In the conclusion I will argue that the choice of an imitation of the royal burial place for Muscovite nobles both represented the chance to symbolically communicate their part in ruling the country and the challenge of the autocratic claims of the rulers, especially of Tsar Ivan IV Vasil'evich, after whose coronation the first burial church was founded and furnished.

Russia in the sixteenth century experienced a time of both consolidation and reform. Russian territory grew as a result of land annexations in the west and the north, which led to economic improvement in the domestic situation as well as in international trade with the English Muscovy Company. All of this growth occurred despite the foreign wars and internal struggles of the time of Ivan IV.[11] The ruling dynasty was the Riurikovichi, who were descendants of the

Moskoviter Rus' des 16. Jahrhunderts und das *Skazanie o knjazjach Vladimirskich*," *Russian History/Histoire Russe*, 28:1–4 (2001), 341–58.

[11] On the economical situation with a focus on the economics before and after the inner struggles introduced by Ivan IV's separation of the land see Janet Martin, "'Backwardness'

legendary Riurik, the alledged founder of Kievan Rus', the first political entity of the East Slavs. After the center of politics shifted to Moscow, the new grand princes moved toward centralizing the government through the appointment of servicemen (*namestniki*) in the provinces, who were remunerated by the local population, a system known as "feeding" (*kormlenie*). At the same time, land became the main source of income for the servicemen from the fifteenth century onward, often granted by the tsar for military service (*pomest'e*).[12] At the center of government, the royal dynasty of Moscow was certainly surrounded by servicemen who formed a hereditary right to counsel and were traditionally serving in the royal or grand princely court. These people—to whom researchers refer as "service aristocracy" or "elite" (*znat'*), servitors, or simply "courtiers" (*dvoriany, dvorianstvo*)—constituted a social stratum that may well be referred to as the "nobility."[13]

During the sixteenth and well into the middle of the seventeenth century, the nobility developed into a hereditary and hierarchical system of titled servitors whose members, as a rule, received their titles when they came of age or gained promotion when related to a higher-ranked clan. While researchers for a long time assumed that the assignment of ranks to certain noblemen was solely due to the grace of the tsar, Nancy Kollmann successfully argued that it was indeed a hereditary system that granted clan members the ranks of their ancestors.[14] Certainly it was a source of self-esteem for nobles that they were part of a single integrated army under the command of the grand prince in which they served as cavalrymen, and were supported by retainers, including slaves. Thus, they were

---

in Russian Peasant Culture: A Theoretical Consideration of Agricultural Practices in the Seventeenth Century," in *Religion and Culture in Early Modern Russia and Ukraine*, eds. Samuel H. Baron and Nancy Shields Kollmann (DeKalb, Ill.: Northern Illinois University Press, 1997), 19–33. On the English trade see Jarmo T. Kotilaine, *Russia's Foreign Trade and Economic Expansion in the Seventeenth Century: Windows on the World* (Leiden: Brill, 2005).

[12]   This is also a source of the serf system, for provision through land meant that the peasants hat to be bound to the soil wherein resulted the restriction of movement for the lower social classes.

[13]   As Andrei Pavlov and Maureen Parrie state in their general overview of sixteenth-century Russia in their biography of Ivan the Terrible. I also would recommend this biography as a general and excellent introduction to the development of sixteenth-century Russia rather than as a biography of the first Russian tsar. See Andrei Pavlov and Maureen Perrie, *Ivan the Terrible* (London: Pearson, 2003), 10–25.

[14]   Kollmann, *Kinship and Politcs*. See also her *By Honor Bound: State and Society in Early Modern Russia* (Ithaca, NY: Cornell University Press, 1999).

directly involved in, and benefited from, Russia's territorial expansion in the sixteenth century.[15]

The interdependence of nobles' and rulers' landowning helped shape their relationship. Living at court was necessary for a Russian nobleman—whose land could be taken or given by the tsar, sold or donated, bartered, or even lost—as Russia's enemies still threatened Moscow throughout the century. Adding to the challenges to noble property was the Russian Orthodox Church, which continued to benefit from lavish donations. This meant that Muscovite nobles lived rather at the center of the country near the tsar's court, some of them inhabiting courts within the Kremlin itself. Only towards the end of the seventeenth century was possession of land stable enough for nobles to begin building residences in the country as well as in the capital, and to develop an interest in architecture.[16] Living near the court and the household of the tsar was vital for the social status of a noble.[17]

As a time of reform, the sixteenth century saw new developments in law, the church, and the ownership of land that were mainly introduced by Ivan IV Vasil'evich, the first Russian tsar crowned by the church and the ruler whose reign, from 1533 to 1584, dominated the century in many ways.[18] Major landmarks were the introduction of a new law code in 1550 and the Russian Orthodox Church council of 1551 dealing with reforms inside the church, instigated by the tsar himself in 100 questions, which gave the council its name "Hundred Chapters" (*Stoglav*).[19]

Tsarism was one of the major developments in sixteenth-century Russia. In 1547 Grand Prince Ivan IV Vasil'evich was inaugurated and crowned tsar in the Moscow Dormition Cathedral by Makarii, the Metropolitan of All Rus'. The coronation can be seen as the culmination of Russia's claim to Byzantine heritage—mainly by church hierarchs—as well as a political necessity in a growing and increasingly centralized state that needed a fixed point at the center of government that was clearly distinguished from the class of nobles. Up to the sixteenth century (in fact until Ivan's father, Vasilii III) Moscow's rulers were referred to as "grand princes," thus distinguishing them from other princes—the rulers of appanage towns and countries. They ruled, as Hartmut Rüß observed,

---

[15]   Pavlov and Perrie, *Ivan*, 24.

[16]   Country houses, as described by Sukanya Dasgupta in this volume in her analysis of the poetry of English country houses, appeared in Russia only in the seventeenth century.

[17]   Therefore the social bonds were rather medieval, as described by Dasgupta for fifteenth-century England.

[18]   See Pavlov and Perrie for a biography of the tsar, and also Isabel de Madariaga, *Ivan the Terrible: The First Tsar of Russia* (New Haven, CT: Yale University Press, 2005).

[19]   See Pavlov and Perrie, *Ivan*, 65–77.

as *primus inter pares*, first among equals.[20] Sixteenth-century Russia obviously needed to distinguish the grand prince of Moscow from other princes and high-ranked counselors by calling him "tsar," a term derived from the Byzantine Empire that had perished in 1453. Although in terms of foreign policy the title was not unchallenged, within Muscovy it represented the legitimation and illustration of an image of the power in the state that had long been put forward by church writers, culminating in descriptions of the tsar as the image of Christ and his people as Christ's flock, sanctifying the whole of Russia ideologically and elevating the Russian government over all other governments.

Although Russian tsarism has always been associated with autocracy, within the Muscovite ruling system we see a tendency toward consensus between the tsar and his noble counselors, which happened simultaneously with a public presentation of the tsar as the sole authority within the state.[21] This discrepancy between representation and real rule must have been hard to live with, not only for the rulers themselves but also for the nobles who ruled in consensus with the tsar.[22]

In the system of representation both tsar and nobles were eager to present their ruler as the most potent in the world. Sigismund von Herberstein, the Holy Roman Emperor's ambassador to the Muscovite ruler in 1516–17, wrote about the power of the tsar in his description of the realm of the Muscovite tsar. Russian nobles described their relationship with the tsar in terms of servility, calling themselves the slaves of the tsar, and thus emphasized his power compared to all other European rulers.[23] Herberstein, being an educated Renaissance nobleman and imperial ambassador, interpreted the representation of the tsar in his own words. First, he made some general remarks about the common people being slaves of the ruler, who were to be sold on his command. This led him to comment that the Russian government was a tyranny (*tyrannis, schwaere Herrschaft, grausame Herrschaft*) derived from the classical doctrine well known to Renaissance scholars. It suggested that there were right and wrong ways to govern, and that tyranny belonged to the latter, while the Western monarchical governments were certainly the right ones. Tyranny was not synonymous with autocracy, but with a government without system and justice, overruling all human and divine

---

[20]   Rüß, *Herren und Diener*, esp. 470f., 438ff., 338, 328ff.

[21]   See Bogatyrev, *The Sovereign and His Counsellors*.

[22]   For a further discussion of Ivan IV's conception of his rule vs reality, see Soldat, *Urbild und Abbild*.

[23]   Marshall Poe, "What Did Russians Mean When They Called Themselves 'Slaves of the Tsar'?" *Slavic Review*, 57 (1998), 585–608. See also his *A People Born to Slavery: Russia in Early Modern European Ethnography, 1476–1748*, (Ithaca, NY: Cornell University Press, 2000).

rights. For a Western humanist, freedom was the fundamental human virtue, enabling one to become aware of one's own value on earth and creating oneself as a human being.[24] If we look at descriptions of Russia from this point of view, we find more of a critique of the governing system than any genuine insight.

Russian nobles made use of the Western point of view, and encouraged the notion that the Muscovite tsar was the most powerful ruler in early modern Europe, who could treat his subjects, including his nobles, the way a master treats his slaves. Slavery, which existed in Muscovy in a mild, household form, provided the elite with a political vocabulary (the "master and slave" metaphor).[25]

As Muscovite nobles in reality were not objects, but rather subjects, of the system who ruled in consensus with the tsar, the political system was quite different from how it appeared.[26] In 1500 we find in Muscovy a system with no institutional or constitutional restraints on the ruler. In fact, shortly afterwards church hierarchs and court officials created the theory of divine autocracy. In the course of the century, powers independent of Moscow and provincial notables were extinguished; the nobles were forced into service classes different from Western European nobilities and gentries. Thus, an elite was created and existed for the state.[27]

As the public display of the tsar's power was autocratic, there was little space for the nobility's representation as decision-makers or even co-rulers; hence the lack of resistance in Muscovy. And indeed, Muscovite nobles had less space for the representation of their participation in decision-making, and in the governmental system at all, than their contemporaries in the West. In the

---

[24] For a recent interpretation of Herberstein's comments in this way, see O.I. Kudravtsev, "'Ugnetennye chrezvychayshchym rabstvom.' Ob odnom stereotipe vosprijatija russkikh evropejtsami pervoi poloviny XVI v.," *Drevnyaya Rus': Voprosy medievistiki*, 3:9 (2002), 24–9. See also Stephen Greenblatt, *Renaissance Self-Fashioning: From More to Shakespeare* (Chicago: University of Chicago Press, 1980).

[25] Richard Hellie, "Thoughts on the Absence of Elite Resistance in Muscovy," *Kritika*, 1 (2000), 5–20, particularly 19.

[26] See Hellie, "Thoughts on the Absence" on this topic, but note that in the other articles in the same volume of *Kritika* the point of resistance for early modern times is discussed controversially: Michael David-Fox, "Whither Resistance?," 161–5, Peter Fritzsche, "On the Subjects of Resistance," 147–52. See also my "Von der Freiheit eines Ratgebers im frühneuzeitlichen Russland, Aufsatz zu Ehren des 75. Geburtstages von Klaus Zernack," *Zeitschrift für Ostmitteleuropakunde*, 57 (2008), 23–33.

[27] Hellie, "Thoughts on the Absence," 19f. See also Daniel Rowland, "Did Muscovite Literary Ideology Place Limits on the Power of the Tsar (1540s–1660)?" *The Russian Review*, 49 (1990), 125–55; and his article "Muscovy," in *European Political Thought, 1450–1700: Religion, Law and Philosophy*, eds Howell A. Lloyd, Glenn Burgess, and Simon Hodson (New Haven, CT: Yale University Press, 2007), 267–99.

opinion of Richard Hellie, Muscovite nobles were indeed abased: they could be dispatched on service assignments at will; they could not travel abroad; their property could be confiscated without any pretense of process; and they could be flogged or put to death by their ruler.[28] However, they could limit the power of the tsar because they controlled the army.[29]

This meant that in public representations, as well as within the governmental system, the space for nobles to communicate their participation and concern was limited. The limited documention of the opinions and daily life of Muscovite nobles of this era only reinforces this impression.[30] Though personal ego-documents of Russian nobles are scarce, other sources, including architecture, provide an alternate narrative of the symbolical communication among Muscovy's ruling ranks.[31] As Barbara Stollberg-Rilinger states, one may open the spectrum of symbolical communication from speech and body language through ritual to conflict management, secret negotiation, and public performances.[32]

Architecture was used by Russian rulers for symbolic communication from the beginning of the Muscovite state until Peter the Great and the tsars of the nineteenth century. For a vast territory by European standards—containing multiple political and cultural units, relatively weak governmental structures, and almost entirely illiterate populations—architecture could be used to demonstrate power and define the image of the ruler. In creating a symbolical unity of the state, architecture worked in harmony with other arts, chronicles, saints' lives, sermons, and monumental paintings. And though we know little of the direct reaction of the people to architectural constructions, they were amply described in the chronicles, pointing at their value for symbolical communication.[33]

---

[28]   Hellie, "Thoughts on the Absence," 6.

[29]   Ibid., 11.

[30]   Cornelia Soldat, "Communicating Self-Awareness in Early Modern Muscovite Russia: The Vorotynskii Mausoleum in the Kirillov Belozerskii Monastery," *Frühneuzeit-Info*, 19 (2008), 10–20; Soldat, "Herrschaft, Familie und Selbstverständnis."

[31]   A case study on the self-awareness of Muscovite nobles expands upon this issue. Soldat, "Communicating Self-Awareness."

[32]   Barbara Stollberg-Rilinger, "Symbolische Kommunikation in der Vormoderne. Begriffe—Thesen—Forschungsperspektiven," *Zeitschrift für historische Forschung*, 31 (2004), 489–527, particularly 512–21. On political rituals in Muscovite Russia, see recently Claudia Garnier, "Die Macht der Zeichen—die Zeichen der Macht. Zur Bedeutung symbolischer Kommunikation in der Politik des Großfürstentums Moskau im ausgehenden 15. und 16. Jahrhundert," *Jahrbücher für Geschichte Osteuropas*, 55 (2007), 331–56.

[33]   See Daniel Rowland, "Architecture and Dynasty: Boris Godunov's Uses of Architecture, 1584–1605," in *Architectures of Russian Identity: 1500 to the Present*, eds James Cracraft and Daniel Rowland (Ithaca, NY: Cornell University Press, 2003), 34.

Timber was the main building material in Russia until the nineteenth century. From the beginning of Christianization in 988, the exceptions were churches that were built of stone from the eleventh century onward. As the art of stone building was not well developed in the fifteenth century, Muscovy invited Italian architects to improve the quality of the ever-increasing church buildings. From the sixteenth century onward, stone buildings came into use more and more not only for the grand princes but also for nobles, and in the sixteenth century many noble families built themselves stone houses. Nevertheless, up until the eighteenth century most buildings were made of timber, a material that suited the climate more than stone but that did not resist time as well as stone.

The building of stone memorial churches at the end of the sixteenth century became a means of showing the self-awareness of Muscovite nobles, as was the case for the Vorotynskii mausoleum in the Kirillov-Belozerski Monastery in the north of Russia.[34] The Vorotynskii clan descended from the Russian Grand Prince St Mikhail Vsevolodovich of Chernigov who, together with his boiar Fëdor, suffered martyrdom in the Mongol Horde in 1246. St Mikhail became one of the national saints of Muscovy, and his relics were transferred to the mausoleum of the grand princely family at the beginning of the sixteenth century, when the church of the Archangel Michael was rebuilt by the Italian architect Alevizo Novo in 1505–08.[35]

The third son of Mikhail of Chernigov became Prince of Novosil' and Glukhov, later of the Odoev and the Vorotynsk principalities. When these principalities were destroyed as a consequence first of the Mongol raid and then of war with Lithuania, in the late fifteenth century Prince Mikhail Fedorovich Vorotynskii went to Moscow into the service of the grand prince. The clan died out in 1679, when Mikhail Ivanovich died without a son.

In the service of Moscow's grand prince most of the Vorotynskii men became boiars (then the top rank in the Muscovite nobility) and served as *voevody* (a kind of military leader) in the Muscovite army. Most of them also fell into disgrace at least once during their service time. Some of them were banished to the Kirillov-Belozerskii Monastery with their families during the fifteenth century. But they all returned to service from disgrace and exile when they were pardoned.

In the middle of the sixteenth century something took place that changed not only the possibilities of symbolical communication for Russian nobles but also the custom of burial. Normally, Russians were buried in graves around churches. Apart from certain church hierarchs, only grand princes and very famous princes

---

[34] The following pages are a summary of my article: Soldat, "Communicating Self-Awareness."

[35] On the architectural history of the cathedral, see T.B. Vlasova, *Arkhangel'skii sobor. Putevoditel'* (Moscow: Kreml', 2005), 6–39.

were buried inside a church.[36] A burial in a church took place in the East in the same way as in the West: it could be either in a niche in the church wall, which was normally reserved for church hierarchs, or under the brick floor in a special brick vault with an overgrave monument on the church floor.

When Vladimir Ivanovich Vorotynskii died in 1553 on a campaign against the Mongols for Tsar Ivan IV, he was buried in the churchyard of the Kirillov-Belozerskii Monastery near the main Dormition Cathedral. In 1554/55 his wife, Princess Mariia Fedorovna, the daughter of boiar Prince Fedor Vasil'evich Lopata Telepnev Obolenskii, dedicated a church to St Vladimir the Baptist of Rus' over the grave of her husband, and thus founded the first mausoleum of a noble family in Muscovy.[37]

After that the male members of the clan were buried in the Church of St Vladimir at the Kirillov-Belozerskii Monastery, while the women of the clan donated to the church and adorned it with icons, memorial plaques, and self-embroidered shrouds. In ornamenting the mausoleum with icons and even embroidered hymns to patron saints of the family, the Vorotynskii women decorated the church in a such a way as to resemble the grand princely mausoleum in the Moscow Kremlin, the Archangel Cathedral. While the Archangel Cathedral had been adorned in the middle of the sixteenth century with murals of the buried princes, many of whom were venerated as saints, St Vladimir Church was decorated with icons of the same princes (St Vladimir, SS Boris and Gleb, St Mikhail of Chernigov, St Aleksandr Nevskii, Aleksii "man of God," Dmitrii Solunskii, and Login Sotnik) and the icon "Council of the Archangel Michael." All these saints are patron saints of the ruling dynasty as well as of the Muscovite state itself.

In this way, St Vladimir Church became a visual bond between the Vorotynskii clan and the rulers of Rus' of old. In the church, the family was presented much in the same way as the ruling princes in Moscow. On the other hand the presentation, right from the choice of the church's patron saint, shows an awareness of the fact that both families were historically connected with the ruling elite of Kievan times. The awareness of this historical continuity was the source for the responsibility of this particular family for the government of Muscovite Rus'; they felt responsible for the government of Muscovy because of their historical legacy and legitimation that lay in their bond to the ruling and saintly family of old. Therefore, the building of family mausoleums became a means of symbolical communication and an uncontested space for the representation of their participation in government.

---

[36]   See Ianin for an example of a church necropolis: V.L. Ianin, *Nekropol' Novgorodskogo Sofijskogo sobora. Tserkovnaia traditsiia i istoricheskaia kritika* (Moscow: Nauka, 1988).

[37]   For the implications of this act in regard to gender, see Ann Kleimola, "A Woman's Gift: The Patronage of Commemoration in the Russian North," *Forschungen zur osteuropäischen Geschichte*, 58 (2001), 151–61.

In a way, the choice of the space for the burial is more than a communication of participation: it is also a challenge and an act of defiance, as the family chose for their mausoleum the very monastery that housed the family in times of disgrace and exile. The space of disgrace thus was changed into a space of honor in the afterlife and memory for the place the family members, even when disgraced, rightfully claimed in the state.

Subsequently, the burial of elite members in churches increased. As it is impossible to explore all Russian churches and look for family graves, finding family burials is somewhat haphazard. However, as a result of the nineteenth-century interest in family history, genealogy, and the history of medieval Rus', some general conclusions can be drawn. The best example of this is the work of Grand Duke Nikolai Mikhailovich, who initiated the search for deceased members of the gentry. Though there had been very few written genealogical lists, he initiated the exploration of cemeteries of Moscow, which took place in July and August of 1904–06, and then of St Petersburg and the Russian provinces as the stone monuments offered an alternative approach to uncovering the history of Russian noble families.[38] As the exploration of the Russian provinces might have been too expensive for the project, the prince involved the Holy Synod, which decreed that the priests of the provincial churches write down the names and dates of the nobles buried in their churchyards and churches.[39] The research culiminated in the publication of eight volumes with the names of Russian princely, noble, and even merchant families, plus their dates of burial and the cemeteries and churches in which they were buried.[40]

In analyzing these volumes I came to the result that, indeed, before the sixteenth century no family burials took place in churches, except for the royal family; though chronicle accounts give evidence of the burial of church hierarchs and princes in churches. By the end of the sixteenth century, we find an increasing number of burials in churches. This goes on until the beginning of the eighteenth century. In the nineteenth century burial in churchyards was more frequent. Also, the sepulchral monuments were apparently better cared for. Until 1775, when the metropolitans looked after the upkeep of cemeteries, and especially of the sepulchral monuments,[41] cemeteries were not tended to, so that

---

[38]   Velikii kniaz' Nikolai Mikhailovich, *Moskovskii nekropol'*, vol. 1, comp. Vladimir Ivanovich Sajtov (St Petersburg: Tip. M.M. Stasiulevicha, 1907), VI.

[39]   Velikii kniaz' Nikolai Mikhailovich, *Russkii provintsial'nyi nekropol'*, vol. 1, comp. V. Sheremet'evskii (Moscow: Tipo-lit. t-va I.N. Kushnerev, 1914), Vff.

[40]   *Peterburgskii nekropol'*, vols 1–4 (St Petersburg: Tip. M.M. Stasiulevicha, 1912–14); *Moskovskii nekropol'*, vols 1–4 (St Petersburg: Tip. M.M. Stasiulevicha, 1907–08); *Russkii provintsial'nyi nekropol'*.

[41]   *Moskovskii nekropol'*, 1: IX.

existing sepulchral monuments perished and even new monuments were lost.[42] I may add that there might also have been only wooden crosses that perished from weathering, as well as the iron crosses of the nineteenth century.

In the form of burials, there are two complementary types of connection between tsar and nobles. First, the nobility started to imitate the burial *ad sanctos*, encroaching on a real space that had been reserved for rulers and high church hierarchs. More significantly, they occupied ecclesiastical spaces in the most important and popular monasteries located in and around Moscow.

Second, rulers and nobles shared similar symbolic spaces linked with certain Christian images and ideas that also convey central concepts of the Muscovite state ideology. The real as well as symbolic spaces claimed by the nobility work towards a redefinition of their position in a reconfigured state—under and alongside a tsar rather than a grand prince.

The nobility's awareness of their place in the state and their inheritance sometimes reached out into the realms of Old Testament history. The ruling dynasty had no choice but to admit this challenge for the penalty of blasphemy: a boiar who was buried in a visible location strengthened his clan's symbolical position in the state, and could not very well be ejected from his prominent tomb. With other symbolic spaces being more closed, for self-representation of the nobility architecture, and more specifically sepulchral architecture, became a landmark of the nobility's claim to political influence. In a time when power was at least outwardly concentrated in the hands of one man, this strategy served the self-assurance of the Russian nobility as a distinct social stratum that was firmly rooted in history and ideology. This means that the place of burial took on a symbolic meaning that was related to patron saints in their eschatological or transcendental significance, as well as to the symbolic meaning of the monastery, church, or saint for the prosperity of the country.

From the sixteenth century onward, Muscovite nobles were buried mainly in churches of the great monasteries around Moscow or even inside the Kremlin. Five noble families chose the Novospasskii Monastery for burials; four the Donskoi, Simonov, and Bogoiavlenskii monasteries respectively; three families chose Novodevichii Monastery (Convent); and two the Vysokopetrovskii, Spaso-Androniev, and Chudov monasteries (Table 6.1). Most of the families or clans belong to the elite families of the sixteenth and seventeenth centuries, many of them having members who directly received the highest rank of boiar, leaving out the rank of *okol'nichii* and exerting the highest influence on the tsar and government politics.[43]

---

[42]   Ibid., 1: III.

[43]   See Sergei M. Solov'ev, *Ob istorii Drevnei Rossii*, comp. A.I. Samsonov (Moscow: Prosveshchenie, 1993), 479ff.

Table 6.1   Monasteries and family burial sites in sixteenth-century Russia

Bogoiavlenskii Monastery	Golitsin, Dolgorukov, Saltykov, Sheremetev[1]
Novospasskii Monastery	Romanov (Zachar'in-Jur'evyi), Sheremetev, Kurakin, Lobanov-Rostovskii, Naryshkin[2]
Simonov Monastery	Golovin, Buturlin, Mstislavskii, Tatishchev[3]
Donskoi Monastery	Golitsin, Dolgorukov, Lopukhin, Saltykov[4]
Novodevichii Monastery	Vorotynskii, Saltykov, Sheremetev[5]
Vysokopetrovskii Monastery	Buturlin, Naryshkin[6]
Spaso-Androniev Monastery	Golovin, Lopukhin[7]
Chudov Monastery	Streshnev, Kurakin[8]

Notes:

[1] *Moskovskii nekropol'*, 1: 283ff, 386ff; 3: 67f, 342ff; *Russkii provintsial'nyi nekropol'*, 1: 764ff; *Drevniaia rossiiskaia vivliofika*, 2nd ed. (The Hague: Mouton, 1970–), XIX, 343, S. 321; P.V. Dolgorukov, ed., *Rossiiskaia rodoslovnaia kniga*, C. 1 (St. Petersburg, 1854), 93.

[2] *Moskovskii nekropol'*, 2: 126f, 177ff, 312ff; 3: 32ff, 342ff.

[3] Ibid., 1: 150 ff, 300ff; 2: 291; 3: 190ff; *Drevniaia rossiiskaia vivliofika*, XIX, 388, 399.

[4] *Moskovskii nekropol'*, 1: 283ff, 386ff; 2: 184f; 3: 67f.; *Drevniaia rossiiskaia vivliofika*, XIX, pp. 321, 343; *Dolgorukov, Rossiiskaia rodoslovnaia kniga*, 93.

[5] *Moskovskii nekropol'*, 1: 150 ff; 3: 67f, 342ff; *Drevniaia rossiiskaia vivliofika*, XIX, 303.

[6] *Moskovskii nekropol'*, 1: 150 ff; 2: 312ff; *Drevniaia rossiiskaia vivliofika*, XIX, 388.

[7] *Moskovskii nekropol'*, 1: 300ff; 2: 184f; *Drevniaia rossiiskaia vivliofika*, XIX, 399.

[8] *Moskovskii nekropol'*, 2: 126f, 3: 164f.

The monasteries chosen for family burials form a ring around Moscow and belong to the fortified monasteries that were established in the vicinity both for reasons of defence and for the burial of fallen warriors.[44] These monasteries are closely related to the ruling dynasty or the founding of the Moscow state.

Chudov Monastery, situated inside the Kremlin, was formally known as the Alexius' Archangel Michael Monastery in the Moscow Kremlin and was founded in 1358 by Metropolitan Aleksii of Moscow (see below on Aleksii and Michael). The monastery was dedicated to the miracle (*chudo*)

---

[44]   The fortifications of these monasteries is discussed in R.A. French, "The Early and Medieval Russian Town," in *Studies in Russian Historical Geography*, vol. 2, eds R.A. French and James Bater (London: Academic Press, 1983), 261. I am indebted to the editors for this reference.

of the Archangel Michael at Chonae. The cathedral[45] was finished in 1365, reconstructed in 1431, and again in 1501–03. The monastery cathedral was the baptismal church of the royal children.

Bogoiavlenskii Monastery was dedicated to the Epiphany (*bogoiavlenie*) of Christ and situated near the Kremlin. Its legendary founder was Daniil, the first prince of Moscow around 1296. It is also believed that the subsequent Metropolitan Aleksii was one of the monks of this monastery. The monastery was under the patronage of the grand princes and later tsars of Moscow.

Novospaskii Monastery in the southeast of Moscow is believed to be the first monastery to be founded in the early fourteenth century. In the seventeenth century Tsar Mikhail Fedorovich built the sepulchre of the Romanov family on the site, and his father, Patriarch Filaret, had his palace there.

Simonov Monastery was established in 1370 on land that had formerly belonged to Simeon Khovrin, a boiar of Greek origin and the founder of the boiar family Golovin. The monastery memorializes the site of the famous Battle of Kulikovo, which Muscovite legends presented as the beginning of the end of Mongol rule, when Grand Prince Dmitrii Donskoi battled Khan Mamai. The bodies of the fallen Russian warriors were buried in the monastery, which was especially founded for this use.

Novodevichii Convent (literally New Maidens' Monastery) was founded in 1524 by Grand Prince Vasilii III in commemoration of the conquest of Smolensk in 1514.[46] Ivan the Terrible granted the convent a number of villages for the commemoration of his late daughters, who were baptized and buried in the monastery.[47] The monastery was both a traditional convent and a prison for many ladies of the royal family in the seventeenth century, such as Irina Godunova (wife of Tsar Fëdor I), Sofia Alekseevna (sister of Peter the Great and former regent on his behalf), and Evdokiia Lopukhina (first wife of Peter the Great).[48]

Vysokopetrovskii Monastery, the High Monastery of St Peter, is believed to have been founded in the 1320s by Metropolitan Peter of Moscow, who

[45]   The Russian word *sobor* is commonly translated as cathedral, though this does not implicate that Russian cathedrals had the same function as a bishop's seat as in the West.

[46]   See E.V. Iurkin, comp., *Novodevichii monastyr'. Al'bom-putevoditel'* (Moscow: Sov. Rossiia, 1970), 7–9; Igor' Bychkov, "Novodevichii monastyr' i predstaviteli carskikh semei v nim," in *Novodevichii monastyr' v russkoi kul'ture. Materialy nauchnoi konferentsii 1995 g.* (Moscow: GIM, 1998), 49–68, here 49. On the building of the cathedral, see V.V. Kavel'makher, "Kogda mog byt' postroen sobor Smolenskoi Odigitrii Novodevich'ego monastyria?" in *Novodevichii monastyr' v russkoi kul'ture*, 154–79.

[47]   See L.I. Shlionskaia, "Tsarskie grobnitsy v Novodevich'em monastyre," in *Novodevichii monastyr' v russkoi kul'ture*, 93–113.

[48]   See M.M. Shvedova, "Tsaritsy-inoki Novodevich'ego monastyria," in *Novodevichii monastyr' v russkoi kul'ture*, 73–93.

Table 6.2   Families buried in the monasteries' main cathedrals

Simonov Monastery	Buturlin, Golovin, Mstislavskii, Tatishchev[1]
Novodevichii Monastery	Vorotynskii, Saltykov, Sheremetev[2]
Donskoi Monastery	Golitsin, Dolgorukov[3]
Novospasskii Monastery	Kurakin,[4] Romanov[5]
Spaso-Andronievskii Monastery	Lopukhin[6]
Bogoiavlenskii Monastery	Saltykov[7]

Notes:

[1] *Moskovskii nekropol'*, 1: 150 ff, 300ff; 2: 291; 3: 190ff; *Drevniaia rossiiskaia vivliofika*, 388, 399.

[2] *Moskovskii nekropol'*, 1: 150 ff; 3: 67f, 342ff; *Drevniaia rossiiskaia vivliofika*, 303.

[3] *Moskovskii nekropol'*, 1: 283 ff, 386ff; *Drevniaia rossiiskaia vivliofika*, 321, 343; *Dolgorukov, Rossiiskaia rodoslovnaia kniga*, 93.

[4] *Moskovskii nekropol'*, 2: 126f.

[5] K.K. Morozov, *Pamiatnik arkhitektury – Novospasskii monastyr' v Moskve* (Moscow: Sov. khudozhnik, 1982), 24.

[6] *Moskovskii nekropol'*, 2: 184f.

[7] *Moskovskii nekropol'*, 3: 67f. Some Saltykov's have been buriedin Kostroma, but also in the Bogoiavlenskii monastery. *Russkii provintsial'nyi nekropol'*, 1: 764ff.

transferred the metropolitan see from Kiev to Moscow in 1325 and thus took place in the process of the movement of the capital of Rus' from Kiev to the Russian lands around Moscow.

St Andronik, or Spaso-Androniev, Monastery is consecrated to the Holy Image of the Saviour Not Made by Hands and contains the oldest extant cathedral of Moscow. It was founded in 1357 by Metropolitan Aleksii in order to thank God for his survival in a storm.

In comparison to the other monasteries, the Donskoi Monastery is relatively young, founded in 1591 in commemoration of Moscow's deliverance from the threat of Khan Kazy-Girei's invasion from the Crimea. It was built on the spot where Tsar Boris Godunov's wartime fortress had been located, and the icon of Our Lady of the Don to which it is dedicated is legendarily connected with Dmitrii Donskoi and the Battle of Kulikovo. Donskoi monastery was the last of the great fortified monasteries founded around Moscow.[49]

---

[49]   Iu. I. Arenkova and G.I. Mekhova, *Donskoi monastyr'* (Moscow: Iskusstvo, 1970), 4ff.

Noble families occupy some of the royal spaces of early modern Muscovy, namely the monasteries connected with significant historical events and persons. Occupation of these spaces underscores the participation in the events and points out the importance of the noble families for the state and its stability and security. To increase visibility, families frequently chose the main cathedral of the monastery as their burial place (Table 6.2).[50]

By comparing the two tables one sees that even in the choice of the burial place there were distinctions not according to single family members but to whole families. As we can see, of the families buried in Chudov Monastery (Table 6.1) nobody was buried in a church, but all family members buried in Simonov Monastery and in Novodevichii Convent were buried in the main cathedral. In Donskoi Monastery the members of the Lopukhin and Saltykov families were not buried in the main cathedrals; in Novospaskii Monastery the Sheremetevs, Lobanov-Rostovskiis and Naryshkins; in Spaso-Andronievskii Monastery the Golovins; in Bogoiavlenskii Monastery the Golitsyns, Dolgorukovs, and Sheremetevs were not buried in the main cathedral.

As there is a clear majority of families who were buried in the main cathedrals, we may suggest that it was quite popular for noble families to obtain places for family burials in the main cathedrals of monasteries. As for the choice of burial place, our data suggests that families tended to bury their members together—this is also new in a society that buried their dead within three days of the death, wherever that occurred.

The main cathedral of Novospasskii Monastery, dedicated to the Transfiguration, was founded in 1491 by Grand Prince Ivan III Vasil'evich and rebuilt in 1645 after the Polish invasion, by Tsar Mikhail Fedorovich. Mikhail took care that the newly built cathedral in its lower part had vast spaces for burials.[51] A description of 1687 shows that until then most members of the Romanov clan—formerly the Zakharin-Iur'ev from whom descended Tsaritsa Anastasiia, wife of Ivan the Terrible—were buried either in the necropolis under the main apsis or under the main nave of the cathedral. Apart from the 114 Romanov burials there are various other members of elite clans buried in the cathedral—such as members of the princes and boiars Obolenski, Sitskii, Trubetskoi, Jaroslavskii, Naryshkin, Gagarin, Dashkov, Masal'skii, Kurakin, Drutskii, Kol'tsov, Eropkin, Buturlin, and Novosel'tsev—though apparently

---

[50]   Sometimes the sources give just the name of the monastery without a certain location, which means that we might suggest that the family burials were also in the main cathedrals without having real proof. We know for certain that some families buried their members in the main cathedrals (*sobornye tserkvie, sobory*).

[51]   Morozov, *Pamiatnik*, 17f.

they were not buried in a family necropolis like the Romanovs.[52] The murals in the main nave, painted in 1689, surround the burials with an imperial as well as modern environment. First, in the right nave near the tsar's place there is a picture of the Tsars Mikhail Fedorovich and his son Aleksei Mikhailovich holding a model of the cathedral, thus depicting their founding. In the vestibule there is a depiction of the spreading of Christianity in Rus', together with the apostle Andrew, who allegedly brought Christianity to Rus'. The torispherical vault of the cathedral sees the family tree of the Russian tsars, beginning with Princess Ol'ga and her grandson Vladimir the Baptist of Rus' and ending with Ivan IV and his sons Tsar Fëdor and Tsarevich Dmitrii.[53] The burial place of the Romanov family in the main cathedral of Novospasskii Monastery thus resembles a justification of their descendants to the throne of Russia, surrounding them with saintly tsars of ancient and recent times. We found the same saints of old, Vladimir and Boris and Gleb, in the instance of the Vorotynskii Mausoleum in Kirillov-Belozerskii Monastery.

A clear connection can be made between the Golitsyn family and the main cathedral of Donskoi Monastery. Built in 1686, the cathedral resembles the Golitsyn palace built in 1687–89, with its lower rows shaped as wedding crowns and its columns. Indeed, the Golitsyn family donated a great amount of money for the building of the cathedral, so that scholars assume that the buildings shared their architect.[54] Still, the monastery became the preferred burial place of the family only after Vasilii Vasil'evich became the favorite (and assumed lover) of Tsarevna Sofiia, sister of Tsar Fëdor Alekseevich and regent for her minor brothers, Ivan and Peter.[55]

The Church of the Archangel Michael in Chudov Monastery was built in 1501 by Grand Prince Ivan III Vasil'evich with two ground floors, of which the one below contains the actual burials while the one above seemed to have been built for the family sepulchre.[56] The northern walls see the sepulchral monuments of the Princes Trubetskoi, Kurakin, Khovanskii, Shcherbatov, and Obolenskii, and the boyars Streshnev, Morozov, Sobakin, and Buturlin—all buried there since the sixteenth century.[57]

---

[52] Ibid., 24ff.

[53] Ibid., 21f.

[54] Arenkova and Mekhova, *Donskoi monastyr'*, 22ff.

[55] On Sofiia and her regency, see Aleksandr Sergeevich Lavrov, *Regentstvo tsarevny Sof'i Alekseevny. Sluzhiloe obshchestvo i bor'ba za vlast' v verkhakh Russkogo gosudarstva v 1682–1689 gg.* (Moscow: Arkheograficheskoi tsentr', 1999).

[56] *Moskovskii kafedral'nyi Chudov Monastyr'* (Moscow: Sviato-troitskaia Sergieva Lavra, 1896), 21.

[57] Ibid., 46.

Family burials in churches dedicated to the Archangel Michael are highly significant for Muscovite Russia, not only given the fact that the royal family had their necropolis in the cathedral dedicated to the Archangel Michael in the Moscow Kremlin. Three of the churches that contain family burials are dedicated to the Archangel Michael, just like the ruling dynasty's burial place in the Kremlin: the Golitsyns in Donskoi Monastery, the Golovins in Spaso-Aondroniev Monastery, and the Kurakins in Chudov Monastery. As the Muscovites considered themselves the image of the chosen people, the Archangel Michael connected them with the Jewish-Christian salvation studies (*Heilsgeschichte*) from the beginning. Already Jewish Septuagint theology knew Michael as guardian angel of the chosen people. The Jewish theology of the Second Temple, the tradition of an angelic heavenly priest, served as background for the Christian High Priest Christology of the Epistle to the Hebrews (1:14). In St John's Apocalypse, Michael is mentioned by name in 12:7; but references to the archangel are quite frequent in chapters 12 and 19–20, where John identifies the one who rides the white horse and leads the armies of Heaven (19:11ff.) with the child of the Heavenly Woman (12:5) and with allusion to Ps. 2:9 (LXX).[58]

St John (Rev. 12:10–12) interprets Michael's victory as dependent upon Christ's victory on the cross. He works with the paradox of conquering through death and suggests that Michael's traditional role of *arkhistrategos* makes him the logical choice for the angelic leader of the Heavenly Host.[59] The New Testament theology of the Archangel Michael led to several transformations of his image in Christianity.[60]

---

[58]   Darrell D. Hannah, *Michael and Christ: Michael Traditions and Angel Christology in Early Christianity* (Tübingen: Mohr Siebeck, 1999), 124ff.

[59]   Ibid., 128f.

[60]   I would like to complete the former with a quotation from ibid., 136f.: "In summary, the picture which the NT documents afford us of the archangel Michael stands in broad continuity with that found elsewhere in the Second Temple period. He leads the heavenly armies (Rev. 12.7), and defends the righteous against the accusations of Satan (Jude 9; cf. Rev. 12.10). His office as psychopomp may stand in the background of Jude 9, and 2 Thess. 2.6–7 may attribute an eschatological role to him. Significantly, in all these texts he is clearly subordinated to Christ. His victory over the dragon in Revelation is limited and dependent upon the victory Christ achieved on the Cross. In Jude 9 he does not condemn the Devil, but defers to the Lord's judgement. Finally, assuming that my proposal indentifying him with 'the Restrainer' of 2 Thess. 2.6–7 is sound, he himself does not destroy the eschatological anti-God figure; that also belongs to Christ. Michael merely restrains him so that his appearance is in accordance with the divine plan."

In Hebrew the names of the archangels are theophoric, the ending "-el" meaning God: Michael means "who is like God."[61] Out of the seven archangels only Michael and Gabriel are depicted frequently in East and West; Michael therefore undergoing transformations as archistrategos, warrior, court official, priest, and rider. According to the Athos icon painter's manual there exist 13 depictions of Michael's miracles, the most popular of which is the miracle of Chonae in which the archangel saves one of his sanctuaries from a flood initiated by the Devil.[62]

In the Byzantine Empire, the chronicler John Malalas (491–565) connected the emperors, and especially Emperor Constantine, with the archangel. From the sixth century, Michael became the patron saint of the governing Byzantine upper strata.[63] In the eleventh century the Byzantine emperor was corroborated by Archangel Michael, and according to the twelfth-century Russian traveller Antonii of Novgorod, the Byzantine war relics, the cross of Constantine and Joshua's trumpet, were kept in the new church dedicated to the archangel in Constantinople. One can also deduce that the Byzantine emperors founded an overwhelming number of churches dedicated to Michael: 45.8 percent of all Constantinopolitan churches founded by the emperors were Archangel Michael churches.[64]

From Constantinople the connection of the Archangel Michael to the government and the ruler were transported along with Christianity into Kievan and, in consequence, Muscovite Russia, as we may conclude from the choice of the burial churches for rulers and nobles as well as from icons and other depictions.[65]

---

[61]   Johannes Peter Rohland, *Der Erzengel Michael. Arzt und Feldherr. Zwei Aspekte des Vor- und frühbyzantinischen Michaelskultes* (Leiden: Brill, 1977), 2.

[62]   B. Rothemund, *Handbuch der Ikonenkunst I*, 3rd edn (Munich: Slavisches Institut, 1985), 297ff.

[63]   Ibid., 118ff.

[64]   Rohland, *Der Erzengel Michael*, 127ff.

[65]   For examples, see Daniel Rowland, "Two Cultures, One Throne Room: Secular Courtiers and Orthodox Culture in the Golden Hall of the Moscow Kremlin," in *Orthodox Russia: Studies in Belief and Practice, 1492–1936*, eds Valerie A. Kivelson and Robert H. Greene (University Park: Pennsylvania State University Press, 2003), 33–57; Michael Flier, "K semioticheskomu analizu Zolotoi palaty Moskovskogo Kremlia," in *Drevnerusskoe iskusstvo. Russkoe iskusstvo pozdnego Srednevekov'ia. Shestnadtsatyi vek*, eds Andrei Batalov et al. (St Petersburg: Dmitrii Bulanin, 2003), 178–87; Michael Flier, "Till the End of Time: The Apocalypse in Russian Historical Experience before 1500," in *Orthodox Russia*, 127–58, Sergei Bogatyrev, "Eternal Apocalypse: The *Church Militant* Icon and the Dynastic Policy of Ivan the Terrible," under review with *Russian Review*.

In using the same patron saint the challenge to the tsar's family position is obvious: if Muscovite and even some Kievan grand princes are buried in a church dedicated to the Archangel Michael, noble families who bury their members in churches dedicated to the same saint elevate them symbolically to a position equal to that of the grand princes. As the position of grand prince is no longer exclusive to the ruler once he assumed the title of tsar, they are now free to occupy this symbolic position, if only in the hereafter.

Burial in churches dedicated to Archangel Michael was not limited to the early modern era. The Golitsyn family created themselves a burial place in the church of the Archangel Michael in Donskoi Monastery, founded in 1806.[66] The families Sheremetev, Lobanov-Rostovskii, and Lopukhin had burials in churches dedicated to the Mother of God of the Sign, the Lopukhins in Spaso-Androniev Monastery, and the others in Novospaskii Monastery.

The churches dedicated to the icon of the Mother of God of the Sign or the Virgin of the Sign (*znamenie*) have significance for the Russian state as well as for the Old Russian town of Novgorod. If, in the case of Archangel Michael, nobles and the ruling dynasty shared a patron saint of church and state, in this case the nobility occupied a patron saint for themselves. But, as in the case of Archangel Michael, the patronage of the Virgin of the Sign links the sixteenth- and seventeenth-century burials with the beginnings of Muscovite history in Kiev and the translation of the Christian faith from Byzantium first to Kiev and then to Muscovy.

The icon of the Virgin of the Sign is still one of the most venerated icons of Russia. It depicts the Mother of God in front view with her hands held up in the prayer posture (*orans*), with a depiction of Christ Emmanuel, usually in a small sphere, on her chest. This icon of the Mother of God is one of the first depictions of the Virgin in Christianity and can be traced back to the fourth century. The icon of the Mother of God orans became the palladium, a safeguard of the town of Constantinople, a sign depicting her special protection of the city. In Russia this type of icon appeared after Christianization in the eleventh century. From the twelfth century onward, the icon was the source of several miracles in Novgorod, which led to the name of the icon "*Znamenie*," meaning in Old Russian "apparition" or "sign." In 1160 and 1170 the icon miraculously saved Novgorod from an attack by Grand Prince Andrei Bogoliubskii; in 1566 it saved

---

[66]   A.M. Riazanov, "Usypal'nitsa kniazei Golitsynykh v tserkvi Arkhangela Mikhaila na territorii Donskogo monastyria," in *Monastyri v zhizni Rossii. Materialy nauchnoi konferentsii, posviashchennoi 600-letiiu prepodobnogo Pafnutiia Borovskogo i 550-letiiu osnovaniia im Rozhdestva Pafnut'ev-Bogorvskogo monastyria*, comp. V. I. Osipov (Kaluga-Borovsk: Borovskii muzei, 1997), 115–20.

the town from fire; and in 1611 from an attack by the Swedes.[67] This shows that the importance of the icon was not restricted to Novgorod, but that from the incorporation of Novgorod into the Muscovite state at the end of the fifteenth century onward the icon served as a miraculous palladium for the whole state—the Swedes in the seventeenth century being not only aggressors in the Russian north but also threatening to seize Moscow and invest their own candidate for the vacant throne of the tsar.[68] Besides personal piety, a family burial in a church dedicated to the Virgin of the Sign also showed the responsibility that a noble felt for the country's safeguarding. It is also a creation of a patronage of the same value and a similar background in ancient history as the patronage of the ruling family, the Archangel Michael.

Among the churches dedicated to various saints and containing noble family burials there are many dedicated to Russian national saints. St George the Dragonslayer is, of course, the patron saint of Russia. The holy Metropolitan Aleksei was the first metropolitan of Moscow after Metropolitan Peter transferred the see to Moscow in 1325. The Kazan' Church in Bogoiavlenskii Monastery is certainly dedicated to the miracle-working icon of the Mother of God of Kazan' that was found in 1579 by a girl after a fire in Kazan'. In the seventeenth century two copies of the icons were made which subsequently worked miracles as well, one against the Poles and one against Napoleon. In the same way the icon of the Mother of God of Bogoliubovo, better known as the Vladimirskaia Mother of God, was a palladium of the Moscow state and used in wars against the Mongols.[69]

The tendency of burying families together in churches began around the end of the sixteenth century and after the coronation of Ivan IV as tsar in Moscow. With the advent of the seventeenth century many of the leading noble families began to create family burials in various monastery churches. This led to a change in architecture, for in the seventeenth century—as we could see in the case of the cathedral of Novospasskii Monastery, built as a family burial place for the Romanov family—churches were already built with spacious basements for burials. The tendency to create family burial places decreased somewhat during

---

[67] For miracle-working icons in Russia, see Aleksei M. Lidov, ed., *Chudotvornaia ikona v Vizantii i Drevnei Rusi* (Moscow: Martis, 1996).

[68] For the Time of Troubles, see Ruslan G. Skrynnikov, *The Time of Troubles: Russia in Crisis, 1604–1618* (Gulf Breeze, FL: Academic International Press, 1988); Chester S.L. Dunning, *Russia's First Civil War: The Time of Troubles and the Founding of the Romanov Dynasty* (University Park: Pennsylvania State University Press, 2001).

[69] On the icons of the Mother of God, and especially the Vladimirskaia icon, see Andreas Ebbinghaus, *Die altrussischen Marienikonen-Legenden* (Berlin: Otto Harrasowitz, 1990).

Table 6.3   Family burials in churches dedicated to various saints

Buturlin[1]	Vysokopetrovskii Monastery, chapel
Naryshkin[2]	Vysokopetrovskii Monastery, Church of the Mother of God of Bogoliubovo
Golitsyn[3]	Bogoiavlenskii Monastery, Church of the Metropolitan Aleksei, Donskoi Monastery, Church of the Mother of God, Church of the Purification
Dolgorukov[4]	Bogoiavlenskii Monastery, St George's Church, porch near the Church of the Mother of God of Kazan', Hospital Church

Notes:

[1] *Moskovskii nekropol'*, 1: 150ff.; *Drevniaia rossiiskaia vivliofika*, 388.

[2] *Moskovskii nekropol'*, 2: 312ff.

[3] *Moskovskii nekropol'*, 1: 283ff.; *Drevniaia rossiiskaia vivliofika*, 321.

[4] *Moskovskii nekropol'*, 1: 386ff.; *Drevniaia rossiiskaia vivliofika*, 343; Dolgorukov, *Rossiiskaia rodoslovnaia kniga*, 93.

the eighteenth century, which may be due to the change in government and the newly created ranks of nobles, a new concept of the service elite, or simply due to the fact that the capital had relocated to St Petersburg. But this will have to be researched in due course.

We also find the tendency to bury members of the family in graveyards in the monasteries and near the churches containing the family necropoles. All the chosen monasteries and churches were connected to the royal family and the state palladia. So we may conclude that, like in Western Europe, in Russia too a usurpation of the imperial patron saints through members of the nobility took place.[70] This usurpation did not take place in an atmosphere of competition but in an atmosphere of congruence. Nobles in Muscovy expressed their self-awareness of their participation in the wealth of the state through the use of the state palladia. However, they had little space to show this awareness. One of their spaces was certainly their burial place, which explains the choice of family necropoles as places for the symbolic expression of their place in the state hierarchy. The increase in such necropoles corresponds with the consolidation of tsarism, beginning with Ivan IV's coronation as tsar in 1547, and continues after the election of Mikhail Fedorovich Romanov in 1613.[71]

---

[70]   On this usurpation in accordance with the Archangel Michael, see Rohland, *Der Erzengel Michael*, 125f.

[71]   We can, of course, interpret this phenomenon in accordance with the pious tendencies of fifteenth- to seventeenth-century Russia that led to a vast practice of donations "for the soul" in Muscovy, as described by Ludwig Steindorff and others in studies on memorial practice. But this tendency towards pious works for the soul and fear of apocalypse does

The cooperative system of governing that existed in Muscovy despite the image of the autocratic tsar displayed in foreign policy and church writings brought with it a lack of space for the development and display of noble positions. Within the ruling system nobles were already displayed as co-rulers or at least as counselors, as Daniel Rowland argued in his analysis of the murals of the Golden Hall of the tsar's palace in Moscow.[72] But as both parties, rulers and nobles, were intermingled in the execution of power as well as in the process of decision-making that always had to result in consensus, it was difficult for nobles to find spaces for themselves and the expression of their view of their participation in the state affairs. The distinction between ruler and counselors of old that had become more acute in 1547 and the coronation of Ivan IV Vasil'evich as tsar certainly influenced the decision of nobles to express their part in the government. Thereby the logical consequence is a close imitation of the legitimizing strategies of the ruling dynasty in a space that the ruler could not contest without appearing blasphemous: the family burial place that formerly had been reserved for the grand prince alone and that had been vastly used for the display of state ideology and the legitimation of the dynasty's rule. In imitating the legitimating strategies of the tsar by creating family burial places in monasteries and churches that—either directly through history or indirectly through the dedication to national saints—were associated with the sacred origin of the Muscovite government and the Muscovite land and in furnishing these burial places with the same symbols, the Russian nobles directly challenged the tsar's assumption of autocratic power. By the means of occupying a sacred space for their display of participation in the rule they secured an incontestable space for themselves,[73] for the tsar could not forbid the burial of people in churches without appearing blasphemous. I think here we can see one step of the Russian nobility to emancipate itself from the royal court and to form a distinguished social stratum for itself.

---

not explain the exclusive use of state palladia and Russian state patron saints. On memorial practice, see Ludwig Steindorff, "Mehr als eine Frage der Ehre. Zum Stifterverhalten Zar Ivans des Schrecklichen," *Jahrbücher für Geschichte Osteuropas*, 51 (2003), 342–65; Ludwig Steindorff, *Memoria in Altrußland. Untersuchungen zu den Formen christliche Totensorge* (Stuttgart: F. Steiner Verlag, 1994); Martin, "Gifts for the Dead."

[72] See Rowland, "Two Cultures, One Throne Room"; Michael S. Flier, "The Iconology of Royal Ritual in Sixteenth-Century Muscovy," in *Byzantine Studies: Essays on the Slavic World and the Eleventh Century*, eds Spyros Vryonis and Henrik Birnbaum (New Rochelle, NY: Aristide D. Caratzas, 1992), 53–76.

[73] Here the Muscovite strategy differs somewhat from the strategy of the Medici as referred to in Katherine Turner's chapter in this volume. The Medici used the sacred space to display their conformity with church reform. Muscovite nobles use the sacred space to explain their distinction from the ruling dynasty.

Like in the West, after the coronation of the first tsar Russian nobles began to occupy the state palladia formerly used by the ruling family, as the Archangel Michael and the family links to the Kievan SS Boris and Gleb. If the creation of the first family mausoleum in Kirillo-Belozerskii Monastery may be considered a gesture of defiance and challenge of the tsar's rule, the creation of family necropoles increasingly became a medium of showing self-awareness and communicating the place of the family within the ruling system and their share in the assumed autocratic power of the tsar. We may also assume that the formation of the Russian nobility as a social stratum in coexistence with the ruling family became more common after the consolidation of the tsardom following the Time of Troubles. If nobles could challenge Ivan IV trying to establish more autocratic power for the tsar only in their afterlife, the existence of family necropoles and the custom of creating them in places significant to Muscovite history reflected the newly found balance. So, from symbolically challenging autocratic power in occupying the same palladia in the sixteenth century, in the seventeenth century occupation of the same palladia became a balanced share of the power and ideology symbolically shared in the state palladia.

Chapter 7

Il monastero nuovo: Cloistered Women of the Medici Court

Katherine L. Turner

Early modern Florence was a confluence of multifarious socio-political ideals and realities complicated by an intense wave of religious reform. The female monastic institution called "*il monastero nuovo*" or "La Concezione" demonstrated these contemporary concerns through its creation and inhabitation. Familial heads, governmental agencies and ecclesiastical authorities variously appropriated the physical and ideological space entangling the cloister and its inhabitants in conflicting political agendas and contested religious interests. This chapter will consider these variances by exploring the intentions of the Medici family in founding the convent, the strategies of noble families who requested admittance for their daughters, and the realities of life for the enclosed women—many of whom entered as teenagers and never left.[1]

The concept and financial backing for the convent was part of the 1562 last testament of Eleonora di Toledo de'Medici, consort of the first Grand Duke of Tuscany, Cosimo I, who began the process of designing and building the convent and church. Historian Giuseppe Richa, in his systematic examination of all of the religious institutions of Florence, recounts how Cosimo and Eleonora established the convent as a sanctuary for the elite women of the city:

> The piety and gratitude that moved the Grand Duke Cosimo I to found in 1561 the Illustrious *Ordine de'Cavalieri di Santo Stefano Papa, e Martire*, equally moved Duchess Eleonora di Toledo, wife of Cosimo, to found under the same Rule a Monastery of *Gentildonne* for those of the finest quality, who before entering were expected to demonstrate Nobility in the same manner as the Cavalieri of the said Order.[2]

---

[1] The terms "monastery" and "convent" are used interchangeably in this chapter as there was no gendered distinction in the early modern era.

[2] Giuseppe Richa, *Notizie istoriche delle chiese fiorentine, divise ne' suoi quartieri* (Florence: Viviani, 1754–62; reprinted Rome: Multigrafica Editrice, 1972), 110–20. Tomo quarto, Quartiere di Santa Maria Novella. Lezione VIII, "Del Monastero Nuovo Detto della

As this history relates, the Cavalieri di Santo Stefano and the convent were closely associated through social ties and through their adherence to the Rule of Saint Benedict. The Order was a military and religious knighthood (now largely remembered only for its naval endeavors) that was the foundation of the court's aristocratic class.[3] Acceptance into the Order or La Concezione required noble quarters and the acquiescence of the grand duke (a *cavaliere* in the family was a prerequisite to entering the convent). The role of the Medici ruler was paramount—he created the opportunity, controlled access, and managed the outcomes of each of these two institutions.[4]

In 1592, with construction completed on the convent, five women processed across town to become its founding members in a display of civic pageantry. The "new" convent quickly became known as the most elite in Florence; it would continue to play an important role in the civic life of the city until its suppression at the beginning of the nineteenth century.[5] Both the foundation of the Order and the convent fall (not coincidently) during the meeting of the Council of Trent (1545–63).[6] The last session included discussion and reforms addressing religious institutions, the ramifications of which would become central to the convent's structure.[7]

Concezione," 110. "La pietà, e la gratitudine, che mossero il Granduca Cosimo I ad istituire nel 1561. L'Illustre Ordine de' Cavalieri di Santo Stefano Papa, e Martire, animarono parimente D[uchessa] Leonora di Toledo moglie di Cosimo a fondare sotto la stessa Regola un Monastero di Gentildonne, le quali prima di entrare fossero tenute di fare le provanze di Nobiltà nella maniera, che lo fanno i Cavalieri di detto Ordine."

[3]   Marco Gemignani, "The Navies of the Medici: The Florentine Navy and the Navy of the Sacred Military Order of Saint Stephen, 1547–1648," in *War at Sea in the Middle Ages and the Renaissance*, eds John B. Hattendorf and Richard W. Unger (Woodbridge: Boydell Press, 2003), 169–85.

[4]   Garfagnini Gian Carlo, ed., *Firenze e la Toscana dei Medici nell'Europa del '500.*, 3 vols, Biblioteca di storia Toscana moderna e contemporanea 26 (Florence: Olschki, 1983).

[5]   Eleonora Baldasseroni, *Le cavaliere dell'Ordine di Santo Stefano: le monache della Santissima Concezione di Firenze* (Pisa: Pisa University Press, 2008).

[6]   The Council met in three sessions, 1545–47, 1551–52, and 1562–63; subcommittees met to discuss assigned issues and prepare legislation for full-council votes. The majority of issues concerned the dogmatic and pragmatic concerns of doctrine and ritual. The standard twentieth-century history has been Hubert Jedin, *A History of the Council of Trent*, trans. Ernest Graf (London and New York: Thomas Nelson and Sons, 1957–61); for a more contemporary reading of the Council of Trent, see John O'Malley, *Trent and All That: Renaming Catholicism in the Early Modern Era* (Cambridge, MA: Harvard University Press, 2000).

[7]   Two primary documents are most useful in discussing the rules for La Concezione. The Constitution guided the women as to the day-to-day operations of the convent and the Charter instructed the Order as to their religious, social, and fiscal responsibilities.

Immediately imbedded in the public sphere of Florence, due in part to its highly visible location within the city walls and its coveted position through the court, the new religious house maintained a parallel private sphere with power hierarchies and equal displays of religious observance and aristocratic opulence to which few were ever admitted.[8] To the ruling Medici grand dukes, La Concezione came to represent the embodiment of wealth, power and Christian ethics. To the average Florentine, it was a visible reminder of the social hierarchy in the new duchy. To noble families it was both a practical solution and a reward—a mark of status and achievement. Lastly, to the women who lived there, this convent was distinct and separate from the secular world but with similar challenges and delights.[9]

Convent Culture

Early modern convents existed across Catholic Europe in many sizes, shapes, and missions. Before the reforms of the Council of Trent, many convents were "open," that is, unrestricted by enclosure; however, the church fathers there decreed mandatory *clausura*, a measure considered necessary to safeguard groups of women, though its enforcement was anything but even.[10] Convents often had a mixture of social classes with corresponding levels of nuns. Servant nuns

---

The "Constitution": Biblioteca Nazionale Centrale Firenze, Mazzatinti Inventari II II 152 (hereafter, BNCF Mazz. Inv. II II 152), "Constituzioni e Ordini del ven[erabile]. Monastero della Concettione della S[anta] Vergine Maria, chiamato il Monastero Nuovo, in via della Scala di Firenze: con approvazione del 3 ottobre 1655 e con modificazioni del 1750." The "Charter": Archivio di Stato, Pisa (hereafter ASPi 2878), "Il Cerimoniere Pratico ovvero un esatto Trattato delle funzioni Pontificali dafarsi dal Prelato dell Ordine Militare di Santo Stefano Papa e Martire: nella Chiesa delle Monache della Santo Stefano Concezione di Firenze. Tomo Secondo."

    [8]   Although not physically attached to the Signoria, Pitti Palace, or other usual spaces of the court, the convent's location next to the prominent Dominican monastery of Santa Maria Novella made it visible to Florentines and guests alike.

    [9]   Katherine L. Turner, "The Musical Culture of *La Concezione*: Devotion, Politics and Elitism in Post-Tridentine Florence" (PhD diss.: The University of Texas, Austin, 2008).

    [10]   For the historic attempts at enclosure and the problems of enforcement, see Katherine Gill, "*Scandala*: Controversies Concerning Clausura and Women's Religious Communities in Late Medieval Italy," in *Christendom and Its Discontents*, eds Scott Waugh and Peter Diehl (Cambridge: Cambridge University Press, 1996); Francesca Medioli, "An Unequal Law: The Enforcement of *Clausura* Before and After Trent," in *Women in Renaissance and Early Modern Europe*, ed. Christine Meek (Dublin: Four Courts Press, 2000), 136–52; Patricia Ranft, *Women and the Religious Life in Premodern Europe* (New York: St Martin's Press, 1996).

took only simple vows, whereas professed or choir nuns took initial and then final vows; children and widows could also make up part of the community, sometimes only on a temporary basis. The size of a community often depended on space and need; it has been estimated that as many as 60 to 70 percent of a town's upper class females lived in convents in the late medieval and early modern periods as rising marriage dowries increasingly strained family finances.[11]

Each convent had a Rule that dictated their religious and social environments. Most convents were associated with a corresponding male house of like Rule that catered to their religious obligations and spiritual needs, as well as practical matters like legal representation and finances. In the seventeenth century, responsibility for oversight shifted away from male religious towards secular authorities; this was largely a matter of defining control of sacred space and women's involvement with that space. Most convents had a private chapel for the community's devotional practices and observation of Mass separate from the public chapel.

The religious obligations of any professed woman included a public commitment to the three solemn vows of poverty, chastity, and obedience, recitation of the Daily Offices, regular Mass, and confession.[12] Other prayers and remembrances were determined by local commission as needed or by the dedication of the community to particular ideals or saints. Only professed nuns could participate in the internal affairs of the convent; like the world beyond the wall, the community had an organizational system with a leader and elected or appointed offices with detailed responsibilities.

Servant nuns did not participate in the running of the convent, nor did they pay much in terms of dowry or upkeep fees, while professing sisters paid a *doti spirituali* similar in function to the marriage dowry. Price varied per institution and increased significantly between the fourteenth and eighteenth centuries, creating a greater variety of institutional options; however, a convent dowry was generally appreciably less than the marriage dowry, encouraging families to send

---

[11]   Gene A. Brucker, "Monasteries, Friaries, and Nunneries in Quattrocento Florence," in *Christianity and the Renaissance: Image and Religious Imaginations in the Quattrocento*, eds Timothy Verdon and John Henderson (Syracuse, NY: Syracuse University Press, 1990), 41–62; Richard C. Trexler, "Celibacy in the Renaissance: The Nuns of Florence," in *The Women of Renaissance Florence* (Binghamton, NY: MRTS, 1994), 6–30; Trevor Dean and Kate Lowe, *Marriage in Italy, 1300–1600* (Cambridge, MA: Harvard University Press, 1998); Stanley Chojnacki, "Daughters and Oligarchs: Gender and the Early Renaissance State," in *Gender and Society in Renaissance Italy*, eds Judith C. Brown and Robert C. Davis (London: Longman, 1998), 63–86.

[12]   An excellent introduction to women religious as one of many roles enacted by early modern women can be found in Olwen Hufton, *The Prospect before Her: A History of Women in Western Europe, 1500–1800* (New York: Alfred A. Knopf), esp. 370–79.

multiple daughters to the nunnery.[13] The membership lists for convents often looked like a family tree. Parents would send their daughter to the convent where her aunts and cousins resided. In effect, house politics, including officer elections, often ran along familial lines with power determined by sheer numbers.

While Eleonora and Cosimo's new monastery had some commonalities with other monasteries and convents, it was an exceptional institution. It promoted itself as a strictly enclosed convent conforming to the most austere reforms of the age. This meant that entrance by outsiders was severely limited—the women did not leave and were rarely seen. This extended to the chapel, where iron grates and curtains prohibited anyone from viewing them, although a small window enabled them to participate in the Eucharist and bidirectional sound could penetrate the coverings. The number of inhabitants was relatively small and convent admittance was so exclusive that the dowry was a formality—hence there was no mixture of classes and only a few dominant families. The grand duke's order of knights had oversight rather than local monastic authorities or the bishop; in fact, the convent had little interaction with anyone outside the Order of Santo Stefano. There was no public church associated with the institution, and even the "outside" chapel was seen only by selective admittance determined by the grand duke or prior of Santo Stefano.

The Medici, Grand Dukes of Tuscany

The Medici, as a young ruling power on an international stage filled with charismatic leaders, influential politicians, and powerful armed forces, created opportunities that presented the Florentine court as a significant military, religious, and political authority, and the family as potent but munificent leaders. Popular means of attracting positive attention included lavish festivals, artistic and musical commissions, grand gestures of state, displays of military prowess, and the foundation of important social, cultural, and religious institutions. Cosimo undertook all of these endeavors during his reign, a pattern that would continue with his descendants.

Politically, a religious establishment of devout, honorable women served as a symbol of the strength and goodness of a city and its governors. It is only logical then, that the grand duke would want to have a convent associated with his rule; if appropriately dedicated to the highest ideals of the church and filled with pious noblewomen, it would project an image of apposite fidelity both to the local populace and to the broader community of religious and secular leaders. Several

---

[13]   Dean and Lowe, *Marriage in Italy*.

convents sought and received the protection and benefice of the Medici court; however, no other institution so heavily relied on the courtiers and the ruling family, a fundamental component of the new institution's original design.

During the founding of the convent in the early 1560s, Cosimo kept abreast of the meetings of the Council of Trent through his many emissaries.[14] The reform of the regulars, including a significant section on the regulation of women religious, had long been on the docket and during the third session of the early 1560s, formal directives came to a vote. The timing of the founding of the convent and the precision of its statutes reveal Eleonora and Cosimo's intentions. First, and most importantly, the "new monastery" was to be strictly enclosed—a contentious issue among monastic communities, but a high priority of the Council. Secondly, the convent's Constitution was based on the new ideas of reform, often quoting from the official mandates of the Council.[15] Thirdly, Cosimo actively sought opportunities for himself and his courtiers to participate in the kind of apposite devotion encouraged by the church through the establishment and promotion of the Order and the convent.

Eleonora may have founded La Concezione, but there is no doubt that Cosimo was intimately involved with the initial conception and, upon the death of Eleonora, Cosimo facilitated its realization. The grand duke clearly gave considerable attention to guiding the public's perception of the convent. He wanted it to have instantaneous status and appeal—he needed not only to build and populate it but also to do so by means that would be immediately tangible to the public. Cosimo cleverly assessed that the maximum benefits of founding a convent could be reaped immediately by appropriating a notable moniker, allocating a prime location, fashioning a positive rapport with an existing establishment, and engaging the community of nobles.

Like many religious institutions, the institution's formal name was quite complex, with layers of symbolism and significance—*Il Venerabile e Nobile Monastero della Santissima Concettione della Santa Vergine Maria in via della Scala di Firenze, detto il Monastero Nuovo.*[16] The contemporary Florentine

---

[14]   The Council of Trent, *Canones et decreta Sacrosancti Oecvmenici et Generalis Concilii Tridentini svb Pavlo III, Ivlio III, Pio IIII*. Pontificibvs Max. CVM Privilegio. Mediolani Apud Antonium Antonianum. Session Tertia, 1564. The Getty Research Institute, Special Collections 93–B14438. Prefatory material includes lists of representatives and their home dioceses.

[15]   Turner, "Musical Culture," Chapter 3.

[16]   This title is in no way standard as the order of the words and the words themselves vary from source to source and even within sources. However, the essential components of *La Concezione, Via della Scala*, and *Il Monastero Nuovo* are the consistent identifying markers of this institution. The most divergent title I found is "*la Immaculata Concettione*

would have immediately understood that this was not a convent for beggars or former prostitutes and that it aligned itself with no one less than the Virgin Mary. While variants of this name are common, reference to the Conception is standard throughout the documents, perhaps reflecting the contemporary move to elevate the event of the Conception as part of a specifically Catholic Church doctrine.[17] *Via della Scala* was a well-known city street on which several important sacred and municipal buildings were located; it would have given a geographical reference as well as an association with other significant features of that neighborhood. Lastly, the title calls this the "new monastery," suggesting that this was an innovative or modern institution not contingent upon the (unreformed) practices of existing institutions; it also implies the existence of an "old monastery." One specific institution is most certainly implied—the two houses had intertwining interests, a fact the Medici would take advantage of while fashioning their convent.

When considering the all-important issue of the founding daughters, Cosimo's son Ferdinando I, as the reigning grand duke, sought women from the convent with the best reputation, one long favored by Florentine citizens and patronized by the Medici family. The rather old and most populated convent called *Le Murate* was just such an institution. Benedictine and of medieval origins, it educated and housed many elite daughters, including Catherine de'Medici; she lived there before her marriage to Henry II and continued to support the institution throughout her life.[18] In 1592, Ferdinando I requested that four of the most pious sisters of Le Murate move across town to become the founding daughters of La Concezione. There was a grand procession of nobility and dignitaries whereby the positive reputation of Le Murate was conveyed upon La Concezione as the latter received its first inhabitants. Among the founding daughters was Laura Aldobrandini, the niece of the newly elected Pope Clement VIII; he had been a prominent Florentine lawyer—an astute and politically motivated decision on the part of the Medici.[19] In the years following

---

della S[antissim]a Genitrice di Dio M[ari]a sempre Vergine." BNCF Mazz. Inv. II II 152 Parte Prima, Delle cose spettanti a tutte le Monache del Monastero in Comune, Capitolo Primo: Delli Obblighi, Efeuzioni, e Priuilegi del Mona.o secondo al sua Fondazione, 5.

[17] See Katherine Crawford, *European Sexualities, 1400–1800* (Cambridge: Cambridge University Press, 2007), esp. Chapters 2 and 3; and Helen Hills, "Iconography and Ideology: Aristocracy, Immaculacy and Virginity in Seventeenth-Century Palermo," *Oxford Art Journal*, 17:2 (1994), 16–31.

[18] Kate J.P. Lowe, *Nuns' Chronicles and Convent Culture in Renaissance and Counter-Reformation Italy* (New York: Cambridge University Press, 2003).

[19] Pompeo Litta, Luigi Passerini, Federico Odorici, Federico Stefani, Francesco di mauro Polvica, and Constantino Coda, *Famiglie celebri italiane* (Milan: P.E. Giusti, 1819), tav. V, D.66, f. 444.

the opening, the population of La Concezione would grow both in terms of the size of the community and the number of important families involved.

Although the institution was a late addition to the city center of Florence, it was not built atop another structure; rather it was constructed around the previously sanctified and historically significant *Sale del Papa* of the prominent Dominican monastery of Santa Maria Novella. The original rooms were the quarters of visiting popes: in the early fifteenth century, the city voted for 1,500 florins to build a new lodging to demonstrate Florentine hospitality. Giuliano Pesello was the painter, Lorenzo di Bartoluccio Ghiberti was the designer, and Donatello the sculptor, among other prominent artists. The Sale del Papa were the upper story on the west side of the Great Cloister, Via della Scala was to the south and provided a separate entrance to the rooms. Notable visitors included Pope Martin V in 1419–20, Eugenius IV stayed there in 1434 for the Ecumenical Council, and Leo X (a Medici Pope) stayed there during his early sixteenth-century visits.[20]

In reappropriating the space to create part of the convent in the 1570s, the Medici made a public gesture that stated the importance of the new convent even before it was built—quarters befitting the Pope were the most suitable housing for the finest daughters of the court.[21] A suitable location procured, Cosimo then wanted to build and outfit the convent to match. He engaged the finest architects and designers, including his personal artistic advisors at court, Vincenzo Borghini and Georgio Vasari, to design the building and oversee the plans.[22]

In his memoirs, courtier Agostino Lapini commented that Cosimo had some of the white marble columns from the choir of the Duomo moved to La Concezione as building materials.[23] Artistic commission abounded, including

---

[20]   Rev. J. Wood Brown, *The Dominican Church of Santa Maria Novella at Florence: A Historical Architectural and Artistic Study* (Edinburgh: Otto Schulze & Co., 1902), 90–92.

[21]   There has been significant research on convent architecture in the last few years. The work of Hellen Hills in Naples and Saundra Weddle in Florence provide a fascinating look into the protection of virtue, the significance of place, and the appropriation of space. Helen Hills, *Invisible City: The Architecture of Devotion in Seventeenth-Century Neapolitan Convents* (Oxford: Oxford University Press, 2004); Saundra Weddle, "Women in Wolves' Mouths: Nuns' Reputations and Architecture at the Convent of Le Murate," in *Architecture and the Politics of Gender in Early Modern Europe*, ed. Helen Hills (Burlington, VT: Ashgate, 2003), 115–29.

[22]   Margaret Daly Davis, *Giorgio Vasari: principi, letterati e artisti nelle corte di Giorgio Vasari, Casa Vasari, pittura vasariana dal 1532 al 1554* (Florence: Edam, 1981), no. 72.

[23]   Agostino Lapini, *Diario Fiorentino di Agostino Lapini dal 252 al 1596* (Florence: G.C. Sansoni, 1900), 164. "À di 14 di giugno 1569 si messono le prime colonne di marmo mistio, ciòè rosse e bianche, e d'altri varj colori, intorno al bel coro di marmo bianc di S[anta]

payments to various painters, sculptors, candlemakers, and leather and ironsmiths for crosses of gold and silver (including the cross of Saint Stephen), decorated tables, altars and pedestals, a bust of Eleonora, and the coat of arms of the duke and duchess painted on the communion window between the sisters and the altar.[24] All of these efforts were designed to highlight the noble character of the convent and its inhabitants, and to demonstrate their close affiliation with the court, the Order and the ruling family. Noble families considering convent life for one or more of their daughters certainly would have been aware of this convent and the prestige it carried.

Early Modern Noble Families of Florence

Politics weighed heavily on the minds of the Florentine elite—radical changes in the politics of Europe as well as the shift in government from a republic to a duchy gave the populace, particularly the wealthy or titled, cause to consider their strategies for continued prosperity.[25] Cosimo I's remedy to this social upheaval was to fashion a social structure that supported him completely; he created a new court around a new nobility shoring up both his local and international political allies.[26] This network was important not only to the grand duke but also to families whose bureaucratic appointments, landholdings, even merchant dealings depended in part on a positive relationship with the ruling family. It was therefore in the best interest of the grand duke to provide opportunities to elevate the status of individuals, families, and the class as a whole, just as it was in the best interest of families to take advantage of such opportunities.[27] In the second half of the sixteenth century, the two institutional opportunities were

---

Maria del Fiore, e si levorno certe colonne di marmo bianco incannellate, che vi erono state qualche anno, e si portorno al nuovo Monistero nella Via della Scala, accanto a S[anta] Maria Novella, di dietro a dove era giá la sala del Papa, per commissione del duca Cosimo suddetto."

[24] ASF CRS 134, Pezzo 32, Libro Giornale, 1592–1605, ff.4–8.

[25] For a study on the granducal era, see Eric Cochrane, *Florence in the Forgotten Centuries, 1527–1800* (Chicago and London: University of Chicago Press, 1973) and Konrad Eisenbichler, *The Cultural Politics of Duke Cosimo I de'Medici* (Aldershot: Ashgate, 2001).

[26] See my dissertation Chapter 1 and John P. Spielman, "Status as Commodity: The Habsburg Economy of Privilege," in *State and Society in Early Modern Austria*, ed. Charles W. Ingrao (West Lafayette, IN: Purdue University Press, 1994).

[27] Spielman, "Status as Commodity," 110–7. The article presents a similar case of social control as a means of gaining/maintaining power.

the creation of the Order of Santo Stefano for Cosimo's local and international supporters and the female counterpart of the "New Monastery."

From the perspective of patrician families, La Concezione was an exceptionally honorable home for daughters destined for the religious life, or, as was often the case, daughters who were *not* destined for the marriage market.[28] The convent was less than a ten-minute walk northwest of the Signoria; although not physically connected to the buildings of the court, it extended the locus of the court as a sort of proxy location. *Cavalieri* could meet in its chapel, the women of the court could gather in the parlor or at the grates, and officials of the Order often assembled to fulfill their ritual requirements to the convent. Furthermore, it served as a site of memorialization and reverence for Eleonora as well as for the feasts of saints such as Stephen and Michael; evidence indicates that feasts throughout the year brought the court to the convent to worship and celebrate.[29]

The close religious, cultural, and financial interactions of the convent, the court, and the Order were a result of a system of familial cross-pollination that ensured unwavering tridirectional support. Cosimo, and subsequent grand dukes, chose among the men of the court those with the requisite qualities to become knights of the court. Those families could then apply for permission to remit a female relative to "the new monastery." The convent in turn protected and elevated the select daughters of the court.

Research has long indicated that women sent to convents were not isolated or cut off from their families; rather their relatives, especially female ones, often had access and interactions with the enclosed daughters.[30] This could take the form of gifts, such as the small monetary amounts recorded on feasts days, letters and material goods, and meetings in the parlor or prearranged visits such as the special luncheon privileges granted to Camilla Martelli, second wife of

---

[28]   Considerable research exists on women's two primary paths — marriage or the convent. See P. Renee Baernstein, "In the Widow's Habit: Women between Convent and Family in Sixteenth-Century Milan," *Sixteenth Century Journal*, 25 (1994), 787–807; Silvia Evangelisti, "Wives, Widows, and Brides of Christ: Marriage and the Convent in the Historiography of Early Modern Italy," *Historical Journal*, 43:1 (2000), 233–47; Samuel K. Cohn, Jr, *Women in the Streets: Essays on Sex and Power in Renaissance Italy* (Baltimore, MD: Johns Hopkins University Press, 1996), esp. chap. 3; Dean and Lowe, *Marriage in Italy*; and Kate Lowe, "Secular Brides and Convent Brides: Wedding Ceremonies in Italy during the Renaissance and Counter-Reformation," in *Marriage in Italy*.

[29]   ASF CRS 134. Account records indicate that joint festivities were held at the convent commemorating Saint Stephen's Day (August 2) as well as other celebrations and commemorations.

[30]   Baernstein, "In the Widow's Habit"; Silvia Evangelisti, *Nuns: A History of Convent Life, 1450–1700* (Oxford: Oxford University Press, 2007).

Cosimo I.[31] Although grates separated the parties and a "listener" nun supervised, such interactions could include feasts, music, and plays.[32] The convent was strictly enclosed, but evidence of such interactions indicates that the women did not abandon the comforts of home and family but rather enjoyed a degree of luxury reflecting their family's status. It was equally important to ensure that the women upheld their status as part of the grand duke's Order—the title *Cavaliera* was used from the convent's earliest days to formally address a sister.[33]

One can easily imagine the admiration bestowed upon *cavalieri* at court and in the city; certainly as ducal knights the crown was partial to the men wearing the Cross of Saint Stephen. A similar statement can be made of the families whose daughters lived at the new convent. The family showed great fidelity to the court by applying for a place in the elite convent and the grand duke displayed his favor by admitting her. The women also wore the Cross of Saint Stephen and throughout the seventeenth and eighteenth centuries, they were in the company of more than a dozen Medici daughters. Most were from non-ducal branches of the family, but one prominent example was Princess Maria Cristina de'Medici, first daughter of Grand Duke Cosimo II and Maria Magdalena of Austria who lived at La Concezione off and on between 1619, when she was ten years old, and her death in 1632.[34] She brought with her a number of servants and "companion" nuns.

The appeal of a wealthy, selective convent for aristocratic daughters was not lost on Florentine nobility seeking strategies to protect their family and their family's assets, maintain or improve their position at court, and strengthen their ties to the powerful Medici family. The sisterhood, like the Order of Santo

---

[31]   ASF MP 6101, f. 205. Documentary sources for the Arts and Humanities, The Medici Archive Project, Inc. MAP DOC ID #15589.

[32]   Elissa B. Weaver, *Convent Theatre in Early Modern Italy: Spiritual Fun and Learning for Women* (Cambridge: Cambridge University Press, 2002). She does not address this convent at length, but the culture of women performing spiritual plays was an important part of convent culture.

[33]   ASF CRS 134, Pezzo 51, Libro Vestiari e Presiori 1592–1734, tomo 2, f. 1r., 28 Febrario 1592 [old dating system]: "Vestim[ent]o [per] n[ost]re Monache Cavaliere ..."; ASPi 2878. The nuns are also referred to as "le dette Religiose, Cavalieresse" in the Tavo Istorico of BNCF Mazz. Inv. II II 152, but as that section is dated 1814, its reliability on this particular is questionable. However, the author refers to herself as "Cavalieressa dell'Ordine di S[ant]o Stefano P[apa] e Martire."

[34]   Bibliographic resources for Maria Cristina: Emilio Grassellini and Arnaldo Fracassini, *Profili Medicei: Origine, Sviluppo, Decadenza della Famiglia Medici* (Florence: SP44, 1982), 110; Pompeo Litta et al., *Famiglie celebri italiane* tav. XV (first published Milan, 1819); Gaetano Pieraccini, *La stirpe de'Medici di Cafaggiolo. Saggio di ricerche sula trasmissione ereditaria dei caratteri biologici* (Florence: Nardini editore, 1986), vol. II, 525–8.

Stefano, read like a roster of Tuscan notables, including daughters from the Aldobrandini, Albizi, Buontempi, Capponi, Falconetti, Malaspina, Malatesta, Piccolomini, Rucellai, Tornaquinci, Ubbaldini, and Vinta families among others.

For some Florentine families, sending a daughter to profess at La Concezione was not just an accepted display of cultural norms—it was a public demonstration of prestige. Acceptance was an acknowledgment of the family's noble lineage; members were so prominent at court that the ruler permitted their kin to enter the court's convent—the most selective and elite female monastic house in Florence. In return, the families helped sustain the daughters in a comfortable lifestyle that ensured the convent's reputation as a house of *"gentiledonne"* and the women concentrated their devotional efforts on the safeguarding and triumph of their families, Florence, and the Medici.[35] The Constitution outlines a stringent regimen of rules and prohibitions as well as the daily schedule which included prayers for present and past Medici rulers and, notably, for Eleonora.

Certainly not every family could expect to send a daughter to this convent; it was quite small, housing only 20 girls initially and about 50 by 1650. Although no records have surfaced detailing the rejection of a particular girl, the ones who were accepted met the criteria of a *cavaliere* in the family, an application in the form of noble lineage documentation, letters attesting to her good and virtuous nature, the signature of the daughter and her family stating her intent to profess, and, finally, the grand duke's approval.

Initiation records indicate that girls were often admitted in small groups of three to six. This demonstrates family strategizing for their children's futures; they may have considered who else might have daughters of the right age, when would be the right time to begin the administrative process, and what might need to be done to ensure the acceptance of their daughter. If successful, the family safeguarded the virtue of their daughter, strengthened their ties not only to the other families in their group but also to the Order and the court, and affirmed their family's religious convictions. The convent projected ardent devotion aligning with the highest ideals of female piety as perceived by the very members of society who wished to sustain or enhance their families' image as not only noble Florentines but also as devout Catholics.

---

[35] Various statutes in the Constitution note the sisters' responsibilities to pray for their families, for Florence, and its leaders.

Enclosed Patrician Women

Across early modern Italy, as in most places in Europe, women had relatively little control over the direction of their lives. Particularly for the elite, parents, brothers, and uncles made the decision as to whether a girl was to marry or to enter a convent. Beyond that, the choice of who to marry or which convent to enter was as much an economic factor as any other. This is not to say that these women had no choice in the matter, only to emphasize that a girl's wishes were not necessarily paramount. Young girls were raised to understand and accept convent life as a natural course. They visited cousins or sisters in their convents, they heard stories about the eternal benefits of taking vows and of female saints, and they played with dolls dressed as nuns. These activities were as much a part of growing up as learning appropriate domestic activities.

Countless decrees and mandates, including those of Trent, insisted that girls and women were not to be committed to a convent against their will. Rules were put in place requiring a prospective nun to have an interview with a priest or confessor prior to taking vows, a verbal affirmation during the ritual, and at La Concezione, each woman signed a statement attesting to her free will.[36] However, this was not uniformly enforced; the most famous example of a woman in revolt of her confinement to a convent is Arcangela Tarabotti. Her 1654 published polemic was scathing.[37] A sound humanist education gave her ample ability and ammunition to cite examples and point out fallacies faulting everyone from her father to her priest to secular and ecclesiastical officials for the state of her imprisonment.[38] Her case was probably not unique but neither was it the rule; although it was common knowledge that many women were not there because of a religious calling, few staged large-scale battles.

No declarations of discontent or unsigned statements of acceptance have been located in the archived documents of La Concezione. It was a small, elite convent with a limited number of openings; it is possible that girls were specifically selected, already having asked to take the habit or having accepted this role. Additionally, one of Tarabotti's complaints rested with the deplorable conditions of her convent, a situation unlikely to repeat itself at this convent. It was relatively new, designed and outfitted by the best designers, furnished to standards of the courtiers, and inhabitants received extra money for items they

---

[36]   ASF CRS 134. These are scattered throughout the documents but usually include a statement of free will, the name of the reigning duke, the abbess, the applicant's signature, and often her parents' signatures.

[37]   Arcangela Tarabotti, *Paternal Tyranny*, ed. and trans. Letizia Panizza (Chicago: University of Chicago Press, 2004).

[38]   Ibid., Book 2, 117–18.

might want beyond their needs. Among contemporary convents, it may very well have been one of the more comfortable convents; records indicate that they had beds and bookshelves, musical instruments, silk cloth, sugared candies, and lap dogs.[39] Necrology records do not indicate concentrations of deaths, implying that disease was not systemic and that food was adequate.

Young girls at court were probably familiar with the convent, having passed by it, perhaps knowing someone there or visiting the parlor; certainly everyone recognized the Cross of Saint Stephen also used by the court and the Order. Its public reputation combined with its private luxuries might have made this a choice house to profess, a fact known not only to young girls but also to their courtier mothers and fathers.

In some ways, life inside the convent was not so different from public life—there were definite social structures, those with authoritative offices set the conditions of life, and the negotiation of power was perpetual. The social and political hierarchies, though intertwined, were not necessarily the same. There were different categories of nuns, often having to do with their vows and the number of years in the community. The most senior members curried the title "*madre*" rather than "*suora*," the usual, informal title for choir nuns—all those who had taken final vows. For the first five years after profession, a woman was considered a junior sister (she could not hold office but she could vote on most matters and she participated in all rituals). After five years, she had full voting and participation rights as well as electability, although some offices were limited to those with 20 or more years in the community.[40] Initiates who had begun the process but were in a transitional year before final vows could attend functions and meetings as part of their training but were probably expected to remain silent, as were servants, students, and temporary members, who likely did not attend meetings and only attended basic rituals. The decision-making class included an elected abbess, priora, secretary, bursar, chapel mistress, choir director, and head of initiates, followed by all manner of readers, recitators, keyholders, and gatekeepers. For a small convent, this many office-holders meant that most of the senior sisters held office consecutively or simultaneously; perhaps, sisters were in a constant battle to get a better job or to move up the political ladder.

Another factor beyond the type of sister and the office she held had to do with her familial status. Technically, when a girl became a nun, she left her earthly family for the heavenly bridegroom; her dowry was her inheritance and she was

---

[39]   ASF CRS 134; ASPi 2878.

[40]   These were usually offices that had to do with outsiders—those who watched the outside gate, handled business interactions, kept an ear out in the parlor, etc.

no longer entitled to any secular privileges.[41] Part of the vow-taking ritual was to take a new name, leaving the secular one behind. Indeed, a few records are extant that give both an initiate's given name and her adopted name; however, convent records usually referred to a sister by her monastic name as well as her family name, indicating that the community continued to value a woman's heritage beyond formal acceptance into the community.[42] The question remains—what practical significance did the name have once inside the convent walls? Perhaps a more prominent or powerful family name insured a woman's successful election or gave her special privileges, such as the nicest room. In a community of socio-economic peers, what gave one an advantage over another?

The formal statutes in the Constitution explicate the prerequisites for holding different offices; all had to do with the ability to carry out the duties and sound judgment rather than a name or a relative's position at court. However, it seems reasonable to assume that having acquired acceptance into the convent through political means, similar political constructs might be at work in organizing both large and small matters of daily life. As mentioned above, male leaders wished to limit the number of women from one family in order to minimize interfamilial cohorts who had the potential to control elected offices. Considering the variety of surnames used within a family and the strength of traditional family alliances, this would seem a tepid mandate. Another means of control imposed by male leaders involved term limits. The most powerful person in the convent, the abbess, could only hold office for three years. However, convent records clearly indicate that a few sisters held power for decades.[43] For example the first abbess, Humliana Lenzi, led from 1592 until 1623, setting a precedent that would continue into the eighteenth century.

A convent easily fits into the recent notion of a "women's sphere" where women are in positions of power and control.[44] Perhaps no woman was more powerful than the leader of a large, wealthy convent. Male religious leaders as

---

[41]   Sharon Strocchia, "Naming a Nun: Spiritual Exemplars and Corporate Identity in Florentine Convents, 1450–1530," in *Society and Individual in Renaissance Florence*, ed. William J. Connell (Berkeley: University of California Press, 2002), 215–40.

[42]   Often she is listed even more explicitly as S. Maria, figlia di Gio. Alberti.

[43]   Various documents in the convent's main body of documents attest to this. Archivio di Stato, Firenze, Compagnie Religiose Soppresse da Pietro Leopoldo, 134 (ASF CRS 134).

[44]   Giulia Barone, Lucetta Scaraffia, and Gabriella Zarri, *Donne e fede: santità e vita religiosa in Italia* (Rome: Laterza, 1994); Silvia Evangelista, "'We Do Not Have it, and We Do Not Want It': Women, Power and Convent Reform in Florence," *Sixteenth Century Journal*, 34 (2003), 677–700; Kate Lowe, "Elections of Abbesses and Notions of Identity in Fifteenth- and Sixteenth-Century Italy with Special Reference to Venice," *Renaissance Quarterly*, 54 (2001), 389–429; Ulrike Strasser, "Early Modern Nuns and the Feminist Politics of Religion," *Journal of Religion*, 84 (2004), 529–54.

well as secular authorities watched her appointment with interest, even though it was technically a matter of purely internal voting. This woman had connections to many powerful families and decisions she made could have an impact on the larger community. In some cities, the induction ceremony for a new abbess included a symbolic marriage between her and a male leader—a monastic abbot, a prince, or an elected leader. Placing them next to each other at once makes them equal counterparts of their respective spheres and subjects her as his "wife."[45] At La Concezione, the abbess was ritually married to the Monsignor of the Order of Santo Stefano as part of her induction. During the ritual, she promised to obey him and he gave her symbols of power and authority, including the keys to the gate, the Benedictine Rule, the Constitution, and the official ring and seal of her office.[46] This further solidified the relationship between the court as a secular entity, the Order as a quasi-religious establishment, and the convent as the female extension of each.

The abbess was certainly the most powerful woman in the convent: she made the major decisions, maintained a relationship with officials of the Order, and led major rituals. Unquestionably, many women sought this highly desired office, even if relatively few held it; the abbess of an important convent such as this one was also one of the most powerful and influential women in Florence. At La Concezione, other officers managed the day-to-day needs of the convent, leaving the abbess free for larger issues. One of the more powerful, if not immediately obviously influential, offices was that of *Corista*, the choir director.

---

[45]   Venice provides an excellent example as one particular abbess "married" the doge. See Mary Laven, *Virgins of Venice: Broken Vows and Cloistered Lives in the Renaissance Convent* (London: Viking Press, 2002), 78–80.

[46]   BNCF Mazz. Inv. II II 152, Parte Prima, Capitolo Primo, 5–10. "12. Che la Superiora per i tempi futura, doppo l'assunzione al Badessato prometta nelle mani di Monsig[no]re o suo sostituto l'osserva n[ost]ra di queste cose, il che per l avvenire non occorerà ma basterà la promessa solita dell'osserva n[ost]ra della Regola, e Constituzioni, mentre che in esse Constituzioni sono inserite come qui aviamo fatto." Parte Secondo, Capitolo Quatro, Della Elezzione della Madre Badessa, 176–81. "Essendo che per Decreto di Papa gregorio decimo quinto, deve a questa elezzione intervenire l'Arcivescovo di Firenze, o suo Vicario; qualche giorno avvanti la M[adre] Bad[ess]a glielo facci intendere; e giunto il giorno destinato, e l'ora che Mons[ignor] Arci[vescov]o o il suo Vic[ari]o con Mons[ignor] Priore di Santo Stefano di Pisa, o altro Sacerdote Cavaliere di detta Religione di sua Comissione assistino alla Grata di Chiesa; tutte le Mon[ach]e che anno voce in Capitolo si aduneranno in detta stanza con le Cocolle in dosso, e la Bad[ess]a inginocchiata a pie di detta grata dirà sua Colpa de mancamenti commessi nel suo Ufizio; e il detto Mons[ignor] Priore, o suo Commissario assistente in abito della Religione impostali la penitenza, l'assoluerà dal'Ufizio, e ella cosi assoluta, baciato terra li porgerà per la finestrella quivi vicina, le Chiavi della Clausura la Reg[ol]a e Const[ituzion]i, l'Anello, e Sigillo, e andrà al suo luogo." ASPi 2878. Libro Secondo, Sessione quarta, 1. Dell'elezione della Badessa, 222–5.

Music was a constant in monastic life. The hours of the day were marked by song, the change of the seasons and the church calendar dictated other musical choices. Monophonic plainsong was most common especially for poor convents without instruments or trained singers; however, polyphony was an inescapably common practice in churches beyond the walls and would have been known to, even desired by, some sisters. Elected by the Abbess, the Corista at this convent was charged with ensuring the appropriateness of not only the music sung each day, but also the readings and lessons. Also under her purview were several deputy officers, indicating that her appointment was probably one of the more prestigious and coveted offices to hold within the convent hierarchy. The Constitution outlines her duties carefully:

> it will be this person's duty to indicate each time the Office that the Choir ought to recite, and to make note of it to the Reader and Singer. It will be her duty to write on a tablet, which shall be attached to the music stand of the choir, who in the choir shall participate in the Office of the Choir, and these shall include the Reader, two Singers, two Antiphoners, and the Readers of the Morning Lessons.[47]

She would have needed to be familiar with a wide variety of hymns and lauda as well as all of the liturgical music of the Daily Offices, the Mass, convent rituals, and the Litanies. She also seems to have been responsible for assigning particular sisters to the choir and to specific jobs in the musico-liturgical context of the convent—certainly a position of power and influence within the community. The Corista assigned a special choir made up of song leaders called *cantore*. This was a position of honor, an acknowledgment of an individual talent that set one

---

[47]   BNCF Mazz. Inv. II II 152, Seconda Parte, Capitolo Decimo Nono: Dell'Ufizio della Corista, p. 222. "Deve dunque la M[adre] Bad[ess]a tra l'altre Uf[fic]i ali eleggere una Mon[ac]a grave di constumi devota e diligente nelle cose Spirituali, pratica, nell'ordinare i Divini Uf[fic]i, e nel Canto fermo quale si chiami Corista; alla quale apparterra l'ordinare volta per volta l'Uf[fic]o che si deve recitare in Coro, e farlo noto all'Eddomedaria e Cantore. Sarà suo Uf[fic]o notare n una tavoletta che si terrà appiccata al Leggio del Coro settimana [per] settimana che a da fare gli Uf[fic]i del Coro, ciòe l'Eddomedaria, due Cantore due Antifonarie, e le Lettore delle Lezzioni Mattutine. Avverta nel distribuire questi Uf[fic]i che la Reg[ol]a nel Capitolo 47 dice che non si commetta il Cantare o leggere a Mon[ach]e che non sieno atte a tali Uf[fic]i con edificazione di che sente, e il medesimo dice della lezzione di mensa nel Capitolo 38 e 47 dice che a tutti quelli che e imposto il Cantare o leggere, o altra cosa, la faccino con umiltà, con gravità e tremore e nessuna senza giusta causa recusi di fare quel che dalla detta Corista glie imposto, etiam che li paressi non essere atta, ma si mortifichi e obbedisca."

woman apart from another in a place where institutional conformity was the rule.

Perhaps because La Concezione was so wealthy, it was assumed that all sisters were literate, as is stated in the description of the education girls received in the convent.[48] Musical literacy, however, was expected of the Corista as well as women who served as *cantore*, if not of all of the professed sisters. This included not only reading notes and rhythms but perhaps also keeping the sisters in tune, providing the starting pitch, or even rudimentary conducting.

Music was uniquely situated within a convent because it could pass freely between the sisters' grated chapel and the main chapel. Singers defined space not only by their physical presence but also through the movement of sound. In this way, chapel singers and instrumentalists could make their presence known. This was perhaps the most common form of interaction between nun and outsider: sisters forbidden from being seen could be heard, just as they could hear the tempting sounds of the outside world.

This uncontrolled permutation made music a contentious issue. While devotional songs had immeasurable benefits, secular song was thought to lead to impurity, materialism, and pride. Some convents, steeped in rich musical heritage, contested that which would suppress their traditions.[49] Although La Concezione had the means and education to support extensive musical experiences, its guiding documents strictly forbid grand musical gestures; it is likely that public musical performances were restrained, while private music was likely inclined towards a certain frivolity.[50] Music certainly could have been an issue, dividing sisters who wished to engage in an activity of entertainment (and spiritual value) and their superiors who wished to display fidelity to the

---

[48]   Stephanie Lawrence-White, "Musical Education at the Ospedale degli Innocenti, Florence" (PhD diss.: Catholic University of America, Washington, DC, 2005); Zannini Masetti and Gian Ludovico, *Motivi storici della educanzione femminile (1500–1650), I: Morale, religione, lettere, arte, musica* (Bari: Editoriale Bari, 1980); Sharon T. Strocchia, "Taken into Custody: Girls and Convent Guardianship in Renaissance Florence," *Renaissance Studies*, 17 (2003), 177–200; Sharon T. Strocchia, "Learning the Virtues: Convent Schools and Female Culture in Renaissance Florence," in *Women's Education in Early Modern Europe: A History, 1500–1800*, ed. Barbara J. Whitehead (New York: Garland, 1999), 3–46; Weaver, *Convent Theatre in Early Modern Italy*.

[49]   See Robert L. Kendrick, *Celestial Sirens: Nuns and their Music in Early Modern Milan* (Oxford: Clarendon Press, 1996); Craig Monson, *Disembodied Voices: Music and Culture in an Early Modern Italian Convent* (Berkeley: University of California Press, 1995); and Colleen Reardon, *Holy Concord Within Sacred Walls: Nuns and Music in Siena, 1575–1700* (Oxford: Oxford University Press, 2001).

[50]   See my dissertation, Chapter 4.

strict reforms of Trent that severely restricted the musical activities of religious women.[51]

The women of the "new" convent incurred many of the same issues as the "old" convents. The social structure was largely predetermined, with a political structure organized around a limited number of offices and office-holders which could be variously elected, appointed, or held indefinitely. As permanent members of a community, many women probably sought various offices, starting with small ones and working their way towards the position in which they could do the greatest good, effect the most change, or harbor the most influence.

What did women in this convent do to sway influence? In what ways did they negotiate power among themselves? There could have been campaigns for votes, although a grand public display seems doubtful. The process of election was suppose to be protected by secret ballot; this was a point stressed by Trent and reiterated in the Constitution, suggesting that open voting had led to unscrupulous wins through manipulation or intimidation. Available documents do not describe actual practices, often only recording the ascension of a new abbess with no details as to how she got there or the results of other elections.

Conclusion

Two specific threads run through any discussion of an early modern convent. The first is the negotiation of devotion. At a time of upheaval and rapid change, the church looked to monastic institutions as the bedrocks of Christianity. Male houses were encouraged to straighten up their practices but continue as founts of education and prayer. Female houses faced more drastic changes. Reining in the hearts, minds, and bodies that represented the "brides of Christ" required increased legislation, enforcement, and oversight. These trends were concurrent with Protestantism's elimination of all forms of monasticism.[52] The second thread has been highlighted in recent decades by a surge in feminist research. Female convents faced specific obstacles, but at the same time they enjoyed power and unusual freedoms for women of their day.

A convent was one of the few spaces largely dominated by women in the early modern era. Although no convent was free of male oversight, assistance,

---

[51] Craig Monson, "The Council of Trent Revisited," *Journal of the American Musicological Society*, 55 (2002), 1–37. For the complex relationship between this convent and the regulations of Trent, see my dissertation, Chapters 1 and 4.

[52] For an immensely readable account of nuns in Geneva during the Protestant conversion, see *Jeanne de Jussie: The Short Chronicle: A Poor Clare's Account of the Reformation of Geneva*, ed. and trans. Carrie F. Klaus (Chicago: University of Chicago Press, 2006).

or control, most communities, especially those following *clausura*, maintained a separate set of practices negotiated internally and fitting their specific community. The sphere of influence was therefore smaller, more concentrated, and, in the case of this convent, guided by well-educated, resource-rich women. The physical space was created by a religious agenda having as much to do with politics as devotion, it was censured and ruled by noble men, but it was inhabited by women who made it their own. As in Erica Bastress-Dukehart's chapter on the womb as under the authority of men but ultimately inaccessible to them, and in Grace Coolidge's chapter on mistresses at once independent and controlled by men, the women of this convent did not necessarily make the decision to inhabit their space; but, once they did, it was something they alone ruled.[53]

The Medici established "*il monastero nuovo*" as a part of a larger strategy to create a strong nobility, provide them with mutually beneficial opportunities, increase the visibility of the Florentine nobility, and elevate the court as a leader of the new devotional climate. Aristocratic families viewed the elite convent as a means of developing their status within the new court, reinforcing their ties to the ruling family and providing their daughter with a legitimacy that bolstered the family's nobility and highlighted her virginity. Daughters, at once at the center of conflicting agendas and at the same time eliminated from the process, perhaps understood their enclosure as a space with the same basic rules of engagement—the secular intermingled with the sacred, power as a negotiation of position, and survival based on a widespread network of family, friends, and allies.

---

[53]   See Bastress-Dukehart and Coolidge, this volume.

Chapter 8

The Question of the Imprescriptibility of Nobility in Early Modern France

Elie Haddad

Pauvres animaux des marais à l'existence jugée méprisable
vous êtes aussi racés qu'un cheval de course à Longchamp
mais votre race ne frappe pas les esprits insensibles
elle remonte pour certain au précambrien pourtant[1]

In 1678, Gilles-André de La Roque published his famous *Traité de la noblesse*, which was widely read until the end of the Ancien Régime. He wrote: "It is a great question that is still not resolved, whether nobility is prescribed or whether it is acquired irrevocably from the right of several generations."[2] A century later, Pierre Guyot wrote a very long article on nobility in volume 12 of his *Répertoire universel et raisonné de jurisprudence*. He devoted Chapter XVI to the question "La Noblesse peut-elle se prescrire?" (Can nobility be prescribed?) He began: "This question is perhaps the most problematic of all those which present themselves in the vast field of law. It is a truly extraordinary thing, of a point so important being left to the vagueness of opinions."[3]

The unsolved problem dealt with knowing whether there was a lapse of time, or a number of generations, able to make legal an ennoblement not conferred by the prince. In other words, could the discovery of *ancêtres roturiers* (ancestors who were commoners) challenge the nobility of a family without any possible

---

[1]   Raymond Queneau, *Courir les rues. Battre la campagne. Fendre les flots* [1968] (Paris: Gallimard, 2002), 182.

[2]   "C'est une grande question non encore résolue, si la noblesse se prescrit, et si elle s'acquiert irrévocablement par la possession de plusieurs générations." Gilles-André de La Roque, *Le Traité de la noblesse et de ses différentes espèces* [1678] (Paris: Mémoire & Documents, 1994), 318.

[3]   "Cette question est peut-être la plus problématique de toutes celles que présente le vaste champ de la jurisprudence. C'est une chose vraiment extraordinaire, qu'un point aussi important soit ainsi livré au vague des opinions." Pierre-Jean-Jacques-Guillaume Guyot, *Répertoire universel et raisonné de jurisprudence civile, criminelle, canonique et bénéficiale; ouvrage de plusieurs jurisconsultes*, t. 12 (Paris: Visse, 1785), 95.

prescription, which means without a limitation period blotting out its common origins? Or at least did it mean the impossibility to claim to be "*noble de race*" (noble coming from a long noble line)?

The importance of these issues is linked to the slow development of a juridical definition of French nobility during the sixteenth and seventeenth centuries, which were connected to major political, juridical, and sociological changes throughout the early modern era.[4] The monarchical state gradually assumed control over the definition of the second order and the ways to attain it. More and more, these criteria were presumed to be only the concern of the king. The rise of the *noblesse de robe* was another element of this debate, creating new conflicts within the second order as regards its boundaries and its definition. Studying the question of the imprescriptibility of nobility offers a way to analyze the contested spaces of the legal definition of nobility during the age of the affirmation of the monarchical state. Indeed, in its full implications, this theory led to the view that the *noblesse de race* was only a presumption, even a fiction, and that "noble" quality came only from the king. Such a definition conflicted with the traditional conception that nobles held of themselves, and with the practice of the investigations into nobility during the sixteenth and the first half of the seventeenth centuries. Even during the eighteenth century, the practice of the king's genealogists, or of the genealogists serving other institutions, did not always subscribe to the theory of imprescriptibility. Moreover, the notion of "imprescriptibility" was ambiguous, for many among the nobles used it to assert that nobility was innate to the people that bear this quality, and that one could not become noble.

Thus, nobility never was an "essence" with a fixed definition recognized by all. On the contrary, it always was the result of social interactions and conflicts, which tested the social representations, social practices, and the juridical elements on which these representations and practices were founded.[5] "Nobility," therefore, was a contested space, and the law was its battlefield.[6] However, the law itself was necessarily conflicting, and it affected society through the conflicts it had to mediate. Since norms describe social practices in the language of the law and social actors do not act outside the normative world, because they know that their actions could be qualified by the law in case of contestation, it is important

---

4   For a juridical approach to French nobility, based on Colbert's investigations, see Alain Texier, *Qu'est-ce que la noblesse? Histoire et droit* (Paris: Tallandier, 1988).

5   Robert Descimon, "Chercher de nouvelles voies pour interpréter les phénomènes nobiliaires dans la France moderne. La noblesse, 'essence' ou rapport social?" *Revue d'Histoire Moderne et Contemporaine*, 46 (1999), 5–21.

6   See Marraud, this volume, whose analysis reaches similar conclusions.

to analyze both the norms and the practices to understand the contested space of the definition of nobility and its evolutions.[7]

In this view, the purpose of this chapter is to understand why no agreement was found on the matter of imprescriptibility. The interpretation of treaties on nobility and of juridical writings, confronted with the studies on noble sociology and ideology, sheds new light on this subject. What follows does not claim to be exhaustive, but only points to the main elements of some major writings of the early modern era on the question of imprescriptibility, and also reveals some changes over time. The first part of the chapter is devoted to the sixteenth century. It shows that imprescriptibility of nobility progressively became a problem during the Wars of Religion because of the calling into question of the bloodline of nobility and because of much ennoblement by arms. The noble response was to stress the ideology of race, but still perceived nobility in a traditional manner. During the first half of the seventeenth century, some jurists drew the basis of a juridical transformation of the definition of nobility, controlled by the monarchy. The second part of the chapter examines how imprescriptibility became an important matter upon which the tensions of the theories of nobility focused. The third part analyzes how these jurists' works were used by the monarchy that had to compromise with the different social practices and with the diversity of nobility. From the 1660s and the great investigations into nobility to the Revolution, the problem of imprescriptibility was never solved because of the internal tensions of the definition and of the sociology of the second order.

Prescription and Noble Autonomy in the Sixteenth Century

During most of the sixteenth century, the prescription of nobility was not a real problem. Noble status was then a matter of customs and local recognition. Royal courts judged this matter only when there was a dispute,[8] but the king generally did not claim the power to establish who was noble and who was not.[9] However,

---

[7]   Yan Thomas, "Histoire et Droit" and "La valeur des choses. Le droit romain hors la religion," *Annales HSS*, 57 (2002), 1425–8 and 1431–62.

[8]   Etienne Dravasa, "'Vivre noblement'. Recherches sur la dérogeance de noblesse du XIVe au XVIe siècles," *Revue juridique et économique du Sud Ouest*, 16:3–4 (1965), 135–93, and 17:1–2 (1966), 23–129.

[9]   Françoise Autrand stresses the importance of the reputation of being noble to obtain letters of ennoblement in fifteenth-century France: the king only confirmed a preexisting social judgment. "L'image de la noblesse en France à la fin du Moyen Age. Tradition et

he sometimes exercised his power to ennoble by letters.[10] In fact, customary nobility was not thought of as a class, but rather as an adjective used in function of the places, the cases, and the events of social life. This explains the various social identities which can be seen in the fourteenth and fifteenth centuries, and even in the sixteenth century, especially in the cities. It also explains the polysemic use of the qualification of "noble."[11]

The *"anoblissement taisible"* was the result of social recognition and domination.[12] It was based on traditional criteria emphasized by Ellery Schalk: the profession of arms, deeply rooted as a mark of nobility, even if it did not correspond to reality in some provinces;[13] virtue, that is the necessary and intrinsic noble quality which gives the ability to command; the way of life and the possession of a fief; and, finally, a *noblesse immémoriale* (nobility beyond memory), passed down through the bloodline, founded on oral memory, except when it was contested.[14] But even in this case, witnesses who were nobles themselves were summoned and, in accordance with customs, they testified that the defendant's ancestors had lived as nobles for two or three generations, or for a 100 years at least (that was the case in Brittany). Ellery Schalk concludes that the medieval definition of nobility still prevailed in the collective representations at

---

nouveauté," *Comptes rendus de l'Académie des Inscriptions et des Belles Lettres* (1979), 340–54.

[10]   On the letters of ennoblement in early modern France, see Jean-Richard Bloch, *L'Anoblissement en France au temps de François Ier. Essai d'une définition de la condition juridique et sociale de la noblesse au début du XVIe siècle* [1906] (Paris: F. Alcan, 1934); and Arundel de Condé, *Anoblissements, maintenues et réhabilitations en Normandie (1598–1790). La noblesse normande sous l'Ancien Régime* (Paris: Sedopolis, 1981). Fulcran de Roquefeuil's work, *Anoblissement et révocation de la noblesse aux XVIe, XVIIe et XVIIIe siècles* (Paris: Patrice Du Puy éditeur, 2005), belongs to a non-scholarly noble historiographical tradition, which does not allow one to go further on these matters.

[11]   Robert Descimon, "Sites coutumiers et mots incertains: la formation de la noblesse française à la charnière du Moyen Age et des Temps modernes," forthcoming in Thierry Dutour, ed., *Les Nobles et la ville* (Paris: Presses universitaires de Paris-Sorbonne, 2010).

[12]   *"Anoblissement taisible"* is the expression used to design a way to become noble by living like a noble, owning a fief, bearing the sword, serving in the army, etc., and being recognized as a noble. Its importance has been showed by Jean-Marie Constant, and so was the mutation of nobility. See "La mobilité sociale dans une province de gentilshommes et de paysans: la Beauce," in Roland Mousnier, ed., *XVIIe siècle*, "La Mobilité sociale au XVIIe siècle", 122, (1979), 7–20.

[13]   For instance in the Beauce, studied by Jean-Marie Constant, *Nobles et paysans en Beauce aux XVIe et XVIIe siècles* (Lille: Service de reproduction des thèses Université Lille III, 1981).

[14]   Ellery Schalk, *From Valor to Pedigree: Ideas of Nobility in France in the Sixteenth and Seventeenth Centuries* (Princeton: Princeton University Press, 1986).

the beginning of the sixteenth century. Of course, an evolution toward a juridical and more precise definition was in progress, and the nobility already formed a social group who were more or less hereditary, but the idea of it was largely based on those traditional criteria and on their continuing military function. Nobility, therefore, was ruled by customs. Like during the Middle Ages, ennoblement by royal letters was rare, and most of the families did not find it necessary to see their status that was locally recognized with local criteria confirmed by the king.[15] The *anoblissement taisible* presupposed prescription, or rather no interest on this matter, since it was out of the question to seek in the past some possible marks of *roture* (common rank) of present noble families.

A more precise royal legislation concerning nobility only arose gradually from the middle of the sixteenth century. The fiscal interests of the state were central in this process, and clearly asserted in the legislation. In 1543, François I promulgated the first declaration by which all who claimed to be noble without proving their quality would pay the *taille*. Three years later, André Tiraqueau, then *conseiller au parlement de Paris* and also a famous Hellenist and jurisconsult, wrote his treatise on nobility.[16] Tiraqueau set the question of nobility using works by jurists of Roman law, especially Bartolo, who had put forward the theory of political nobility in *De Nobilitate* during the fourteenth century. According to this theory, noble status essentially issued from royal power and its legislation, and from office-holding, and not from lineage or virtue. Bartolo's theory was clearly elaborated against the traditional conceptions which linked nobility to lineage and virtue. Only political nobility, which was given by the prince, was legal: all other claims for nobility were considered as a *crimen falsi*.[17] Tiraqueau resumed this idea in his own treatise, but he adapted it to the French situation, and he brought it inside the tradition of the *scientia juris*, which borrowed from various sources of the law. Therefore, his writing drew upon different conceptions of nobility, creating a new synthesis.

Tiraqueau thought that nobility was primarily a social recognition: "*Hic nobilis qui populi opinione est nobilis.*"[18] But also he said it was a dignity given by the

---

[15]   Jan Rogozinski, "Ennoblement by the Crown and Social Stratification in France 1285–1322: A Prosopographical Survey", in *Order and Innovation in the Middle Age: Essays in Honor of Joseph R. Strayer*, eds William C. Jordan, Bruce McNab, and Teofilo F. Ruiz (Princeton: Princeton University Press, 1976), 273–91.

[16]   On Tiraqueau, see Giovanni Rossi, *Incunaboli della modernità: Scienza giuridica e cultura umanistica in André Tiraqueau (1488–1558)* (Turin: Giappichelli, 2007).

[17]   Armand Arriaza, "Noblesse politique et anoblissement: conception émergente au XIIIᵉ siècle en France," *Revue d'Histoire du Droit*, 84 (2006), 333–51.

[18]   André Tiraqueau, *Commentarii de Nobilitate et jure primigeniorum* [1549] (Lyon: Guillaume Rouille, 1602), 65.

prince, and who claimed to be so must prove it. Thus, Tiraqueau was keeping his distance from Cesare Ripa, for whom nobility could not be prescribed. According to the jurisconsult, the *anoblissement taisible* was accepted if several generations showed virtue, and lived and were recognized as nobles. Prescription, in this sense, was due to a "*possession immémoriale*," which meant having no conflicting memory of any witness.[19] It did not prevent Tiraqueau from thinking that the older the nobility, the more it was esteemed, in conformity with a deeply rooted ideology. The various sources of the law on which his treatise was based removed his definition of nobility from Bartolo's idea of political nobility. Adding the fact that he did not emphasize bloodline as an element of nobility, compared to social recognition, his acceptance of the prescription of nobility was logical.

Tiraqueau's treatise was a watershed moment in noble history. Subsequent jurists could not fail to engage with its arguments. But political developments during the second half of the sixteenth century were also of great consequence for theories of nobility. During the Wars of Religion, some of the Ultra-Catholics strongly challenged the idea that nobility was passed on through bloodline. In the meantime, constant warfare favored ennoblements by arms.[20] As a reaction, nobles tended to ask for restrictions in the access to the second order.[21] Theoreticians defended both positions.

For François de L'Alouete, seigniorial judge then *maître des requêtes de l'Hôtel du roi*, and Jacques de Coucy's private tutor, the answer was to assume that nobility was nothing other than virtue. His treatise is above all a teaching book for his pupil, and more generally for all noblemen, written to restore nobility as prudence, force, temperance, and justice, which fell into decline because of ignorance and the disparagement of sciences and virtue.[22] If L'Alouete said that kings had originally distinguished those of their subjects who had a more excellent nature, he however admitted that behavior was the source of nobility. This fact justified not only ennoblement but also loss of nobility in case of lack of virtue. L'Alouete did not talk about prescription, but the notion was underlying, given the importance of the way of life to claim to be noble: to be recognized as a noble, you had to prove four degrees of nobility, said

---

[19]   Ibid., 72.

[20]   For instance Jehan de Caumont: "Je sçay qu'il y a une Noblesse perverse, Noblesse serpentine, Noblesse bastarde, vilaine, degenereuse, prevaricatrice, blasphematrice, n'ayant rien du bien de noblesse que l'origine de la race, ayant tous les effects contraires aux effects de vraye noblesse," *De la Vertu de Noblesse. Aux Roys et Princes Tres-Chrestiens* (Paris: Frédéric Morel, 1585), f. 6.

[21]   Schalk, *From Valor to Pedigree*.

[22]   François de L'Alouete, *Traité des Nobles et des Vertus dont ils sont formés* (Paris: Robert le Manier, 1577).

L'Alouete. However, he also thought that those who came from an ancient race, *"vrais nobles,"* were more excellent than the others, and he rejected usurpations, asking for a clear difference between nobles and commoners. He regretted that the ignorance of the second order had made possible for the commoners to challenge it concerning the offices that should have normally been allotted to it, since virtue consists in devoting oneself to noble things, which means to the king's service. Consequently, L'Alouete recommended that each noble "have the description and genealogy of his race" for four degrees at least, and more for those who could, so that they proved their excellence and antiquity, and so that they encouraged the imitation of their ancestors' virtues. He added:

> As much as the ancient genealogies are normally the most esteemed, at all times, those who undertake these discourses and descriptions ... are well advised not to discover or research too much before the first source and origin of [noble] race, which could be, perhaps, a vicious, infamous, and dishonest beginning, which will cover all posterity with infamy rather than with the crown of honor one wants to acquire.[23]

L'Alouete encouraged the hiding of common origins, in accordance both with his recognition of ennoblement and with the greater excellence he attached to the antiquity of nobility.

Another answer to the question of the second order prevailed over L'Alouete's equivalence between nobility and virtue. It consisted in stressing the traditional idea of *race*.[24] The balance between nobility-virtue and nobility-blood was reversed,

---

[23]   "Combien que les anciennes Genealogies soient ordinairement les plus estimées, toutesfois il faut que celui qui entreprend d'en faire le Discours & Description, s'i comporte & i garde cette mesure avec telle prudence, qu'il avise bien de ne découvrir ne rechercher trop avant la premiere source & origine de la Race, laquelle aura, peut étre, un commencement vicieux, infame & deshonneste, qui donnera une fueille d'ignominie à toute la posterité, au lieu de la couronne d'honneur qu'il lui veut acquerir." Ibid., f. 74.

[24]   The notion of *race* should not be seen through a modern biological framework, as André Devyver did in *Le Sang épuré. Le préjugé de race chez les gentilshommes français de l'Ancien Régime (1560–1720)* (Brussels: Éditions de l'Université de Bruxelles, 1973). Arlette Jouanna has precisely analyzed the meaning of this word, which refers to patrilineage, in *L'Idée de race en France au XVIe siècle et au début du XVIIe siècle (1498–1614)* (Lille: Service de reproduction des thèses Université Lille III, 1976). However, her book draws the notion towards a biological thought which was not the nobles' one. For an analysis of the traditional noble ideology, see Diego Venturino, "L'ideologia nobiliare nella Francia di Antico Regime. Note sul Dibattito storiografico recente," *Studi Storici*, 29 (1988), 61–101. The medical and scientific aspects and their evolutions during the Renaissance and the seventeenth century are of course fundamental for this matter. For an example of the juridical implications they had,

leading to the preeminence of the second, agreeing that neither of them was ever found without the other at this time.[25] This transformation changed the terms in which the problem of prescription was formulated. It can be seen in Florentin de Thierriat's treatise, written in 1606. He was a lawyer in Lorraine coming from Champagne, but he just presented himself as "seigneur de Lochepierre." There are two different nobilities, he said: the *noblesse de race* which is natural, and the civil nobility, "which is a quality given by the sovereign prince, one that is not natural but has its customs and usages."[26] The last one is inferior to the first one: "not only is the gentleman preferable to the 'political' noble; but to all other gentlemen if their nobility is not as ancient, or at least as illustrious."[27] Thus, he stood against all the Bartolean tradition and he modified strongly the definition of nobility towards nature and bloodline. Unlike L'Alouete, he distinguished clearly between race and virtue: if civil nobility can be lost, it is not the case in *noblesse de race*, even in case of *dérogeance* (loss of nobility): nobility was then just "*mise à l'estoufée*," or hidden.[28] Thierriat wrote about prescription but only for civil nobility. He recognized prescription for those who had been ennobled by possession of a fief, provided that there was no contrary memory, that the title had been taken in the presence of a royal officer, or that it had been confirmed by a contradictory judgment. Prescription was then not an effect of time, but an effect of the law of the prince.[29] The distinction between civil nobility and natural nobility, and the importance given to old nobility, were not without tensions. Indeed, natural nobility was presumed if it was proved that the father and the grandfather were nobles, but it was also supposed to be imprescriptible. At the

---

see Bastress-Dukehart, this volume. For an approach of the conceptions of heredity in the Middle Ages and in early modern times, see Maaike van der Lugt and Charles de Miramon, eds, *L'Hérédité entre Moyen Âge et époque moderne. Perspectives historiques* (Florence: SISMEL-Edizioni del Galluzzo, 2008).

[25]   See Michel Nassiet's criticism addressed to Ellery Schalk, "*Pedigree AND valor*. Le problème de la représentation de la noblesse en France au XVIe siècle," in *La Noblesse de la fin du XVIe au début du XXe siècle, un modèle social?*, t. I, eds Josette Pontet, Michel Figeac, and Marie Boisson (Anglet: Atlantica, 2002), 251–69. It must be said however that Ellery Schalk does not deny that both aspects were present in the sixteenth century.

[26]   "qui est une qualité donnée par le Prince souverain à celuy qui ne l'avoit pas de nature, ains de ses mœurs & usages." Florentin de Thierriat, *Trois Traictez. Sçavoir, 1. De la noblesse de Race, 2. De la noblesse Civille, 3. Des Immunitez des Ignobles* (Paris: Lucas Bruneau, 1606), 4–5.

[27]   "non seulement le Gentil-homme est preferable au Noble Politique: mais à tout autre Gentil-homme dont la Noblesse n'est si ancienne, ou est moins illustrée." Ibid., 10.

[28]   Ibid., 77.

[29]   Ibid., 149–50.

same time, civil nobility could be prescribed, and then its origins forgotten. So how was it to be distinguished from the *noblesse de race*?

The proof demanded by Thierriat was still the result of the customary thought of nobility. He took up Jehan Baquet's words, who considered that witnesses were sufficient to justify *immémorialité*, which was still perceived as what was out of reach of men's memory:

> Because we in France hold that to verify if a man is noble, witnesses must testify that they knew his grandfather and father, and he who claims nobility, that they have lived nobly: carrying arms, going to war, even had command of military companies, having been Captains, Lieutenants, Ensigns, standard-bearers, or men-at-arms, that they followed Gentlemen, dressed like Gentlemen and their wives like Ladies, and performed other noble acts, without having been assessed for the *taille*, like nobles, and that all the people of the country where he has been taxed estimated and considered them noble.[30]

From this view, prescription was obvious, and nobility was still fully a matter of social recognition, locally anchored, and founded on the exercise of arms. But the insistence on the importance of blood to be noble, linked to a demand of social closure, wanted by Thierriat and many nobles paved the way to the transformations of the seventeenth century.

Political Nobility and the *Noblesse de Race*

The juridical elaboration of the definition of nobility combined: first, customary laws; second, criteria coming from royal taxation; third, social changes among elites—particularly socio-political demands of the second order asking for a control of ennoblement; fourth, influences of Aristotelian thought and of the Roman model of hereditary nobility; and fifth, the conception of political

---

[30]   "Car nous tenons en France que pour vérifier que un homme est noble, il suffit que les tesmoins deposent qu'ils ont cogneu son ayeul et son père, les ont veu vivre noblement, suivre les armes, aller aux guerres, mesme avoir eu charge de compaignees, avoir esté Capitaines, Lieutenans, Enseignes, Guidons, hommes d'armes, hanter les Gentils-hommes, porter habits de Gentils-hommes, leurs femmes porter habits de Damoiselles, et faire autres actes de nobles, sans avoir esté assis à la taille comme nobles, et que au païs ils ont esté censez, estimez et reputez nobles, par tous les habitans, ensemble celuy qui se pretend noble." Jean Bacquet, *Quatriesme traicté des droits du domaine, de la Couronne de France, concernant les francs fiefs, nouveaux acquests, anoblissemens et amortissemens* (Paris: S. Nivelle, 1582), f. 72r–v.

nobility held by jurists.[31] Jurists contributed to the reorganization of the conceptual field of nobility during the first half of the seventeenth century: they stressed the importance of bloodline to belong to the second order, at the time when social practices concerning passing on of nobility were also reinforcing patrilineages.[32] Charles Loyseau and Cardin Le Bret were two jurists of great influence as regards nobility. The first one was *bailli* of Châteaudun between 1600 and 1610. He profited from his position, but he never held a royal office, probably because of his relationships with the Catholic League.[33] In contrast, Le Bret succeeded remarkably in his career. He was the son of a lawyer and was a lawyer too, before becoming an *avocat général à la cour des Aides*, then at the *parlement de Paris*, between 1590 and 1624. He ended his career as a *conseiller d'Etat*. Nonetheless, Loyseau's work was far more read than Le Bret's *Traité de la Souveraineté*, pubished in 1630. Yet, as a lawyer at the *cour des Aides*, Le Bret had had to judge on noble matters and had drawn a doctrine from his experience. Some aspects of this doctrine can be found in his *Actions publiques*.[34]

According to Le Bret, Nature did not create men equals. He used the Platonic argument of metals to justify this point of view, as Thierriat had done before. Concerning bastards, this natural distinction led Le Bret to argue that the prince could not confer noble race on those who did not have it. The prince had no power on blood right and race came only from the grandfather. That was saying that the prince could make a noble, but not a *gentilhomme*. However, this natural conception went hand in hand with the idea that all nobility came from the king, either tacitly by the fiefs and offices he gives, or expressly by letters of ennoblement. Considering a fief concession as a king's tacit ennoblement allowed Le Bret to make the *noblesse immémoriale* glorious, because it took its origins from the beginning of the monarchy and derived from the king. The coherence of the whole argument was based on the prince who distinguished as nobles only those who showed a more excellent nature than others through their deeds, and so acquired race through the passing on of this nature publicly

---

[31]   Robert Descimon, "L'invention de la noblesse de robe. La jurisprudence du Parlement de Paris aux XVIᵉ et XVIIᵉ siècles," in *Les Parlements de Province. Pouvoir, justice et société du XVᵉ au XVIIIᵉ siècle*, comps Jacques Poumarède and Jack Thomas (Toulouse: FRAMESPA, 1996), 677–90.

[32]   Claire Chatelain, *Chronique d'une ascension sociale. Exercice de la parenté chez de grands officiers (XVIᵉ–XVIIᵉ siècles)* (Paris: Éditions de l'EHESS, 2008); Elie Haddad, *Fondation et ruine d'une "maison". Histoire sociale des comtes de Belin (1582–1706)* (Limoges: PULIM, 2009).

[33]   Robert Descimon, "Les paradoxes d'un juge seigneurial. Charles Loyseau (1554–1627)," *Cahiers du CRH*, 27 (October 2001), 153–76.

[34]   See particularly the 7th, 35th and 36th *actions*, and Chapter X of *De la souveraineté*, in *Les Œuvres de Messire C. Le Bret conseiller ordinaire du Roy en ses Conseils d'Estat et Privé* (Paris: Toussainct du Bray, 1643).

recognized. The juridical fiction of royal ennoblement was then true to Nature. It was an attempt to merge the theory of the *noblesse de race* and the theory of political nobility in support of royal sovereignty.

Loyseau's logic was different because he rejected the idea of a natural distinction between nobility and *roture*, since the rational soul comes to man directly from God. To explain French nobility, he relied on the Roman law and distinguished gentility, or generosity, corresponding to the *noblesse de race*, improving with age, and the nobility of dignity, conferred by the king, which was personal.[35] No doubt that for Loyseau, the second one was the only true nobility. Yet, he could not avoid using the word at his disposal, which mixed up gentility, that he called the *simple noblesse*, and the nobility of dignity.

The first one, Loyseau said, was old and beyond memory, founded as early as the institution of the monarchy: the *gentilshommes* had been destined to defend the state, the *roturiers* to plough, to trade, and to craft. Loyseau took up the idea that the beginning of the *simple noblesse* could not be known, adding that it had to be without any trace of *roture*. If he recalled that the nobility beyond memory was proved by the father's and the grandfather's nobility, he added that it was on the condition that no contrary proof was found. *Immemorialité* only gave a presumption of nobility.[36] Placing Bartolo against Tiraqueau, Loyseau introduced the idea of imprescriptibility of the *simple noblesse*, which was more or less the *noblesse de race*, except that he did not argue that this nobility came from Nature, but from royal power. Though the foundations of their arguments were different, Loyseau's and Le Bret's theories were close. Both were based on the power of the prince. But while Le Bret only resolved the question of the antiquity of nobility by recalling the customary law imposed to prove its possession over three generations, Loyseau drew from the conception that all the nobilities come from the king the idea that only one mark of *roture* found in the past of a family was a sign of an usurpation of sovereign power.[37] If Loyseau did

---

[35]   Charles Loyseau, *Traité des simples ordres et dignitez* (Paris: veuve L'Angelier, 1613 [1610]), chapter IV, "De l'Ordre de Noblesse en general."

[36]   "Car je suis bien d'accord avec eux [nos Docteurs], que la Noblesse, ou pour mieux dire, l'ingenuité est presumée asseurement & peremptoirement, par le moyen de la possession immemoriale ..., mais il faut prendre garde, que c'est quand la possession est immemoriale, c'est-à-dire quand il n'y a mémoire, ny preuve, ny par consequent certitude du contraire." Ibid., 30.

[37]   However, he accepted the prescription after three generations for the possession of a *fief de dignité*, because of the *édit des tailles* (1600) and because he thought that the idea of such a possession was abhorrent to *roture*. Besides, it could be seen as an *anoblissement taisible* coming from the king, as Le Bret said.

not demand an investigation of each family's past to determine whether it was truly noble or not, the possibility to do so appeared.

Since the *simple noblesse* was a consequence of state law, the nobility of dignity—which was obtained by being in charge of a great office of the crown, either of the royal household or government—was better according to Loyseau, even if it could not be passed on. However, the jurist explained, common opinion esteems less the ennobled because the beginning of the *simple noblesse* cannot be known, whereas the nobility of dignity obviously proceeds from royal fiction. That is why families want to hide their noble origins. Loyseau argued that ennoblement affected all the ancestors of the ennobled who were retrospectively also ennobled: such a power had the juridical fiction! Yet, his treatise is also a sign that the hereditary conception of nobility strengthened. Indeed, he asserted that it was impossible to lose the *noblesse de race* in case of vile actions: "as for the nobility of race which is as though natural to man, I oppose Tiraqueau—it is not lost at all because of infamy."[38] While the tensions between these two conceptions of nobility that the jurist tried to unite were not resolved, his attempted juridical dogmatism accompanied some ideological flexibility, which was able to explain social reality and its evolutions.

Le Bret's and Loyseau's treatises helped strengthen the idea that all the nobilities came from the king, including ancient nobility. Paradoxically, these two thoughts, which were based on the notion of political nobility, also reinforced the conception of bloodline nobility at the same time. In this, they were congruent with noble social practices and with the demand of a social reorganization, based on sharp distinctions between the orders. Louis XIV's reforms leant on this demand.

The Impossible Imprescriptibilty of Nobility

The juridical practices establishing the great investigations into nobility from the time of Colbert in the middle of the seventeenth century were far from the science of the law which characterized the treatises of the preceding century, which considered many subtleties.[39] The *traitants* in charge of the investigations applied a politic with financial stakes that were soon denounced by some nobles, but that were also supported by a general will desiring social control. For the

---

38   "... quant à la noblesse de race, qui est comme naturelle à l'homme, je tiens contre Tiraqueau, qu'elle n'est point perdue tout à fait par l'infamie." Loyseau, *Traité des simples ordres et dignitez*, 77.

39   Robert Descimon, "Élites parisiennes entre XVe et XVIIe siècle. Du bon usage du Cabinet des Titres", *Bibliothèque de l'École des chartes*, 155 (1997), 607–44.

monarchy, this control required a clear delimitation of the second order. In this purpose, it used the work of some jurists and rigidified the Bartolean tradition which inspired their definition of nobility. However, the investigators were somewhat forced to compromise because of the general outcry the first wave of investigations caused in 1661, among other reasons.[40] They also had to come to terms with the local forms of noble recognition which had always prevailed.[41] Therefore, the investigations into nobility came to a compromise which took seriously the noble ideology of *race*, but undermined it by the idea of the nobility of service.[42]

By imposing the year 1560 as a limit to the proof of nobility which had to be given, the monarchy fixed a tacit recognition of prescription before this

---

[40]   Analyses coincide concerning the great investigations and their mixed results in comparison with the strict definition that governed their implementation. See Jean Meyer, *La Noblesse bretonne au XVIIIᵉ siècle* (Paris: Éditions de l'EHESS, 1985), 2 vols; Jean-Marie Constant, "L'enquête de noblesse de 1667 et les seigneurs de la Beauce," *Revue d'Histoire Moderne et Contemporaine*, 21 (1974), 548–66; Anne Blanchard, "Une approche de la noblesse languedocienne: la maintenue de 1668–1672," in *Sociétés et idéologies des Temps modernes. Hommage à Arlette Jouanna*, eds Joël Fouilleron, Guy Le Thiec, and Henri Michel (Montpellier: Université de Montellier III, Centre d'histoire moderne et contemporaine de l'Europe méditerranéenne et de ses périphéries, 1996), t. 1, 15–35; Valérie Piétri, *Famille et noblesse en Provence orientale de la fin du XVIIᵉ siècle à la Révolution* (thesis under Francis Pomponi's direction, Université de Nice-Sophia Antipolis, 2001), 3 vols, and "Bonne renommée ou actes authentiques: la noblesse doit faire ses preuves (Provence, XVIIᵉ–XVIIIᵉ siècles)," *Genèses*, 74 (2009), 5–24; Daniel Hickey, "La remise en cause d'une élite: la noblesse de Poitou et les recherches de noblesse de 1667–1668," *Cahiers du Gerhico*, 1 (2001), 63–72; Jérôme Loiseau, "Much Ado About Nothing? The *Intendant*, the *Gentilshommes* and the Investigations into Nobility in Burgundy (1664–1670)," *French History*, 22 (2008), 275–94.

[41]   The commissioners in charge of the investigations might have different approaches from one place to another, which made some specific local aspects of noble definition last. For a juridical analysis of the particularities of the reforms in Provence, see François-Paul Blanc, "Vivre noblement en Provence—Essai de définition juridique sous le règne de Louis XIV," *Provence historique*, 230 (2007), 331–48, and "Le statut juridique de la noblesse de robe dans la Provence du XVIIᵉ siècle", in *Etudes offertes à Alfred Jauffret* (Aix-en-Provence: Faculté de droit et de sciences politiques, 1974), 81–97. See also the case of Languedoc in Arlette Jouanna, "Mémoire nobiliaire. Le rôle de la réputation dans les preuves de noblesse: l'exemple des barons des Etats du Languedoc," in *Le Second ordre: l'idéal nobiliaire. Hommage à Ellery Schalk*, eds Chantal Grell and Arnaud Ramière de Fortanier (Paris: Presses de l'Université de Paris-Sorbonne, 1999), 197–206.

[42]   Descimon, "Élites parisiennes" and "Chercher de nouvelles voies." This compromise can be understood by the fact that the monarchy acted mainly for fiscal reasons: David D. Bien, "Manufacturing Nobles: The Chancelleries in France to 1789," *The Journal of Modern History*, 61 (1989), 445–86.

date. But it also lengthened the time ordinarily presumed for prescriptibility (three generations). Moreover, it instituted a fixed point in time which divided "true" and "false" nobility. The very logic of customary *immémorialité* was thus demolished. Now, one had to prove nobility at least since 1560. Some of the opponents of Colbert's investigations contested precisely this fact. For instance, the magistrates of Provence denounced a juridical abuse:

> The aforementioned commissioners to the detriment of the orders of the crown and of your predecessors, and to the distinctions that French authors and practitioners like Bacquet, Carondas, Loiseau and others have remarked on the chapter on nobles and non-nobles, not only request proof beyond that of father and grandfather but also beyond that of a century, without considering reception in the Knights of Malta, and without reception of witness testimony in lack of written evidence ...[43]

Some of the investigators did not hesitate to draw all the juridical consequences of the investigations as regards the definition of nobility. That was the case of Alexandre de Belleguise, who published a treatise addressed to the nobility of Provence, explaining the principles that had been followed to verify noble titles.[44] He clearly claimed that Nature does not make nobles, and that nobility is only an effect of sovereign authority which publicly recognizes virtues. Consequently, a letter of ennoblement conferred the most glorious nobility. Logically, Belleguise added that all the nobles had common ancestors, and asserted the imprescriptibility of nobility, even if he was conscious that asking for proof as regards the *noblesse de race* was a new practice which changed the social order. However, while commenting on the decision of the *Conseil d'Etat* in 1667, which granted the *noblesse de race* to those who could prove their nobility

---

[43]   "... lesdits Commissaires au préjudice des ordonnances des Roys, vos prédécesseurs et des distinctions que Bacquet, Carondas, Loiseau et autres auteurs et praticiens français en ont remarqué sur le chapitre des nobles et non nobles, ils ont non seulement demandé des preuves au-delà du père et de l'ayeul mais au-delà de la centenaire, sans avoir égard à la réception des Chevaliers de Malthe, sans réception des preuves par témoins au deffaut de la littérale ... ." Quoted by Valérie Piétri, "Vraie et fausse noblesse: l'identité nobiliaire provençale à l'épreuve des réformations (1665–1718)," *Cahiers de la Méditerranée*, 66 (2005), accessed <http://revel.unice.fr/cmedi/document.html?id=117>.

[44]   Alexandre de Belleguise, *Traité de la noblesse suivant les préjugez rendus par les commissaires députez pour la vérification des titres de noblesse en Provence* (1669), published by François-Paul Blanc, "Un traité de droit nobiliaire au XVIIᵉ siècle. Alexandre de Belleguise et le statut juridique de la noblesse provençale," *Recueil de mémoires et travaux publiés par la Société d'histoire du droit et des institutions des anciens pays de droit écrit*, fasc. IX (Faculté de droit et des sciences économiques de Montpellier, 1974), 33–65.

since 1560, he made it clear that it was only then a presumption: to prove *roture* before 1560 destroyed the *noblesse de race* without any prescription. By bringing the logic of the reform to its ultimate consequence, Belleguise made obvious the principle of doubt that it carried about the *noblesse de race*. It was a very powerful attack against noble theories of nobility, paradoxically just when blood inheritance was strongly asserted.

Among the writings reflecting on nobility and taking into account the large Colbertian reorganization, André de La Roque's treatise was the most influential.[45] His book took a position about the contested problems, but it reorganized them following both the new juridical definition of nobility and the ideology of antiquity. Indeed, he defended the idea that nobility was passed on through bloodline and was attached to Nature: "Original nobility cannot be lost as it is inalienable; because it is attached to nature, it remains on the condemned, who can only be stripped of it by legal fictions."[46] And at the same time, he declared, "it belongs only to sovereigns to ennoble."[47] La Roque took up the Aristotelian distinction between nobility as an essence and nobility as an accident. This distinction informed most of jurists' theory of ennoblement and established the noble theory of blood. La Roque also took up from Aristotle the idea that the more the age of one's nobility is proved, the more it is honorable and illustrious. It was, according to La Roque, the foundation of hierarchical inequality inside the second order. Therefore, he distinguished the nobles of four generations, called *gentilshommes* or *nobles de race*, and the *gentilshommes de nom et d'armes*, nobles by essence, whose quality came from the beginning of the fiefs, and whose perfection lay in the oblivion of their origins. If the king was a creator of nobility, he obviously could not make a *gentilhomme*, even less a *gentilhomme de noms et d'armes*. Those two qualities could not be prescribed. However, La Roque was not clear about the means to prove natural nobility, since he took up the customary model of three generations that the monarchy had dismissed and that was contradictory to the importance attached to antiquity in the hierarchical organization of the second order. Besides, imprescriptibility presupposed that

---

[45]   La Roque, *Le Traité de la noblesse*. On La Roque, see Dinah Ribard, "Livre, pouvoir et théorie. Comptabilité et noblesse en France à la fin du XVIIᵉ siècle," *Revue de synthèse*, 128:1–2 (2007), 97–122, and "Travail intellectuel et violence politique: théoriser la noblesse en France à la fin du XVIIᵉ siècle," in *Le Mot qui tue. Une histoire des violences intellectuelles de l'Antiquité à nos jours*, eds Vincent Azoulay and Patrick Boucheron (Seyssel: Champ Vallon, 2009), 353–68.

[46]   "La noblesse originelle ne peut se perdre, étant inaliénable; car comme elle est attachée à la nature, elle demeure aux condamnés, qui n'en sont dépouillés que par une fiction de droit." La Roque, *Le Traité de la noblesse*, 574.

[47]   Ibid., 160.

no trace of *roture* could be found in the past. Now, the fundamental stake really was the antiquity of nobility and the families' capacity to prove it. La Roque was proposing to his readers a compromise, which was largely followed, between an extreme vision of the political nobility and the vividness of the idea of race and antiquity.

But this compromise, which was equally borne out by the relative flexibility of the investigations which led to local negotiations, was a source of contradictions. Since the definition of nobility was henceforth controlled by the monarchy, and since the only possible ennoblement was the one conferred by the king, the question of noble essence was set with a great accuracy. This essence could only be the result of an *immémorialité* that the investigations into nobility precisely sought to uncover, and that they often succeeded in exposing as nonexistent. Therefore, social practice was of great importance, because it permanently put at stake the question of imprescriptibility. The trouble is that all the socio-political evolutions reinforced the contradictions of the Colbertian compromise by giving more and more weight to the antiquity and to the proof of nobility supplied by the king's genealogists. Loyseau's distinction between the *simple noblesse* and the nobility of dignity was not taken up by the royal power, which, on the contrary, asked for more and more proof of antiquity to accede to charges of dignity. From 1760 onwards, getting the honors of the court required one to prove one's noble line as far back as 1400 at least, without any principle known, which means without any trace of ennoblement, even if it was prior to this date.[48] And as regards the investigations into nobility, the trend was to ask for more and more proof. The d'Hoziers generally recognized the nobility of a family who was able to prove a little more than a hundred years of peaceful possession (of fiefs, mainly, and without any non-noble behavior). Later, in the 1740s, the families had to give proof from 1600 or so; and from the 1750s, the king's genealogists asked that peaceful possession, when it was not proved before 1560, should be ratified by an *arrêt de maintenue*. Louis-Nicolas-Hyacinthe Chérin even went on to consider that a trace of *roture* prior to the possession of noble qualifications annulled them, no matter how long they had been held. This rejection of all acquisitive prescription of nobility contrasted strongly with the common practice followed until then.[49]

---

[48]   François Bluche, *Les Honneurs de la Cour* (Paris: L'Intermédiaire des chercheurs et curieux, 1998).

[49]   Benoît Defauconpret, *Les Preuves de noblesse au XVIIIe siècle. La réaction aristocratique. Avec un recueil de tous les ordres, honneurs, fonctions, écoles, chapitres, réservés à la noblesse* (Paris: L'Intermédiaire des chercheurs et curieux, 1999).

This reinforcement of the lineage ideology and of the monarchical control on nobility had cultural,[50] but also social, consequences.[51] With the new definition of nobility and the great investigations, it was no longer possible for those who had been ennobled after 1560 to claim *immémorialité*; and whoever claimed it was enjoined to furnish his proof and was confronted with the "instability of his antiquity,"[52] since genealogical investigations precisely sought to detect traces of ennoblement. The system created resentment[53] at the time when the "culture of merit" prevailed,[54] and placed the king in a position to decide the contentious cases in a way that was convenient for him by the exercise of his grace.[55]

However, for jurists, the idea of imprescriptibility, linked to their conception of political nobility, was prevailing. For Louis Astruc, a law professor in Toulouse in the 1730s, the possible contradiction between the *noblesse de race* and the nobility conferred by the prince was eventually simple to solve:

> We have often said and repeated that there is no other nobility in France than that which comes from the King by express or tacit concession. What of, therefore, nobility of race and extraction, whose origins are hardly known and who carry no other proof than possession? The response is easy. Nobility of race and extraction do not constitute a type of nobility different than the other, because, in effect, it does not and cannot have any other origin than princely concession, which is always assumed. In consequence, it does not have anything over what we, properly

---

[50]   Jonathan Dewald, *Aristocratic Experience and the Origins of Modern Culture: France, 1570–1715* (Berkeley: University of California Press, 1993).

[51]   See also Marraud, this volume, who analyses the social consequences of monarchical control over hierarchy and nobility for the ennobled *bourgeois*, and the persistence of other social spaces and forms of domination.

[52]   The expression comes from François-Joseph Ruggiu, "Ancienneté familiale et construction de l'identité nobiliaire dans la France de la fin de l'Ancien Régime," in *La Noblesse de la fin du XVI*, t. I, 309–25.

[53]   For example, the case of Boulainvilliers is well known. See Harold A. Ellis, "Genealogy, History, and Aristocratic Reaction in Early Eighteenth-Century France: The Case of Henri de Boulainvilliers," *The Journal of Modern History*, 58 (1986), 414–51.

[54]   Jay M. Smith, *The Culture of Merit: Nobility, Royal Service, and the Making of Absolute Monarchy in France, 1600–1789* (Ann Arbor: University of Michigan Press, 1996). See also Sarah Maza, *The Myth of the French Bourgeoisie: An Essay on the Social Imaginary 1750–1850* (Cambridge, MA: Harvard University Press, 2003), 27–36.

[55]   According to Jean Nagle, of the thousand families given honors of the court, half were without regular proof and had only the king's agreement. *Luxe et charité. Le faubourg Saint-Germain et l'argent* (Paris: Perrin, 1994), 109.

speaking, call concessions, except that its origins are older and in public opinion it is more esteemed than the other.[56]

The *noblesse de race* was thus referred to opinion, even if the author added that this opinion was found in all the nations where nobility was recognized. Astruc drew the obvious conclusion:

> Possession, no matter how long, is less a title of nobility than a presumption. Possession since time immemorial withstands investigation, but be careful to not discover imperfect origins, because if imperfection is discovered, presumption ends and possession is regarded as an usurpation. In effect, it is an uncontestable principle that personal nobility is imprescriptible ...[57]

According to Astruc, the imprescriptibility of nobility was certain, and the presumption of race always susceptible to be questioned: nobility was definitely entered in the era of suspicion.

Yet, in practice, even Chérin, who argued on the imprescriptibility of nobility,[58] had to admit that the legislation declared that the possession of noble qualifications over a century was sufficient to recognize the nobility of a family.

---

[56] "Nous avons dit et souvent repeté qu'il n'y a d'autre noblesse en France que celle qui emane du Roy par concession expresse ou tacite. Qu'est-ce donc, dira-on, que la noblesse de race et d'extraction, dont on ne recouvre point l'origine et dont on ne peut rapporter d'autre preuve que la possession? La réponse est aisée, la noblesse de race et d'extraction ne constitue pas une espece de noblesse differente de l'autre, parce que en effet elle n'a et ne peut avoir eu d'autre origine que la concession du prince, laquelle est toujours présumée, elle n'a par consequent d'autre avantage sur celle que nous appellons de concession proprement dite, qu'en ce que son origine est plus eloignée, et que dans l'opinion du public elle est plus estimée que l'autre." Louis Astruc, *Instituts de Justinien conférés avec le droit françois par noble Louis Astruc, professeur en droit françois de l'Université de Toulouse tome 1*. This is a legal lesson, probably published from notes of students. Pierre Bonin has produced an annotated edition of it: "Construire un cours de droit français: le manuscrit de Louis Astruc, Toulouse, C. 1737–1738," in *Histoire de l'enseignement du droit à Toulouse*, ed. Olivier Devaux (Toulouse: Presses de l'Université des Sciences sociales de Toulouse, 2007), 217–310. The quotation is on 285.

[57] "... la possession, quelque longue qu'elle soit, est moins un titre de noblesse qu'une présomption de titre; la possession immémoriale met à l'abry de toute recherche, mais bien entendu qu'on ne decouvre pas le vice de l'origine, car si le vice est decouvert la presomption cesse et la possession n'est plus alors regardée que comme une usurpation. C'est en effet un principe incontestable que la noblesse des personnes est imprescriptible ... ." Ibid., 287.

[58] Louis-Nicolas-Hyacinthe Chérin, *Abrégé chronologique d'édits, déclarations, règlements, arrêts & lettres patentes des Rois de France de la troisième race, concernant le fait de noblesse précédé d'un discours sur l'origine de la noblesse ses différentes espèces, ses droits &*

That led him to lament on usurpations, which he said were innumerable, and to seek beyond the required 100 years any unjustified ennoblement in the families whose proof he had to check. But how to conciliate imprescriptibility with the researches of titles proving nobility, and with royal ennoblement? Chérin's intellectual solution can be seen when he treats the question of *dérogeance*. The problem was to know if *lettres de relief* could be given when *dérogeance* exceeded three generations. The genealogist asserted three principles. First, that nobility was a right of sovereignty, and thus was imprescriptible. Second, that nobility also was imprescriptible as regards the rights of blood, which were as strong as those of sovereignty. Third, that the granted nobility "is actually the only one that can finish as it began."[59] Surprisingly, Chérin asserted imprescriptibility both of the *noblesse de race* and of political nobility, which was contrary to the rest of his book. Indeed, at the beginning of his work, Chérin specified that there was no natural inequality between men, and that any inequality was anchored in history. As for inequality in the kingdom of France, it was linked with the military function of the Franks—that is with the king's service—at the beginning of the monarchy. Besides, a little further in his text, he asserted: "nobility is a distinction of the state necessary for the constitution of the realm,"[60] and he quoted Montesquieu to sustain his words. Chérin did not take part in the debate that opposed the Germanists and the Romanists regarding the origins of nobility,[61] but he seemed to hold both views at the same time, without trying to hide their contradictions. It is possible, in fact, that Chérin intentionally demonstrated these contradictions in order to reveal the impossible foundations of nobility.

Conclusion

Jurists' and theoreticians of nobility's hesitations on the question of the imprescriptibility of nobility during the Ancien Régime have to be understood as the result of a fundamental tension in the very definition of French nobility: tension between the idea that it came only from the king and the idea that it was natural and transmitted through the bloodline. Those two ideas functioned

---

prérogatives la manière d'en dresser les preuves & les causes de sa décadence [1788] (reprinted Versailles: Mémoires et documents, 2002), 11.

    [59]   Ibid., 12.

    [60]   "La noblesse est une distinction d'Etat nécessaire à la constitution du Royaume." Ibid., 14.

    [61]   On this debate, see Harold A. Ellis, *Boulainvilliers and the French Monarchy: Aristocratic Politics in Early Eighteenth-Century France* (Ithaca, NY: Cornell University Press, 1988).

together, but their combination was modified during the early modern period, which reconfigured the very definition of the second order.[62] In this process, the investigations and the proof required by the monarchy to delimit the borders of the second order, on a demand that originally came from nobles themselves, played an essential role. The monarchy and the second order were both agents of these changes, which could be seen as a modernization of the legal system. However, the purposes they had were not the same (and were also different within these pluralistic groups), and the ideas which supported their purposes were not those of a rationalization, but the old ideas of blood and service.[63]

Similar to Pierre Guyot's quote at the beginning of this chapter, Gilles-André de La Roque remarked that this fundamental question of the prescription of nobility was not resolved. But it could not be without challenging the compromise on which the Colbertian definition of nobility was based. This compromise guaranteed both monarchical control on the second order and the ideology of race, which was so important in noble views. Leaving this question unsolved was, after all, allowing the king to decide about the cases that came up, through his courts or his council. Thus, it was supporting the flexibility of the social and political game, while promoting the idea of a strictly royal nobility of service. But it was also founding a system on tension that became more acute as the guarantees given by the monarchy to the ideology of antiquity were reinforced, just when the changing noble sociology did not correspond to this representation anymore. The social contradiction that resulted from this debate was a source of conflicts, misunderstandings, and resentment among the nobility.

---

[62]   The reforms of nobility and the debates over its definition in France should be compared to those in Spain: see Gaston, this volume.

[63]   For another example of the complexity of the positions taken by the social and the political groups vis-à-vis what historians usually call "modernization," see Lukowski, this volume. The will to reform was real in a part of the Polish nobility, and the main other part, which was hostile to it, could quote Rousseau to justify its views! Moreover, like in Poland, the French monarchical reforms never put in danger the social domination of nobility as a whole. The conflicts about the limits of the second order disqualified some families, but they did not challenge nobility itself as the elite of the kingdom.

Chapter 9

All the King's Men:
Educational Reform and Nobility in Early Seventeenth-Century Spain

Ryan Gaston

As the month of March turned to April in 1621, the Spanish monarchy, once the most powerful state in Europe, changed rulers. On the last day of March, Philip III succumbed to illness, putting Spain in a state of mourning and placing control of the monarchy in the hands of his 16-year-old son. Sadness for the loss of a king, however, mixed with hope that the crowning of a new ruler might bring a brighter future. Since Philip III's ascent to the throne in 1598, Spanish authors and officials had grown increasingly concerned with what appeared to them as a loss in Spain's power. They lamented waning agriculture and population, and took intermittent military and commercial successes as indicators of decline. A fear of the eventual collapse of the monarchy permeated political writings, but as Philip IV took the throne (ruling from 1621 to 1665) these anxieties were allayed in part by a widespread belief in the ability to reform Spain. Reform efforts began less than a week into Philip IV's reign and continued with varied intensity throughout the next two decades, earning this young ruler the moniker the "Reformer King."

In addition to an array of financial, fiscal, and military reform strategies, Philip IV and his ministers—most specifically his closest advisor (*privado* or *valido*), the Count-Duke of Olivares—turned their attention to educational reform, especially of Spain's nobility. What made nobles the primary focus of these reform efforts was their role as the natural leaders of Spanish society. Traditionally nobles had served the monarchy as government officials and military officers. The king, Olivares, and many other officials alleged that nobles had begun to neglect these duties, paying closer attention to their own needs than those of the monarchy. The once industrious and honorable behavior of the nobles, lamented Olivares, had turned to "a lack of obedience and tepid love [for Spain] and an obsession with one's own ends."[1] By educating the children of Spain's nobles and imparting knowledge, skills, and a greater sense of duty, the monarchy and its officials hoped to stave off the threat of decline.

In order to effect these changes, the monarchy would have to compete with nobles' allegiance to their families. Being a noble in early modern Spain called for commitment to both family and crown. In addition to filling crucial offices for the monarchy, a good nobleman sought out honors at court and other ways to advance family name and reputation. Family interests consistently influenced his actions and decisions. Service to family and the monarchy were not incompatible, but for a government that feared its impending collapse, the priority of these obligations was clear: the conservation of the monarchy should be the first concern of the nobles. In an effort to secure the loyalty and service of the nobility, Philip IV and royal officials would wage an educational campaign for nearly 20 years, skillfully navigating the contentious notion of nobility. These educational reforms, as this chapter will show, stressed service to the crown as the key tenet of nobility, plotting duty to the king against prominent noble concerns with legacy and lineage. Through these programs the king and his ministers made nobility itself a contested space.

The early modern understanding of nobility was complicated and contentious. The nobility was a social rank comprised of a complex hierarchy of titled and non-titled subjects, who perpetuated those titles and that social group by carrying on their lineage. The new generations of each noble family inherited the titles earned by their ancestors. At the same time, nobility had long been considered a distinguished trait or set of traits, which became manifest through deeds done in the service of the king or for the public good. Such noble qualities served as impetus for the ruler to grant a title of nobility to a valorous man, and thus to his family in perpetuity. Debates in the era considered which of these two elements reflected the true source of nobility. Those writing on the topic in France placed a growing emphasis on nobility

---

[1]   This chapter was presented at the Early Modern and Latin American Seminars at the Hall Center for the Humanities on the campus of the University of Kansas in December 2009. It has benefited from the comments of the directors of the Early Modern Seminar, Luis Corteguera and Patricia Manning, as well as continued readings by Marta Vicente and my wife, Emily Gaston.

This statement appears in a September 1632 letter from the Count-Duke of Olivares to the Cardinal-Infante Fernando, the brother of Philip IV. See Document XI in *Memoriales y Cartas del Conde Duque de Olivares*, Tomo II, eds John Elliott and José de la Peña (Madrid: Editoriales Alfaguara, 1978), 75.

through birth, intending to quash or rein in the independent actions of nobles.[2] These same questions of family and public service were woven deeply into the Spanish understanding of nobility, but Spanish authors, perhaps influenced by a sense of crisis, took a slightly different view.

In his *Discourse on the Spanish Nobility* (1622), Bernabé Moreno de Vargas recognized the importance of both family and service to the concept of nobility. However, his analysis of this relationship stressed action over heredity. Moreno argued repeatedly that nobility was a natural trait that manifested itself in one's actions. "Those that possess natural and true nobility," Moreno maintained, "have it in their very spirit [*ánimo*]."[3] This meant that anyone with these traits could become a noble if recognized by the king as a noble due to their honorable deeds. The titles and honors that marked members of the nobility, the author diligently reminded his readers, were merely acknowledgments of these natural traits and their expression through service; they marked society's leaders, but they did not comprise nobility. Subsequent generations received these same titles, but did not necessarily possess the same noble spirit as their ancestors, who had earned these admirable distinctions from their rulers.

With these qualifications in mind, Moreno reluctantly admitted that the legitimate inheritance of noble titles was also a "natural" form of nobility. But quickly quelling the notion that lineage was more important than service, he clarified, "That which is natural is the familial bond, bloodline or ancestry, and not the nobility." Again, this was because Moreno viewed the inheritance of noble titles as less "effective" than the noble qualities with which some were born. Many of the nobles inheriting titles and honors did not possess the truly noble qualities of their ancestors. Despite this difference, the author claimed, people frequently conflated these natural and hereditary forms of nobility. For him, true nobility was an inclination toward and execution of service to king and kingdom, but he recognized that the antiquity of noble families garnered great respect in Spanish society.[4]

The notion that nobles owed allegiance to both king and family appears throughout early modern Spanish society. One has only to look at the life of Olivares for proof. Although known for serving as the king's *privado*, much of his life was shaped by family interests. Olivares abandoned studies at the University of Salamanca and an ecclesiastical career to go to Valladolid, then

---

[2]   Ellery Schalk, *From Valor to Pedigree: Ideas of Nobility in France in the Sixteenth and Seventeenth Centuries* (Princeton: Princeton University Press, 1986). For more on this debate, see Haddad, this volume.

[3]   Bernabé Moreno de Vargas, *Discursos de la nobleza de España* (Madrid: Viuda de Alonso Martín, 1622), 9r, 13v.

[4]   Ibid., 13r–v, 48r.

the site of Philip III's court. Called there after the death of his older brother, his father wanted him to seek honors and rewards (*mercedes*) in order to advance the family name and reputation. The same quest for social status had also underpinned Olivares' arranged marriage with his cousin, Doña Inés Zúñiga y Velasco, a strategic marriage that strengthened the alliance of these two houses. After being relieved of office as the *privado* to Philip IV in 1643, Olivares worried that his dismissal meant that he had failed his family, tarnishing the reputation of his ancestors.[5] His worries reflected the guidance given in a debate published in Madrid in the 1630s. It reminded its readers that a proper nobleman not only dedicated himself loyally to his king but also remained always "advantageous to his family" [*provechoso a su familia*].[6]

This debate, set for discussion at the Imperial College (*Colegio Imperial*) in Madrid, offered a perspective absent from Moreno's work. It maintained that noble behaviors could be learned. Less condemning of hereditary nobles than Moreno, the unknown authors of the debate—alleged to be government ministers—made the following statement: "Nature gives nobility, and for the virtue of the heir to a noble title there are ways of teaching him the 'what,' and 'when,' and the 'where' that a noble should know."[7] Once again, these authors attributed nobility to a natural root, but as they termed it later, this was only a "remote foundation." Lacking inherent noble traits, the heir of a noble title could "cultivate" (*grangear*) his nobility by learning how to carry out noble tasks and serving the king.[8]

Requisite training, they clarified, included either military drilling or formal schooling. For the sons of nobles seeking a military career, they encouraged travel and gaining experience by joining the king's armies. The authors exempted only the first-born sons of Spain's titled nobles from either travel or rigorous studies, excepting of course that the king requested them to represent him abroad. Family was important, but as these authors saw it, service was the top priority. This publication presented some of the re-emerging and debated strategies for noble education, arguing for example the virtues of practical learning over theory. The monarchy embraced some of these pedagogical tactics in its own educational reforms. More importantly, its reforms also reflected an awareness of the contentious division in the lives of nobles between public service and duty

---

[5] John Huxtable Elliott, *Count-Duke of Olivares: The Statesman in an Age of Decline* (New Haven: Yale University Press, 1986), 18–19.

[6] Agustín Castro, "Conclusiones políticas ... defendiéndose en los Reales Estudios de Colegio Imperial de la Compañía de Jesús." (Madrid) Biblioteca Nacional de España (BNE), VE/12/5.

[7] Ibid.

[8] Ibid.

to family. As they crafted their educational programs, the monarchy followed one key principle offered by Moreno and his cohort: service was the true essence of nobility.[9]

Less than three years after the start of Philip IV's reign, the king and the Count-Duke of Olivares put into action a plan to start a school of "general studies" in Madrid. In early 1624, the king and his *privado* sent a letter to Rome to the administration of the Society of Jesus, better known as the Jesuits. Aware of the successful establishment of Jesuit schools throughout the European continent and in the New World, Philip IV and Olivares hoped that the Society would direct the new school. The Jesuits eventually agreed, and with the designation of Madrid's *Colegio Imperial* as the site for the new institution, the "Reales Estudios" took a few steps closer to becoming a reality.[10]

Over the next few years, the monarchy and the Jesuits hashed out details about the Reales Estudios. Funding would come from taxes levied in the Indies as well as from the so-called "chest of the dead" (*caja de difuntos*), a collection of state-owned possessions left by those who died intestate.[11] At this time, Father Aguado, the provincial of the Society and the confessor of Olivares, sought out candidates for the school's 23 teaching chairs. Presumably due to connections between funding and taxes from the Indies, the president of the Council of the Indies, Juan de Villela, received the post of superintendent of the school.

On 23 January 1625, Villela finished an official plan for and description of the school. This plan became public the following year, but only in an effort to placate the complaints of the local Castilian universities, who had heard rumors about the new school.[12] In his plan, Villela explains the motivations behind its creation. According to the author:

> Although there is great interest in extending education to common people, it is much more important that education not be lacking among the children of princes and nobles because as they are the most principal part of the Republic; with good or bad customs this group will forcibly drag along the rest of society, and with the passage of time, control of the government and administration of the Kingdom will eventually rest in their hands before they are rid of the vices they developed as children.[13]

---

[9]   Ibid.

[10]   José Simón Díaz, *Historia del Colegio Imperial de Madrid*, 2nd edn (Madrid: Instituto de Estudios Madrileños, 1992), 149.

[11]   Ibid., 156.

[12]   Ibid., 149, 157.

[13]   This study uses a reprint of the 1625 plan, which appears in a publication defending the school against attacks by the universities of Salamanca and Alacalá de Henares. See page

The Reales Estudios would educate young nobles and mold them into the next generation of leaders—*cabezas*—who would govern the Spanish state. As the natural leaders of their people, nobles were expected to serve in this role. Thus, Villela justified the school on grounds of saving and cultivating the "superior potential of their souls."[14]

Although Villela failed to mention it directly, the service of nobles also included duty as officers in the military. This responsibility did not escape the founders of the school. The lower divisions of the curriculum consisted of liberal arts courses, including studies in ancient languages and philosophies. The school's upper division continued liberal studies but added courses in mathematics, astronomy, hydraulics, and geometry. Supplemented by lessons on building fortifications, the curriculum reflected the monarchy's desire to teach young nobles the art of seafaring and give them greater technical and tactical knowledge of warfare.[15]

The exclusion of non-noble Spaniards from the new school aligned with other educational reforms of the 1620s. The earliest educational reforms of Philip IV's rule sought to conserve the monarchy by having men fulfill jobs commensurate with their social station. Thus in February 1623, Junta Grande de Reformación, a special committee directed by the Count-Duke of Olivares for the restoration of social order and general reform of conduct in Castile, sought to reduce the number of grammar schools in Spain to one school in each of its largest cities. The committee argued that common Spaniards had fruitlessly invested in education, distracting them from "other occupations and positions that were more useful to them and the Republic."[16] Orphanages and charitable hospitals should abandon lessons in grammar. Administrators and caretakers should instead direct their young charges toward other forms of training, particularly that of becoming sailors "for which they would be very useful given the lack of sea captains in these kingdoms."[17] A 1627 order from Philip IV to Spain's major cities made similar attempts. Based on a memorandum (*memorial*)

1v of the document titled "Por los Reales Estudios que el Rey Nuestro Señor ha fundado en el Colegio Imperial de la Compañía de Jesús de Madrid," in Archivo General de Simancas (AGS), Gracia y Justicia 972.

[14]   Ibid., 2r.

[15]   Ibid., 3r, 6v. Similar curricula also appeared in French military academies of the era; see Jonathan Dewald, *Aristocratic Experience and the Origins of Modern Culture: France, 1570–1715* (Los Angeles: University of California Press, 1993), 54.

[16]   Ángel González Palencia, *La Junta de Reformación: Documentos procedentes del Archivo Histórico Nacional y del General de Simancas, 1618–1625* (Valladolid: Academia de Estudios Histórico-Sociales de Valladolid, 1932), 452.

[17]   Ibid., 453.

by a noble from Palencia by the name of Andrés Gutiérrez de Haro, the order called for the formation of municipal boards that would tend to the care and professional training of Spain's growing population of orphans. These children could be treated for illnesses, clothed, and have their skills assessed. From there they could be assigned to a master to learn a trade. The effort, Gutiérrez assured his king, was worth "the fruit it is bound to bear."[18] If properly cared for and given basic training, these children could turn into a good, inexpensive form of labor, bolstering the workforce and improving Spain's economic situation. This was provided that these future apprentices focused on their careers and not on frivolous lessons in grammar or other such studies.[19]

By contrast, the failure to provide children—noble or non-noble—with the proper education or training left them vulnerable to vice and deprived the king of their service. Gutiérrez de Haro assured his ruler that the neglect of Spain's parentless children would result in their corruption. Rather than useful subjects contributing to the welfare of the kingdom, they would merely spread "sickness and vices, being a greater detriment than benefit to the Republic."[20] As seen above, Villela offered a similar assessment of noble children in this plan for the Reales Estudios. To reiterate his previous statement, he claimed that young nobles, "With good or bad customs ... will forcibly drag along the rest of society, and with the passage of time, control of the government and administration of the Kingdom will eventually rest in their hands before they are rid of the vices they developed as children." Like Gutiérrez, Villela noted the susceptibility of children to corruptive influences. He feared that young nobles would take their positions as the leaders of Spain guided by improper customs or habits (*costumbres*). Villela may have worried that nobles would be poor exemplars of virtue and conduct for the rest of Spanish society, but based on the latter portion of this statement, it seems most likely that his greatest concern lay with the inability of decadent nobles to properly guide the people. As he later pointed out, reforming profligate and corrupted nobles to make them suitable for government service would take a great deal of time, costing the king years of valuable service from these elite subjects or leading to countless errors by vice-ridden officials. Fearful of the impending collapse of the monarchy, reformers like Villela knew that the state could neither afford nor endure such mistakes or lapses in duty.[21]

---

[18]   Archivo Histórico Nacional (AHN), Osuna, legajo 3620, 25–1.

[19]   See document titled "Propuesta de don Andrés Gutiérrez de Haro, Caballero del Hábito de Calatrava, sobre la crianza y aplicación de los niños desamparados," in AHN, Osuna, legajo 3620, 25–2.

[20]   Ibid.

[21]   AGS, Gracia y Justicia 972, 2v.

The key to avoiding these undesirable behaviors and assuring greater service to the king was education. Only by teaching children from an early age could they be saved from an otherwise inevitable life of vice and sloth, and develop proper conduct and habits for the rest of their lives. The Jesuit and royal chronicler Juan de Mariana explained the role of education in his 1599 *De Rege et Regis Institutione*.[22] According to Mariana, children are pure by nature, but if not tended to while young they become ruined by vice as they age. He maintained that youthful attraction to the flesh and other pleasures always threatened to "invade" and corrupt the *ánimo* or *espíritu*, the spirit or soul of the child. Still impressionable, children internalized lessons, giving shape to a particular spirit and affecting conduct throughout their adult life. Well educated and endowed with a good spirit, these children would continue to fend off vice. Beginning this education early was crucial. "No matter the precepts given," Mariana claimed, "at no other age will people admit any outside change or reform."[23]

The 1620 novel *El Caballero Perfecto*, by Alonso Gerónimo de Salas Barbadillo, illustrates these principles clearly. The novel, which touts the virtuous effects of education, recounts the life of a nobleman referred to as Don Alonso. During his childhood, Don Alonso undergoes an education of both "military drill and studies" (*armas y letras*). In addition to practicing military arts, he gains theoretical knowledge for navigation and combat from mathematical studies. He completes his education with liberal arts lessons meant to instill in him virtue and good customs. Studies in disciplines such as history, which Salas Barbadillo divides into the fields of divine and secular history, provided Don Alonso with a better understanding of past societies as well as models of proper behavior. The result of this comprehensive education is the protagonist's "perfection of spirit" (*perfeción del ánimo*), a quality which makes him an invaluable servant to his king and helps him to fend off vice and temptation throughout his life. This is especially true when Don Alonso is faced with the death of his family. Salas Barbadillo comments, "possessing a wealthy estate, without parents or siblings, and with a free disposition [Don Alonso] could have given in unconditionally to vice, if he had not possessed in his spirit and understanding so many internal weapons with which to defend himself."[24] Despite a loss of guidance and a tremendous increase in wealth and power, the young noble is able to withstand the temptations that surround him as a result of his education. Without an

---

[22]   Mariana's text, created in Latin as an educational text for the new King Philip III, was translated to Spanish in 1981. The translation is used here. Juan de Mariana, *La Dignidad Real y la Educación del Rey* (Madrid: Centro de Estudios Constitucionales, 1981).

[23]   Ibid., 135, 179, and 208.

[24]   Salas Barbadillo, *El Caballero Perfecto*, ed. Pauline Marshall (Boulder: University of Colorado Press, 1949), 6, 9.

edifying education, such as that provided by the Reales Estudios, Villela feared that Spain's young nobles would not fare as well upon inheriting power or money.[25]

As seen earlier, the curriculum planned for the Reales Estudios had similar content and objectives to the studies completed by Salas Barbadillo's protagonist. The schedule for the Reales Estudios lacked practical lessons in military skills, but mirrored Don Alonso's education in most other areas. In addition to the training necessary for the formation of a good military officer, it also included similar studies in liberal arts disciplines and theology. The study of Scripture, supporters of the Reales Estudios pointed out, was a way to shape the customs and character of young men. Villela averred that lessons learned from the Bible could "mold" and "work" (*labrar* and *cultivar*) young nobles the same way that an artisan crafted a finished product or the farmer cultivated land. That is to say that these lessons yielded moral adults and dutiful subjects to serve the king.[26]

Toward the middle of his plan, Villela offered his readers an additional justification for forming the school. He felt the schooling of young nobles was insufficient. Most nobles received an education through private tutors.[27] To Villela, tutors could provide only an incomplete education. Unlike public schools, which offered a variety of classes taught by specialists in each field, tutors had a limited scope of subjects they could teach. He added that students taught by tutors lacked motivation to succeed academically. After all, privately tutored pupils lacked the competition which pushed students to excel in public schools.[28]

Villela also argued that some noble parents even neglected their children's education entirely. He commented disapprovingly that noble parents "[did] not provide for or hope for anything more than for their sons to live in order to carry forward the antiquity of their families ... they conserve them by not engaging them in study or any other activity that might cause them pain or annoyance."[29] In particular, he meant that nobles refused to educate their first-born sons. By choosing not to educate their eldest sons, noble parents hoped to protect them from the obvious perils of military training as well as the strain of

---

[25]   AGS, Gracia y Justicia 972, 2r.

[26]   Ibid., 1v, 9r.

[27]   Richard Kagan, "Olivares y la Educación de la Nobleza Española," in *La España del Conde Duque de Olivares: Encuentro Internacional sobre la España del Conde Duque de Olivares celebrado en Toro los días 15–18 de septiembre de 1987*, eds John Elliott and Ángel García Sanz (Valladolid: Universidad de Valladolid, 1990), 232.

[28]   AGS, Gracia y Justicia 972, 2r.

[29]   Ibid., 1v.

rigorous studies, which were believed to have an unhealthy effect if pursued too vigorously.[30]

As Villela noted, nobles protected first-born sons because they represented the future and perpetuation of noble families. They inherited *mayorazgos*, or entails, which held the majority of the family fortune. They were also the children upon which the family depended for the continuation of the bloodline. Having an heir to carry on the family name and title meant more than leaving a legacy. The perpetuation of lineage, as Moreno de Vargas had clarified, was the basis for tremendous public esteem.[31] Motivated by these reasons to protect their eldest sons, noble parents withheld their children from a potentially perilous education.

Salas Barbadillo's novel *El Caballero Perfecto* lends credibility to Villela's claim. Because he is the second son in the family, Don Alonso receives what the author refers to as "a *mayorazgo* in a virtuous upbringing."[32] By this the author means to reference Don Alonso's comprehensive education, which stands in contrast to the true *mayorazgo* that his older brother, Luis, will inherit. While he provides a lengthy description of Don Alonso's education, Salas Barbadillo makes no mention of any formal schooling or military training for Luis. In fact, he shows the family's desire to shelter Luis, writing that the boys' parents and servants discourage Alonso from inviting his brother to hunt with him. Resisting this protection, Luis leaves to hunt on his own and, realizing his family's greatest fears, suffers a fatal fall from his horse. The author seems to allude to the dangers of noble education in his book, but he also traces the successful career of his protagonist as a soldier and statesman, elucidating the importance of education to the creation of a "perfect noble."[33]

Through his criticisms of neglectful parents, Villela hoped to make the same point. Priority should be placed on raising and training nobles to be loyal subjects, not on their isolation and protection as the primogenitures of their families. Endowed with a good education, the children of nobles could carry out their public duties, but without they would become useless to the monarchy and unable to serve the king in their traditional capacities. They could only serve to perpetuate their families, conserving their lineage but not the monarchy. Claiming that the self-interest of nobles had always caused problems for the monarchy, Villela firmly asserted "It is because of this that no well-governed

---

[30]   Stated somewhat vaguely, Juan de Mariana likens intensive study to, or perhaps equates it with, spending too little time in the sun and fresh air, without which he felt the student's body would physically degrade; see his *Dignidad Real*, 192–3.

[31]   Moreno, *Discursos*, 13r–v.

[32]   Salas Barbadillo, *Caballero Perfecto*, 5.

[33]   Ibid., 5–7.

republic has trusted the education of its children to the diligence and care of their parents; for this reason they invented public schools."[34]

With this statement, he laid bare the deep tensions between the expectations placed on noblemen by their kings and by their families. Villela's attempts to emphasize the importance of noble service not only dismissed the role of family, it also encroached upon parental authority. According to the era's authors, the education given to children was the prerogative of their parents. In his seventeenth-century text *Monarquía Perfecta*, Fray Juan Márquez protested the state's interference in disciplining children. It was the preserve of fathers or the tutors they hired to educate children and teach them right from wrong.[35] Gil González Dávila offered a similar view in his 1623 *Teatro de las Grandezas de la Villa de Madrid*, referring to the *Ayo*, or the private tutor to the prince, as "an extension of the authority of the father, in order to prepare, reform, mold, and correct the spirit and thoughts of [his child]."[36] Aggressive and paternalistic, Villela's statement attempted to subjugate parental prerogative to the monarchy's needs. It called for the unwavering loyalty and dedication to the king of both noblemen and their sons. If the monarchy was to survive, sons would have to become the military and government leaders they were born to be, and fathers would have to put aside their familial concerns, giving the king their sons to train for the good of the monarchy.

But while the monarchy and its agents deemphasized the importance of preserving noble lineage in the plan for the Reales Estudios, they may not have discounted entirely the needs of noble families. Proponents of the school may have intended to bolster the reputation of the Reales Estudios not only to bring it prestige but also to encourage nobles to enroll their sons in the new institution. As noted earlier, nobles sought opportunities to build their families' public honor and reputation. If it was not enticing enough for nobles to place their children in a school personally endowed and endorsed by the royal family, its creators surrounding the opening of the Reales Estudios with pomp that might tempt them to enroll their children. Attended by the king and queen, the inaugural ceremony appears to have included a reading of Lope de Vega's poem *Isagoge a los Reales Estudios* ("Preamble to the Reales Estudios") as well as a presentation from the students of the recently opened school. The latter was very well received, and its multiple performances granted the children of nobles the opportunity to impress the royals and the general public. Meanwhile, the former provided a further dimension of popular recognition for the school, as

---

[34]   AGS, Gracia y Justicia 972, 1v.

[35]   Juan Márquez, *El Gobernador Christiano* (Madrid: Teresa Junti, 1625), 65, 208–9.

[36]   Gil González Dávila, *Teatro de las Grandezas de la Villa de Madrid* (1623) (Valladolid: Maxtor, 2003), 321.

Lope de Vega was a highly celebrated literary figure in the era.[37] In both cases, the Reales Estudios provided nobles with a chance to affiliate themselves with the new institution and raise their families' public esteem.

The king's attempts to hire renowned scholars to teach at the school served similar purposes. Correspondence from the late 1620s relates the king's negotiations over the appointment of academic chairs. In 1628, Father Francisco Aguado and Philip IV communicated about who to hire for the remaining teaching positions. The king obdurately resisted Aguado's suggestions to hire certain instructors, holding out for the appointment of some of Europe's most prestigious, Jesuit scholars. When, in December 1628, the Jesuit administrator informed the monarch of the poor health of Juan de Matos, who held the chair in politics, the king responded, "I have to insist that Sirmond come to teach this course ... tell the Count-Duke what it will take so that I know and it gets done."[38] Philip IV certainly hoped to provide a top-shelf education for the pupils at the Reales Estudios. However, his demand for the Frenchman Jacques Sirmond, a renowned Jesuit professor of ecclesiastical history, was also a move to give the school noteworthiness.[39] In another December 1628 memorandum, the king again insisted that Aguado get Sirmond on faculty. "For as soon as that vine is planted," argued the king, "the resulting fruit will be extremely reputable for this foundation, to see the prime subjects from every land coming to serve in this school."[40] After all, Philip intended this school to be "the best in the world to be at and attend ... [a] seminary like none seen before by the world's most prominent men."[41] To be sure, the king was attuned to the effect that the school could have on his own reputation and on the political and military acuity of Spain's nobles. Yet it seems likely that he also hoped that the reputation of the Reales Estudios would entice nobles to enroll their sons, entrusting their formation to the state and permitting it to mold them into the statesmen and soldiers that Spain needed.

If this was the king's intention, it met with severely limited success. Within a few years of opening in 1629, the school's failure became evident. By 1634,

---

[37]   Simón Díaz, *Colegio Imperial*, 90–91.

[38]   See Philip IV's response to the 12 December 1628 memorial from Father Francisco Aguado in the packet titled "Habiendo propuesto al Rey Felipe Cuarto algunas personas aficionadas a las buenas letras muy grandes utilidades y conveniencias en que hubiese en Madrid unos estudios públicos." AGS, Gracia y Justicia 972, 21–2.

[39]   For more on Sirmond and the other scholars selected, see José Martínez de la Escalera. "Felipe IV: Fundador de los Reales Estudios," in *Anales del Instituto de Estudios Madrileños*, t. XXIII (Madrid: Consejo Superior de Investigaciones Científicas, 1986), 175–97.

[40]   AGS, Gracia y Justicia 972, 22.

[41]   Ibid., 28–9.

attendance was as low as 60 students in the school's upper division. The school had mustered neither the number of students nor the kind of social status the king had desired. The protests of the universities may have dulled its luster.[42] Concerned with their own loss of power and reputation, the universities of Salamanca and Alcalá de Henares had waged a vicious campaign against the school before it even opened, publishing criticisms late in 1626 and early the next year.[43]

But with the enrollment of nobles in certain universities on the rise during this time, the lack of students enrolled in the Reales Estudios certainly also reflected recalcitrance among nobles.[44] Quite simply, noblemen may have sought to educate their children and operate their families as they saw fit. The monarchy was asking for great sacrifice. It was not enough for noble families to devote their younger sons to the king's service. Villela and other representatives of Philip IV were asking for nobles to contribute all of their sons, risking the very extinction of their lineage. This was apparently a sacrifice they were unwilling to make.

Eventually, government support for the project began to dry up. In 1634, the Royal Council of Castile suggested closing the Reales Estudios.[45] This reform was clearly faltering, but before the school had closed its doors, the Count-Duke of Olivares had begun to put together another educational program. The new plan consisted of a peninsula-wide educational system and a series of public exams by which students gained admission to an elite military academy and trained to become royal pages.[46] In 1632 and again in 1635, Olivares, who was no novice to advising on matters of education, produced memoranda supporting and describing the network of schools.[47]

This new educational program started with early education and tended to its pupils well into their twenties. The plan consisted of four stages. The first three focused on formal schooling and corresponded fairly closely with Spain's existing educational divisions.[48] The first stage targeted the development of children three to five years of age. Like most early education, it focused on

---

[42] Elliott, *Count-Duke*, 188.

[43] Simón Díaz, *Colegio Imperial*, 158.

[44] Kagan, *Nobleza*, 235.

[45] Ibid., 228.

[46] AHN, Consejos, 50113.

[47] Olivares played at least a nominal role in the formation of the Reales Estudios. Kagan also offers evidence of Olivares' efforts to write a curriculum in 1624 for his 12-year-old brother-in-law, the Marqués de Toral. Kagan, *Nobleza*, 227.

[48] For more on the stages of education in early modern Spain, see Richard Kagan, *Students and Society in Early Modern Spain* (Baltimore, MD: Johns Hopkins University Press, 1974).

basic literacy and church teachings, hoping to influence the spirit and habits of children. The second phase included students aged six to 14, the ages of students attending grammar schools, or *colegios*. This stage included lessons in writing and mathematics. Olivares also expected students to obtain reading proficiency in Latin during this stage. For the first 14 years, or during these initial two stages, students could receive their education from local educators or clergy in preparation for entrance to an academy. Municipal leaders, diocesan clergy, or figures such as the Royal Chaplain, for those living in Madrid, could test students and vouch for the quality of their education. Students wanting to enter into the "pages' academy"—as Olivares had termed it—had to receive certification for each completed level. At the age of 14, students could opt to enter vocational training or the universities as desired, or they could apply to enter one of the academies. At this point, they entered the third stage of Olivares' plan.

Planned for Madrid and a few other Spanish cities, the academies were the centerpiece of his program. Hosting students for a period of five years—beginning around the age of 14 and ending by the age of 20—the academies would teach students from a curriculum that included both academic and military exercises. Their goal was to form *pajes* and *meninos*. The former served as pages for the king and the latter tended to the queen and the rest of the royal family. Highly coveted for their prestige and placement in the king's inner circle, these positions had traditionally been the preserve of the nobility. As with the Reales Estudios, Olivares once again intended to train those who surrounded the king and reverse what he saw as a lack of service in government and military. Summing up the description of his program, Olivares boasted that the plan was neither impractical nor costly. It was, in his estimation, the perfect plan to "reestablish the nobility" (*recrecer a la nobleza*).[49]

His reasons for reforming the nobility differed little from those given by Villela in the plan for the Reales Estudios. Olivares cited the neglected education of young nobles as justification for enacting the proposal.[50] He expressed similar views in a letter written to the President of Castile, Miguel Santos de San Pedro, on 18 September 1632. "Few noblemen," complained Olivares, "the masters of minor and major households, deal with the study of the good letters that shine and prepare for any profession."[51] Asked to review Olivares' proposal by Philip IV in the summer of 1635, the *Junta de Educación* reached the same conclusion.[52]

---

[49]   This phrase appears in the plan for the academies in AHN, Consejos, 50113.

[50]   Ibid.

[51]   Elliott and Peña, *Memoriales*, Tomo 2, 81.

[52]   For more on their ordered review of Olivares' plans for the academies, see Juan Francisco Baltar Rodríguez, *Las Juntas de Gobierno de la Monarquía Hispánica (siglos XVI–XVII)* (Madrid: Centro de Estudios Políticos y Constitucionales, 1998), 426–8.

In their assessment, the education provided for the children of nobles was "short and careless."[53] Both called for the monarchy to act paternally and compensate for the neglectful nobles, who had failed to educate their children and deprived the monarchy of men trained to carry out traditional noble duties. "Without a good upbringing and education [*crianza*]," Olivares maintained in his proposal, "there are no good subjects, just as it is impossible to have the ideal people in the government, the state, and the military without a good education."[54]

Olivares and the members of the Junta de Educación felt confident that the academies could prepare young men to fulfill these roles successfully. The Junta anticipated that the proposed academies would "instruct the spirit for public and domestic governance."[55] This reference to gaining knowledge in "domestic governance" was most likely meant to accentuate the overall leadership qualities that pupils stood to gain. Throughout early modern Europe, the household was often conceived of as a scale model of the state. Placed in control of this idealized view, men were to order and rule the household with the same firmness and fairness as a good monarch would his people.[56] Since the ability to effectively govern a household mirrored the ability to govern a larger body of people it may have translated to better leadership in the minds of the Junta's members. This claim may also have reflected the need to govern one's self or control one's desires. Advocates of noble education writing in France at this time called for lessons in ethic and politics to teach young nobles how to govern themselves and others.[57] Proponents of the Reales Estudios had also promoted self-control and resistance to temptation as critical to greater focus and efficiency as a leader.

For Olivares, the development of these leadership qualities came not only from formal studies but also from travel, which he proposed students take after graduation as the fourth phase of the education. The son of the Spanish ambassador to Rome, Olivares' worldview had been forged in part by experiences abroad.[58] Consequently, he regarded highly the pedagogical value of experiences obtained outside the classroom. Olivares maintained that exposure to the lands inside and outside of Spain would help students build on the education they received in the academies. Embracing a belief expressed by many authors of the

---

53   AHN, Consejos, 50113.

54   Ibid.

55   Ibid.

56   For two brief reflections on this comparison, see Merry Wiesner, *Women and Gender in Early Modern Europe*, 2nd edn (New York: Cambridge University Press, 2000), 293; and Gisela Bock, *Women in European History* (Oxford: Blackwell, 2002), 27. Katherine Turner points out in this volume that these idealized images overlook the agency of women in the era.

57   Dewald, *Experience*, 58–60, 80.

58   Elliott, *Count-Duke*, 15.

era, Olivares felt a combination of travel and study would reveal to graduates the nature of certain people as well as the proclivities of mankind in general, facilitating their understanding of the people they would later govern.[59] The common behaviors and inclinations observed comprised a "political science" that could be applied by those in power.[60]

There was no doubt that the academies could remedy a shortage of "ideal people" in military positions. The curriculum for the academies reflected a substantial commitment to military training. In fact, this was its greatest difference from the Reales Estudios. Rather than relying solely on texts to educate students on military situations, Olivares focused his academies on military skills both "theoretical and practical," stressing physical activity much more than Villela had.[61]

The list of proposed exercises included a variety of activities meant to form an elite corps of physically and military trained young men. When not training, students should play games with a ball. Admitting a personal fondness for such activities, Olivares also clarified that passing recreational time in sport would strengthen students' bodies. Otherwise, students would practice riding horses and using a lance, as well as learn to fence and dance.[62] In a schedule drawn up by Olivares for the house of pages in 1639, he lists fencing and dancing courses, as well as their exams, adjacent to one another, suggesting perhaps a connection between dancing and developing footwork in fencing.[63] His insistence on teaching dancing also may have indicated a desire to groom pages for formal social interaction at court and temper their combat training. Dancing was part of the curricula in French academies for this very reason; courtly conduct promoted grace and self-control.[64] Whatever the reason, Olivares saw fencing and these other lessons as critical to the formation of the pages and of the Spanish nobility.

---

[59]   AHN, Consejos, 50113.

[60]   This call for a "political science" appears in the work of the Toledo Profesor of Theology, Sancho de Moncada. See his *Restauración Política de España* (1619), ed. Jean Vilar Berrogain (Madrid: Instituto de Estudios Fiscales, 1974), 229–30. For other examples of this view, see Baltasar Álamos de Barrientos, *Aforismos al Tácito Español* (1614) (Madrid: Centro de Estudios Constitucionales, 1987); and Antonio de Herrera, "Discurso y Tratado que la Felicísima Monarquía Castellana Fue Acrecentando su Imperio por los Mismos Modos que la República Romana," in *De las Varias Epístolas Discursos y Tratados de Antonio de Herrera* (Madrid, 1622).

[61]   See pages 97v–98r in the Count-Duke of Olivares' 1639 plan for the house of pages titled "Representación del Conde-Duque de Olivares hecha al Rey don Felipe IV sobre la educación de los caballeros pajes de SM," BNE mss 10994.

[62]   AHN, Consejos, 50113.

[63]   BNE mss 10994, 98r, 99r.

[64]   Schalk, *Valor*, 180.

In his 18 September 1632 letter to Santos de San Pedro, Olivares declared without the mastery of such skills "one cannot be a nobleman."[65]

Although it did not hash out the curriculum in the same detail as Olivares, the Junta de Educación imagined the academies having the same effect. They wrote the king that the academies could become a "university of cavalry," clearly reflecting a desire to craft a well-disciplined and martially spirited group of men that could carry out the traditional military roles of the nobility. The quest to "re-establish the nobility," it seems, meant the revival of a corps of battle-ready men prepared to serve the king and imbued with an active, martial spirit through rigorous physical training.[66]

Through his proposals, Olivares made clear that this increased emphasis on physical training and actual military drill was a response to Spain's involvement in the Thirty Years War.[67] Toward the end of the 1620s, Spain's initial success in the war had faded, and as the conflict progressed into the next decade, Spain faced new battlefronts and continued having difficulties in marshalling resources.[68] Undoubtedly frustrated by the turn of events, Olivares declared that Spain had lost its martial spirit. Of course, in his mind the most culpable were the nobles. He offered proof of their recent abandonment of duty. In the spring of 1633, the brother of the king, the Cardinal-Infante Ferdinand, received orders to lead Habsburg troops out of Italy and into the Netherlands. Reflecting on this assignment, Olivares sourly wrote that "With the passage of the king's brother *in person* to Flanders neither a single high-ranking nobleman nor gentleman [*caballero*] budged to accompany him, showing quite clearly the state to which the martial spirit of our people has been reduced as a result of neglect and disregard."[69] Through an education replete with military exercises, Olivares hoped to rekindle Spain's "inclination for military endeavors."[70] He also proposed another way to attract young men into the military.

Olivares offered an alternative to an education in the academies for those hoping to become pages. After reaching the age of 14 and completing the second phase of education, students could opt to serve in the king's army for five years instead of training in an academy. Undergoing evaluation by their superiors and receiving certification of this alternative form of education, these young men

---

[65]   Elliott and Peña, *Memoriales*, Tomo 2, 81.

[66]   AHN, Consejos, 50113.

[67]   Kagan, *Nobleza*, 231.

[68]   John Elliott, "Spain and the War," in *The Thirty Years' War*, 2nd edn, ed. Geoffrey Parker (New York: Routledge, 1997), 92–8.

[69]   AHN, Consejos, 50113.

[70]   Ibid.

could then petition to become pages.[71] This option corresponded to Olivares' view on experience as a critical part of education. Through their service in the military these young men would gain first-hand knowledge of combat, and introduced into the ranks of the court, they might later serve as advisors on military issues. A clever enticement, this alternative path would not only endow future leaders with military knowledge but also bolster the numbers of men serving the king in his armies.

For Olivares and the Junta de Educación, the academies seemed also to have diplomatic connotations. This too may have resulted from the tensions on the continent. With the king's troops overextended and notoriously underpaid, diplomacy might necessarily resolve some conflict, saving the monarchy some expense and preserving the lives of Spain's undermanned military. Olivares and the Junta alluded to this goal through repetitive admiration of the diplomacy prompted by military academies in France.[72] They pointed out that these academies not only drew the best students from France but also from Germany and Italy; the exchange had improved diplomatic relations between these countries. Perhaps anticipating similar results in Spain, the Junta saw the enrollment of foreign students in Spanish academies as an opportunity for them to "drink in the customs and affection for the people." "With good training," its members continued, "they will develop an affinity to and inclination toward [Spanish] things and lose the fear gained from looking at Spain from a distance."[73] The Junta believed that the academies could foster good rapport with neighboring lands and even win their allegiance.[74] Perhaps endearing the future generations of foreign lands to Spain and its people might decrease their military obligations, a trouble which had consistently plagued the Spanish Habsburgs.

While the shift toward diplomacy was a new addition to the educational reforms, Olivares proposed another significant change from the program implemented in the Reales Estudios. He proposed to open his entire network of schools to children of all social strata. His academies, Olivares boasted, would give "a path to anything, for anyone."[75] One would earn admission to the academies and appointment to the esteemed position of page based solely on merit.

---

[71]   Ibid.

[72]   Ibid.

[73]   Ibid.

[74]   Some French authors believed that studying in France maintained cultural identity and allegiance. Studying in Italy, where many academies had been established, taught young nobles the perspectives of and loyalty to Italy and Spain. Schalk, *Valor*, 184, 189–90.

[75]   AHN, Consejos, 50113.

It should be understood that Olivares was not seeking to overturn the established social order. In fact, he claimed that his educational plan would not offend subjects of any social class. This claim was debatable, but his stated plans made clear that he did not intend to introduce a great number of non-nobles into these prestigious positions. Olivares remained certain that the rigorous curriculum leading into the academies would separate the wheat from the chaff. Non-noble children living in rural areas would never have to sever ties with the farm. With a school in close proximity, he imagined they could conduct their early studies "without the hoe leaving their hand." In the instance that they failed to advance to an academy, these students could undertake an agricultural or artisanal career. They would be none the worse for their experience, returning to cultivating the land but having been taught better customs and given a primary education.[76]

Olivares had many possible motivations for this decision. It has been suggested that he intended to put haughty nobles in their place.[77] Truly, his relationship with Spain's highest-ranking nobles was tense. Olivares had taken steps to remind them of their subordination to him and the king in a reform order, which clarified the hierarchy of titles at court and the proper titles by which noble courtiers should be addressed.[78] It is quite possible that this struggle for power may have crossed the *privado*'s mind, but it is most likely that he intended his programs to improve the quality of military and government leaders and revive the nobility by infusing it with loyal subjects committed to serving the monarchy. This had been the impulse behind the efforts to start the Reales Estudios, and was an urge that could only have grown stronger with the reversal of fortunes in the Thirty Years War.

It is also probable that Olivares intended to incite competition within the nobility. He was certainly mindful of the benefits such competition could bring to Spain. In his 1624 *Gran Memorial* (Great Memorandum) he had encouraged Philip IV to foster a competitive environment among Spain's notables and to rely on what he termed "emulation" (*emulación*). This is to say that by offering opportunities for service and honors to lower-ranking nobles, the monarchy would prompt them to compete with their social superiors for honors and esteem and to fulfill the political and military roles needed by the king.[79] It seems that Olivares' plan for the academies once again counted on social competition to restore the nobility's sense of service to the king. He recognized the tremendous

---

[76]   Ibid.

[77]   Kagan, *Nobleza*, 231.

[78]   This reform was a repetition of an order issued in 1611. See González Palencia, *La Junta de Reformación*, 434–40.

[79]   Elliott and Peña, *Memoriales*, Tomo 1, 61.

social promotion he was offering non-nobles, and claimed that their inclusion in a social circle traditionally preserved for nobles would have the "greatest effect and public benefit."[80]

In his plan for the academies, Olivares made clear his belief that Spain's nobility had lost its motivation and loyalty to the crown. He claimed that nobles sought prestige only through the actions of their ancestors. To use his words, audacious nobles felt as if with "the greatest vice, the loosest lifestyle and most repugnant behavior they can obtain the highest rewards and request them only to complain if they do not receive them."[81] Turning to a merit-based system would hopefully reverse these trends. Awards and offices would regain their value, motivating men—noble or common—to serve the king in order to receive these honors.

The Junta de Educación agreed with this view. Its members complained that many honors were being given to undeserving recipients, stripping these rewards of their true significance and depriving the monarchy of the brave actions which merited reward. In their estimation, this was especially true of the habits awarded as recognition in one of Spain's prestigious military orders. The Junta argued that they no longer represented military prowess and service as they had in past eras. Now entrance to the military orders was being granted indiscriminately. Even the daughters of deceased officials, the Junta complained, received habits, offering these titles to suitors as part of their dowries.[82] Members of the Junta saw the need to restore the true meaning of Spain's honors in order to stimulate virtuous service to the monarchy. To solve this problem, they delved into Spain's ancient past and its shared history with the Roman Empire, proposing the revival of the "knighthood of the band" (*Caballería de la banda*). Its members would consist of military heroes, who would be distinguished by a gold collar that only they would be allowed to wear. By resurrecting this honor, the king would not have to remove unmerited members of the military orders, but could elevate an elite class of warriors above those wearing the habit of one of the orders. The urge to belong to such an elite group could reignite the martial spirit that had brought Spain to the same imperial heights as its Roman predecessor.[83]

In their writings on the academies, Olivares and the Junta de Educación even called into question blood purity (*limpieza de sangre*) as a determining factor for some honors. As with opening the academies to Spaniards of all social ranks, these discussions shook one of the foundations of noble superiority. In most cases, having "pure" blood meant that one could prove that his or her lineage

---

[80]   AHN, Consejos, 50113.

[81]   Ibid.

[82]   Ibid.

[83]   Ibid.

consisted for several generations of only Christians. In some instances, this was also extended to questions of non-Spanish heritage. Having pure blood was a distinction enjoyed by the nobility. As one author of the era put it, those with nobility always had pure blood, but the reverse was not always true.[84] Because many of the era's prestigious institutions and organizations accepted members only if they could prove the purity of their blood, nobles became the nearly exclusive recipients of certain honors and awards. Deviating from these traditions, Olivares and the Junta proposed that habits for the military orders be given automatically to soldiers serving in an active war for 16 to 20 years, regardless of the candidate's *limpieza*.[85] This proposal not only stripped nobles of an elevating social distinction but, as with the decision to open the academies to all Spaniards, it also privileged service and merit over considerations of lineage.

In this regard, the plans drawn up by Olivares and the Junta de Educación for the academies paralleled the educational reforms of the previous decade. Subtle differences distinguished them, but the principles that guided them were the same. The plans for the Reales Estudios had prioritized noblemen's obligations to family below their duty to their king. Olivares' program targeted noble families in a slightly different way. With merit as the sole source of promotion, lineage and blood purity, two of the nobility's preserves, became increasingly irrelevant. Young nobles could no longer depend on heritage and inheritance to gain public esteem. It was up to them to establish their name and advance family reputation by performing honorable deeds to the benefit of king and kingdom. Even with these subtle differences, the educational reforms emphasized service as the basis for the nobility and relegated issues of lineage and family to a position of near insignificance. All that mattered was the conservation of the Spanish monarchy, which in their minds was predicated on service to the king.

The educational reforms of these two decades also sought similarly to restore Spain's nobility and fulfill the much needed roles traditionally held by nobles. Again, there were shifts in policy over the two decades. While proponents of the Reales Estudios turned to existing nobles to carry out their natural roles in society, Olivares and his cohort considered the possibility of talented non-nobles holding posts and honors commonly granted to nobles. Indeed, Olivares made no mention of granting titles of nobility to meritorious non-nobles, but implied in his plan was the view expressed the previous decade by Moreno de Vargas. The plans for the academy allowed for anyone to show their inherent noble qualities and to strive for the honors that distinguished nobles. Valued for

---

[84]   Castro, "Conclusiones."

[85]   AHN, Consejos, 50113.

their ability and their service to the monarchy, those of humble origin selected to become pages would be part of the "re-established nobility."

The educational programs studied here give us only a glimpse into the contested space of nobility in early modern Spain; much is left to be discovered. As Susannah Humble Ferreira has shown, the educational policies of early sixteenth-century Portugal resemble the programs created by Philip IV and his ministers. Did the Spanish monarchy also intend to bring order to an unruly court the way that Manuel I had done in the previous century by mandating that courtiers receive an education before considering them for a post at court?[86] M. Safa Saraçoğlu also points out that nobles in the nineteenth-century Ottoman Empire found ways to preserve their power in spite of attempts by the central government to usurp it.[87] The response of nobles to the Reales Estudios reflects similar resistance, but with the perspective of nobles largely absent from the monarchy's educational proposals, the exact steps Spanish nobles took to protect their threatened interests remain undiscovered. Only with further investigations into the contentious idea of nobility in early modern Spain will the actions and intentions of all the king's men become clear.

---

[86] See Humble Ferreira, this volume.
[87] See Saraçoğlu, this volume.

Chapter 10

"Of polish'd pillars, or a roofe of gold": Authority and Affluence in the English Country-House Poem

Sukanya Dasgupta

In Shakespeare's *King Henry IV, Part II* (1598), Lord Bardolph describes to Hastings, the process of building a house:

> When we mean to build,
> We first survey the plot, then draw the model;
> And when we see the figure of the house,
> Then must we rate the cost of the erection.[1]

This chapter will focus on one strategy used by the English nobility in the seventeenth century to assert their authority, affluence, and legitimacy: the commissioning and building of country houses. The kind of painstaking effort and expenditure that went into the building of a house and is described by Bardolph in Shakespeare's text suggests the symbolic importance that was invested in a country house in early modern England.

Katherine Turner has argued how the Florentine nobility used the "Medicean strategy" of establishing the exclusive, elite convent of La Concezione to highlight their patrician standards and noble lineage. The public display of religious devotion as well as artistic taste demonstrated the noble character of the convent and its inhabitants.[2] The English nobility too needed to consider strategies for continued prosperity, but these had to be strategies that could not be matched by the lower ranks of society. At a time when the whole notion

---

[1] William Shakespeare, *King Henry IV, Part II*, I, iii, 41–4, in *Complete Works*, Quatercentenary edition, ed. Peter Alexander (London and Glasgow: The English Language Book Society and Collins, 1964), 520.

[2] See Turner, this volume. Turner points out how, in a lavish display of wealth, artists and sculptors were commissioned to paint, make candles, marble columns, and coats of arms to decorate the convent.

of "nobility" was being contested by upwardly mobile merchants, the English nobility was negotiating a literal and architectural "space" for themselves through the building of country houses. This was a space which could be "uncontested" economically, politically, and culturally: property and a conspicuous and deliberate consumption of property became a means by which the English nobility distinguished itself and established its status. As the country house lost its military role, it became a site of elegant comfort where the nobility could show the world their wealth, good taste, and breeding. This was different from the situation in France, where, as Mathieu Marraud points out, it was mercantile activity which was responsible for an economic and elitist stability; this in turn became a means to attain nobility.[3]

While nobles dominated early modern societies by their wealth and social esteem, there were many aspects of their economic situation that were complex. Current historiography on early modern European consumption has focused on the combined influence of political, economic, religious, social, and aesthetic ideologies, including the cultural development of taste, politeness, and "respectability."[4] What needs to be analyzed is the response of the English nobility to economic and cultural change and to what extent this change really affected them. How did they adapt to a modernizing world where their orientation to warfare and chivalric ideals seemed incompatible with the economic agility demanded by modern capitalism? More significantly, how did they use the strategy of building architecturally opulent, aesthetic country houses and patronizing poets to celebrate these houses and their inhabitants as a means of negotiating this change? Was this an attempt at stabilizing and consolidating their positions in the wake of enormous economic and social transformations that threatened the cultural mythos of legitimacy? Traditional paradigms were being redefined and the country-house poem emerged as part of this restructuring and redefinition of older feudal notions. It mediates the renegotiation of social and economic relationships, frequently through the articulation of modes of power, legitimacy, status, and authority. To illustrate this, three country-house poems will be analyzed: Æmilia Lanyer's *The Description of Cooke-ham*, Ben Jonson's

---

[3] See Marraud, this volume, who argues that the Six Corporations (*Six Corps*) personified the entry of commerce into the great functions of the state and thereby helped merchants to acquire the dignity of the nobility and to draw a distinction between the "common" people and themselves.

[4] See Woodruff D. Smith, *Consumption and the Making of Respectability, 1600–1800* (New York: Routledge, 2002), 3. Smith merges the historiographies of consumption and politeness by asserting that "Respectability gave meaning—moral and political as well as social and economic—to consumption, thereby permitting the construction of a host of connections between purchasing commodities and thinking and action appropriately."

To Penshurst, and Andrew Marvell's *Upon Appleton House*. In my analysis of seventeenth-century country-house poetry, I will attempt to show how the English nobility attempted to make the image of the house and the land a visible domain of property and of identity and thereby legitimized their status. At the same time they attempted to create what Bourdieu has called a new "aristocracy of culture."[5]

This practice of building country houses cannot be defined as an event; nor can it be understood as the result of a particular conjuncture of factors over a short period of time. Instead, an examination of the changing economic status of the English nobility and its social and cultural consequences in the *longue durée* would provide a better understanding of the development of country houses as a complex architectural and ideological practice. Since Braudel conceived of history as the dialectic of time span, it is legitimate to read the history of country houses as an intervention at the level of superstructure, necessitated by the dialectic of the *longue durée*.[6]

There has been endless debate over Tawney's thesis of the "rise of the gentry" in sixteenth- and seventeenth-century England at the expense of a declining peerage, due to differences in the degree of adaptability of estate management to rising prices and agricultural techniques. Following him, Lawrence Stone puts forward his "crisis thesis" with regard to the aristocracy in early modern Europe, where he contends that the decline of the aristocracy was not due to inefficient land management but to over-expenditure that brought many of the earls and barons to the brink of financial ruin. This theory too has been challenged, with an emphasis on the remarkable resilience of the nobility, who despite drastic social and economic changes, amassed fortunes and monopolized royal offices. In 1951, H.R. Trevor-Roper launched an assault on the Tawney thesis, arguing that the condition of the "mere" gentry worsened and that "the whole distinction between the peerage and the gentry, upon which so much has been built, becomes again what it has always been in England; a distinction of nomenclature and legal rights, not a difference of either habits of mind or economic practice."[7] P. Zagorin, in turn, offered a critique of the Trevor-Roper

---

[5]   See Pierre Bourdieu, *Distinction: A Social Critique of the Judgement of Taste*, trans. Richard Nice (Cambridge, MA: Harvard University Press, 1984), 11–96.

[6]   Fernand Braudel, *On History*, trans. Sarah Matthews (London: Weidenfeld & Nicolson, 1980), 68–9.

[7]   R.H. Tawney, "The Rise of the Gentry, 1558–1640," *Economic History Review*, 1st Series, 11 (1941), 1–38; Lawrence Stone, *The Crisis of the Aristocracy, 1558–1641* (Oxford: Clarendon Press, 1965); H.R. Trevor-Roper, "The Decline of the Mere Gentry," *Economic History Supplement*, I (1953), reprinted in *Social Change and Revolution in England, 1540–1640*, ed. Lawrence Stone (London: Longmans, Green and Co. Ltd, 1965), 21.

theory, suggesting that the condition of the "mere" gentry did not worsen and that they could not have been responsible for the Civil War.[8] However, despite these contending views, most of which are based on conflicting terminologies rather than concepts, there seems to be little doubt that the English social structure was being broadly reshaped in the sixteenth and seventeenth centuries. The demarcations between old and new nobility were increasingly blurred: there were ancient grandees like the Cliffords and Russells, new grandees like the Sidneys, and provincial nobles like the Fairfaxes. As Jonathan Dewald points out, all over Europe members of the nobility survived by adapting and fitting themselves to a modernizing society: "Despite numerous fluctuations and variations, nobles became richer and more powerful over the early modern period, and their impact on European culture deepened."[9] Nobility of birth was set aside, and the aristocracy was, to use Tocqueville's phrase, "thrown open."[10] With the feudal system substantially abolished, and spiraling prices, fixed rents, and nascent capitalism challenging the feudal conceptions of property, social ranks inevitably overlapped. English nobles adapted with alacrity to the newly available economic opportunities. Many of them survived and adapted to the realities and challenges of the modern age with a striking increase in real income, consumption, and accumulation of capital. As the later discussion of country-house poems will illustrate, the English nobility played a key role in contemporary culture; but cultural adaptation also brought with it divisions within the nobility and segregated rich and poor nobles.[11] Similarly in France, as Guy Chaussinand-Nogaret has argued, the monarchy and the nobility cannot be seen as a single entity; he has illustrated how, by the eighteenth century, French nobles were actively involved in banking, mining, land speculation, and joint stock concerns and "were far from a class of lightweights ... On the contrary, they were a dynamic class, confident in the future and well aware of the opportunities offered by the decline of a faltering, unrespected monarchy, the stimulus of burgeoning political thought, and technological changes whose rapid progress

---

[8]   P. Zagorin, "The Social Interpretation of the English Revolution," *Journal of Economic History*, 19 (1959), 376–401, reprinted in *Social Change and Revolution in England*, 45–56.

[9]   Jonathan Dewald, *The European Nobility, 1400–1800* (Cambridge: Cambridge University Press, 1996), 201.

[10]   A. Tocqueville, *L'Ancien Regime*, trans. M. Patterson (Oxford: Basil Blackwell, 1947), 21.

[11]   See Dewald, *The European Nobility*, 198–9. Dewald sees this as a European phenomenon and argues that the reason behind this "disaggregation of the nobility" was that access to culture was expensive.

they followed with interest."[12] While the economic preeminence of the nobility was seen throughout Western Europe, England had a much larger number of aristocratic fortunes than any other country and the English nobility dominated a much higher percentage of land than in any other part of Europe.[13]

In his seminal work *The Production of Space*, Henri Lefebvre contends that space is not an inert, neutral, and preexisting given, but an ongoing product of spatial relations. Thus:

> Visible boundaries, such as walls or enclosures in general, give rise for their part to an appearance of separation between spaces where in fact what exists is an ambiguous continuity. The space of a room, bedroom, house or garden may be cut off in a sense from social space by barriers and walls, by all the signs of private property, yet still remain fundamentally part of that space.[14]

Anna Bryson has pointed out that the identity of the nobility in early modern England was not a simple matter of wealth and blood but involved complex considerations of lifestyle and social image. This "status group" was committed to cultural practices, which defined and attracted social esteem.[15] From the late sixteenth century onwards, gentlemen were expected to possess some knowledge of architectural theory: in 1607 James Cleland advised the gentry to acquaint themselves with the principles of architecture.[16] The stream of architectural treatises available, such as Palladio's *First Book of Architecture*, were equally complicit in establishing a symbolic function of the country house. The country estate signified an economically self-sufficient, socially stable (and hierarchical) microcosm within which the aristocratic owners dominated as patriarchs and attempted to negotiate and stabilize the profound social and economic changes taking place around them. This would make it, as Lefebvre would say, "as much a work as it is a product" and thus social space is produced in connection with

---

[12]   Guy Chaussinand-Nogaret, *The French Nobility in the Eighteenth Century: From Feudalism to Enlightenment* (Cambridge: Cambridge University Press, 1985), 85.

[13]   Dewald, *The European Nobility*, 62.

[14]   Henri Lefebvre, *The Production of Space*, trans. Donald Nicholson-Smith (Oxford: Blackwell, 1991), 87.

[15]   Anna Bryson, "The Rhetoric of Status: Gesture, Demeanour and the Image of the Gentleman in Sixteenth and Seventeenth Century England," in *Renaissance Bodies: The Human Figure in English Culture, 1540–1660*, eds Lucy Gent and Nigel Llewellyn (London: Reaktion Books Ltd, 1990).

[16]   Malcolm Airs, *The Making of the English Country House* (London: Architectural Press, 1975), 37.

the forces of production and with the relations of production.[17] The country house became a site of elegant luxury where powerful new aesthetic and cultural aims began to shape its design. Between 1575 and 1625 outmoded castles were often replaced by airy country houses with long galleries filled with paintings, extensive gardens, and parks. This was part of a long-standing desire to project to the outside world the image of status, wealth, power, and a new concern for privacy. The emphasis on privacy and the creation of parks around these houses clearly separated the nobility spatially, culturally, and ideologically from lesser classes. As Simon Schama points out in *Landscape and Memory*, "Landscapes are culture before they are nature; constructs of the imagination projected onto wood and water and rock." Schama further asserts that the embellishment of estates with rural meadows, architecture, Italian villas, and ruins create contrived, narrativized landscapes that function as "arcadian theme parks."[18]

The dissolution of monasteries and the enclosure of land in the sixteenth century brought with them the economic revolution of the seventeenth century as well as radical changes in the entire notion of the "nobility" in England. Between 1538 and 1553, perhaps a quarter or more of all English land was transferred from institutional to private hands through the massive redistribution of church and royal property.[19] Many of the new Tudor nobility received these lands as gifts from the crown; many members of the existing gentry bought these lands and were thus elevated into positions of power and status. The transfer of property invariably favored the nobility, simply because they had the purchasing power to buy vast amounts of land. While political connections allowed the English nobility to enjoy the fruits of state power and to make advantageous purchases, powerful members of the bureaucracy who held important official positions were also competitors for these lands on which they could now lead lives similar to that of the older aristocracy. These land sales were thus instrumental in cementing the assimilation of the new, rich bureaucrats with the old noble families as official families quickly entrenched themselves firmly within the old nobility, obscuring differences between the two groups. As Jonathan Dewald has cogently argued, a very small minority of the nobility could actually claim medieval roots for their family trees, and the "biological pretensions of early modern aristocratic ideology were simply false" and indeed misleading.[20] When one speaks of the "nobility" in early modern England, one has to take into account that this was a group that included some old aristocratic

---

[17]   Lefebvre, *The Production of Space*, 83.

[18]   Simon Schama, *Landscape and Memory* (New York: Alfred A. Knopf, 1995), 2, 541.

[19]   Lawrence Stone and Jeanne C. Fawtier Stone, *An Open Elite? England, 1540–1880* (Oxford: Clarendon Press, 1984), 296.

[20]   Dewald, *The European Nobility*, 13.

families, but also middling nobles and wealthy members of the gentry who had accumulated wealth, status, and power. Among the English "nobility" only the peer and his immediate family were considered noble (sons of younger sons were not, whereas they would be on the continent), facilitating the mixture of lineage and wealth.

As the most influential and powerful landed elite in Europe, members of the English nobility and gentry rearranged landholdings as well as increased their share of village acreage in order to make the transition from a pre-capitalist to a market economy. Through the twin economic-political strategies of private agreements and parliamentary legislation, English landowners exchanged parcels of land with each other to create compact blocks of property that entailed the dismantling of entire villages. Thomas Fuller, historian and churchman, later complained "Rich men to make room for themselves, would jostle the poor people out of their commons."[21] When James I passed through Northamptonshire in 1603, crowds protested against the recent enclosures by Sir John Spencer and other "wolfish lords that have eaten up poor husbandmen like sheep."[22] In his sensitive reading of economic shifts at the beginning of the seventeenth century, Don Wayne contends that long before the establishment of a "bourgeois ideology" in England, images and values identified as "middle class" had begun to appear in the transformation of the aristocracy's own self-image:

> This was a "new aristocracy" in a double sense. Chronologically families had been elevated as part of the Tudor policy of eradicating potential opposition from the remnants of an older feudal baronage that had largely destroyed itself in the Wars of the Roses ... they saw to the management of their own vast landholdings accumulated through the combined efforts of the enclosures and the dissolution of the monasteries. They constituted an agrarian capitalist class with strong links to the trading community ... Architecture and landscape, and subsequently the poetry in which these were celebrated, constitute stages in the preliminary "mapping" as it were, of an ideological domain ...[23]

The controlling interests of the country house-owning class were now shared by those immediately below them in the social hierarchy and the concept of

---

[21]   David Underdown, *Revel, Riot and Rebellion: Popular Politics and Culture in England 1603–1660* (Oxford: Clarendon Press, 1985), 19.

[22]   C.H. Firth, "The True Narration of the Entertainment of his Royal Majesty 1603," in *Stuart Tracts, 1603–1693* (Westminster: Constable, 1903).

[23]   Don E. Wayne, *Penshurst: The Semiotics of Place and the Poetics of History* (Madison: University of Wisconsin Press, 1984), 24–5.

"nobility" was becoming increasingly permeable. As Kari Boyd McBride points out in her admirable study of country-house discourse, even apparently noble families like the Sidneys were "social arrivistes whose tenure dated only from Edward VI's reign."[24] The individualistic act of commissioning buildings and luxurious houses was one way by which the "landed elite" (comprising the survivors of the old *noblesse d'epée*, the new *noblesse de robe*, and powerful country squires) invested themselves with legitimacy, power, and authority.[25] Many members of the nobility, through shrewd business enterprises and entrepreneurial investments of land, managed to display lavish standards of living. As Stone points out correctly enough:

> Since ownership of a country house was a *sine qua non* of elite membership, and since this would provide a coherent framework within which to operate, it was decided to try to formulate a meaningful definition in terms of ownership of (and residence in) a country house ... The ownership of a house of a certain size was a suitably reliable status indicator for membership, or aspiration to membership of the county squirearchy.[26]

A country house became a visible and concrete means of displaying and confirming one's status as a member of the local elite.[27]

It was in sixteenth-century England that members of the nobility began to view their country residences from a new perspective. Before that, the development of the country house was thwarted by the prevailing insecurity of the countryside. In a feudal society the country house played an important military role and defense took precedence over aesthetic or artistic needs. The landed gentry lived in well-guarded, fortified houses, usually under the patronage of a rich and politically powerful magnate who provided security and protection from the violence that often occurred in the medieval countryside. There was hardly need for privacy here, given the fact that these houses had a significant military function. The medieval nobility lived surrounded by retinues of servants, gardens were small to optimize security, and farm buildings often adjoined the main house. During the Middle Ages, kings and nobles "retained" local knights,

---

[24] Kari Boyd McBride, *Country House Discourse in Early Modern England: A Cultural Study of Landscape and Legitimacy* (Aldershot: Ashgate, 2001), 49–50.

[25] The "landed elite" was a term used in Stone and Stone, *An Open Elite?*

[26] Stone and Stone, *An Open Elite?* 11.

[27] See Soldat, this volume. Soldat points out how architecture was used by Russian rulers for symbolic communication to demonstrate power and define the image of the ruler. She focuses on how the building of stone memorial churches and ornate mausoleums were a means of showing self-awareness on the part of the Muscovite nobles.

via the household, to act as reserve military recruiters. In return for this service, householders and kings practiced good lordship either by annuities or by sponsoring the knights' extra-military activities. Political loyalty in the sixteenth and early seventeenth centuries, as during the medieval period, was expressed in England in terms of service and good lordship. But by now, monarchs were more interested in recruiting judges than knights into service, and aristocratic military retinues were too reminiscent of the overreaching nobles of the Wars of the Roses to be tolerated by the Tudor and Stuart monarchs. Defense needs were now minimal and fortification was no longer a primary architectural need. Nevertheless, political loyalty was still expressed in terms of service within an economic context. It was this dimension that enabled Elizabeth, James, as well as the members of the English nobility to articulate their political ambitions through material culture and hospitality. Moreover, the economic function of the household—processing and distributing landed revenues—enabled the nobility to recruit political clients both within and without the household. Servants, tenants, and neighbors were dependent on the local elite household for economic employment and political patronage. Country houses served as retreats from the turmoil of public or court life, but they also served as power centers for the administration of a large landed estate of several thousand acres. The revenues from these properties allowed the nobility to use their households for the purposes of display and authority. It also endowed them with legal and political status. In this period, politicians reinforced their status through land acquisition and property testified to a politician's ability to dispense patronage. For the nobility and upper gentry, land was a measure of her or his standing in society and in the political arena. As Kate Mertes contends, "By keeping a luxurious home and a generous table, by dressing servants in fine livery ... a lord was able to assert his nobility, proclaim his wealth and advertise his power, thus attracting clients and gaining respect."[28] In as early as the fifteenth century, one sees foreigners commenting on the openness to new wealth of the established landed elite in England and the reluctance of the nobility to live in cities. Poggio Bracciolini pointed out that "the English think it ignominious for noblemen to stay in cities. They live in the country, cut off by woods and fields ..."[29] The period between 1570 and 1615 also saw the advent of "prodigy houses" built by influential public servants whose main objective was to obtain favor from

---

[28]   Kate Mertes, *The English Noble Household, 1250–1660* (Oxford: Basil Blackwell, 1988), 103.

[29]   P. Bracciolini, *Opera 69*, in *The Florentine Enlightenment, 1400–50*, George Holmes (London: Weidenfeld & Nicolson, 1969), 146.

the monarch by showering lavish hospitality during royal visits.[30] Christopher Hatton maintained an ostentatious house at Holdenby. Sir Percival Willoughby spent £8,000 on Wollaton House, but this was a modest amount compared to the £39,000 that Robert, Earl of Salisbury, spent on Hatfield House in Hertfordshire. Salisbury also built a garden with a stream containing shells, artificial leaves, fish, and snakes.[31] Tudor gardens were elaborate affairs with topiary work, obelisks, painted handrails, and geometric Elizabethan grounds, such as the one constructed by Lord Burghley at Theobalds.[32] All of them had a common objective: a celebration of the symbolic glory of the owner and his family.

In this connection it is worth considering how far building country houses by the English nobility can be explained by Veblen's theory of conspicuous consumption.[33] In general, it may be accepted that the sociological explanation of such consumption as an imperative for the leisure class remains true for the English aristocracy of the time. In his analysis of the "crisis of fashion," David Kuchta has argued that the English aristocracy in the sixteenth and seventeenth centuries not only indulged in such consumption but also defended such a practice. Kuchta points out that for defenders of the old sartorial regime, the maintenance of social order depended on the maintenance of a court of conspicuous consumers. Uneasily straddling the challenges from the new gentry on the one hand and criticism from political adversaries on the other, defenders of the crown and court constructed a definition of masculinity that argued for the morality of sumptuous display, yet made it theoretically inaccessible to all but the nobility:

> This defense of aristocratic men's consumption drew on a hierarchical social theory, royalist propaganda, Anglican theology, and a mercantile economic policy to argue that men's conspicuous consumption was properly masculine, politically necessary, socially useful, ethically neutral, economically beneficial, and consistent with aristocratic definitions of manliness.[34]

---

[30]   See Mark Girouard, *Life in the English Country House: A Social and Architectural History* (New Haven, CT: Yale University Press, 1994).

[31]   Stone and Stone, *An Open Elite?*, 354, 334.

[32]   For an excellent analysis of Tudor gardens, see Roy Strong, *The Renaissance Garden in England* (London: Thames and Hudson, 1979).

[33]   Thorstein Veblen, *The Theory of the Leisure Class* (1899) (New York: Macmillan, 1915).

[34]   David Kuchta, *The Three-Piece Suit and Modern Masculinity: England, 1550–1850* (Berkeley: University of California Press, 2002), 19.

During the seventeenth century, examples of spectacular noble wealth, concretely represented by the building of houses both in the country and the city, abounded everywhere in Europe. The Swedish baron Magnus Gabriel de la Gardie had an annual income that equaled one-fifth of the Swedish state and owned several castles; the Duke of Lesdiguières had an enormous townhouse in Paris, but nevertheless built a huge country house in Dauphiné. In England, Robert Sidney had staterooms and a Long Gallery added to Penshurst, while Lady Elizabeth Wilbraham undertook the task of rebuilding Weston Park, Staffordshire, with the help of Palladio's *First Book of Architecture*. Such was the vogue and desire for country house building, that in his *Golden Grove Moralized* (1600), the poet Henry Vaughan disparagingly points out that "sooner shall we see a gentleman build a stately house than give alms and cherish the needy."[35]

The transformation of the country house from a locus of political and military leadership into a concrete space for the display of authority, good taste, wealth, and social status was instrumental in the development of the seventeenth-century literary genre known as the country-house poem. This is an apt genre to elucidate how economic history is closely linked with literary production. These poems are a manifestation of the socio-economic condition of the nobility and demonstrate the validity of Braudel's comprehensive view of history and his interest in the cultural-historical significance of space. In *A History of Civilizations*, Braudel examines how the space of Europe was a site for artistic and cultural processes of production belonging to the superstructure that coexisted with economic processes.[36]

The concept of country-house life and the role of the landlord as the apex of a manageable power structure was a vivid metaphor of control for writers and readers. As the country house lost its military power, standards of aristocratic building also underwent a dramatic change. After a long period of social chaos and aristocratic factional violence, the building of these country retreats symbolized a return to law and order in the countryside. The desire to build was shared by the older noble families as well as the newer ones, the latter of course driven by the impulse to establish their new presence in the countryside as owners of luxurious estates. This impetus to build throughout the late sixteenth and seventeenth centuries caused what Hoskins termed "the rebuilding of rural England."[37] The importance and significance of presenting a splendid exterior

---

[35]   See Dewald, *The European Nobility*, 60. Also see Nicole Pohl, *Women, Space and Utopia, 1600–1800* (Aldershot: Ashgate, 2006), 66, 55.

[36]   See Fernand Braudel, *A History of Civilizations*, trans. Richard Mayne (New York: Penguin Books, 1993).

[37]   W.G. Hoskins, "The Rebuilding of Rural England, 1570–1640," *Past and Present*, 4 (November 1953), 44–59.

to the world became a political and social necessity. In his *Breviary of Suffolk* (1618), Robert Reyce draws one's attention to contemporary buildings with their lavish exteriors: compared to older houses and styles of building with their thick walls of rough stone, brick or timber, small windows or large chimneys, "... our building at this day is chiefly to place the houses where they may be furthest seen, have best prospect, sweetest air and greatest pleasure; their walls thin ... their lights large, all for outward show ..."[38] The country house thus became a field for strong personal identification. With its grand setting, usually on a hill, elaborate and towering "frontispiece" (as in Burghley House), and the imposing Great Hall and public rooms, the country house clearly spelled out the hierarchical structure of society, with the owner of the house at the apex of the pyramid.

Ever since the 1956 publication of G.R. Hibbard's article "The Country House Poem in the Seventeenth Century," much has been written on this unique and short-lived genre. Hibbard focuses on the symbolic function of the country house and its architecture as the center of an organic, harmonious community and locates Ben Jonson's *To Penshurst* (1616), Thomas Carew's *To Saxham* (1640), and Andrew Marvell's *Upon Appleton House* (1681) as being part of a homogenous body of poetry with common ideals of good housekeeping, responsible use of wealth, and hospitality.[39] Since Hibbard's article, a number of literary scholars have analyzed the socio-political context of the country-house poetry tradition and have expanded the range of texts and literary forms that may be categorized under this genre. The evolution from the archaic Old Hall to the Palladian country houses of the seventeenth century, according to William McClung, "suggests many metaphors and analogies: from communities to the individual, from anonymous to idiosyncratic design, from utility to display, from timelessness to 'modernity' and stylistically from horizontal to vertical thrust."[40] This movement from the growth of a communal hall to the individualistic act of commissioning private houses was in keeping with the gradual erasure of the bonds between lord and tenant in an increasingly mercantile society. This is recognized by Nicole Pohl in her book *Women, Space and Utopia*, where she argues that the genre of the country-house poem is a "utopian discourse" that reflects the socio-economic transition from feudalism to monetary land ownership and its consequent possessive individualism symbolized by the

---

38   Robert Reyce, *Breviary of Suffolk* (1618), ed. Francis, Lord Hervey (1902), in *Social Change and Revolution in England*, 128.

39   G.R. Hibbard, "The Country House Poem in the Seventeenth Century," *Journal of the Warburg and Courtauld Institute*, 19 (1956), 159–77.

40   William A. McClung, *The Country House in English Renaissance Poetry* (Berkeley: University of California Press, 1977), 90.

Palladian style of architecture.[41] Pohl's emphasis, however, is on how feminist writers of the eighteenth century revised country-house literature, sometimes creating fictional separatist communities that adapted the country house to its own uses. The literary manifestation of the country-house ethos as a mirror of socio-political changes in history has been explored by scholars such as Don E. Wayne, who in his reading of Jonson's *To Penshurst* points out that the country-house genre:

> represents a stage in the emergence of a national culture closely identified with the land and with the values associated with land tenure. In it the pastoral conventions of Elizabeth's reign are transformed into a more domestic, historical and a relatively naturalistic mode. It is a type of "nature poetry" better fitted than its courtly antecedents to serve as the cultural accompaniment to a developing agrarian capitalism.[42]

Raymond Williams, in *The Country and the City*, strategically places the country-house poems between a residual ideology of an organic feudal community and an emerging bourgeois and agrarian capitalist order, pointing out that while poems like Jonson's *To Penshurst* entail a nostalgic idealization of a pre-capitalist economy and social relations, they also make oblique references to the requirements of an emerging capitalist agriculture—an exploitation of the land and its creatures, "a prolonged delight in an organized and corporative production and consumption..."[43] Increasingly after 1600, nobles sought to create large private spaces around their houses, separating themselves from ordinary villagers. This obviously served ideological ends. Walled parks insistently made visible the ideals of privacy with their uninterrupted vistas and linked these to ideas of class where ordinary villagers would be excluded from the views enjoyed by the estate owners; it also made visible absolute property rights that the decline of feudalism had ushered in.

Æmilia Lanyer's *The Description of Cooke-ham* (1609–10) was written in honor of Margaret Clifford, Countess of Cumberland, who was not the mistress of the manor at Cookham in Berkshire, but a visitor who was staying there by the generosity of her brother, Sir William Russell of Thornhaugh, during her estrangement from her husband.[44] Strangely enough, despite being a country-

---

[41]   Pohl, *Women, Space and Utopia*, 53.

[42]   Wayne, *Penshurst*, 16.

[43]   Raymond Williams, *The Country and the City* (New York: Oxford University Press, 1973), 39, 30.

[44]   Barbara K. Lewalski, "The Lady of the Country House," in *The Fashioning and Functioning of the British Country House*, eds Gervase Jackson-Stops, Gordon J. Schochet,

house poem, there is hardly any mention of the house itself. The poem is set almost exclusively in the grounds of the house and, as Kari Boyd McBride points out correctly enough, Lanyer has "omitted mention of either walls or domestic interiors" and has freed Cumberland from "both the hall and domestic spaces that cloistered aristocratic women and attendants."[45] The poem establishes a relationship between Cumberland and nature in such a way that her legitimacy and status is constantly reinforced.[46] Her privileged position and nobility are constantly on display: not only is she of noble lineage, descending from the Russells of Bedford (l.94), but even the elements of nature are given a life of their own to pay deference to her. Thus birds obediently chirp to entertain her (l.30) and the trees turn themselves into "beauteous Canopies" to shade her eyes from the sun (ll.25–6). Even the landscape assumes a position of subordination:

> The very Hills right humbly did descend,
> When you to tread upon them did intend.
> And as you set your feete, they still did rise,
> Glad that they could receive so rich a prise.
> The gentle Windes did take delight to bee
> Among those weeds that were so grac'd by thee.
> And in sad murmure uttered pleasing sound,
> That Pleasure in that place might more abound:
> The swelling Bankes deliver'd all their pride,
> When such a *Phoenix* once they had espide.
> Each Arbor, Banke, each Seate, each stately Tree,
> Thought themselves honour'd in supporting thee. (ll. 35–46)

The plants, the flowers, the trees are described almost in terms of a retinue of servants who hasten to welcome her with decorum and civility. The terminology of obedience permeates the text; particularly telling is Lanyer's use of the term "liveries": the "Walkes put on their summer Liveries" (l.21). Similarly, the birds who come to "attend" upon her fly away in case they "offend" her, small creatures that approach her from their burrows are intimidated by "the Bowe in your faire Hand ..." (ll. 47–52). Yet, the Countess is never seen to respond to these elements and the ordered reactions of the flora and fauna at all: she maintains

---

Lena Cowen Orlin, and Elisabeth Blair MacDougall (Washington, DC: National Gallery of Art, 1999), 267.

[45]   McBride, *Country House Discourse*, 112.

[46]   Æmilia Lanyer, "The Description of Cooke-ham," in *The Penguin Book of Renaissance Verse*, eds David Norbrook and H.R. Woudhuysen (London: Penguin Books, 1993), 414–20. All references are to this edition and line numbers are given parenthetically in the text.

her distance and her privacy and creates for herself an inviolable personal space as she continues like a monarch on a royal progress. If Cumberland's male counterparts created their private spaces and established their legitimacy as powerful men through the construction of houses, enclosed parks, and grounds, she does so within the confines of the woods around the country house at Cookham. Alice F. Friedman contends that in early modern country houses "each area carried a status designation and each 'belonged' to a specific group defined by gender … and degree," while only the master had complete access to all parts of the house and estate.[47] Given that, as a woman, she may have been under strict surveillance within the confines of the country house, Lanyer deliberately celebrates Cumberland's nobility outside the portals of the manor at Cookham. The privacy that she constructs for Cumberland is constantly camouflaged by a façade of public display. Yet, it is precisely this which allows the Countess's privacy to become a hallmark of noble privilege where she maintains a distance from all that is around her, including the writer, who grieves at the fact that she cannot be near the Countess, because "so great a difference is there in degree" (l.106). What is interesting is that Lanyer poeticizes such elements as "liveries," which, according to Veblen, represented vicarious consumption and were irksome as a mark of slavery or servility. The Countess is not only a guest but also a woman, thus not the ideal representative of the patriarchal master of the house. Therefore it is doubly imperative for the poet to indicate her class by emphasizing the distance, the aura, and the private space that the Countess enjoyed.

Cumberland's authority is legitimized and her privacy is ensured with a sense of finality at the moment when she approaches the stately oak tree at the top of a hill. Here the oak is represented as a hospitable and generous host,

> Which seeming joyfull in receiving thee,
> Would like a Palme tree spread his armes abroad,
> Desirous that you there should make abode:
> Whose faire greene leaves much like a comely vaile,
> Defended *Phebus* when he would assaile:
> Whose pleasing boughs did yeeld a cool fresh ayre,
> Joying his happinesse when you were there.
> Where being seated, you might plainely see,
> Hills, vales, and woods, as if on bended knee
> They had appeard, your honour to salute,
> Or to preferre some strange unlook'd for sute … (ll. 60–70)

---

[47]   Alice F. Friedman, "Architecture, Authority, and the Female Gaze: Planning and Representation in the Early Modern Country House," *Assemblage*, 18 (1992), 41–61: 44.

Figure 10.1　Penshurst Place

Source: Wikimedia Commons, <http://en.wikipedia.org.uk/wiki/File:Penshurst_Place_2008.jpg>, accessed on 19 February 2010.

The language of supplication is evident here again: the hills and woods salute her on "bended knee" for preference and "sute." The oak now metamorphoses into a kind of throne on which the Countess is invited to sit like a monarch and survey "a Prospect fit to please the eyes of Kings" and "thirteene shires" that are more delightful to the eye than any scene that Europe can provide (ll. 72–4). Free of the constraints that might otherwise be imposed on her by her gender, the Countess of Cumberland is no longer a guest at Cookham: she can now rise to the stature of a king. The hierarchical order is maintained, but the patriarchal order is subverted by her elevation to the stature of a monarch. Her admission into an exclusively male elite circle allows her to participate in activities of public significance and to contribute to the construction of dominant discourse. Once her authority is legitimized, she can resort to private meditation and her contemplation on the Bible in these woods.[48]

---

[48]　For an analysis of the nature of early modern patriarchal authority, see Tim Stretton, "Marriage, Separation and the Common Law in England, 1540–1640," in *The Family in*

To Penshurst, by Ben Jonson, was probably written some time before 1612 though it was published along with Jonson's other works in 1616. Penshurst (Figure 10.1) in Kent was the family home of the Sidneys; at the time of the poem's composition, the "great lord" referred to was Robert Sidney, Viscount L'Isle, later the Earl of Leicester. Many critics have recognized the fact that Jonson's poem celebrates a retrospective ideal of feudal obligation and responsibility and idealizes a hierarchical social order where there is no class conflict. Yet what has often not been emphasized is how Jonson encodes a new tradition by celebrating certain values that are indicative of the rise of capitalism. Aristocratic families like the Sidneys were, after all, involved in shipping and mining industries and were pioneers of a "nascent capitalism."[49]

The first part of the poem puts forward a number of negative constructions about what Penshurst is *not*.[50] Although this is conveyed through architectural metaphors, there are clear ethical and ideological connotations. Jonson emphasizes that Penshurst is not one of the new-fangled Elizabethan "prodigy houses" built by Tudor officials like the Cecils. It is, on the contrary, an "ancient pile":

> Thou art not, Penshurst, built to envious show,
> Of touch, or marble; nor canst boast a row
> Of polish'd pillars, or a roofe of gold:
> Thou hast no lantherne, whereof tales are told;
> Or stayre, or courts; but stand'st an ancient pile,
> And these grudg'd at, art reverenc'd the while.
> Thou joy'st in better markes, of soyle, of ayre,
> Of wood, of water: therein thou art faire. (ll. 1–8)

It is suggested here, of course, that there is a deliberate strategy on the part of the family being celebrated. By choosing to maintain the old architectural or Gothic style at Penshurst, which is incidentally made of "country stone," and by rejecting the new architectural styles found in the Palladian villas, Sir Henry Sidney and his sons may have been drawing attention to the past to highlight their lineage

---

Early Modern England, eds Helen Berry and Elizabeth Foyster (Cambridge: Cambridge University Press, 2007), 39.

[49] Geoffrey Walton, "The Tone of Ben Jonson's Poetry," in *Metaphysical to Augustan: Studies in Tone and Sensibility in the Seventeenth Century* (London: Bowes and Bowes, 1955), 23–4.

[50] Ben Jonson, "To Penshurst," in *The Penguin Book of Renaissance Verse*, eds David Norbrook and H.R. Woudhuysen (London: Penguin Books, 1993), 420–23. All references are to this edition and line numbers are given parenthetically in the text.

and descent: their accession to the estate is apparently part of a natural historical continuity. As Don Wayne argues, "the buildings of a new nobility, brought to power largely through the policies of the new royal line, reflect a[n] ... attempt to legitimize power and authority with identification with a ruling class of an earlier epoch through an association of architectural forms." In 1585, the coat of arms of Edward VI and an inscription was added along with the Dudley and Sidney badges on the screen of the Great Hall to draw attention to the Tudors and their genealogy.[51] The different aspect of Penshurst and its contrast to other country houses is reiterated: it is conspicuous in its lack of architectural ornamentation compared to other "proud, ambitious heaps" (l.101). Of course by the time Jonson wrote his poem, staterooms and a Long Gallery had been added and Robert Sidney had every intention of turning it into a "prodigy house." But in Jonson's text, it is not made of marble or gold; more significantly it has no "stayre," a symbol of hierarchy and power. Jonson depicts the Sidneys as a family that participates openly and directly in a community outside the confines of the house. The Sidneys obviously wish to be represented as just, generous, hospitable, and powerful and Jonson distinguishes them from other families of the Jacobean aristocracy by identifying them and their home not only with the land but also with the families and homes of their subjects.

After distinguishing Penshurst from the ostentatious display or "show" of other country houses, Jonson highlights what Penshurst does have in terms of natural elements: soil, air, woods, and water. There is a natural order suggested here, which is epitomized in the patriarchal family and the home. There is an association of myth and history—the pagan deities are evoked to create the atmosphere of a Golden Age:

> Where Pan and Bacchus their high feasts have made,
> Beneath the broad beech, and the chest-nut shade;
> That taller tree, which of a nut was set
> At his great birth, where all the Muses met. (ll.11–14)

Into this magical, mythical world is introduced both Philip Sidney (the "his" referred to) and Barbara Gamage, wife of Robert Sidney, the owner of Penshurst at the point when Jonson was writing the poem. Nature's attributes are itemized: it is an estate governed by Nature's laws where the birds and fish voluntarily sacrifice themselves for the Sidneys' table. The pheasant and the partridge are "willing to be killed," fat carps "run into thy net," pikes "themselves betray," eels

---

[51] Wayne, *Penshurst*, 89, 102. Robert and Philip Sidney were the nephews of Robert Dudley, Earl of Leicester.

jump into the fisherman's hand, and the orchard yields the fruits of the season: cherries, plums, apricots, and peaches (ll.28–44). Wayne highlights the depiction of a "natural" chain of events here, where the land gives of itself voluntarily, where the "chain of being" is a "chain of giving."[52] The walls of Penshurst have no barriers: all are welcomed. Jonson provides a considerably long passage on the relationship between the Sidneys and the peasants on their land:

> But all come in, the farmer, and the clowne:
> And no one empty-handed, to salute
> Thy lord, and lady, though they have no sute.
> Some bring a capon, some a rurall cake,
> Some nuts, some apples; some that thinke they make
> The better cheeses, bring 'hem; or else send
> By their ripe daughters, whom they would commend
> This way to husbands; and whose baskets beare
> An embleme of themselves, in plum or peare. (ll. 48–56)

Yet, this is clearly an idealization of rural relations between the feudal lord and his subjects. These apparent "expressions of love" (l.57) on the part of the peasants could well be gifts based on obligation or rents paid in kind. Particularly revealing is the fact that along with the rural cakes and cheese is sent the "ripe daughters." The sexually-charged image cannot be ignored: like the fruits they bear and resemble, these daughters are commodified and gifted, so to speak, to the Sidneys.

A little later in the poem, Jonson portrays himself as a guest at Penshurst and the generosity and hospitality of the Sidneys are such that he, though untitled, is treated as an equal. He can partake of "the same beere, and bread, and selfe-same wine" (l.63), unlike Lanyer, whose difference of degree prevents her proximity to the Countess of Cumberland.[53] But the waiter serving the food "knows, below, he shall find plenty of meate" (l.70). The waiter clearly has to go "below" the stairs to the servants' hall for his meat, despite the fact that Penshurst apparently does not have a "stayre." Unlike Margaret Clifford in Lanyer's poem, Barbara Gamage, the quintessential good housewife, is "noble, fruitfull, chaste" (l.90) and fits perfectly into the patriarchal mold of the Sidney family. Moreover, her children are invited to "Reade, in their virtuous parents noble parts" all the "mysteries of manners, armes and arts" (ll.97–8). What the children will read is in fact the virtues of Robert and Barbara Sidney that are enumerated by the poet

---

[52]   Ibid., 75.

[53]   For an account of hospitality in noble households, see Felicity Heal, *Hospitality in Early Modern England* (Oxford: Clarendon Press, 1990).

himself. Nobility is defined here not in terms of lineage or descent, but natural virtue.

The poem therefore legitimizes the nobility of the Sidneys in keeping with the primary and ideological function of country-house poetry. But Jonson also presents a veiled conflict here. By receiving patronage he is obliged to write an encomium to the Sidney family, their virtues, and their hospitality, but there are qualities about the house and landscape that embrace the essential aspect of a capitalist ideology. Penshurst the historically-specific location is merged with Penshurst the idealized social model. Wayne's comment is particularly germane to the issue here: the poem, he points out, is an examination of how "a culture, caught between two epochs" represented itself and an attempt to rationalize and sanction the accumulation of wealth, though this wealth is idealistically viewed as being gifted by nature and not collected by acquisition.[54]

Jonson's poem is unusually rich in its exposition of class distinction as conceived by Pierre Bourdieu. The primary thesis of the poem—that Penshurst is distinct from other country houses in terms of the culture that it embodies— is reinforced throughout the entire poem. In his work *Distinction*, Bourdieu contends that "class fractions teach aesthetic preferences to their young."[55] He asserts the primacy of cultural capital by claiming that social capital and economic capital, though acquired cumulatively over time, depend upon it. As Bourdieu argues:

> A work of art has meaning and interest only for someone who possesses the cultural competence, that is the code, into which it is encoded ... A beholder who lacks the specific code feels lost in a chaos of sounds and rhythms, colors and lines, without rhyme or reason.[56]

In *To Penshurst* Jonson is making visible the class distinction of the owner of the house by decoding the codes, not just architectural, but symbolic and moral. The denial of an ostentatious display of wealth, the "walks of health," the Muses meeting at the birth of the owner of the house, the display of humanistic learning by references to Greek mythology, the plentiful flora and fauna, the generous hospitality, and a general impression created about the house that it is an abode of wholesome and moral life distinguish Penshurst from other country houses and their masters in a remarkable way.

---

54   Wayne, *Penshurst*, 28, 118.
55   Bourdieu, *Distinction*, 466.
56   Ibid., 2–3.

Andrew Marvell's *Upon Appleton House* (1681) deals with Lord Fairfax's retirement to Nun Appleton in Yorkshire from the Civil War. Fairfax, the Parliamentary General and founder of the New Model Army, had constructed Appleton House to replace an earlier house built on land that had been acquired by the Fairfax family after the dissolution of a priory in Appleton. The poem is permeated with architectural references. Fairfax's home is built with local materials and is perfectly proportioned, a "Vitruvian building."[57] In the first stanza itself, Marvell suggests that the poem should be treated as a piece of architecture where one should expect the "work of no foreign architect" within this "sober frame" (ll.1–2).[58] Each space in the house is carefully controlled and regulated; every part of the estate is composed "like Nature, orderly and near" (l.26), all of which contribute to the prospects of the Fairfax dynasty.

The poem is preoccupied with the complex moral decisions demanded of its owner. Marvell explores the value of retreat and the character of a man who has retired to the countryside at a time of civil strife. Once again, Fairfax's social status and the legitimacy of his nobility is asserted, but in a completely different manner compared to Cumberland and the Sidneys. Unable to cease his "warlike studies," the gardens are designed by Fairfax to resemble a fort fenced with five bastions; the flowers display their "silken ensigns" and let "fly their fragrant volleys" when the master passes by; the blossoms form "regiments," the bees are "sentinels" (ll. 285–320). We are never allowed to forget Fairfax's military background. The class difference that excludes Lanyer from the Countess also denies Marvell the access to privacy in Fairfax's country house. The "order" that Marvell extols is one that is designed solely for Fairfax himself. When "the laden house does sweat" (l.49) and the "swelling hall/Stirs" (ll.51–2), it is for the Master. The subject matter of the poem according to Marvell was "the progress of this house's fate" (l.84). The entry of Maria, Fairfax's daughter, later in the poem is significant, for it is only through this "sprig of mistletoe,/On the Fairfacian oak" (ll.731–2) that progress can be made. The true virtue of the Fairfax heir is examined here: she inherits the ancestral virtues in every sense, but while her male ancestors were renowned throughout Europe for their military prowess, she must accept the bonds of matrimony and limit her triumphs to fruition and procreation.

Although Fairfax is commended for his hospitality, the "stately frontispiece of poor" and the "daily new furniture of friends" (ll.65–8) suggest a deliberate

---

[57]   See James Turner, *The Politics of Landscape: Rural Scenery and Society in English Poetry 1630–1660* (Oxford: Basil Blackwell, 1979), 79.

[58]   Andrew Marvell, "Upon Appleton House: To my Lord Fairfax", in *Andrew Marvell: Selected Poetry and Prose*, ed. Robert Wilcher (London and New York: Methuen, 1986). All references are to this edition and line numbers are given parenthetically in the text.

and careful control of space within the confines of the house where individuality is constantly threatened. The narrator has to pass beyond the confines of the actual house to the woods beyond. Like Cumberland, it is this outdoor space that gives him a freedom denied indoors. As he crosses the meadows that are subject to "massacre" by the scythe of the mower (ll.93–4), he moves towards the "double wood of ancient stocks" which symbolically represents the union of the pedigreed Veres and Fairfaxes (ll.489–92). Although the wood is part of the Fairfax property, it offers the poet a space that is governed along completely different lines than the house itself. Here "all creatures" are allowed (l.487) and the poet need not bother about the codes of civility:

> Then as I careless on the bed
> Of gelid strawberries do tread,
> And through the hazels thick espy
> The hatching throstle's shining eye,
>
> ...
>
> Then languishing with ease, I toss
> On pallets swoll'n of velvet moss;
> While the wind, cooling through the boughs,
> Flatters with air my panting brows. (ll. 529–96)

An egalitarian social environment is presented here, where all get their due share and where nature is not subject to the relentless massacre of the mower in the meadows. It is here that the poet can assert his autonomy away from the authority of the Master. The metaphysical wit of *Upon Appleton House* thus "demonstrates the ambiguities faced by the civic humanist in forming concepts about the use of power and wealth with the passing of the age of analogical thinking and the development of empirical modes of thought."[59]

In conclusion, one can see that the assertion of authority by the English nobility and their response to changing notions of "nobility" and respectability is done in different ways in the three poems considered. In Lanyer's text, differences in degree are maintained and a Countess's authority is legitimized in privacy; in *To Penshurst* Jonson maintains a precarious balance between the depiction of a pre-capitalist feudal household and the pressures of a burgeoning capitalist economy; in Marvell's poem, with its depiction of Fairfax's military background, autonomy can only be achieved outside the country house. The country-house poem may therefore be seen as a product of the desire of the nobility to mark its

---

[59]   Virginia C. Kenny, *The Country-House Ethos in English Literature, 1688–1750* (Brighton: The Harvester Press, 1984), 11.

Figure 10.2 Daniel King, "Nun Appleton House, Yorkshire," woodcut
c. 1655

location in the ambit of a socio-economic power struggle; by recasting the rural environment through the building of elegant and stylish country houses they intervened at the level of the "superstructure."[60] Architecture, art, and poetry were used as durable signs that would breathe their semiotic meaning over the *longue durée*.

At the same time, the country-house poems also vividly demonstrate the complex process of change in the English nobles' relations with their monarchs and reflect not only the turmoil of contemporary politics but also the attempt of the English nobility to carve out a niche for themselves within a highly "contested space." In Lanyer's *A Description of Cooke-ham* (1609) the projection of the Countess as a kind of monarch to whom nature subordinates itself is particularly telling, given the fact that James I had already embarked on a course of entertaining court favorites that would have disastrous political consequences. By the time Jonson wrote *To Penshurst* (around 1612), there

---

[60] Fernand Braudel, *The Identity of France*, vol. II, trans. Sian Reynolds (London: Fontana Press, 1990), 415–59. Braudel refers to a dialectic between "rural infrastructures" and "urban superstructures."

were frequent confrontations between the king and Parliament over the question of royal prerogative. In July 1610, the Commons presented a Petition for Grievances to the king and council where they referred to a "general fear conceived and spread amongst your Majesty's people, that Proclamations will by degrees grow up and increase to the Strength and Nature of Laws."[61] By highlighting the importance of tradition, inheritance, and, most of all, virtue, Jonson distinguishes the Sidney family from other members of the Jacobean aristocracy. *To Penshurst* reasserts the elegance, culture, and refined tastes of this family at a time when the reigning monarch was trying to extend his rights and privileges. On the other hand, Marvell's *Upon Appleton House*, written on Lord Fairfax's retirement from the Civil War and with its constant emphasis on domestic interiors, suggests that the Fairfaxes must reconcile themselves to a world where the only prospects are domestic ones. Although the moral decisions of the owner are alluded to, the solid values of the past are upheld in this country estate and it is these values that may heal the body politic at a time of civil strife. Thus early modern nobles in England confronted changes in the functioning of political power in various ways, one of which was through the strategy of building country houses. Often excluded from the easy relationship they had hitherto enjoyed with the monarchy, the English nobility survived, prospered, and grew stronger in wealth and power by reinventing itself in a modernizing society. The building of spectacular country houses and commissioning poems to celebrate these architectural marvels was a social, psychological, and cultural assertion of authority and affluence on their part, but simultaneously it may be viewed as a distinctly "English" form of claiming noble rights in the face of radical economic and political change.

---

[61]   Robert Steele, ed., *A Bibliography of Royal Proclamations of the Tudor and Stuart Sovereigns 1485–1714*, vol. I (Oxford: Clarendon Press, 1910), xci.

Chapter 11

Nobility as a Social and Political Dialogue: The Parisian Example, 1650–1750

Mathieu Marraud

Historians have described nobility as a definable category, delimited by a series of juridical status. Nobility accumulated with every person fulfilling, at a given time, at least one of the legal conditions the regime recognized or produced.[1] Inheritance and ownership of this status made possible hereditary completion and recognition, extending nobility over centuries and providing it with all kinds of exclusive cultural signs. Nobility can be studied across historical periods as a single phenomenon of distinction and as an unvarying product of the *société d'ordres* (society of orders).

However, as regards Old Regime France, there are some other ways to describe nobility, mainly as a system of relations built upon a double process: the construction of the state through delegation of the public authority from the prince to private individuals; and the impact of family practices on holding and transferring such authority, that means on its own terms. Thus, nobility was nothing but an everlasting negotiation, a fight for political belonging rather than a predefined and intangible social group.[2] These stakes could only be stated in absolute terms: the monarchy sought always to include all forms of hierarchy, giving individuals progressive access to royal prerogatives,[3] while people sought to guarantee, in ways symbolic and patrimonial, their position in the state machinery, trying this way to limit its sphere of activity,

---

[1]   Alain Texier, *Qu'est-ce que la noblesse? Histoire et droit* (Paris: Tallandier, 1987); François Bluche and Pierre Durye, *L'anoblissement par charges avant 1789* (Paris: Les Cahiers nobles, 1962).

[2]   Robert Descimon, "Chercher de nouvelles voies pour interpréter les phénomènes nobiliaires dans la France moderne: La noblesse 'essence' ou rapport social?" *Revue d'histoire moderne et contemporaine*, 46 (1999), 5–21.

[3]   Mathieu Marraud, *De la Ville à l'Etat, la bourgeoisie parisienne, XVIIe–XVIIIe siècle* (Paris: Albin Michel, 2009), 317–440; Laurence Croq, "Privilèges sociaux et hiérarchies sociales: le déclassement des 'bourgeois de Paris' du milieu du XVIIe siècle à la Révolution," *Etudes et documents*, 11 (1999), 55–95.

to dominate its outward signs.[4] Either through theory or behaviors, nobility stands on the point where these two opposite motions meet and run into strained connections. Here, nobility is in a relation to the sacred as well as in a relation to things material.

In regard to court ceremony, it is obvious that rivalries between different foundations of the *second ordre* (fief, office, immemoriality) assure their efficiency more so than stability or fixity.[5] The monarchy did not hesitate to set principles contrary to others. By turns, it justified aristocracy and its validity by the prince's service or by the customary prescription of nobility. Some families could gain benefits from one to the detriment of the other.[6] Therefore, antagonism between all components of rank, more than their unity, made noble wealth possible as well as its hierarchical superiority, thanks to different sources, almost all in conflict, from which nobility drew its legitimacy. The corporate and ideological frontiers of the *second ordre* always varied according to particular places and periods.

Because of its closeness to the royal court, the example of Paris between the 1650s and the 1750s makes this noble "multivalence" plain, helping us to understand its presence in a continuous conflict between local and central powers. Based on several great families of the capital that were located at the edge of nobility and *roture* (commons), this chapter intends to describe how nobility cannot contain all social and political preeminences, though claiming its capacity to do it ideally so. Studying families, and the urban institutions they dwelt in, nobility can be "derealized" and brought out of ontology (nobility as the sum of all noblemen). It becomes an instrument, a social and political practice more than an immemorial essence gaining social superiority.

Ennoblement: The Urban Nobility

Thanks to several hundred ennobling offices linked to urban courts, ennoblement became an urban phenomenon around 1600. During previous centuries, nobility was renewed in tacit ways, with the help of the *ban*

---

[4]   Sarah Hanley, "Engendrer l'Etat, formation familiale et construction de l'Etat dans la France de l'époque moderne," *Politix*, 132 (1995), 45–65.

[5]   Fanny Cosandey, "L'insoutenable légèreté du rang," in *Dire et vivre l'ordre social en France sous l'Ancien Régime*, ed. Fanny Cosandey (Paris: Éditions de l'EHESS, 2005), 169–89.

[6]   Elie Haddad, "Les Mesgrigny ou le coût social et moral des prétentions à l'épée," in *Epreuves de noblesse, les expériences de la haute robe parisienne (XVIe–XVIIIe siècle)*, ed. Elie Haddad (Paris: Belles Lettres, 2010), 211–31.

(vassals' duty to serve in the army) and of rural fief ownership.[7] More and more families were ennobled through charges of *secrétaire du roi*, united with the Great Chancellery or with the parlements, which were located in urban environments.[8] When Jean-Baptiste Colbert decided to hold an inquiry into the kingdom's nobility in order to search for usurpers, his attempt had an amazing outcome: for 60.5 percent of Parisian families originating in ennobling office-holding, there were only 29.5 percent originating from noble extraction and just 10 percent from ennobling letters. At the end of the seventeenth century, the great majority of the nobility living in Paris stemmed from a typically urban process.[9] Throughout France, a strong urban movement characterized the *second ordre* and led it to take up residence in towns. In the mid-eighteenth century, 45 percent of noblemen's regular domicile was an urban one (which does not mean they did not retain some country ones).[10] In its specific nature, nobility came gradually to depend on mechanisms of social rise connected to the purchase and the practice of civil offices. In this way, city expansion and royal office expansion were closely connected.[11] When a locality rose to the status of a city, or when it acquired related rights and privileges, it gained in honor. Nothing was more natural than a city redistributing honor in return.

In fact, most of the historiography focuses upon this kind of transfer to ennobling offices in order to explain the mechanisms of social mobility during the Old Regime, as well as to explain its major significance: people's admission into the "regime of dignities." Every office granted a hierarchical value to its purchasing, according to the monarchy's common belief stating that an office is at one and the same time function and dignity to all buyers and owners. It is to say that each fragment of public authority, through delegation, gave access to the king's majesty. Venality was at the heart of this system of exchange.[12] That meant a double involvement for office-holders: in a process of "dignification"

---

[7]   Georges Huppert, *Bourgeois et gentilshommes: la réussite sociale en France au XVIe siècle* (Paris: Flammarion, 1972).

[8]   David Bien, "Manufacturing Nobles: The Chancelleries in France to 1789," *The Journal of Modern History*, 61 (1989), 445–86.

[9]   Bibliothèque Mazarine, ms 1222, *Journal de M. de Clairambault, procureur du roi, pour la recherche de la noblesse de la généralité de Paris, faite en exécution de la déclaration du 4 septembre 1696, élection et ville de Paris*, s.l.n.d.

[10]   Mathieu Marraud, *La noblesse de Paris au XVIIIe siècle* (Paris: Seuil, 2000), 23–33.

[11]   Jean Nagle, *Un orgueil français: La vénalité des offices sous l'Ancien Régime* (Paris: Odile Jacob, 2008), 297–320.

[12]   Robert Descimon, "Dignité contre vénalité: L'œuvre de Charles Loyseau (1564–1627) entre science du droit et science des saints," in *Historische Anstöße: Festschrift für Wolfgang Reinhard zum 65.Geburtstag am 10. April 2002*, eds P. Burschel, M. Häberlein, V. Reinhardt, W.E.J. Weber, and R. Wendt (Berlin: Akademie Verlag, 2002), 326–38.

and in a specific political order. This order is a public organization summed up in the king's person, the only one capable of placing authority in private hands, the only one to make people participate in the original sacrality of any power. Here is where the ennobling nature of offices lies. The patrimonialization of offices, with the *Paulette* of 1604, allowed the birth of what is called the *noblesse de robe*.[13] This established dignity principles in the city while the old nobility established them in the countryside.

Nevertheless, this social investment in offices, which was a capital investment too, needed to confront family practices. The reality of often complex usual practices sheds light on another intention than climbing up the social ladder. By searching for offices, families could express needs coming from very different sources: private finances or the defense of political territories, and so on. Finally, they did not take systematically the way of social fulfillment through ennobling themselves, because of the bankruptcy that followed and because of the rejection of noble codes they exposed. Families accepted ennoblement without subscribing to every attached cliché. In this way, they complicated the linear vision of the Old Regime social mobility. They challenged the unity of a nobility imagined as a doctrinal body.

Ennoblement and Family Compromise

The case of the great Parisian merchant families is an instructive one. Many of them entered the nobility during this period. It is clear that their ennoblement occurred for particular reasons. For example, descendants of a single couple from the hosiery guild (the Nau family), married in 1655, made 15 *secrétaires du roi* until the Revolution. In the same way, a couple from the drapery guild (the Brochant family), married in 1644, saw five of its male descendants entering an ennobling court as the *Chambre des comptes*, and 23 of them entering a sovereign court of the capital city.[14] The trend is evident. However, these kinds of charges obeyed a logic, dependent on the divisions of positions among brothers and heirs, contrary to primogeniture, as one might expect.

---

13   Robert Descimon, "The Birth of the Nobility of the Robe: Dignity versus Privilege in the Parlement of Paris, 1500–1700," in *Changing Identities in Early Modern France*, ed. Michael Wolfe (Durham, NC: Duke University Press, 1997), 95–123.

14   Nicolas Lyon-Caen, "Au Petit Paradis des Brochant: transmission et reproduction familiale chez des marchands drapiers parisiens, XVIIe–XVIIIe siècles," in *Mobilité et transmission dans les sociétés de l'Europe moderne*, eds Anna Bellavitis, Laurence Croq, and Monica Martinat (Rennes: Presses Universitaires de Rennes, 2009).

For instance, in their mutual will, a Boucher couple cared about handing down their drapery business in 1725 to the older son, after having married six of their daughters into the office nobility (two others having taken religious vows) and purchasing a noble office for their younger son. While he was not ennobled as well, the older brother was viewed as the main heir of the family, and of its merchant tradition. That was put into material form with the shop sign, the house name, as well as the goods he now owned.[15] In the previous generation, the elder of the family had to make his way in business, while the younger was compensated for his loss with an *office de robe*. Consequently, the latter was introduced into the ennobling process as early as 1692, 30 years before his older brother could do so.[16] Another example: when René Marsollier bought a charge of *secrétaire du roi* for his younger brother in 1732, it was expressly to compensate his sibling for having inherited the family silk commerce to his brother's cost. Marsollier made amends for the loss his younger brother was subjected to at the time of the inheritance, offering him instead this charge. The capital was then consolidated into real estate which would not depreciate in the future, sheltered as it was from currency devaluations. In remaining a commoner and merchant, the older brother simply played his role as head of the family, protecting the interests of the clan at large.[17] One can see that the financial reliability of ennobling offices is strong enough to serve often as a guarantee in patrimonial or matrimonial exchanges: when the dowry was paid in cash, the money could be converted into real estate to give it security and to protect the wife's dower. Ennobling offices helped serve to make it so. This is what Pierre Nau was compelled to do by his marriage contract in 1732, when this younger son of an old merchant household had to transform his wife's dowry into an office of *secrétaire du roi*.[18] All his older brothers were maintained in commerce by the family. In this way, the venal dimension of noble office made them part of a larger household economy of which the end, paradoxically, might be the maintaining of the family in commerce. This practice brought into the *second ordre* some people who did not respond to the appeal of elite distinctions. Their daily deeds did not inevitably ratify the hierarchical predominance of one profession above another.[19]

---

[15]   Archive nationales, Paris (hereafter A.N.), MC LIX 196, 6 décembre 1725, testament mutuel de Louis-Paul Boucher et de Marie-Anne Legallois.

[16]   Christine Favre-Lejeune, *Les secrétaires du roi de la grande chancellerie de France, dictionnaire biographique (1672–1789)* (Paris: Sedopols, 1986), t. I, 252–4.

[17]   A.N., MC LXXXV 442, 11 octobre 1732, traité d'office de secrétaire du roi.

[18]   A.N., MC CX 299, 3 décembre 1719, contrat de mariage Nau-Delarue.

[19]   For quite extensive analysis of bourgeois marriage contracts, see Barbara D. Diefendorf, *Paris City Councillors in the Sixteenth Century: The Politics of Patrimony*

It must be specified that all the wealth these families possessed propelled them to the greatest fortunes of the city. Thanks to this financial situation, they could well afford any noble office they wanted. They all could spend enough to maintain their rank as noblemen. At the height of his business, the draper Boucher displayed a patrimony over 3,500,000 livres, almost the same as a duke's fortune.[20] Other families like the linen merchants the Brochants, the silk merchants the Marsolliers, the cloth merchants the Boucarts, and the braid merchants the Boursiers could produce equivalent fortunes. The cost of ennobling charges seems to be quite low from the viewpoint of their means. Every one of them agreed to become noblemen. But they did so without being prejudiced against social impurity, against merchant properties to the advantage of land or office ones. None of these men ever tried to buy a fief. Most continued living in their ancient shop house, or the nearest they could.

It is even hard to notice a dynastic intention of passing on offices within these families of the bourgeoisie. When his father died in 1752, Charles Guiller d'Héricourt had to fight for the possession of his father's office of *secrétaire du roi* against his brothers and sisters who found another buyer for it, a complete stranger who offered a better price than the older brother offered. Guiller d'Héricourt had to then raise his bid, with a bribe to his joint legatees of 2,000 livres more than the total value of the office, in order to put them off their plan. The problem was that the amount of the office, around 110,000 livres, was mortgaged by the three sisters' dowries up to 89,000 livres. The sisters expected the exact payment of what came to them on this office, on its value, thanks to the new owner's solvency. Nothing was as unsure as the brothers' capacity to do it.[21] Once again, the price of an office could surpass the dignity that it contained or conferred. The patrimonial administration did not aim to ennoble families above all, but to respect customary law and the principle of equality between heirs.[22] It had a concern for preservation before accumulation. Ennoblement was often but a fragile agreement between kinsmen. Starting from this part of bourgeoisie, the renewal of the nobility could not be compared to a quest to break with a former social identity.

(Princeton: Princeton University Press, 1983).

[20]   A.N., MC LIX 200, 8 juillet 1727, partage des biens de Marie-Anne Legallois épouse Boucher. For an example of a duke's fortune, see Robert Forster, *The House of Saulx-Tavannes: Versailles and Burgundy 1700–1830* (Baltimore, MD: Johns Hopkins Press, 1971).

[21]   A.N., MC XCVIII 517, 18 avril 1752, inventaire après décès d'Etienne Guiller; ibid., 29 avril 1752, comparution des héritiers d'Etienne Guiller.

[22]   Jérôme-Luther Viret, "La reproduction familiale et sociale en France sous l'Ancien Régime: Le rapport au droit et aux valeurs," *Histoire et Sociétés Rurales*, 29 (2008), 165–88.

Ennoblement and Bourgeois Notability

As large as it was, the number of bourgeoisie entering the nobility was built less upon the overstepping of social boundaries than patrimonial continuities, as well as on areas of purely bourgeois distinction. Here lay the only way of property transmission. Bourgeois notability was a political space, supported by positions of power, urban institutions like the greatest guilds (called the *Six Corps*),[23] the town council (*échevinage*), the merchant court (*Consulat*), the fabric committees, and the hospital administration. These types of urban authorities remained effective everywhere in the kingdom until the end of the Old Regime. Oligarchy survived there, facing the ascendancy of royal absolutism over the city.[24] Also urban ennoblement became more possible with the harsh discipline that families forced themselves to adopt, in a way to stay at the top of urban society. The conveyance of shops and goods was totally linked to the conversion of profits into noble offices. Obviously, releasing the needed sum or credit for ennoblement was conceivable and, thanks to the vitality of great shops and stores, able to produce enough long-term profits for their owners. The ability of ennoblement depended on the way merchant places succeeded in creating constant wealth. As a consequence, it depended on political foundations where such prosperity took root. The one was connected to the other. As long as bourgeois structures were in a state of activity, and as notability structures were still protecting wide-ranging trade and defending commercial monopolies (through the leadership of the *Six Corps* or of the *Consulat*), then all merchant affairs found such economic stability, in order to build up a continuous way to nobility.

The example of a drapery firm, located in the center of Paris at the corner of Prouvaires and St Honoré streets, throws light on this double process (Figure 11.1). A single shop managed to secure the transmission of power positions within the guild (with charges of *garde* and *grand garde*), within the merchant court (with charges of *consul*), within the parish (with charges of churchwarden), all joined to the high bourgeoisie. And it managed also to transfer a part of the profits into ennobling offices, that is, placing their buyers into the nobility. A double filiation was occurring there. On one hand, owners followed owners at the head of the commercial house, often established by apprenticeship after they received their social bourgeois capital from their masters. On the other hand, patrilineal families progressively left the commercial house after ennobling

---

[23]   Since the early sixteenth century, the *Six Corps* were composed of the following guilds: drapers, grocers, haberdashers, furriers, hosiers, and goldsmiths.

[24]   Laurent Coste, *Les lys et le chaperon: Les oligarchies municipales en France de la Renaissance à la Révolution* (Bordeaux: Presses Universitaires de Bordeaux, 2007).

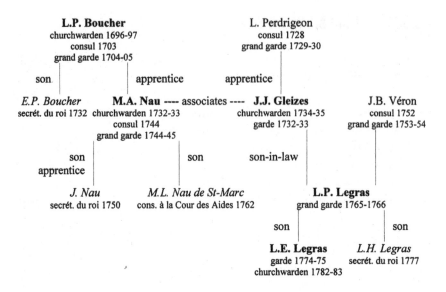

Figure 11.1   Bourgeois notability and ennoblement in a Parisian drapery shop, parish of St-Eustache

Note: In bold are mentioned the masters/owners of the shop, in italic the ennobled men. Only churchwardens of the parish where the shop was established are mentioned.

Source: A.N., MC XXVI 363, 1 septembre 1732, acte de société Nau-Gleizes; A.N., MC LXXXV 502, 30 juillet 1744, acte de société Nau-Legras; A.N., MC LXXVIII 712, 6 juillet 1750, dissolution de la société Nau-Legras.

themselves, and after providing for the continuity of their business with an apprentice or a son-in-law taking it over.

Through shops, space began producing social distinction by itself. If there was no will of founding dynasties by birth, shop spaces got around this lack of intention, creating rules and social regularity inside of them. Both dimensions were promoting merchant honor and ennoblement. Each one filled up the other. It did so at a high level, since flourishing shops were a path to sovereign courts and the *noblesse de robe* for the owners' sons. Table 11.1 details the Great Louis shop in the heart of the merchant quarter that demonstrates this fact over a century and a half.

In this way, the demographic renewal of the nobility over the period partly came through the continued strength of bourgeois institutions. Both spaces were linked by particular families that were divided into noble branches and *roturier* ones. Nobility and bourgeoisie also communicated organically by chains

Table 11.1   Merchants and *nobles de robe* in a Parisian drapery shop, St Honoré Street

Merchant owners	Years in practice	Bourgeois charges held by owner	Sovereign courts office held by sons
R. Coustard	1636–49	*Garde*	
J. Ledoubre	1649–68	*Grand garde, consul*	Master at the *Chambre des comptes*
G. Coustard C. Debemy (associate)	1668–97	*Garde* *Grand garde, consul*	Counsellor at Parlement Master at the *Chambre des comptes*
J. Devin	1697–1741	*Grand garde, consul*	
J.R. Devin	1741–59	*Grand garde, consul*	Counsellor at Parlement
E. Cavillier	1759–63		
E.J. Cavillier L.J. Cavillier (associate)	1763–80	*Garde* *Garde*	

Sources: A.N., MC XVI 144, 27 novembre 1675, inventaire après décès de Catherine Leroy veuve Coustard; A.N., MC CXV 266, 22 septembre 1689, reconnaissance de biens par Julien Ledoubre; A.N., CXV 312, 24 décembre 1701, transport de Madeleine Coustard veuve Devin à ses fils; A.N., MC XIV 237, 24 février 1719, dépôt de l'inventaire après décès de Gabriel Coustard; A.N., MC XCVIII 536, 29 décembre 1756, vente du fonds par Jacques-René Devin à Emmanuel Cavillier.

of mutual obligation that made coherent and continuous the social framework within the city.

Noble Dignity and Merchant Dignity

Simultaneous processes took place in Paris around the preservation of the bourgeois organization and the conversion of movable assets into immovable offices. Ennoblement stood where these two processes met, on a tense point between two political models that had coexisted from the Fronde (1648–1653) until the liberalization of commerce in the 1760s and 1770s. Actually, two systems of government confronted each other: an emerging centralized state leaning on the city as a relay, and an old medieval administration of the city by its own. The first system joined the state and the civic nobility together. The second one joined the city and the corporatist bourgeoisie together.[25] The city still perpetuated an upward delegation of authority from the community to its elected members, through annual non-transferable charges. For its part, the monarchy established a downward delegation of authority from the prince to his counselor, through hereditary offices. In doing this, the monarchy broke with its medieval inheritance and put into competition two distinctive figures of the king: the one of the suzerain one versus the one of the sovereign.[26]

But the system strengthened when it took that turn, leading to the king becoming the first magistrate of the realm. It happened thanks to the notion of dignity that the sacred king now conferred on private individuals, office-holders, against any other sort of public authority. As nobility was a distinction mode opposite to the ordinary people, its exclusivity slowly came to be based on this immediate participation in the sacrality of the system, against any external way outside of royal intercession. Of course, the monarchy itself was torn between two aims: the jurists' attempt to found stable state duties and the royal finances' attempt to collect more and more money by creating and taxing offices.[27] Still, the way office-holders saw their civilian worth clashed with the way sword nobility used to define its own role. Justice was becoming one of the main justifications for noble status the state advanced, besides the kingdom's defense. The jurist Gilles-André de La Roque noticed that clash in his famous *Traité de la noblesse*, in 1678:

> Military virtue is not the only noble profession of the civil society: peace has its renowned men as well as war, and the science that makes justice reign does not deserve less from the public than the strength that keeps preserving the state.[28]

Urban powers were troubled by all the changes that the monarchy imposed on juridical and symbolical policies. Noble officers tried to confiscate social value to their own advantage. Bourgeois institutions could do nothing but reply by constructing a merchant dignity that could be worthy of themselves. From the early seventeenth century, the *Consulat* (the merchant court) and the *Six Corps* (the main guilds) actually developed a set of justifying discourses to support their

---

[25] Ann Catherine Isaacs and Maarten Prak, "Cities, Bourgeoisies, and States," in *Power Elites and State Building*, ed. Wolfgang Reinhard (Oxford: Clarendon Press, 1996), 207–34.

[26] Robert Descimon, "La royauté française entre féodalité et sacerdoce: Roi seigneur ou roi magistrat?" *Revue de synthèse*, 3–4 (1991), 455–73.

[27] Alain Guery, "Raison financière et raison politique d'Ancien Régime," in *Ecrire l'histoire du XXe siècle: La politique et la raison* (Paris: Gallimard-Le Seuil, 1994), 229–41.

[28] Gilles-André de La Roque, *Traité de la noblesse, de ses différentes espèces* (Paris: Michallet, 1678), 122.

superiority over every other community, over the arts and crafts, over all trading professions that had not been raised to *jurande* status. They sought to mark out a frontier separating them from the "common," a discrete line that could take from heredity and delegated authority all their social effectiveness, as nobility already succeeded in.[29] The *Six Corps* intended to be the embodiment of the commercial capacity to enter the great state functions, just like the justice and army clearly did. They wanted this so as to be a political body, just like the royal courts:

> There is no other body in the Bourgeoisie as appropriate for representing the City, after the town hall, as these *Six Corps* ... They must be considered like the canal from where all of Paris's commerce comes. They are the ones that maintain the abundance of goods contributing to the usefulness, convenience, and splendor of all Citizens. Their commerce seems to be so wide, the men they employ so numerous, as men depending on them, that this draws on them all the consideration they do naturally enjoy among the People. After that, there is no surprise to see all honors, meant for the high Bourgeoisie, particularly reserved for them.[30]

As regards the parlements, they constantly reinterpreted and rewrote the law, through all the jurisprudence they produced, as a means of building a *de facto* role of representing the whole subject's face to the king.[31] There is no doubt that the *Six Corps* and the *Consulat*, on their level, tried to include the entire merchant sphere by this kind of political mediation and advising role they held close to the king's court. Their dignity was established on this. La Roque himself asserted that all the members of the *Six Corps*, in spite of their ordinariness, belong to the lowest categories deserving of purchasing nobility:

> The honorable ones are men whose vocations are beyond those of ordinary people, and these ones who gain city charges have personal or real dignities ....

---

[29]   Mathieu Marraud, "La juridiction consulaire de Paris aux XVIIe–XVIIIe siècles, entre dignité royale et notabilité bourgeoise," in *Les corps intermédiaires économiques, entre l'Etat et le marché*, ed. Clotilde Druelle-Korn (Limoges: Presses Universitaires de Limoges, forthcoming).

[30]   *Guide des corps des marchands et des communautés des arts et métiers, tant de la ville & fauxbourgs de Paris que du royaume* (Paris: veuve Duchesne, 1766), Bnf V 25 836, p. 10.

[31]   Francesco Di Donato, "Le concept de représentation dans la doctrine juridico-politique de Louis-Adrien Le Paige," in *Le concept de représentation dans la pensée politique* (Aix-en-Provence: Presses Universitaires d'Aix-Marseille, 2003), 53–73.

> The ordinary ones have less lofty professions, but without vileness: these ones can relate to the main *six corps* of the Parisian trade.[32]

Of course, none of these urban institutions claimed the same authority that the higher courts of justice were responsible for. They knew what their political level was. The fact remains that the ennobled men mentioned earlier (the Boucher, Nau, and Guiller families) all belonged to the first of the *Six Corps* of the capital, the drapers. More than its wealth, the merchant dignity of this guild—its closeness to the royal court and to the royal supplies—placed it at the top of the whole urban hierarchy. There was nothing surprising about these men perfecting their social life with a noble office that set them apart from popular indignity, the unworthiness their ancestors left behind a long time ago. In a paradoxical way, the corporatist reaction against royal offices encroaching on the city autonomies led the bourgeois elite closer to the great state dignities that the nobility still embodied.

However, rising up this way, the bourgeois elite understood its place right in the chain of the body politic that had to structure, according to them, the whole society. This point of view made them feel attacked when monarchical repression struck the sovereign courts, which were composed of the highest *noblesse de robe*. That was the case in 1754, when the *Consulat* refused to start new elections because he did not want to take the oath while the Parisian Parlement had been banished. Barbier's diary mentions:

> There have been several *lettres de cachet* sent to the judges and *consuls* that would have left their charges, condemning them to continue their functions, to stay in charge in order to avoid the election of two new *consuls*. This occurred because of the oath they have to take before the Parlement, that they would not have taken before the Royal Chamber [i.e. the commission that stands in for the banished Parlement].[33]

It would be the same in 1771, when the *Consulat* could not elect judges who elected to take the oath before the new Parlement, which Chancellor Maupeou had just completely reorganized using brute force. They agreed to take the oath, but only before taking the traditional one. Thus, the "dignitarization" that the bourgeois bodies took advantage of at the turn of the seventeenth and eighteenth centuries incited them to enter the great conflicts of the late-eighteenth century,

---

[32]   de La Roque, *Traité de la noblesse*, 232.

[33]   *Chronique de la Régence et du règne de Louis XV, ou Journal de Barbier* (Paris: Charpentier, 1857–66), t. 6 (1754–57), 5.

with regard to the limitation of sovereign powers and to the very definition of political society.

Hierarchy and Bourgeois Liberties

The monarchy just wanted to bring under control this capacity of the main guilds to stand against integrating into the state. It had to in the mid-eighteenth century because it gave cause for such a claim in the past. After the Fronde, the monarchy rewarded all the powers that had rallied (for instance, the *Six Corps* implored the king in 1652 to come back to the city), giving them more and more privileges and juridical stability. The monarchy no longer needed that much to win urban powers, given that the Versailles administration was strengthening. If urban institutions carried on using the language and sources of public authority, then the king would find his own way to retaliate. He would try, on many occasions, to model the bourgeois charges on the pattern of royal offices. How did the king set about doing this? As the master's letter was the real mark for registration and reception into the community, nothing was easier than to compare it with the direct service to the king even more than to the community, as the king was the ultimate base of public incorporation. Nobility itself, against its will, became based on that kind of analogy.

The king desired to create and sell masters' letters without having first obtained the agreement of the guilds which should have been the only ones able to control their enlisting rules. An edict of March 1691 already wanted to set charges of *garde* and *juré* up as office titles for all bodies and communities. This was the way of combining the elected chiefs of the guilds with plain office-holders coming under the Great Chancellery and the royal *parties casuelles*. The threatening measure reappeared in 1747 when the king planned to make all the masteries hereditary ones, then again in 1759 when he wanted to convert the masteries straight into offices. He planned the same thing in 1771. Whereas Maupeou's reform of 1771 attacked offices, as it could no longer tolerate them as the authority aids into the main courts of the kingdom, it carried on enforcing this political model within every space where royal interference was contested.[34] The *noblesse de robe* was in danger with such a reform. But the office remains the usual way of supporting the state's expansion.

Introducing such a model has many consequences, above all on the structure that bourgeois organs were founded, especially temporary mandates. At the end

---

[34]   David Bien, "Every Shoemaker an Officer: Terray the Reformer," in *L'Histoire grande ouverte: hommages à Emmanuel Le Roy Ladurie*, eds André Burguiére, Joseph Goy, and Marie-Jeanne Tits-Dieuaide (Paris: Fayard, 1997), 100–107.

of the seventeenth century, the former *consuls* and the former *gardes* of the *Six Corps* attempted to raise them to a *collège* form. That means they wanted to form themselves into groups definitively distinguished from the communities they came from, and by the common charges they carried out. These charges gave them now a superior voice over all their ordinary peers, the "commons" to which they could no longer revert. The collegiality of the "ancient ones" established the consistency of bourgeois jurisdictions that gradually saw themselves as like royal companies.[35] As within the nobility, dignity reaches men after it has reached their functions.

In fact, creating offices was a powerful instrument. It was how the king established urban institutions in a hierarchical linearity deriving only from him. It was the way to contain these institutions within a strong dependence upon honor and social quality, which could imitate the dependence on which the nobility suffered: taking part of the royal sovereignty only by direct delegation. It was the way to present the king as the only source of authority, not so much as the one that sheds and protects privileges, as the one that can always interpret them. So the guilds struggled against these reforms for years. They began to see in this struggle the loss of liberty, of the status and privileges they possessed, and the end of their autonomy. They avoided it by accepting debt and the payment of the special taxes the *Trésor* asked them for.[36] That occurred generally in time of war. Creating offices remained above all a fiscal instrument. However, in conferring nobility in 1706 on the *échevinage*, the first members of the municipality elected annually, the monarchy proved that it could assimilate any urban power into royal hierarchies. Instead of raising these bourgeois charges to offices, the king brought them down. He did it thanks to their new noble nature. Actually, this new municipal nobility, called the *noblesse de cloche*, was placed lower on the whole honor scale. Political distinction was due to the highest charges of the army and of the magistrature. Attaining nobility served as a kind of demonstration: the king demonstrated how he could absorb every power into his own person, how he legitimated them by his own authority, and how the last to have been ennobled stood at the lowest rank. Therefore, admission to the nobility was about to depreciate. It disparaged the old autonomous powers of the city.

But the ministry dispatched other dangers towards the guilds that were even more disturbing for them. After granting the nobility the right to wholesale commerce in 1669 and 1701, the king liberalized commerce in the 1760s and threatened the guilds again, not only by withdrawing their monopolies but

---

[35]   A.N., H2 2102, Mémoire servant de remontrances au sujet des élections des juge et consuls, v.1730.

[36]   Steven L. Kaplan, *La fin des corporations* (Paris: Fayard, 2001), 51–62.

also by deleting the social nature of the trade, its identity, in order to make it compatible with the values nobility based its income on. Of course, the relaxing of the *dérogeance* (disparagement) laws did not mean they were totally removed, as they were maintained for the retail trades. The liberalization of commerce stigmatized as never before retail commerce, which was the main business of the *Six Corps*. A hierarchical barrier was installed at the heart of merchant dignities and their ancient unity. The communities had to counter the dilution of their privileges into noble privilege, and to counter the reinforcement of *dérogeance* too. They answered thus in 1762:

> Wishing to take advantage of the fatherly dispositions of His Majesty, to benefit from them, *Messieurs* of the *Six Corps* have decided to present a memorandum to the General Lieutenant of Police, aiming to implore His Majesty that he be inclined favorably in interpreting the edicts of 1629, 1669, and 1701, to declare that these edicts invited noblemen to do some particular kinds of commerce without losing their rank, but that his intention never was to punish men doing other kinds of commerce by a sentence of *dérogeance*, even less the commerce that the members of the *Six Corps* of Paris are dealing with every day, wholesalers as much as retailers, consequently that he declares everybody dealing with them, today or in the future, able to enjoy, with their descendants, all the privileges that belong to them because of their birth rights [i.e. to enjoy nobility].[37]

The *Six Corps* did not win the case, of course. The king was only seeking to upset the old political structure of the city, forcing it to make its stance on the nobility clear, to assess its own value compared to the overall hierarchy. Retail business remained an impassable frontier between bourgeoisie and nobility. The Duke of La Force's proceedings (he was accused of owning a soap shop) revealed in 1720 the symbolic strength of such a frontier.[38] Besides, the royal legislation proved its ability to shift or to block categories. It stirred up quarrels between different spaces of social distinction which did not think a hierarchical relatedness could exist between them, thinking they rested on different legitimacies. Slowly it modified what social *états* or status contained and protected. While they were called by the same terms by lawyers or jurisconsults, amounting to the same historical and juridical functions, social *états* saw their political value change. Nobility was now like a sliding scale where they all move along.

---

[37]   A.N., KK 1343, 30 mars 1762, registre des délibérations des Six Corps.

[38]   It is possible to grasp the repercussions of this affair in the *Journal de Mathieu Marais*, annotated by Henri Duranton and Robert Granderoute (Saint-Etienne: Publications de l'Université de Saint-Etienne, 2004), t. I (1715–21), 339–420.

Nobility and Social Unsteadiness

The political utility assigned to categories was shifting, as was the concept of *vie noble*. All this treated the social lives of individuals and families roughly. People were affected by the difficulties they had in traveling through ranks or status whose continuity remained so uncertain. Many left the merchant business as a means of freeing up the shops they ran and to engender their turnover, thus assuring the renewal of their guilds, but they all discovered that their new nobility hardly produced positive outcomes.

Problems piled up quickly against ennobled men: it was difficult for them to enter a new culture of pomp, to still apply the customary rules of equality between heirs with the immovable and indivisible offices they now owned, to prolong the familial discipline with individual properties (the office) and without any shared one (the shop). The end result was the financial unsteadiness of many young office-holders, who were driven back to hard solutions: sudden separation of properties between husband and wife, bankruptcy, sale of offices. In 1754, magistrate of the *Chambre des comptes* and draper's son, Mr Guiller de Gerville, had to give up the community of property he had with his wife before he ceded her his own office with all the income that proceeded from it in order to pay back all her dowry.[39] The heirs of another magistrate, Mr Pocquelin, had to sell his office in 1714 because they could not pass this too important amount on to one son without infringing on the other son's rights.[40] The two sons entered the army and there spent all of their slim fortune. The last of one of Paris's greatest names in haberdashery, Pocquelin, one renowned for its banking activities as well, ended this way in 1762: a man died in a hotel room, owning nothing but a shirt and his captain sword.[41] A century before, the family had numbered among the most taxed and, thus, wealthiest merchants of Paris.[42]

Though a shapeless social category, the new nobility was still confronted with the tough demarcations of hierarchy. All disturbances that families were experiencing derived from those demarcations. They prevented ennoblement from being an "any case" fulfillment. Ennoblement became a sort of breakaway into a social world that traditional institutions and rules did not structure

---

[39] A.N., MC XCVIII 526, 18 avril 1754, transaction entre les époux Guiller de Gerville.

[40] A.N., LXXXVIII 431, 22 novembre 1714, inventaire après décès de Charles-Henri Pocquelin.

[41] A.N., LXXXVIII 664, 19 janvier 1762, inventaire après décès de Charles-Thomas Pocquelin.

[42] A.N., H2 2102, contribution du corps de la mercerie à la Compagnie des Indes Orientales, 1665.

anymore. As a draper's son, *maréchal des logis* Guiller lived with a woman without being married, to whom he bequeathed all his fortune in 1773.[43] His brother Guiller d'Héricourt, *secrétaire du roi*, did the same thing in 1781, in favor of a kinswoman he was living with for years.[44] His heirs sought advice from at least five lawyers before they gave up taking action against her. Before he died, their late brother made a point of producing a certificate which specified he was not married: he could make this woman his sole legatee.[45] The Guiller's cousin, Etienne-Paul Boucher, was an ennobled former draper as well, and had a love affair for 30 years after losing his wife. He had seven illegitimate children with his mistress.[46] As regards the ancient merchant Judde, directly ennobled from the king's hands for the commerce he conducted with the Baltic region, he remained single, ostentatiously living in his Parisian mansion and in his château of Soisy-sous-Etiolles. In the meantime, the police kept watch on him because of his close and dissolute contact with prostitutes.[47] He invited several of his noble nephews to his side in Paris, offering them the same comfort of a willful and definitive celibacy.[48] His family is still well known in Paris and Rouen for its overseas trading affairs. As for the *secrétaire du roi* Antoine-Edouard Nau, he left the old drapery business of his family, previously a distinguished one within all the great guilds of the city, of the *Six Corps*, in 1770 as a means of marrying an impoverished girl behind his kin's back, and to withdraw from the merchant quarter to a small and smart apartment in the north of Paris.[49] Endless examples could be related. None of these men had legitimate children. In spite of being noble, they all strove towards the progressive extinction of their names, without planning any dynastic foundations or any status perpetuation.

They confined their ennoblement to material pleasures, enjoying some properties suddenly devoid of any symbolical meaning. They suddenly used

---

[43]   A.N., MC XXIX 548, 21 mai 1773, dépôt du testament de Paul Guiller; ibid., 27 mai 1773, inventaire après décès du même.

[44]   A.N., MC XCVIII 680, 29 août 1781, inventaire après décès de Charles Guiller d'Héricourt.

[45]   Ibid., 4 juillet 1781, acte de notoriété du même.

[46]   Samuel Gibiat, *Hiérarchies sociales & ennoblissement: Les commissaires des guerres de la Maison du roi au XVIIIe siècle* (Paris: École des Chartes, 2006), 564–5.

[47]   Gaston Capon, *Les maisons closes au XVIIIe siècle: Académies de filles et courtières d'amour, maisons clandestines, matrones, mères-abbesses, appareilleuses et proxénètes: Rapports de police, documents secrets, notes personnelles des tenancières* (Paris: Daragon, 1903), 139.

[48]   A.N., MC XLVI 431, 27 avril 1770, inventaire après décès de Nicolas-Michel Judde.

[49]   A.N., MC C 805, 24 avril 1778, inventaire après décès d'Antoine-Edouard Nau.

luxury to express their individuality much more than their social rank.[50] While their former bourgeois status raised them up in a whole system of distinction, and of reputation and responsibilities, their nobility hurled them down in an urban total anonymity. At best, their fortune is captured by older families through marriage. They no longer knew how to manage with their social mobility in a time when prejudice was fixed, unchanging, and giving every preeminence to ancientness, to an antecedence they did not fit.[51] A lot did not experience social domination, but rather, the incapacity to harmonize their life with the canons of nobility.

Abandoning all thought of standard social life, these men created the modern category of individualism from the side of nobility they were members of. Inside Parisian society, individualism could not rest on a bourgeois lifestyle that could throw out collectively organized ways of thinking. The bourgeoisie was as socially structured as nobility always had been. On the other hand, it was within all the setbacks that nobility gave rise to that individualism could emerge, through hedonism and consumerism resulting from social disabilities, from social obstacles, much more than through feelings of personal fulfillment. Here, individualism was a reaction of social frustration in front of a non-integrating group that can be classed as the aristocracy.[52]

So, nobility sheds light on the way French society was longing for a social mobility that was true in theory. But it reveals all the difficulties and failures this mobility brought about in practice.

Conclusion

The relationships between monarch and society never did succeed in superimposing perfectly public holding and noble dignity. Questioning nobility is about putting it back in its real power of forcing things and deeds, of breaking off, of doing it in truly functional ways. Until urban institutions remained steadfast in countering the king's plans over the merchant guilds or the merchant court of Paris, families took advantage of maintaining themselves there, even the noble ones, even leaving the bourgeoisie to keep

---

[50]   Michael Kwass, "Big Hair: A Wig History of Consumption in Eighteenth-Century France," *The American Historical Review*, 111 (2006), 631–59.

[51]   Nicolas Lyon-Caen and Mathieu Marraud, "Le prix de la robe: coûts et conséquences du passage à l'office dans la marchandise parisienne, v.1680–v.1750," in *Epreuves de noblesse, les expériences de la haute robe parisienne (XVIe–XVIIIe siècle)*, ed. Elie Haddad (Paris: Belles Lettres, 2010), 233–56.

[52]   Marraud, *De la Ville à l'Etat*, 358–60, 435–40, 457–67.

it precisely open-populated. This variety that usages have respect for, in fact, shows how permanently conflicting legitimacies, jurisdictions, and juridical systems prevented the nobility from forming itself into a globality of action and meaning. They require thinking about it almost in a changing ideal way. More than a category, nobility can be seen as a dual mode of dialogue in Old Regime Paris: a social dialogue within families dividing up economical and patrimonial roles among themselves, and a political dialogue between monarchy and civil organization about defining how people can take part honorably in the state.

In spite of belonging to nobility or to its fringes at the same time, families can be distinguished by the way they invested in it, by the way they felt involved through their adhesion or their refusal to adhere to noble archetypes, or to the doctrine of political representation that absolutism was establishing. Since the Fronde, the monarchy heightened some charges or positions against others in order to heighten the king's favor against his older role of guarding franchises and privileges. Even if they did it in a fictitious way, several parts of the city persisted in showing a unity of values that the nobility was unable to embrace, to annex to hierarchy. Even outside noble status, the institutions could find efficiently their place in a political continuity linking the smallest urban powers to the highest sovereign courts. It is how society had always known to describe itself, much more than calling for the opposition between nobility and *roture*.[53] At this point, all offices, even ennobling ones, look like a system of exchange: complex exchange between desires of public credit and hierarchical annexation, on the part of the state; desires of perpetuation through properties and dignities, on the part of individuals; and lastly desires of perpetuation through historical and traditional foundations, on the part of institutions.[54]

In consequence, holding any fraction of common authority did not lead to ennobling processes. Seeking any social distinction did not lead to a concern for assimilation into the *second ordre*. Evolutions of the state and of its numbers could not avoid weakening nobility in the capacity it should have to signify naturally all the preeminence and hegemony. Consequently, historians have to continue describing the Bourbon monarchy as a system of exchanges and rivalries. In the center of it, nobility did not exhaust the variety of all political

---

[53]   Jacques Revel, "Les corps et communautés," in *The Political Culture of the Old Regime*, eds Keith Baker and François Furet (Oxford: Pergamon Press, 1987), 225–42.

[54]   Mark Potter, "Good Offices: Intermediation by Corporate Bodies in Early Modern France," *Journal of Economic History*, 60 (2000), 599–626; Wolfgang Reinhard, "Puissance étatique: un problème de crédit? Structure et fonction du commerce des offices à l'époque moderne," in *Papauté, confession, modernité* (Paris: Éditions de l'EHESS, 1998), 137–53.

languages and social maturities the period took in. It would not be the case after 1750, when the second absolutism defeated the ancient forms of incorporation inside the city, when it imposed on them by aristocratic ideals the wild dream of an ultimate perfection brought out by the king's immemorial service.

Chapter 12

Challenging the Status Quo: Attempts to Modernize the Polish Nobility in the Later Eighteenth Century

Jerzy Lukowski

On the eve of the First Partition of 1772, there may have been roughly 1 million nobles in the Commonwealth of Poland-Lithuania—out of a total population of some 14 million. In 1792, one year before the Second Partition, the number stood at some 750,000 in a population of around 11 million. Between 6 and 7 percent of the population enjoyed noble status, comparable to the figures for Hungary, Spain, or Portugal, and with much the same disparities of wealth within the noble (*szlachta*) estate. Perhaps only one in six might qualify as a truly independent country gentleman, topped by a handful of magnates of immense wealth; most of the rest wallowed in poverty or relied on some form of service with or patronage from their wealthier "elder brethren." In 1790, some 100,000 adult males made up an active citizenry—inevitably dominated by a small minority of more substantial landowners. In theory, all nobles—or at least, all landowning nobles, no matter how small their properties—were equal. All felt themselves superior to commoners; all felt themselves to be the real rulers of the Commonwealth: they elected their kings, who, in turn, could undertake no legislation or even, supposedly, any form of domestic or foreign policy initiative without the approval of the central parliament, the Sejm.[1] Poland's extreme republicanism amounted to what commentators began calling in the 1770s

---

[1]   For an accessible introduction, see Robert I. Frost, "The Nobility of Poland-Lithuania, 1569–1795," in *The European Nobilities in the Seventeenth and Eighteenth Centuries*, vol. 2, ed. Hamish M. Scott (Basingstoke: Palgrave Macmillan, 2007), 266–310. See also J.T. Lukowski, *Liberty's Folly: The Polish-Lithuanian Commonwealth in the Eighteenth Century, 1697–1795* (London: Routledge, 1991). The best estimates of the noble population after 1772 are to be found in Emanuel Rostworowski, "Ilu było w Rzeczypospolitej szlachty," *Kwartalnik Historyczny*, 94 (1988), 3–40.

"*szlachta* democracy."[2] It meant that little could be achieved in Poland unless a significant proportion of the nobility could be called on to give its approval.

The dominance of the *szlachta* was never more secure from domestic challenge than in the eighteenth century. The wars of the later seventeenth and early eighteenth centuries so debilitated commercial and urban elements that they could never even begin to contemplate rivaling the nobility—ambitious commoners (as, indeed, in most of Europe) sought to join nobles, not to displace them. The sort of family strategies pursued by bourgeois elements in Paris, as described by Matthieu Marraud, were practically unthinkable.[3] At best, the predominantly Germanophone elites of the three "Great Towns" of Polish Prussia (Danzig/Gdańsk, Elbing/Elbląg, and Thorn/Toruń) regarded themselves as the social equals of the nobility. Their determination to preserve their own and their province's wide legal autonomy became largely irrelevant after the bulk of the region was swallowed up by Prussia under the First Partition of 1772. Most Polish "towns" were large villages, inhabited above all by peasants and Jews. The latter had no formal political role at all in the country. They were excluded from almost all municipal magistracies. A truly significant urban sector, capable of agitating for expanded political rights, existed only in Warsaw, whose population by 1790 hovered at around the 100,000 mark—a giant metropolis by Polish standards, but it was the only one.[4]

The traditional values and world of the Polish nobility, where political liberty was their exclusive preserve and their economic security was assured through an obedient serf labor force, did not, however, go without questioning from within the *szlachta* estate itself. It occurred above all at an ideological level, but occasionally too it was backed up by attempts at practical political action. The apogee of noble freedoms was, of course, the *liberum veto*, the right of any one nobleman to disrupt the proceedings of the Sejm and of local assemblies by his sole "*Nie pozwalam!*" (I will not allow it!). Recourse to that destructive liberty was questioned almost from its first fully fledged manifestation in 1652, even if early efforts were directed towards its regulation rather than its extirpation.[5]

---

[2]   Antoni Popławski, *Zbiór niektórych materyi politycznych* (Warsaw, 1774), 241, 243, 247.

[3]   See Marraud, this volume.

[4]   Emanuel Rostworowski, "Miasta i mieszczanie w ustroju Trzeciego Maja," in *Sejm Czteroletni i jego tradycje*, ed. Jerzy Kowecki (Warsaw: PWN, 1991), 138–51.

[5]   Stanisław Dunin Karwicki, "Egzorbitancje we wszystkich trzech stanach Rzeczypospolitej krótko zebrane ...", [ms. c. 1703], in Karwicki, *Dzieła polityczne z początku XVIII wieku*, eds Adam Przyboś and Kazimierz Przyboś (Wrocław: Ossolineum, 1992), 23–79; Karwicki, *O potrzebie urządzenia Rzeczypospolitej albo o naprawie defektów w stanie Rzeczypospolitej Polskiej* [usually known as *De ordinanda Republica*, first published 1746],

Likewise, throughout the first 60 years or so of the eighteenth century, individual voices, wrapped inside major treatises urging a greater or lesser degree of political reform, were raised calling for better treatment of the peasant population. Any change in their legal situation as *glebae adscripti* was bound to have repercussions for the nobility, even for those who did not own serfs. But neither a questioning of the veto, nor handwringing over the oppression of the peasantry, offered any kind of threat to the position of the nobility. Had the suggestions proposed in Stefan Garczyński's eccentric *Anatomia Rzeczypospolitey Polskiey* of 1753 been implemented, peasant labor duties would have been halved, but the dominant position of the nobles left intact. Garczyński advocated compassion and moral renewal, not structural reform. Only in oblique terms did he propose a transition from labor duties to rentals.[6] The thorny issue of serfdom was tackled in the most far-reaching reform treatise of the first half of the eighteenth century, the *Free Voice, Freedom Announcing* of 1743. Usually attributed to the exiled ex-king of Poland, Stanisław Leszczyński, it advocated peasant emancipation and moving to a system of rents in kind, but, in the Polish context, its arguments were quite exceptional for its time. The author had almost nothing to say about Poland's towns. He was quite emphatic that the "commonalty" (*pospólstwo*) were to be kept out of politics.[7] The public life of the Polish-Lithuanian Commonwealth remained reserved for the *szlachta* alone.

There was an external wild card: the role of Russia, which since the early eighteenth century had exercised an increasingly strong influence on Polish affairs, to the point where it was decisive in securing the elections of the Commonwealth's last two kings, Augustus III in 1733 and Stanisław Poniatowski in 1763. But Russia had no interest in challenging the dominance of the *szlachta* as such— it sought to use Poland as an instrument of its own geopolitical ambitions. It had little truck with the reformist ambitions of Catherine the Great's protégé, Poniatowski, after 1763, whose refusal to toe the Russian line at all times was to bring about all sorts of complications.

---

ibid., 87–189. But see Bronisław Natoński, "Walenty Pęski" in *Polski Słownik Biograficzy*, eds W. Konopczyński et al. (Kraków: Polska Akademia Umiejętności, 1935–), 25, 446–8.

⁶ Stefan Garczyński, *Anatomia Rzeczypospolitey Polskiey* (Breslau, 1753), *passim* and 126–9.

⁷ Stanisław Leszczyński, attr., *Głos Wolny Wolność Głosujący* (Nancy, 1733 [=1743]), esp. 100–106 and cf. 125–6. The authorship of the treatise has been questioned by Emanuel Rostworowski, "Czy Stanisław Leszczyński jest autorem *Głosu Wolnego*?" in Rostworowski, *Legendy i fakty XVIIIw.* (Warsaw: PWN, 1963), 68–144, but the issues raised remain unresolved. For an accessible, scholarly account of Leszczyński, see Anne Muratori-Philippe, *Le roi Stanislas* (Paris: Fayard, 2000).

The first real "challenge" to the established self-portrait of *szlachta* ideology emerged in the 1740s—not an outright ideological questioning as such, but the establishment in Warsaw, in 1741, of a Collegium Nobilium, an exclusive boarding establishment aimed at the education of the sons of the wealthier nobles by the Reverend Stanisław Konarski. He was one of the most outstanding eighteenth-century representatives of the teaching order of "clerks regular of the Pious Schools of the Poor of the Mother of God," more succinctly known as the Piarists. In Poland, the order had long since concentrated its energies on teaching the nobility rather than the poor, and was second only to the Jesuits as a purveyor of education to the *szlachta*.[8] The fee-paying establishment offering a modernized curriculum inspired by the *Ritterakademien* of Germany and the more progressive Piarist and Jesuit colleges of France and Italy seems to have initially aroused little comment, perhaps because of its modest beginnings.[9] No serious criticism of it appears to have surfaced before 1758, when Felix Czacki published (anonymously) his *Complaint of the poor nobility at the boarding schools opened in Poland*.[10] By then, not only had the Polish province of the Piarist order adopted the new educational program but also the Jesuits, the principal purveyors of education to the *szlachta*, had opened several similar elite schools. It was during the 1750s that great magnate families began sending their sons to Konarski's establishment in any numbers. The new colleges were a challenge precisely because they were exclusive, charging hefty fees for supervised boarding on the premises. They deliberately sought to provide an education for the sons of those nobles who might reasonably aspire to holding the leading offices of state. Hitherto, at most, noble families might have had to spend only on some kind of accommodation near the schools attended by their offspring.[11] Felix Czacki painted a picture of an imaginary *szlachta* world, bound in an idyllic brotherhood, whose fundamental equality transcended all division:

---

[8]   Konarski's undoubted attainments in other fields may have led to an underplaying of what others were also achieving. Similar initiatives were at least under consideration by the Jesuits from the late 1730s, held back by lack of funds and suitable accommodation. See Ludwik S.J. Piechnik, "Jezuickie Collegium Nobilium w Warszawie," in *Z dziejów szkolnictwa jezuickiego w Polsce*, ed. Jerzy S.J. Paszenda (Kraków: WAM, 1994), 151–82.

[9]   Konarski's establishment initially took in only some 20 boarders: even in 1754, when it received new, purpose-built accommodation, their number had barely reached 50. Stanisław Bednarski, *Upadek i odrodzenie szkół jezuickich w Polsce* (Kraków: Wyd. Księży Jezuitów, 1933), 442–3.

[10]   Felix Czacki, *Skarga ubogiej szlachty na otworzone w Polsce konwikty, podczas sejmików zaniesiona* (n.p. [1758]).

[11]   See the measured appraisal by Kazimierz Puchowski, "'Collegium Nobilium' Stanisława Konarskiego a elitarne instytucje wychowawcze zakonów nauczających w Europie," *Wiek Oświecenia*, 20 (2004), 11–69.

> In those happier times, when the poorer and wanting sons of nobles were able in
> large numbers to attend public schools alongside more substantial young lords,
> waiting on them in their service, and in their domestic employ; and thus could
> one see the beautiful rulings of Divine Providence, how in a common mutuality
> the poor nobility served wealthier lords, who, in turn, provided them with the
> means to acquire an education at their side and then gave them their hand and
> assistance to further fortune.[12]

This picture of a nobility woven together in virtue exercised a powerful hold
on the Polish noble mind: if society was not like this, it should have been like
this; if it had strayed from this, it had done so through the moral failings of
individuals, not through deficiencies in the constitution of the Polish-Lithuanian
Commonwealth. Those who sought reform wanted to expose such imaginings
to a cold blast of realism and begin to get the nobility to view things as they
were, not how so many of them wished them to be. The new elite schools were
only the beginning of that process.

Outright, open questioning of the noble Arcadia on anything like a
significant scale began in 1765. That year saw the launch of a new periodical,
the *Monitor*, a vehicle for the dissemination of the reform hopes of the new
monarch, Stanisław August Poniatowski, elected in 1764. The *Monitor*, which
had a regular subscription list of around 500, and which continued to appear
until 1785, tackled a range of controversial subjects in its early issues: the reform
of serfdom; prejudices against foreigners, religious minorities, and commercial
enterprise; and the need for more effective government—which inevitably
involved support for the abolition of the *liberum veto*. Here, the ground had been
already laid by Stanisław Konarski, whose *On the Means to Successful Counsels*
of 1761–63 constituted a detailed intellectual demolition of that destructive
device,[13] although the widespread interest it aroused, unprecedented for a Polish
political treatise, had been overtaken by the tumultuous events of the 1763–
64 interregnum. During that interval, reformers made use of a Confederacy
(*konfederacja*) to push through some of their objectives—that is, of a league with
a proclaimed program to which nobles subscribed, leaving the leadership free to
take decisions unencumbered by the *liberum veto*. King Stanisław August opened
up another front in the war against entrenched prejudices. In November 1765,
a National Theatre (*Teatr Narodowy*) opened in Warsaw, in a country where a
theatrical tradition barely existed. Although Italian opera and French plays were
a staple part of the *Teatr Narodowy*'s repertoire, new Polish plays were more

---

[12] Czacki, *Skarga ubogiej szlachty*, 3r.
[13] Stanisław Konarski, *O Skutecznym Rad Sposobie albo o Utrzymywaniu ordynaryinych Sejmów*, 4 vols (Warsaw: u XX. Scholarum Piarum, 1760–63).

important. These consciously didactic performances were meant to encourage new attitudes and ideas, urging a reexamination of traditional "Sarmatian" ways of being and advocating the embrace of a wider European culture. Envoys to the 1766 Sejm were given free tickets to performances of Franciszek Bohomolec's *Ceremoniant*, an adaptation of Philippe Destouches' *Fausse Agnès*, in which the boorishness of provincial nobility was much ridiculed. The heavy-handed send-ups of the nobility which characterized the earliest performances were more likely to offend than to win hearts and minds.[14]

The nobility were left in no doubt after the mid-1760s that their world was under challenge—not only from the forces of external, principally Russian, intervention but also from within their own ranks. It was the defenders of the old order who had to respond to reforming initiatives. On the one hand, the search for reform could make no headway amid the chaos which engulfed Poland between 1768 and 1772, in a confused mixture of civil war and anti-Russian guerrilla campaigning which was to culminate in the First Partition. On the other hand, the conservative, anti-royalist camp, represented by the *frondeur* Confederacy of Bar, chose to bolster its ideological credentials by turning to the *philosophes* of France for support. In 1770, the Confederacy's agent to Versailles, Michał Wielhorski, contacted, among others, Gabriel Bonnot de Mably and Jean-Jacques Rousseau for advice and succor. The results were far from what Wielhorski and his kind were hoping for.

Mably was forthright in his condemnation of Poland's failings: its laws were highly defective; they, and in particular the *liberum veto*, lay at the root of Poland's woes. He proposed strong medicine: not only abolition of the veto but also the creation of a more vigorous parliament and a strong executive in the Senate under a figurehead king. He also urged the introduction of hereditary monarchy. He wanted something totally at variance with long centuries of practice and tradition: "une puissance publique, qui peut intimider par des force supérieures" (all citizens not prepared to observe the law).[15] Mably's proposals became even more radical once he embarked on a discussion of Polish society. He wanted to admit commoners to real share in the Commonwealth's public life. Townsmen were to be given a much greater role in the administration of justice. They (and even Jews) would be given the right to own land (a right largely removed in 1496). He wanted to give the peasantry direct access to state courts. Only when these groups were given a real interest in the country could Poland flourish.[16] He

---

[14]   Mieczysław Klimowicz, *Początki teatru stanisławowskiego (1765–1773)* (Warsaw: PIW, 1965), 50, 79–219, 265–70.

[15]   Gabriel Bonnot de Mably, *Du gouvernement et des lois de la Pologne: Oeuvres complètes de l'abbé Mably*, vol. 8 (Bossange: Masson et Besson, 1797), 176.

[16]   Ibid., 114.

was sufficiently conscious of the strength of noble prejudice to counsel delaying such measures of social reform until the nobility had been made aware of where their true interests lay. Ultimately, Mably hoped for a free peasantry, perhaps by starting with the emancipation after 20 years' service of peasant conscripts in a reformed army.[17]

Rousseau was less radical: he would have retained the *liberum veto* and elective monarchy, even if in recast form. But he agreed with Mably on social reform and on the emancipation of the peasantry, even if he was, in the final analysis, reluctantly prepared to retain serfdom if the peasantry showed itself unworthy of liberty. But, in principle, he wanted their emancipation; as for townsmen, he would not only have greatly extended their rights but also would have seen them armed and eligible for incorporation in a national militia, the better to be able to defend a country to which they would feel a renewed attachment.[18]

Mably and Rousseau posited a long-term program of reeducation in order to enlighten the nobility into accepting reform—that too had been the aim of Stanisław Konarski and King Stanisław August Poniatowski. It was also the aim of the Commission for National Education, set up in 1774 in the wake of the First Partition and Pope Clement XIV's dissolution of the Jesuit order in July 1773. As one of the Commission's early correspondents put it, "If we had good education, would we be in the condition in which we are today?"[19] Those involved in educational reform, with the king to the fore, all accepted the need for a better-educated and public-spirited noble community. In the Commission's own words, it had been given the opportunity "for a more perfect education of posterity ... let us go about this salutary undertaking and lift up the more quickly the wholly fallen hopes of our Commonwealth."[20] The French physiocrat, Pierre Samuel du Pont de Nemours, briefly secretary for foreign correspondence to the Commission in 1774, defined its task as that of "créer une nation par l'instruction publique."[21] A modernized curriculum emerged in 1783, with less emphasis on

---

[17]   Ibid., 137.

[18]   Jean-Jacques Rousseau, *Considérations sur le gouvernement de Pologne*, ed. Jean Fabre, reprinted in *Oeuvres Complètes de Jean-Jacques Rousseau*, vol. 3, eds Bernard Gagnebin and Marcel Raymond (Paris: Gallimard, 1964), 951–1041.

[19]   Franciszek Bieliński, *Sposób edukacji w XV. Listach opisany, które do Kommissyi Edukacyi Narodowey od bezimiennego autora były przesyłane* (Warsaw, 1775), 52.

[20]   From the Proclamation of the Establishment of the Commission, 24 October 1773, ed. Stanisław Tync, *Komisja Edukacji Narodowej (pisma Komisji i o Komisji). Wybór źródeł* (Wrocław: Ossolineum, 1954), 29. See also *Volumina Legum*, 11 vols (Warsaw, 1732–92), reprinted (St Petersburg and Kraków, 1859–89), 8: 152–3.

[21]   Ambroise Jobert, *La Commission d'Éducation Nationale en Pologne (1773–1794)* (Paris: Droz, 1941), 27, 185.

instruction in Latin and in religion (though neither were neglected) but with a much greater emphasis on "moral sciences" (such subjects as modern and classical history, geography, law), natural sciences, mathematics, and modern languages.[22] Ostensibly, once more, no challenge to the status quo was involved. It was explicitly geared towards "the *szlachta* youth" (*młódź szlachecka*).[23]

More subversive of the established order was the ethos driving the educational reformers. The Commission for National Education asked du Pont to draft a memorandum on how serfdom might be gradually abolished.[24] To Michał Wielhorski and to the great majority of his fellow nobles, "The *szlachta* alone are honored with the name of citizens."[25] But it was at around this time that the concept of citizenship began to be extended to commoners. In 1773, the *Monitor*, taking its cue from fashionable physiocracy, proclaimed that "Agriculture alone enriches and gives life to kings, nobles, merchants, craftsmen, laborers and all peasants, or, more briefly, all the citizens of the state, from the first, to the last."[26] Such sentiments were increasingly echoed, above all by close associates of the Commission. For Franciszek Bieliński, there were four categories of citizen: clergy, nobles, townsmen, and *rolnicy* ("farmers" in the English sense of the word). Significantly, he consistently eschewed the use of terms such as *chłopi* and *poddani*, that is, "peasants" and "serfs."

> These are all citizens; these should all be good citizens, the four wheels forming the machine (*machinę*) of our country so perfectly fashioned that, aiming for one goal, they assist but do not impede one another.

All were to be the beneficiaries of "public education." These were not of course "citizens" *tout court*. Citizens came in different categories, each with its own set of rights and duties—citizens "of all conditions."[27] Nonetheless, "citizens" was how commoners were, by some, acknowledged. For Antoni Popławski, one of the most distinguished Piarist successors of Stanisław Konarski, the *obywatel* (the citizen)—the mature, economically active adult male individual—formed the

---

[22] Tync, *Komisja Edukacji Narodowej*, "Ustawy Komisji Edukacji Narodowej," 571–723.

[23] Ibid., 25, 572. See also *Volumina Legum*, 8: 152. In practice, the new schools were also open to young townsmen, just as the old Jesuit and Piarist schools had been.

[24] Jobert, *La Commission*, 186–7. Du Pont's memorandum has been lost, but, in the manner of Mably and Rousseau, it envisaged emancipation after military service.

[25] Michał Wielhorski, *O przywróceniu dawnego rządu według pierwiastkowych Rzeczypospolitey ustaw* (Amsterdam, 1775), 165–6.

[26] *Monitor*, 100 (15 December 1773), 783.

[27] Bieliński, *Sposób edukacji*, 10, 15. See also Adolf Kamieński, *Edukacya obywatelska* (Warsaw, 1774), 10–11, 14, 84–5, 160–64.

basic building block of the state. Popławski did not avoid the word "peasants," but he preferred the more neutral, bordering on the abstract "farmers" (*rolnicy*), making it clear that these comprised a wide range of agricultural occupations: "landowning farmer, holders of land, tenants, renters or rent-paying administrators of land, peasants, servants, hired laborers"—all were citizens.[28] Citizenship was not yet equal, but, for some, all commoners were coming to be embraced in it.

In 1776, the Sejm entrusted a reform of Poland's chaotic judicial processes to ex-crown chancellor Andrzej Zamoyski. He was to be guided by "natural justice" and "to amend all things which might leave citizens and judges in doubt as to their duties."[29] An early proponent of political reform, he was something of a model paternalistic landowner. A physiocratic sympathizer, he experimented cautiously with the replacement of labor dues by cash rentals on some of his estates.[30] He and his team of advisors interpreted their brief in 1776 in the widest possible manner—not merely to reform judicial procedures, but to secure wider structural changes in Polish society.

The *szlachta* estate itself was to be transformed by being made formally open to talent and productive wealth creation. Under Article XIV of his proposed law code:

> To encourage the desire to foster industry which will bring public benefits, We decree that if anyone should discover mineral or salt deposits in the lands of the Commonwealth, or excel in learning or some particular art, from which a public benefit to the nation as a whole might follow.

Such a person could be ennobled, as indeed could anyone purchasing landed property to the value of 200,000 zlotys.[31] Although some traditional activities

---

[28] Popławski, *Zbiór niektórych materyi politycznych*, 4, 7–8, 19–20.

[29] *Volumina Legum*, 8: 543.

[30] See Zamoyski's speech to the Convocation Sejm, 16 May 1764, in *Historia Polski 1764–1795: wybór tekstów*, ed. Jerzy Michalski (Warsaw: PWN, 1954), 65–78. Ryszard Orłowski, *Działalność społeczno-gospodarcza Andrzeja Zamoyskiego (1757–1792)* (Lublin: UMCS, 1965), 182–203, 212–30; Józef Kasperek, *Gospodarka folwarczna Ordynacji Zamoyskiej w drugiej połowie XVIII wieku* (Warsaw: PWN, 1972), 18–19, 37–8, 164, 170. For a positive, if overstated, contemporary assessment of his landownership regime, see William Coxe, *Travels in Poland and Russia* (5th edn, London, 1802), reprinted (New York: Arno Press, 1970), vol. 1, 114–18. See also Ewa Borkowska-Bagieńska, *'Zbiór Praw Sądowych' Andrzeja Zamoyskiego* (Poznań: UAM, 1986), 20–31; and Jerzy Michalski, "O rzekomych i rzeczywistych pismach Andrzeja Zamoyskiego," *Przegląd Historyczny*, 61 (1970), 452–75.

[31] A. Zamoyski et al., *Zbiór Praw Sądowych na mocy konstytucyi 1776 roku ... ułożony ...* (Warsaw: Gröll, 1778), 45, 48.

leading to derogation of nobility were reaffirmed (acceptance of municipal citizenship, the pursuit of retail trades), *szlachectwo* was to be formally made much more porous, and the boundaries between nobles and commoners blurred, by encouraging the former to pursue manufacturing enterprises in towns and allowing them to practice professions not subject to guild regulation—including medicine, painting, engraving, architecture and construction (*professye ... mularskie*), the manufacture and retailing of "physical, geometric and astronomical instruments," and printing.[32] The provisions relating to jurisprudence were so framed as to allow, or not to prevent, commoners from using the practice of the law as an avenue to acquiring noble status and offices ordinarily reserved to *szlachta*.[33] This was no longer to be a nobility based on mythical, ancestral martial prowess, but a nobility of economic substance, enterprise, and talent.

Far more striking, however, were the Code's proposals relating to serfdom. "I have ... put the peasants under the protection of the law" stated Zamoyski in the preamble, since it was in "the general interest" that Poland should be populous and its agriculture flourish.[34] This in itself was a major step: peasants had hitherto not enjoyed the protection of the laws at best; the Sejm of 1767–68 had removed the seigneurial right of capital punishment—such cases would be heard by the nearest noble or urban court.[35] But more meaningful, and more alarming to the great majority of nobles, were the Code's proposals to recast serfdom. Under article XXXI, *glebae adscripti* were now linked explicitly to the working of landholdings and the use of agricultural equipment and livestock (*załoga*) provided by the seigneur. Those, however, who had any kind of contractual relationship with the landowner, written or oral, and who received no *załoga*, were free to leave on the expiration of their contract as *non adscripti glebae*. Included in this category were cottagers—those who received no landholding from the landlord. At a stroke, non-landed laborers were to be released from their serf status.

Furthermore, processes were to be set in process which would, over time, make serfdom untenable. The eldest and third sons of a serf would remain bound in life service to the estate. Second and younger sons "can be given, at the age of ten, by their father to the practice of learning, crafts and trades; they will require no specific permission for this from their seigneurs" beyond a certificate

---

[32] Ibid., 72–3, 81–2.

[33] Ibid., 33–4, 38.

[34] Ibid., viii–ix.

[35] This was classed as a "Cardinal Law"; the same provision also emphasized that apart from this, seigneurial jurisdiction and rights over their serfs would be fully preserved in perpetuity. *Volumina Legum*, 7: 280.

from their parish priest stating that, under the law, they were entitled to "acquire true freedom." But even if such sons remained on the estate and continued to practice agriculture, "they will be equally free." Seigneurs were entitled to recover runaway serfs, but, under a law (supposedly) of 1386, they would lose that right after the lapse of just one year; after four years, they would not only lose the right to recover any *załoga* the absconding peasant had taken, but "prescription will make the person of the peasant, his wife and children, with whom he had absconded, free." And after ten years, the aggrieved landlord would lose the right to any compensation for movable property the peasant might have taken with him.

As if this were not enough, even serfs who had undertaken any kind of contractual agreement with the landowner were to be free to summons him before the local court if the landowner failed to observe his side of the contract— something quite unheard of for private landlords. A landlord's jurisdiction over serfs would be weakened by the transfer of criminal hearings to state courts; nor would he be able to incarcerate a serf for more than 24 hours. Should a seigneur kill a serf, not only would he be liable to the death penalty and his heirs have to pay the victim's family pecuniary compensation, but the entire extended (*poboczna*) family of the victim would receive its freedom. As for those serfs remiss in the performance of their obligations, they could be punished by their seigneur with a public lashing only with the approval of the local court.[36]

Zamoyski paid only lip service to the preservation of serfdom. His motivation was avowedly economic (physiocratic), to encourage freedom as a means to boosting the nation's industry and wealth. "We see the principal cause of the poverty of our country in the lack of that estate of persons, which through the various arts and crafts enriches the country, keeps money circulating in it, thereby encouraging agriculture itself, so that, through an increase in population, it will flourish through the consumption of goods and the circulation of monies."[37] For that reason, the legal rigidities of serfdom had to go. Zamoyski's proposals punched so many holes in the institution that it is difficult to see how it could survive. Up until then, the "normal" commoner in agriculture had been a serf; were the proposals to be accepted, the new norm would be a free citizen.

The proposed code was published in the summer of 1778 but its submission to the Sejm was deferred until 1780, in order to give the nobility more time to digest its contents. It was the first major test in the confrontation between enlightened reform and the old-established structures of the Polish-Lithuanian noble polity. It was a fiasco. The *Patriotic Letters* of 1777 of Józef Wybicki, one of

---

[36]   Zamoyski, *Zbiór Praw Sądowych*, 89–94, Article XXXI.
[37]   Ibid., 90.

Zamoyski's closest collaborators, which aimed to win noble opinion over to the code, failed utterly to do so. Wybicki himself abandoned all thought of standing for the constituency of the palatinates of Poznań and Kalisz as envoy to the Sejm in 1780 after threats to his life. The *sejmiki* were overwhelmingly hostile, foreseeing the ruin of the *szlachta* estate. Not one supported the Code. The Sejm rejected the proposals and forbade their reintroduction in the future. Outraged envoys trampled copies of Zamoyski's Law Code underfoot.[38] It was as emphatic a rejection of the call to reform as could be.

The 1780s were largely a period of political torpor in the Commonwealth. There was no scope for grand initiatives after the Zamoyski debacle. *Sejmy* which had enacted major reforms such as the creation of the Commission for National Education had been able to do so only because they had functioned under the aegis of a Confederacy. It was thanks to this device that the *Sejmy* of 1767–68 and 1773–75 had reformed parliamentary procedures to the point where minor individual items of legislation could go through without being subjected to the veto—but since major items remained within its purview, the non-confederated parliaments of the 1780s could agree only routine, quasi-administrative bills. The fact that the Sejm of 1780 had not been confederated would almost certainly have led to the wrecking of the Zamoyski proposals by use of the individual veto, even if feeling had not run so powerfully against it.

Most of the political writers of the 1780s did little more than tread ideological water, advancing little, if at all, beyond the arguments of their predecessors. Hieronim Stroynowski OSP's textbook of 1785, *The Science of Natural Law* (*Nauka Prawa Przyrodzonego*) combined physiocracy with Rousseau, but only the most dedicated could have followed its cumbersome calculations on monetary circulation and national wealth distribution—there is absolutely nothing to suggest its abstruse ratiocinations had any impact whatever on a conservative nobility. Konstanty Bogusławski's *On perfect legislation* (*O doskonałym prawodawctwie*), of 1786 argued more accessibly and perhaps more desperately that "perfect legislation" could only ensue once an educational system had been perfected. The education he envisaged was clearly that laid down by the Commission for National Education—but it could only compete if its beneficiaries went through the curriculum in its entirety.[39] Consciously or not, Bogusławski had put his finger on a major problem. *Szlachta* society was deeply suspicious of the new schools. If nothing else, the gradual creation of a lay teaching profession under the Commission's aegis led to immense friction and

---

[38]   Józef Wybicki, *Pamiętniki Józefa Wybickiego*, 3 vols, ed. Edward Raczyński (Poznań: Stefański, 1840), 2: 36–43. See also *Volumina Legum*, 8: 588–9.

[39]   Konstanty Bogusławski, *O doskonałym prawodawctwie* (Warsaw: Drukarnia J.K. Mci, 1786), 35–6, 49.

misunderstandings. The downgrading of Latin was met by incomprehension and a widespread resort to illegal schools where it retained its old primacy. Probably fewer than 10 percent of all pupils completed the curriculum in its entirety, most missing out entirely on the senior classes where those subjects—the "moral sciences" intended to form the new, enlightened patriotic citizen—were most intensively taught.[40]

When in 1788, with the stifling Russian protectorate undermined by war with Turkey, Poland-Lithuania's parliament had its first genuine opportunity to debate freely for a prolonged period for almost a century, noble society was ready to contemplate only the most sporadic change. The *sejmiki* envisaged limited increases in the size of the army; increased taxation of non-nobles, principally the church; the dismantling of much of the administrative machinery introduced in 1773–76; but no serious thought was given to constitutional reform; social reform barely featured on the noble electorate's horizons.[41] The status quo was to remain.

The Sejm that met in October 1788 remained in session until June 1792. With the loss of Russian control, a massive outburst of desire for genuine independence was unleashed, but what form that independence was to take was the subject of unprecedented debate. Something akin to a genuine "public sphere" focused on the confederated parliament emerged. For almost the first time, even commoners—principally Warsaw townsmen, occasionally even Jews—joined in polemical exchanges.[42] Around 600–700 printed political tracts appeared during those fours years, excluding numerous manuscript circulations, the most popular appearing in two or three editions and print runs reaching 5,000.[43] The Commonwealth of the two nations had never seen anything like

---

[40]   Kamila Mrozowska, *Funkcjonowanie systemu szkolnego Komisji Edukacji Narodowej na terenie Korony w latach 1783–1793* (Wrocław: Ossolineum, 1985), 188–233.

[41]   Jerzy Michalski, "Sejmiki poselskie 1788 roku," *Przegląd Historyczny*, 51 (1960), 52–73, 331–67, 465–82.

[42]   The most comprehensive modern treatment of the political literature generated by the Four-Year Sejm is Anna Grześkowiak-Krwawicz, *O formę rządu czy o rząd dusz: publicystyka polityczna Sejmu Czteroletniego* (Warsaw: IBL, 2000). The main accounts of the Sejm remain W. Kalinka's unfinished *Sejm Czteroletni*, first published posthumously in 1888. The latest edition is Walerian Kalinka, *Sejm Czteroletni*, ed. Zofia Zielińska (Warsaw: Volumen, 1991), 2 vols. Much of the key legislation is analyzed in Bogusław Leśnodorski, *Dzieło Sejmu Czteroletniego 1788–92* (Wrocław: Ossolineum, 1951). For accessible accounts in English, see R. Butterwick, *Poland's Last King and English Culture: Stanisław August Poniatowski, 1723–1798* (Oxford: Clarendon Press, 1998), 275–309; Lukowski, *Liberty's Folly*, 239–52; J.T. Lukowski, *Disorderly Liberty: The Political Culture of the Polish-Lithuanian Commonwealth in the Eighteenth Century* (London: Continuum, 2010), 173–250.

[43]   Grześkowiak-Krwawicz, *O formę rządu*, 39–50.

this. The bulk of this literature focused on political and constitutional matters—what shape the Polish-Lithuanian polity and its institutions was to take. The most hotly debated issue was whether it should retain elective monarchy or opt for hereditary succession. Of social or socio-political issues raised by reformers during the preceding two decades, only that of political rights for townsmen gave rise to any significant, prolonged discussion. Though individual reformers continued to raise the matter of serf reform, within the context of the Sejm's debates and of political literature as a whole, it remained an emphatically marginal concern.[44] Events in France, of which the reading public was well informed by an active press, amounted to "noises off," utilized by political groupings for their own purposes—even the most vocal commoners remained so politically weak that they posed no real threat to the nobility's dominance.[45]

There is space here only to consider a few of what have come to be regarded as the principal texts. Something of a trailblazer was Stanisław Staszic's *Observations on the Life of Jan Zamoyski* (*Uwagi nad życiem Jana Zamoyskiego*), published before the Sejm assembled, in 1787. While much of it echoed the writings of reformers from the 1760s onwards, in its pleas for emancipation of serfdom and widening the political rights of townsmen (not least through their admission into the legislature), it was most remarkable in a call for "enlightened despotism" (*oświecony despotyzm*—Staszic was one of the first writers anywhere to use the phrase) as a desperate remedy for Poland's ills. No such call had ever been made in Poland. In fact, Staszic's plea was almost certainly a rhetorical device to shock—what he really wanted was a form of constitutional, hereditary monarchy. It is still unclear how much impact his ideas had—a number of responses to his work came out in the first year of the Sejm, but he did raise the very issues which were dearest to the hearts of reformers.[46]

Debate surrounded the form of government which Poland should take. There was almost no dispute over the merits of the *liberum veto*—apart from among some diehards,[47] it was taken as almost axiomatic that it would disappear.

---

[44]   Ibid., 60–61. Emanuel Rostworowski, "'Marzenie dobrego obywatela', czyli królewski projekt konstytucji," in his *Legendy i fakty XVIIIw.* (Warsaw: PWN, 1963), 421–2.

[45]   Rostworowski, "Miasta i mieszczanie," 138–51.

[46]   Stanisław Staszic, *Uwagi nad życiem Jana Zamoyskiego*, ed. Stefan Czarnowski (Wrocław: Ossolineum, 1951); and Grześkowiak-Krwawicz, *O formę rządu*, 180–88.

[47]   The most notable of these was Seweryn Rzewuski, author of "A short discourse on the succession in Poland," *O sukcessyi tronu w Polszcze rzecz krótka* (1789), in which he equated majority voting with royal absolutism. It was a theme he pursued in numerous other, often anonymous, pamphlets. See Zofia Zielińska, *Republikanizm spod znaku buławy: publicystyka Seweryna Rzewuskiego z lat 1788–1790* (Warsaw: Uniwersytet Warszawski, Wydział Historii, 1988).

The prospect of its abolition gave rise to numerous alternative proposals for more or less cumbersome mechanisms which sought to reconcile effective government with safeguards for noble freedoms against any hint of tyranny by the majority. Almost all political writers of any note insisted on the introduction of voting systems by qualified, as opposed to simple, majorities. Even the most seemingly progressive could not bring themselves to shake off the fears of what simple "counting," as opposed to "weighing," of votes might lead to. The age-old preference for securing as large a majority as possible, indeed, of striving for unanimity of decision-making, was too psychologically engrained to be shaken off, no matter how ready many might have been to acknowledge the disastrous consequences of the veto. In this respect, the main reform tracts of the years 1788–92 represent a retrograde step on the *On the Means to Successful Counsels* of 1761–63, for there Konarski had argued forcefully and at length for the introduction of simple majorities. That remained a step too far.

The clearest evidence of this comes in three documents: the "Principles of the Form of Government" debated and passed by the Sejm in December 1789; the "Project for the Form of Government" introduced into the Sejm in August 1790; and the Law on *Sejmy* passed on 16 May 1791, barely a fortnight after the enactment of the Constitution of 3 May.[48] That Constitution, the so-called "Statute on Government," formally rescinded the veto: "Everything, at all times, should be decided by a majority of votes; therefore, we abolish the liberum veto ... forever." It did not however, specify what should replace it. One thing that both committed ideologues and rank-and-file nobility had taken on board since the First Partition was the idea of the "popular will," the "will of the palatinates/constituencies" as laid out by Rousseau—though the only "people" whose "will" mattered were the nobility.[49] So much was this taken to heart that the "Principles of the Form of Government" specified that fundamental or "cardinal" laws could be amended only with the backing of an unanimity of instructions from the local constituencies; declarations of peace and war, approval of foreign treaties would require approval by a three-quarter majority of all instructions. The "Project for the Form of Government" of 1790, a monstrously long document which the Sejm never got around to debating in its entirety, repeated these stipulations and even went beyond them. It specified that constitutional and money bills (the resolution of which the "Principles" had left open) required endorsement by three-quarters of all instructions; only ordinary civil and criminal laws were to be decided by a simple majority of instructions. For the "Project," even at

---

[48]   "Zasady do Formy Rządu," *Volumina Legum*, 9: 157–9; *Proiekt do Formy Rządu* (Warsaw, 1790); "Ustawa Rządowa," *Volumina Legum*, 9: 220–25; "Seymy," ibid., 250–66.

[49]   Jerzy Lukowski, "Recasting Utopia: Montesquieu, Rousseau and the Polish Constitution of 3 May 1791," *The Historical Journal*, 37 (1994), 65–87.

the level of executive, ministerial boards, majority decision-making, although accepted, was clearly a *faut de mieux*.[50] While the king succeeded in weaning Rousseau's more enthusiastic devotees from binding instructions before the acclamation of the "Statute on Government" on 3 May 1791, their reluctance to embrace straightforward majority voting remained unshakeable. The Law on *Sejmy* of 16 May specified that while "civil" laws could be passed by a simple majority, constitutional and criminal laws had to be passed by a majority of two to one; and tax bills required a majority of three to one.[51]

While constitutional matters were paramount, reformers continued to press for change in the position of peasants and townsmen, which, if carried through, would have their own impact on the position of the nobility. Most arguments in favor of peasant freedoms did not progress beyond those made in the 1770s and earlier 1780s. It was above all calls for amelioration of the rights of townsmen which were far more systematically developed and aroused far more debate. The principal advocate of increased urban rights was Hugo Kołłątaj, an ambitious ecclesiastic who had made a name for himself with the overhaul of the University of Kraków. He argued that Poland's towns could only be revived economically by enlarging their political rights—to the extent of giving townsmen their own chamber in the Sejm and making the passage of any legislation dependent on its consent. At the same time he favored breaking down the old barriers which, at least notionally, continued to distinguish townsmen from nobles. He wanted to abolish the centuries-old ban on the purchase of landed properties by townsmen, to facilitate their ennoblement, and also to open urban occupations to nobles (though, as with almost all writers, he did not consider Poland's Jews as members of the urban community). Stanisław Staszic, though far less systematic in his approach than Kołłątaj, was more radical—he would have given townsmen equal representation to the *szlachta* in the Sejm (Kołłątaj wanted his proposed Chamber of Nobles to be twice as strong as the Chamber of townsmen).[52]

But what of the noble rank and file? In 1791, the Polish nobility as a whole numbered some 750,000, some 7.5 percent of the Commonwealth's entire population. Over half, some 425,000 (56.7 percent of all nobles) would have made up families owning land outright, but of these, 300,000 would have made up families owning less than an entire village. Owners of one village or more (or

---

[50]   *Proiekt do Formy Rządu*, ff. 4v, 33r–v, 86v, 98v, 109v.

[51]   Rostworowski, "Marzenie," 265–464; *Volumina Legum*, 9: 259.

[52]   Hugo Kołłątaj, *Listy Anonima i Prawo Polityczne Narodu Polskiego*, 2 vols (1788 and 1790), reprint, eds Bogusław Leśnodorski and Helena Wereszycka (Warsaw: PWN, 1954), 1: 286–8, 314–16, 351–8; 2: 97–101, 176, 202–7, 282–3. Staszic, *Uwagi nad życiem*, 54; Stanisław Staszic, *Przestrogi dla Polski* (1790), reprint, ed. Stefan Czarnowski (Kraków: Krakowska Spółka Wydawnicza, 1926), 177–83, 230.

some 135 hectares of land and above), with their families, accounted for around 20,000 persons. Most remaining nobles, just under half of the whole, would have been landless, or minor and petty leaseholders, in domestic service or practicing (often at the risk of a notional *dérogeance*) some form of urban-based profession or occupation. At most, according to Emanuel Rostworowski's estimates (the most convincing), the number of "active" citizens would have accounted for some 100,000 adult males—inevitably dominated by a small minority of more substantial landowners.[53]

Parliaments were meant to meet once every two years for a six-week period. As the term for a new Sejm approached, that elected in 1788 ruefully faced up to how little it had achieved: in October 1790, the Sejm resolved that it would remain in being, but that new envoy elections would go ahead on 16 November, and the new tranche of envoys would sit alongside the old complement. So anxious was it to hear the "will of the nation" that on 18 October it ruled that the instructions, normally drawn up after the election of envoys (and after many electors had drifted away), would, at the coming *sejmiki*, be formulated before the envoys were elected.[54] Of course, the tenor of instructions normally reflected the views of the more influential and the more powerful—though even they were unlikely to permit themselves anything which significantly diverged from their understanding of their fellow nobles' views. The procedures decided on for the November 1790 assemblies meant that they were bound to be more representative of *szlachta* opinion than usual.[55]

It was these instructions which played a major role in weaning enlightened reformers away from their idealization of the will of the nation,[56] for they were conservative through and through. On the major issue of political reform confronting the electorate, should the monarchy be transformed from an elective to an hereditary one, only nine of the Commonwealth's 55 *sejmiki* supported the proposed change. Thirty-six (two-thirds) wanted to retain elective kingship. Almost all, however, accepted the designation of the elector of Saxony, Frederick Augustus III, as successor during Stanisław August's lifetime. But reformers could have been forgiven for thinking it was a poor return for the oceans of ink spilt

---

[53]   Rostworowski, "Ilu było," 3–40.

[54]   Kalinka, *Sejm Czteroletni*, 2: 294–8, 405–8; *Volumina Legum*, 9: 176–7, 184–5. Attendance of 200–300 was around the "average" for a *sejmik*, though some might exceptionally attract participation in the thousands. Rostworowski, "Ilu było," 35–6; Wojciech Kriegseisen, *Sejmiki Rzeczypospolitej szlacheckiej w XVII i XVIII wieku* (Warsaw: Wyd. Sejmowe, 1991), 131–5.

[55]   Rostworowski, "Marzenie," 343–4.

[56]   Ibid., 344; Kalinka, *Sejm Czteroletni*, 2: 418–28; Zofia Zielińska, *"O sukcesyi tronu w Polszcze" 1787–1790* (Warsaw, PWN, 1991), 219–20.

on advocating outright hereditary succession.[57] Two instructions, those of the county of Zakroczym and the palatinate of Wołyń, went so far as to enjoin their envoys to use the *liberum veto* should the Sejm opt for hereditary succession— but there seem to have been no further calls for its use; and the Pinsk *sejmik* condemned it for having "caused no little harm to the nation." Otherwise, it barely attracted any notice.[58]

The same cannot be said of anything threatening the nobility's social and political dominance. Either explicitly or implicitly, all instructions agreed with the county of Dobrzyń in rejecting any "law harmful to ... the liberties and prerogatives harmful to the *szlachta* estate." The Dobrzyń constituency would even have maintained the centuries-old ban on the purchase of landed property by townsmen.[59] Not a single assembly supported the full admission of urban representatives to the Sejm. Three assemblies only were prepared to grant towns restricted rights to be consulted in the Sejm on purely commercial matters.[60] The palatinate of Podole was the most generous, inasmuch as it was prepared to extend to the towns the principle of *Neminem Captivabimus nisi iure victum*,[61] the Polish *Habeas Corpus*, hitherto restricted to the nobility. It was little enough and merely served to demonstrate the gulf between reformers and the run of the mill nobility. Particularly wounding to key exponents of reform, most of whom were heavily involved with the Commission for National Education,

---

[57]   The fullest study of this issue is Zielińska, *O sukcesyi tronu*, esp. 207–21.

[58]   The analysis that follows is based on a sample of 41 (74.5 percent) of the 55 instructions issued in November 1790. Here, the Zakroczym instruction, Biblioteka Polskiej Akademii Nauk, Kraków (hereafter BPAN), 8354, f. 334r; Wołyń instruction, Archiwum Główne Akt Dawnych, Warsaw (hereafter AGAD), Roś, Publica 94/4/5, unpaginated; Pinsk instruction, Lietuvos Mokslų Akademijos Biblioteka, Vilnius (hereafter LMAB), F233–126, f. 138r.

[59]   F. Kluczycki, ed., *Lauda sejmików ziemi dobrzyńskiej*, Acta Historica res gesta Poloniae illustrantia, vol. 10 (Kraków: Akademia Umiejętności, 1887), 400. The call for a ban on land purchases was echoed by the *sejmiki* of Liw (BPAN, 8332, f. 611 r), Wołyń (AGAD, Roś, Publica 94/4/5), and Pinsk (LMAB, F233–126, f. 141r).

[60]   The Wołyń assembly was prepared to allow the more important towns to submit commercial proposals to the Sejm, but only through *szlachta* envoys, since townsmen themselves were to have no direct parliamentary representation. AGAD, Roś, Publica 94/4/5. The Livonian *sejmik* would have admitted urban delegates to the Sejm, but for municipal business only. LMAB, F233–126, f. 78r. Pinsk would have allowed a maximum of six urban delegates to the Sejm for consultation purposes only, ibid., f. 141r. The *sejmik* of Brześć Litewski would have allowed a very restricted townsman participation in the chief organs of local government, the newly created civil-military commissions of the peace, ibid., f. 19r.

[61]   Podole instruction, Wojewódzkie Archiwum Państwowe, oddział na Wawelu, Kraków (hereafter WAP Kraków), Archiwum Podhoreckie, X 2/ 24, unpaginated.

were widespread demands for cutting back on its jurisdiction, funding, or even its outright abolition.[62]

Directly or indirectly, the overwhelming majority of constituencies came out against serf emancipation. The conservative tenor of the five instructions that did not allude to the issue – those of Kiev, Czersk, Liw, Wizna, and Wyszogród – hardly suggests their electorates to have been hotbeds of enlightened social thought. On the other hand, some assemblies, notably those of the Grand Duchy of Lithuania, were clearly capable of turning the fashions of enlightened ideologies to their advantage. The *sejmik* of Brześć Litewski could call on the sacred rights of property:

> All men should be assured of security of life and property by their country's laws, just as they have by divine law ... Therefore our envoys will insist that the ownership of the land and the serfs settled on it, will remain subject to the free disposition and usage of their seigneurs, in accordance with the laws.[63]

At Pinsk, the *sejmik*, in insisting on the preservation of landlords' rights over their serfs, pointed out that "the commoner estate ... in this enlightened age experiences no indecencies."[64] The assembly at Słonim railed against reformers' tracts, which "hold out hidden delusions, clad in the mask of virtue and humanity, deliberately suggesting supposedly burning issues, under cover of which they seek to hide the creation and construction of a framework for our perpetual destruction." Chief among these was the "disease" of "proposals for the emancipation of serfdom."[65] The Minsk *sejmik* took issue with proposals contained in the "Project for the Form of Government" of the previous August. Among its provisions was the proposal (repeated from the ill-fated Zamoyski law code) that where a landlord's actions led to severe injury, maiming, or death of a peasant, then the victim and "all his relatives" (or, in the case of death, all the inhabitants of the village) were entitled to leave the property as freed individuals. The Minsk nobility wanted to restrict those who could so leave to the victim's immediate household, otherwise "such punishment will have a greater impact on the innocent children of the murderer or guilty party than on the perpetrator himself." They did, however, agree that the death penalty should apply to culpable landlords, the only assembly to do so.[66]

---

62 Thirty-two of a sample of 41 available instructions carried such stipulations.
63 LMAB, F233–126, f. 17r. The Lida *sejmik* made a very similar point, ibid., f. 72r.
64 Ibid., f. 139r.
65 Ibid., ff. 201v–202r.
66 *Proiekt do Formy Rządu*, f. 12v; Minsk instruction, AGAD/Zbiór Popielów 130, 532–3.

A few other *sejmiki* were prepared for "concessions" to peasants, although in the main these were meaningless cosmetic. The Chełm *sejmik* felt that

> Justice and humanity cannot fail to make us conscious of the tyranny with which, in many places, seigneurs treat their serfs. Our envoys, after assuring the serfs of their lives and [moveable] property are not to allow any restriction of seigneurial jurisdiction.[67]

The assemblies of Orsza and Wołkowysk identified Jews and their wiles as a particular source of peasant exploitation and suggested they should be banned from the retail of alcohol "and, in removing [peasants] from occasions of luxuriating, their condition will improve and will be able to be of greater benefit to the needs of the Commonwealth." That Jewish innkeepers, on tenancies from noble landlords, "exploited" peasants to supply seigneurial pockets was not a connection that the two *sejmiki* chose to make.[68] The *starostowie*, nobles holding leases on crown lands, were identified as another source of exploitation.[69] Abuses were to be curbed, taxation burdens were not to be increased—but there was no hint of any kind of betterment of serfs' legal status and any such suggestions (as in the "Project for the Form of Government") were firmly slapped down.[70]

The Constitution of 3 May 1791 proved acceptable to the Polish nobility because it left them, more firmly than ever, the dominant grouping within the state. Those behind the Constitution, foisted on the nobility in what amounted to a peaceful *coup d'état*, took one major risk—notwithstanding the widespread reservations of the *sejmiki*, they declared the monarchy to be hereditary in the Saxon house of Wettin. But the dominance of the nobility remained unscathed. It is true that the Statute on Towns of 18 April 1791 (declared to be an integral part of the new Constitution on 3 May)[71] gave townsmen representation in the Sejm. But it was highly restricted: the towns could elect 22 plenipotentiaries "well endowed with property and capable undertaking public functions," who would attend not the plenary but the so-called "provincial" sessions of the Sejm (that is consultative sessions held at provincial level). Only at these would each of the *Rzeczpospolita*'s three great provinces (that is Wielkopolska, Małoplska, and

---

[67] WAP Kraków, Archiwum Podhoreckie, X 4/B, unpaginated. A similar sentiment was voiced by the Łęczyca *sejmik*, BPAN, 8330, 802.

[68] Wołkowysk instruction, LMAB, F233-16, f. 244r–v; Orsza instruction, ibid., f. 127r; H. Levine, "Gentry, Jews and Serfs: The Rise of Polish Vodka," *Review*, 4:2 (1980), 223–50.

[69] Ciechanów instruction, BPAN, 8318, f. 368v.

[70] See especially the Wołyń instruction, AGAD, Roś, Publica 94/4/5, unpaginated.

[71] *Volumina Legum*, 9: 215–18, 221.

Lithuania) elect two urban plenipotentiaries to the new central commissions of the Police and of the Treasury; and three to the Assessory courts, where appeals from royal towns were heard. Urban plenipotentiaries could fully participate in the proceedings of these bodies in business concerning commercial and municipal affairs. In plenary sessions of the Sejm, these same plenipotentiaries could present and speak only to the *desideria* of the towns. This was a world removed from the calls for direct urban parliamentary representation made by Staszic or Kołłątaj. Moreover, the chances of any kind of urban agitation against *szlachta* dominance were neatly decapitated: all urban plenipotentiaries sitting on the commissions and assessories would be automatically ennobled after completion of their two-year term. Each Sejm was to ennoble 30 freeholder townsmen. The bar on townsman purchase of landed property was lifted— indeed, any townsman buying an entire village was entitled to ennoblement. In effect, any reasonably wealthy townsman could reasonably look forward to becoming a *szlachcic*.

The towns, or at least their elites, welcomed this. Such was their economic and political debility that the "Statute on Towns" represented a more realistic level of aspiration than the dizzy heights which reformers had demanded. The relative generosity of ennoblement provision was almost inevitably going to prove attractive to ambitious townsmen, not least because "the practice of crafts and ownership of factories" was not to derogate (*derogare nie ma*). The main requirement of *anoblis* was the payment of hefty chancery fees—in practice, often ignored. In fact, each of the *Sejmy* of Stanisław August's reign had agreed to the ennoblement, on average, of some 80 persons—by comparison, the facilities created under the Statute on Towns were less than generous, but at least they were placed on a formal footing. The substantial nobles who sat in Polish parliaments had far fewer reservations about ennobling townsmen than admitting them into the legislature. In the space of three weeks in November 1790, the Four-Year Sejm itself had ennobled over 400 persons.[72] The Statute on Towns also worked in the opposite direction: it allowed nobles to receive municipal citizenship, and hence avail themselves of municipal office, with no loss of status. In reality, prohibitions on nobles holding urban office had long been ignored. The Sejm of 1775 had permitted them to pursue "every variety of commerce" with no loss of status.[73] The Statute on Towns represented an advance on the ill-fated Zamoyski

---

[72] Krystyna Zienkowska, *Sławetni i urodzeni: ruch polityczny mieszczaństwa w dobie Sejmu Czteroletniego* (Warsaw: PWN, 1976), 12, 130–47, 169–71; Jerzy Jedlicki, *Klejnot i bariery społeczne: przeobrażenia szlachectwa polskiego w schyłkowym okresie feudalizmu* (Warsaw: PWN, 1968), 91–126; *Volumina Legum*, 9: 189–200.

[73] *Volumina Legum*, 8: 113; Jedlicki, *Klejnot i bariery społeczne*, 67–74. See also Kazimierz Maliszewski, *Jan Kazimierz Rubinkowski: szlachcic, mieszczanin toruński, erudyta*

proposals of 1780—for they had preserved the ban on nobles taking up urban citizenship. The effect of the Statute was not only to open up wide avenues of ennoblement on a formal basis to non-Jewish townsmen but also to allow the nobility to broaden the scope of their public life by removing the last barriers to their holding of municipal office. The Statute was, in practice, less a concession to the towns, more a device to enable the *szlachta* to strengthen their dominance of society.

The Constitution of 3 May also looked to the peasantry. It made two provisions—one almost meaningless, the second, surprisingly, far less so. Article IV placed the peasants "under the protection of the law and the national government." By this, the government pledged to uphold all existing and future voluntary agreements, contracts, and liberties. Since most Polish laws relating to serfs were there to keep them in their due place, this meant little. No independent judicial organ existed to which peasants could appeal, save for seigneurial courts and the so-called referendary courts, for peasants settled on crown lands. On the other hand, Article IV went on to announce

> full freedom for all those both newly arrived, and those who have earlier left the country and now wish to return, so much so, that every person arriving in or coming back to the territories of the Commonwealth, as soon as he places his foot on Polish soil, is entirely free to use his industry as and where he wishes, is free to make contracts of settlement, employment or lease as and when he can, is free to settle in a town or in the countryside, is free to live in Poland or to return to whichever country he wishes, provided he has discharged the obligations which he has voluntarily assumed.[74]

How this would have worked in practice is impossible to say, if only because Russian intervention barely a year after the enactment of the new constitution rendered it nugatory. There were certainly cases of peasants fleeing abroad and returning, supposedly as free men, but how many there were and how far their claims could be made good remains an open question. There were instances of peasant unrest, so much so that on 2 August 1791, the king issued a Proclamation, condemning all such turbulence.[75] The peasantry, as so often with eighteenth-century reforms, was all too prone to exaggerate their real import. Those who had been agitating for peasant reform for the past two decades or so secured

---

barokowy (Warsaw: PWN, 1982).

[74] *Volumina Legum*, 9: 221.

[75] Władysław Smoleński, *Ostatni rok Sejmu Wielkiego* (Kraków: Gebethner, 1897), 95–111.

far less from the new Constitution than they had been hoping for, but about as much as *szlachta* society was prepared to concede.

In the end, it was the *szlachta*, or more specifically the substantial landowning gentry, who were the principal beneficiaries of the Constitution of 3 May 1791. They had always formed the great bulk of parliamentary representatives; and during this, the longest and most significant parliament of Poland's history, they had gained a new self-awareness and confidence. Their position remained intact and strengthened, by opening up new legal avenues of advancement—the way was open to their dominating Polish society more than ever. The *sejmiki* of February 1792, pressed by the king, basking in the illusory hope that the reforms of the Sejm had solved the Commonwealth's problems, gave a resounding endorsement to the new Constitution.[76] But the *szlachta* were no longer the nobility that existed before the Four-Year Sejm. It was not only the sacred cow of elective monarchy which had been slaughtered. The much-vaunted "equality" and "brotherhood" of the nobility had always been fictions, even if powerful ones. The law on *sejmiki* of 24 March 1791[77] (the only part of the "Project for the Form of Government" that was, after debate and amendment, enacted) formally excluded landless nobles from active participation in these local assemblies—but their role had always been peripheral or, on occasion, that of increasing the muscle of great landowners who wished to influence the course of deliberations. That law was accompanied, for the first time in Polish history, by a system of registration of landholding nobles—essential for active participation in the *sejmiki*.[78] It was a blow against magnate clientage and patronage, as much as a slapping down of the impoverished, petty *szlachta*. At one level, ennoblement was becoming more exclusive, more difficult—*annoblissement taisible*, the kind of prescriptive nobility identified by Elie Haddad, such a feature of "ennoblement" among so many nobilities in the past, would no longer be feasible. But this new nobility was to be one of merit and achievement in a wide range of fields: industrial, commercial, civic, cultural—all well beyond the traditional and respectable avenue of valor on the battlefield. But as nobles gained legal access to ever greater numbers of occupations, as entrepreneurship and *enrichissement* replaced military virtue, or, at least, came to stand alongside it as measures of nobility, so the character of that nobility had to change. With time, its social and economic activities would be so far flung as to make the notion of any pedigree-based exclusivity redundant. To those genuinely committed to meaningful reform,

---

[76]   Ibid., 259–300; Maria Wisińska, "Sieradzkie wobec Konstytucji 3 Maja," *Rocznik Łódzki*, 33 (1983), 39–61; Wacław Szczygielski, *Referendum trzeciomajowe. Sejmiki lutowe 1792 roku* (Łódź: Wyd. Uniwersytetu Łódzkiego, 1994).

[77]   *Volumina Legum*, 9: 233–40.

[78]   Ibid., 240–41.

this, of its nature, long-term transformation, was an essential precondition to the modernization of the state and society as a whole. First, the *szlachta* had to change. Only then could state and society follow.

It is therefore not wholly surprising that the polemics around the Four-Year Sejm threw up the occasional writer who thought in terms of a fusion of the whole nation into a single ennobled community.[79] Maurycy Karp so despised townsmen as idlers and parasites he would have preferred to see, in a distant, perhaps never attainable, future, peasant, rather than urban representation in the Sejm.[80] While advocates of such extreme change remained a tiny minority, and while such change was envisioned in very nebulous terms, the late eighteenth-century Polish-Lithuanian nobility were indeed in the process of a transformation—but only at the slow, measured pace which their elites were prepared to accept. The Russian invasion of May 1792 was to end that particular luxury of choice.

---

[79] Rostworowski, "Marzenie," 293–4; Rostworowski, "Ilu było," 38; Zienkowska, *Sławetni i urodzeni*, 179–81. A similar prospect was periodically contemplated, not always positively, in later eighteenth-century France. Jay M. Smith, *Nobility Reimagined: The Patriotic Nation in Eighteenth-Century France* (Ithaca: Cornell University Press, 2005), 121, 128–9, 180, 230–31, 252–3, 273–4.

[80] Maurycy Franciszek Karp, *Pytanie i odpowiedź, czy do doskonałości konstytucyi polityczney państwa naszego koniecznie potrzeba, aby gmin miał uczęstek w prawodawstwie? ...* (Warsaw: Drukarnia Wolna, 1791), 2 editions.

Chapter 13

Resilient Notables: Looking at the Transformation of the Ottoman Empire from the Local Level[1]

M. Safa Saraçoğlu

Bulgarian lands were part of the Ottoman Empire from the fifteenth to the end of the nineteenth century.[2] As Crampton noted, "the vigorous but self-righteous Christians of the Victorian era created the impression that their co-religionists under Ottoman domination had suffered continual persecution for five hundred years. It was not so."[3] A half millennium of Ottoman administration of the Balkans was more dynamic and complex than was perceived by the Victorians—and by some modern historians;[4] its military, fiscal, and administrative institutions evolved as the nature of power

---

[1] I would like to thank Virginia Aksan, Heather Almer, Bogaç Ergene, and the editors of the volume for their comments and help. Parts of this research were funded by The American Council of Learned Societies, The Institute of Turkish Studies, and PASSHE Faculty Professional Development Grants.

[2] R.J. Crampton, *A Concise History of Bulgaria* (New York: Cambridge University Press, 2005), 28; Dennis P. Hupchick, *The Balkans: From Constantinople to Communism* (New York: Palgrave, 2002), 107–13; Hüdai Şentürk, *Osmanlı Devleti'nde Bulgar Meselesi (1850–1875)* (Ankara: Türk Tarih Kurumu, 1992), 4–5.

[3] Crampton, *A Concise History*. For a more nuanced approach, cf. Mariia Nikolaeva Todorova, "The Ottoman Legacy in the Balkans," in *Imperial Legacy: The Ottoman Imprint on the Balkans and the Middle East*, ed. Carl Brown (New York: Columbia University Press, 1996). Also see Mariia Nikolaeva Todorova, "Afterthoughts on *Imagining the Balkans*," *Harvard Middle Eastern and Islamic Review*, 5 (1999–2000); and Fikret Adanir and Suraiya Faroqhi, eds, *The Ottomans and the Balkans: A Discussion of Historiography* (Boston: Brill, 2002).

[4] For example Şevket Pamuk notes that the Ottoman "empire cursorily depicted in these accounts is a centralized, monolithic entity lacking in internal dynamism and differentiation." Şevket Pamuk, "Institutional Change and the Longevity of the Ottoman Empire, 1500–1800," *Journal of Interdisciplinary History*, 35:2 (2004), 225–47, here 227.

and rule within the empire changed from the sixteenth to the early twentieth century.[5]

It would be impossible to think of the transformation of the socioeconomic structure in the Balkans without considering this region as part of a larger empire. Nevertheless, as Faroqhi and Adanir aptly observed recently:

> Generally, the historians of most states located on previously Ottoman territory
> tended, and still tend, to concentrate upon the lands situated within the borders
> of the modern country within which they happen to operate. ... Yet it is a major
> anachronism to assume that relations between regions were what they are today,
> when the territorial units under consideration, along with many others, formed
> part of a large-scale empire such as the Ottoman.[6]

This chapter focuses on local notables and administrative practices in Vidin County (in the northwest corner of modern-day Bulgaria) during the eighteenth and nineteenth centuries. Conventional accounts of Ottoman administration in this county emphasize how certain regulations on land tenure—issued in 1850 as part of Ottoman centralization attempts—marked an end of local notables' supremacy. Distancing myself from this perspective, I show how some notables such as Ma'ruf Ağazade Ahmed Bey or Sevastaki Ivanov Gunzovyanov negotiated a space for themselves in Vidin as influential members of the administrative institutions within the Ottoman and Bulgarian modern states in the second half of the nineteenth century. These notables were members of a multitiered elite network that adjusted to the fiscal and institutional transformations in the seventeenth and eighteenth centuries and remained powerful throughout the nineteenth century. Their prominence in the judicial and administrative institutions of the county was not a secret. Analyzing provincial documents, I point out how such notables maintained a relatively consistent presence in these institutions and argue that local correspondence coming from the region was shaped and should be read in this light.

---

[5]   Some of the works that capture this transformation in its complexity include: Dina Rizk Khoury, *State and Provincial Society in the Ottoman Empire: Mosul, 1540–1834* (New York: Cambridge University Press, 1997); Virginia H. Aksan and Daniel Goffman, *The Early Modern Ottomans: Remapping the Empire* (New York: Cambridge University Press, 2007); Karen Barkey, *Empire of Difference: The Ottomans in Comparative Perspective* (New York: Cambridge University Press, 2008); Jane Hathaway and Karl K. Barbir, *The Arab Lands under Ottoman Rule, 1516–1800* (Harlow: Longman, 2008).

[6]   Suraiya Faroqhi and Fikret Adanir, "Introduction," in *The Ottomans and the Balkans*, eds Adanir and Faroqhi, 25–6.

As part of the nineteenth-century Ottoman provincial administrative framework, Vidin County was governed by a complex of councils and committees. This particular framework was introduced as part of centralization attempts of the modern Ottoman state and often is perceived as reflective of the imperial administration's attempt at limiting or eliminating the strong notables of the eighteenth century. This chapter, as part of a comparative attempt at understanding how "nobility" adopt to the changing socio-economic dynamics, will point out how nineteenth-century reforms contributed to the construction of a judicio-administrative sphere that allowed local "notables" to be a part of politics of administration.[7] While I focus on "Ottoman notables"—as opposed to "nobility"—in the Ottoman Empire, the ways in which they were involved with processes of continuous negotiation and adaptation to maintain their socio-economic privileges are somewhat similar to what Haddad and Marraud describe in the context of French nobility in this volume. And as Lukowski's contribution to this volume explains, the boundaries between the old classes and the new bourgeoisie were not that clear cut.

Vidin

Modern-day Vidin is a town where the borders of Romania and Serbia meet along the Danube. During the Ottoman period of administration Vidin served as a center for a larger administrative unit expanding further south and east. This study focuses on the county of Vidin, bordered by the Iskar River to the east, the Stara Planina mountain range to the south and west, and the Danube River to the north.[8] Fertile soil, moderate climate, temperatures, and precipitation made these lands suitable for agricultural production, mostly cereal and fodder crops, vegetables, fruit, and grapes. An Ottoman survey published in 1873 indicates that 81 percent of the population lived in rural areas.[9]

---

[7]   For an interesting discussion on the compatibility of terminology emanating from early modern European history, see Ariel Salzmann, *Tocqueville in the Ottoman Empire: Rival Paths to the Modern State* (Leiden: Brill, 2004), 1–30.

[8]   In connection with a provincial regulation issued in 1864, the boundaries of Vidin County were redesigned to include the districts 'Adliye (modern-day Kula), Belgradcık (Belogradchik), Berkofça (Berkovitsa), İvraca (Vratsa), Rahova (Oriahaovo), and Lom (Lom). Today, three separate Bulgarian districts (Vidin, Montana, and Vratsa) cover the approximately 4,092 square miles (10,600 square kilometers) that was Vidin County in 1864.

[9]   Milen V. Petrov, "Tanzimat for the Countryside: Midhat Paşa and the Vilayet of Danube, 1864–1868," (PhD dissertation: Princeton University, 2006), 63.

The Danube Province, including Vidin County, was a region where diverse ethnic groups lived and interacted with each other in towns and countryside.[10] The county was predominantly non-Muslim in the 1860s and 1870s—with a Muslim population below 20 percent. This was the general character of the western counties of the Danube province.[11] However, the demographic composition was reversed in the town of Vidin—the fourth-largest town in the province—where a survey of 1866 reported 51.6 percent of the population as Muslim, 34.1 percent as Bulgarian, 6.2 percent as Roma, and 8.2 percent as Jewish.[12]

In the history of Ottoman administration, Vidin was not a frontier zone. As Ottoman control over the Balkan region contracted, Vidin essentially moved toward the frontier. This is merely one aspect of the complex matrix of Ottoman state–province relations.[13] In order to contextualize local notables' access to power we must consider interconnected military, fiscal, and social institutional transformation within the Ottoman Empire between the seventeenth and nineteenth centuries, focusing particularly on the landholding practices and local administration.

Scholars of Bulgaria and the Balkans have explained the transformation of landholding practices in this region between seventeenth and nineteenth centuries differently. In her article on Vidin, Ivanova has explained how the rapid expansion of sultanal lands (*hass-ı hümayun*—lands proprietorship of which belonged to the ruling family), in the Vidin area after the seventeenth century led to limited claims on property by the military elite (*sipahis*) and increased possessions by Janissaries and local notables (*gospodar*—lit. "master").[14]

---

[10]   Petrov, "Tanzimat for the Countryside," 75–81. This does not imply that confessional politics were absent from the picture altogether. I do not wish to deny the existence of such self-identifying processes and politics revolving around them; however, the focus of this chapter is more modest.

[11]   Ibid., 69–70.

[12]   Ibid., 76. Most of Petrov's demographic information comes from Nikolai Todorov, *The Balkan City, 1400–1900* (Seattle: University of Washington Press, 1983). For these particular figures Petrov adopts the ethnic identifiers used by Todorov.

[13]   For a discussion of the general historiography on this topic, see Suraiya Faroqhi, "Coping with the Central State, Coping with Local Power: Ottoman Regions and Notables from Sixteenth to the Early Nineteenth Century," in *The Ottomans and the Balkans*, eds Adanir and Faroqhi, 351–82.

[14]   Svetlana Ivanova, "Widin," in *Encyclopaedia of Islam*, 2nd edn, ed. P. Bearman et al. (*Brill Online, http://brillonline.nl*: Brill, 2009). Accumulation of land was neither the only way nor a sufficient condition to become a local notable; however, there is a relationship that I explore below between the rise of a particular land regime—known as *gospodarlık*— and the peculiarities of military composition and transformation in the Vidin region. In

Palairet, on the other hand, argues that initially low exploitative capacity of the *sipahis* in the sixteenth century had increased by the eighteenth century due to "manifest decay" of Ottoman fiscal institutions.[15] Whether one explains the transformation in Vidin by the peculiarities of the Ottoman military composition in northwestern Bulgaria or by the "manifest decay" of imperial fiscal institutions,[16] by the nineteenth century this reconfiguration resulted in the predominance in this region of a land-tenure pattern known as *gospodarlık*, in which local notables were given extensive control over administration and authority over tax collection from entire villages,[17] leading to overexploitation

---

discussing the prominence of Janissaries—in relation to the rise of *gospodars*—Ivanova notes that "the role of the *sipahi* [cavalry] troops in the [Vidin] area was reduced at the expense of the rise of the Janissaries and the local troops, which *ca.* 1750 numbered 5,500, more than in any other Ottoman city of the Balkans. ... [After the sixteenth century, Vidin] could safely be called a Janissary town. We find Janissaries in all spheres of public life, beginning with the economy and the craftsmen's guilds and ending with the professional witnesses in the courts" (ibid.). For a more detailed explanation of the tension between cavalrymen and the Janissary corps, see Virginia H. Aksan, *Ottoman Wars 1700–1870: An Empire Besieged* (Harlow: Longman/Pearson, 2007), 45–82; Rhoads Murphey, *Ottoman Warfare, 1500–1700* (New Brunswick, NJ: Rutgers University Press, 1999), 35–63. Janissaries were more than a standing army; their rise, presence, and demise had significant impacts on socio-economic dynamics of the Ottoman provinces. In a recent interesting article Radushev reveals the connection of Janissary troops to local agricultural economy in the Balkans: see Evgeni Radushev, "'Peasant' Janissaries?" *Journal of Social History*, 42 (2008), 447–67. For their involvement with ports and commercial activity see Hathaway and Barbir, *The Arab Lands*, 60, 163–4.

[15]   Palairet's explanation is based on the assumption that *sipahis* were more numerous than Janissaries in this region: "Despite numerous smaller perquisites owed by the peasant population to the [*sipahis*], the system imposed a fairly shallow level of exploitation upon the labor of the peasantry, and upon the usufruct of the land. This was wholly intentional, as it limited the ability of the [*sipahis*] to command resources which might render him independent of the Sultan. ... By the eighteenth century this system has fallen into manifest decay. The fiefs had become hereditary, and this in itself weakened the hold of the Porte over their holders." M.R. Palairet, *The Balkan Economies, 1800–1914: Evolution without Development* (New York: Cambridge University Press, 1997), 35–6. The emphasis on the power of *sipahis* contradicts what Ivanova notes about their relative numbers.

[16]   For a critique of the "decline literature" see Hathaway and Barbir, *The Arab Lands*, 60–62. Most of the English-written literature on the rise of the *gospodarlık* regime unfortunately subscribes to the "decline literature," which fits all too well with the identification of the Ottoman rule in the Balkans as stagnant and exploitative. The fiscal institutions of the empire in such explanations are decaying simply because they cannot change.

[17]   Ortaylı argues that the local autonomy of the *gospodars* were more *de facto* than *de jure*. İlber Ortaylı, "Gospodarlık," in *Islam Ansiklopedisi* (Istanbul: Türkiye Diyanet Vakfı, 1988). What emerges from the limited amount of literature on this group of landlords is that

and irritation of peasants in the nineteenth century, as commonly accepted in the literature.[18] Visiting the Balkans in 1850, Edmund Spencer had this to say about the rise of *gospodars*:

> The Turkish Government, during the reign of the late Sultan [Mahmud II {r. 1808–1839}], and that of the present Prince [Abdulmecid I {r. 1839–1861}], has done much towards ameliorating the condition of the [peasants], by abolishing several military pachaliks and spahiliks, which by long prescriptive right had arrogated an authority in some degree independent of the sovereign, and highly obnoxious to the [peasants].
>
> In carrying this measure into effect, the [palace], always arbitrary, was in many cases unjust, seeing that it deprived certain families of a privilege which they had enjoyed unquestioned for centuries, and in some instances secured to them by treaties since the Turkish conquest. This, however, has been the means of introducing here and there a new race of glebe landlords, who, employed as civil or military officers, usually reside in towns, and seldom or never visit the land whence they derive their revenues, save at harvest time ...[19]

Spencer's description of the rise of *gospodars* seems to correspond with Ivanova's conclusions in that these "glebe landlords" replaced the old *sipahi* class[20] in the course of imperial fiscal transformations in the nineteenth century. The historical evidence on how this process took place in Vidin does not necessarily lend itself to a definitive conclusion on whether there was a clear division

---

they were local and they were less powerful than the more significant notables who were mostly *sipahis*. In the case of Vidin, *gospodars* come into the picture following the demise of Pasvanoğlu Osman Paşa of Vidin (1758–1807), as discussed below.

[18]   Halil İnalcık, *Tanzimat ve Bulgar Meselesi: Doktora Tezinin 50. Yılı* (Istanbul: Eren, 1992), 83–107; Şentürk, *Osmanlı Devleti'nde Bulgar Meselesi*, 92–6; Traian Stoianovich, "Land Tenure and Related Sectors of the Balkan Economy, 1600–1800," *The Journal of Economic History*, 13 (1953), 398–411; Crampton, *A Concise History*, 56–8; Hupchick, *The Balkans*, 164–70.

[19]   Edmund Spencer, *Travels in European Turkey, in 1850*, vol. 1 (London: Colburn & Co., 1851), 253.

[20]   Cf. Pinson, who notes that "since the Ottoman government had to secure the position of the *sipahis* after the abolition of *sipahilik*, once the finance ministry had repossessed the *sipahilik* lands, it made them over to the *agas* again with 'documents of private ownership' (*chastnosobstvenishki dokumenti*) in which the villages the *agas* held were designated, *aga koyleri* (*aga* villages, or in Bulgarian *gospodarski sela*). The new system of landholding acquired the designation *gospodarlik*." Mark Pinson, "Ottoman Bulgaria in the First Tanzimat Period: The Revolts of Nish and Vidin," *Middle Eastern Studies*, 11 (1975), 118. Pinson, rather problematically, seem to treat *sipahis* and Janissaries as the same.

between *gospodars* and the more powerful *sipahis*.[21] What seems to be certain is that Vidin's best-known notable, Pasvanoğlu Osman Paşa (1758–1807), died at the beginning of the nineteenth century[22] and the *gospodarlik* system was abolished in 1850 with hopes that it would help prevent popular unrest in Vidin.[23] The *gospodars* were issued inheritable treasury certificates, *esham*, in exchange for villages that were under their control, while arable lands in those villages were offered, for sale, to their inhabitants.[24] The sale process, however, proved difficult in practice and was accompanied by problems.[25]

Be that as it may, conventional accounts of the Ottoman rule in Bulgaria during the eighteenth and nineteenth centuries focus on the gradual demise of local notables as the imperial administration eliminated the big notables, the *sipahis*, and finally the *gospodars* by 1850s. This was accompanied by Ottoman centralization aimed, among other things, at protecting the rights of an agitated non-Muslim populace in these lands, but was doomed to fail due to secessionist movements, foreign (Russian) intervention, and lack of funds and personnel to apply the reforms. As the notables were forcibly removed from the administrative space in the Balkans, they were replaced by Balkan nationalists, foreign spies, and constrained Ottoman bureaucrats. In what follows, I focus on the socioeconomic transformation in nineteenth-century Vidin as I reconstruct a local story of how some former *gospodar* families maintained their prominence in the administrative space by adapting to the nineteenth-century reforms.

---

[21] Works on notables in other parts of the Ottoman Empire indicate a complex, multitiered notable structure. Adanir, for example, notes the relationship, in the later part of the eighteenth century, between a landowning *sipahi* family responsible for public security in northeastern Bulgaria and the Janissaries (Adanir, "Semi-Autonomous Provincial Forces," 176.) Nagata's work on the Karaosmanoglu family reveals similarly complex relations in Yuzo Nagata, *Muhsinzâde Mehmed Paşa ve Âyânlık Müessesesi* (Izmir: Akademi Kitabevi, 1999).

[22] I discuss Pasvanoğlu below.

[23] Prime Ministry Ottoman Archives (BOA) A. MKT. MHM. 84/24 (dated 23 October 1850).

[24] The process is explained in an imperial decree sent to Vidin: BOA İ.DH. 13733 (15 February 1851). Another imperial decree, BOA İ.DH. 19124 (20 June 1854), refers to a dispute regarding the heirs of former *gospodars* who were issued such certificates.

[25] It appears that villagers were not willing to "buy" these lands and eventually some land was auctioned to merchants: BOA A .MKT. MVL 48/25 (12 December 1851). Other documents point to different problems continuing a decade after the initial decree was issued in 1851.

Contexts of Official Correspondence

Nineteenth-century Vidin was an important economic center stimulated by navigation on the Danube.[26] The economic revitalization in Ottoman Bulgaria from the 1830s to the 1860s led to more land being brought under cultivation.[27] Changes in the political arena reflected this transformation. One of the better-known *a'yans*—a term that can loosely be translated as "notable"[28]—of the whole empire, Pasvanoğlu Osman Paşa of Vidin, died in 1807.[29] His successor, Molla Idris, the last *a'yan* that "controlled" the region, did not cause much trouble for the imperial administration. "When one looks at Vidin in the years following the death of Pasvanoğlu," notes Zens, "there is very little evidence that the city was home to one of the most notorious *a'yans* in the Ottoman state, apart from buildings and other public works that bore his name."[30] From 1814 onward, the region's administrator was directly appointed from the imperial center. Gradeva, on the other hand, explains the significance of the memory of Pasvanoğlu for other agents in Vidin: "it was among the Janissaries and the rank-and-file Muslims that [Pasvanoğlu] earned his real and lasting fame. They created and circulated songs for him in which he emerges as a true hero. The age of nationalism had set in the Balkans."[31] The rise of a centralized Ottoman state and emergent Bulgarian nationalist movements seem to have provided a framework for studies that explain the uprising that happened only a few decades later in 1849.

Works on the 1849 uprising seem to agree that "the land tenure regime and the highly exploitative relations between cultivators and landlords in the Vidin area" instigated discontent particularly among non-Muslims.[32] At the center of this

---

[26]   Ivanova, "Widin." This was closely related to increased stability in the region which eventually led to increased agricultural production. See Palairet, *The Balkan Economies*, 62.

[27]   Ibid., 41–5.

[28]   See H. Bowen, "A'yan," in *Encyclopaedia of Islam*.

[29]   Recent accounts of his life include Robert W. Zens, "The *Ayanlık* and Pasvanoğlu Osman Paşa of Vidin in the Age of Ottoman Social Change, 1791–1815" (PhD dissertation: University of Wisconsin, 2004); Rossitsa Gradeva, "Osman Pazvantoğlu of Vidin: Between Old and New," in *The Ottoman Balkans, 1750–1830*, ed. Frederick F. Anscombe (Princeton, NJ: Markus Wiener Publishers, 2006); F. Bajraktarević, "Paswanoghlu," in *Encyclopaedia of Islam*.

[30]   Zens, "The *Ayanlık* and Pasvanoğlu Osman Paşa," 193.

[31]   Gradeva, "Osman Pazvantoğlu of Vidin," 149.

[32]   Erden A. Aytekin, "Land, Rural Classes, and Law: Agrarian Conflict and State Regulation in the Ottoman Empire, 1830s–1860s" (PhD dissertation: State University of New York-Binghamton, 2006), 36. Aytekin's discussion of the 1849 uprising relies mostly on İnalcık, *Tanzimat ve Bulgar Meselesi*, 58–74. (This is a reprint of İnalcık's dissertation from 1942.) Hüdai Şentürk argues that these uprisings should be seen as the origins of the

problem were the large estates owned by the *gospodars*, to which I have referred above. Large estates became common in the Balkans and western Anatolia as early as the seventeenth century due to certain political and military developments.[33] The situation began to change when new opportunities opened there: "towards the end of the 18th century Vidin became the seat of [Pasvanoğlu Osman Paşa] and the centre of one of the most important secession movements and [a'yan] rule in Rumeli."[34] Vidiners in the seventeenth and eighteenth centuries witnessed the gradual accumulation of usufruct in the hands of a military class, who chose to ally with Pasvanoğlu against the imperial administration during the military reforms of Selim III (r. 1789–1807).[35] The particular land regime that benefitted the military class and eventually led to uprisings was established earlier than the nineteenth century, and was further solidified during Pasvanoğlu's rule in Vidin when the Janissaries supported him in his resistance.[36]

The uprising in 1849 is an ideal starting point for a discussion of the state–society relations and roles/structure/transformation of local notables in Vidin County. Pinson explains these events as stemming from improper application of nineteenth-century *Tanzimat* reforms of the Ottoman Empire. These reforms were "concerned with creating a stronger centralized state with more effective organs of state power such as the army, [and] opened the way for an intensification of the struggle between [*gospodar*] and peasant for land"[37] in the countryside. Pinson's conclusions on this revolution rely almost exclusively on İnalcık's 1942 dissertation on the provincial application of the *Tanzimat* reforms,[38] which influenced most of the works on this rebellion. Consider how Pinson refers to

---

Bulgarian independence movement (Şentürk, *Osmanlı Devleti'nde Bulgar Meselesi*, 101–24, 82–99). Regardless of the differences they attribute to the role of nationalist movements and foreign powers, all three authors agree that the existing land regime in Vidin instigated a lot of discontent, particularly among the non-Muslim populations.

[33]   Huri İslamoğlu-İnan, "State and Peasants in the Ottoman Empire: A Study of Peasant Economy in North-Central Anatolia During the Sixteenth Century," in *The Ottoman Empire and the World-Economy*, ed. Huri İslamoğlu-İnan (New York: Cambridge University Press, 1987), 101–59; Bruce McGowan, *Economic Life in Ottoman Europe: Taxation, Trade, and the Struggle for Land, 1600–1800* (New York: Cambridge University Press, 1981), 73–9; Zens, "The *Ayanlık* and Pasvanoğlu Osman Paşa," 20.

[34]   Ivanova, "Widin."

[35]   Strashimir Dimitrov, *Vustanieto ot 1850 Godina v Bulgariia* (Sofia: BAN, 1972), 13–28.

[36]   Gradeva, "Osman Pazvantoğlu of Vidin," 120.

[37]   Pinson, "Ottoman Bulgaria," 117.

[38]   İnalcık, *Tanzimat ve Bulgar Meselesi*.

the latter's dissertation: "The eminent Turkish historian, İnalcık, in his very solid study of this revolt based almost entirely on Ottoman archival material."[39]

Pinson is correct in noting that İnalcık's work is predominantly based on Ottoman archives. However, Pinson himself notes that Mahmud II (r. 1808–39) adopted a policy to rotate provincial officials "at times more frequently than once a year" and that they "brought no knowledge of local conditions with them to the job and did not remain at the post long enough either to acquire such knowledge or a feeling of identification with the interests of the area in question."[40] İnalcık, Pinson, and other scholars appear to be unsuspicious of such provincial officials' reports in claiming that "local landholders [*gospodars*] who had long been a major component of the Ottoman provincial administration and army"[41] were not happy with the nineteenth-century reforms of the Ottoman Empire. Provincial correspondence, however, needs to be treated as an artifact of "politics of administration."[42] Reports written by inexperienced administrators lacking "a feeling of identification with the interests of the area in question" might be blurring how local notables were using the administrative structure of the nineteenth century. Furthermore, these reports could be designed particularly to filter out sensitive information. In a recent study, Meeker emphasizes how such reports might be selective in the way they provide information:

> The [central government] was always kept in the dark about certain matters by provincial governors. Provincial governors were always kept in the dark about certain matters by chief notables and district governors. No doubt the chief notables and district governors were also kept in the dark by the greater and lesser aghas of the outlying villages. All centralized bureaucracies work by filtering out information as it passes upward. Still, a centralized bureaucracy vertically segmented by tiered circles of interpersonal association could be expected to filter out information even more reliably and consistently.[43]

Critical approaches to provincial dynamics reveal a sense of continuity between the eighteenth and nineteenth centuries. In order to understand local notables' response to the transformations of the nineteenth century we need to

---

[39]   Pinson, "Ottoman Bulgaria," 114.

[40]   Ibid., 103.

[41]   Ibid., 104.

[42]   Huricihan İslamoğlu, "Politics of Administering Property: Law and Statistics in the Nineteenth-Century Ottoman Empire," in *Constituting Modernity: Private Property in the East and West*, ed. Huricihan İslamoğlu (New York: I.B. Tauris, 2004), 277.

[43]   Michael E. Meeker, *A Nation of Empire: The Ottoman Legacy of Turkish Modernity* (Berkeley: University of California Press, 2002), 260.

contextualize the changing dynamics of the environment that produced such reports of discontent instead of readily accepting the reports at face value. This requires understanding the transformation in the eighteenth and nineteenth centuries as a continuum and locating local notables in that context as agents.

Changing Land Tenure Patterns and "State–Society" Relations in Vidin

In her elaborate work on Mosul, Khoury notes that:

> Mosuli urban and rural societies were better integrated into the Ottoman "system" in the late eighteenth century, the century of decentralization, than they were in an earlier period when state controls were said to be more stringent. ... This approach to the eighteenth century makes dealing with the modern period somewhat less problematic. Instead of viewing the *Tanzimat* reforms as a rupture with the old order and as an initiative coming from a central state bureaucracy inspired by European models, we now can look at the internal social and political bases of the modern period. To be sure, not all of Mosul's gentry and merchants were supportive of the liquidation of political households and the old order. Nor were they enthusiastic about the model for reform espoused by the stronger elements among the state elite. However, they were engaged in the political debates of the time, and offered their own agendas for reform.[44]

Following a similar line of argument, Quataert notes that the "long nineteenth century" (1789–1922) "continued processes of change and transformation that had begun in the eighteenth century and sometimes before."[45] The nineteenth-century transformation of the Ottoman provincial administration should be understood in the context of "the dynamics inherent in seventeenth- and eighteenth-century decentralization, which can no longer be regarded as a manifestation of 'Ottoman decline' and a precondition for proto-nationalism."[46]

---

[44] Khoury, *State and Provincial Society*, 214.

[45] Donald Quataert, *The Ottoman Empire, 1700–1922*, 2nd edn (New York: Cambridge University Press, 2005), 54. Also see Rifa'at 'Ali Abou-El-Haj, *Formation of the Modern State*, 2nd edn (Syracuse, NY: Syracuse University Press, 2005), 81–90; Iris Agmon, *Family and Court: Legal Culture and Modernity in Late Ottoman Palestine* (Syracuse, NY: Syracuse University Press, 2006), 9; Ehud Toledano, "Social and Economic Change in the 'Long Nineteenth Century,'" in *Modern Egypt from 1517 to the End of the Twentieth Century: The Cambridge History of Egypt*, ed. M. W. Daly, vol. 2 (New York: Cambridge University Press, 1998), 252–3.

[46] Suraiya Faroqhi, "Introduction," in *The Later Ottoman Empire, 1603–1839*, ed. Suraiya Faroqhi (New York: Cambridge University Press, 2006), 11.

Understanding this continuum would allow us to see the transformation in the long nineteenth century as one led predominantly by internal factors, as opposed to a series of reforms that were designed by the imperial administration to superimpose "Western" institutions on Ottoman society.

Delineating the "internal social and political bases of the modern period" in their continuity over the last two centuries of the Ottoman Empire requires a different framing of Ottoman state–society relations: one that will account for the agency of certain local notables as part of emergent state institutions of the nineteenth century rather than opponents of the Ottoman modern state. Until recently, the literature on state–society relations in the Ottoman Empire in general has been dominated by two models: a strong state mitigating or co-opting oppositional groups or a weak state that existed separate from a relatively independent civil society.[47] The historiography on Ottoman administration in Bulgaria is no exception to this.[48] However, the relationship between state and society was not that simple. Scholars following Hourani's influential work on the "politics of notables"[49] pointed at the importance of building alliances with the local power elites for Ottoman imperial rule.

> [P]erhaps most critical for relations between the provinces and the central government, was the local social matrix within which the prerogatives of the government were played out. Although we have as yet relatively few and unevenly distributed studies of provincial Ottoman history, what is available points to the centrality of local familial and group networks in shaping the central state's relations with provincial societies.[50]

[47]　Khoury, *State and Provincial Society*, 213.

[48]　For an example of those who argue for a strong Ottoman state, see Valentina P. Dimitrova-Grajzl, "The Ottoman Economic Legacy on the Balkans," *SSRN* Working Paper Series (2 January 2007). As Fikret Adanir notes, "such research remain[s] more or less focused on the 'classical' Ottoman regime, subscribing thereby rather uncritically to what the Weberian archetypal concept of 'sultanism' implied—that is, a kind of patimonialism that left little room for negotiated solutions on the basis of popular acceptance" (Adanir, "Semi-Autonomous Provincial Forces," 157). For the second model that argues for a weaker Ottoman state see İnalcık, *Tanzimat ve Bulgar Meselesi*. For a more detailed discussion of this historiography see Faroqhi and Adanir, "Introduction."

[49]　Albert Habib Hourani, "Ottoman Reform and the Politics of Notables," in *The Modern Middle East: A Reader*, eds Albert H. Hourani, Philip S. Khoury, and Mary C. Wilson (New York: I.B. Tauris, 2004).

[50]　Dina Rizk Khoury, "The Ottoman Center versus Provincial Power-Holders: An Analysis of the Historiography," in *The Cambridge History of Turkey*, ed. Suraiya Faroqhi (New York: Cambridge University Press, 2006), 137.

Local social matrixes appear to have constituted the gray zone where the boundaries between the Ottoman state and its provincial society were blurry. Explicating this complex relationship is essential in understanding the local response to the *Tanzimat* reforms.

In explaining Ottoman state–society relations, Anderson notes "the historical significance of corporate, lineage, and tribal groups in exercising political authority alongside—*and sometimes within*—centralized bureaucratic administrations."[51] In nineteenth-century Vidin we see "a single government of state officials and local elites"[52] thanks to an election system that allowed local notables to serve as members in provincial councils for two-year periods.[53] This procedure was designed, primarily by Midhat Paşa,[54] to systematize local participation while preventing local administration from being an extension of provincial notables. Midhat Paşa traveled, for six months, to Paris, London, Vienna, and Brussels "with a view to the study of certain points of European

[51]   Lisa Anderson, "The State in the Middle East and North Africa," *Comparative Politics*, 20:1 (1987), 14. Emphasis is mine. Karen Barkey makes a similar note about the state–society relations in the Ottoman Empire during the seventeenth century. Karen Barkey, *Bandits and Bureaucrats: The Ottoman Route to State Centralization* (Ithaca, NY: Cornell University Press, 1994).

[52]   The phrase is from Meeker, *A Nation of Empire*, 210. For the later nineteenth century Meeker notes that "a tactic of sovereign power based on interpersonal association had continually reproduced the collusion of local elites and district officials generation after generation. An Ottomanist state society had come to occupy a place and play a role in the governmental structure of the westernized imperial system. Local elites and district officials were not representatives of two different political systems, but rather still part of a single governmental structure." Ibid., 256.

[53]   For diagrams explaining the administrative and the judicial structure in the provinces, see Petrov, "Tanzimat for the Countryside," 439–41. For a discussion of these councils and the election process in Vidin, see Mehmet Safa Saraçoğlu, "Some Aspects of Ottoman Governmentality at the Local Level: The Judicio-Administrative Sphere of the Vidin County in the 1860s and 1870s," *Ab Imperio*, 8:2 (2008), 233–54.

[54]   Midhat Paşa was one of the key figures, if not *the* key figure, behind the Ottoman provincial regulation of 1864, which transformed provincial administrative practices. The structure introduced in 1864 centered on offices and bureaucratic practices that, in theory, allowed members of the local populace to participate in provincial administration but prevented them from gaining permanent powerful positions. Provincial councils were established earlier in the nineteenth century; however, in 1864 the administrative and the judicial councils were connected to a variety of offices that controlled administrative, judicial, military, and financial affairs. For Midhat Paşa's role in the devising of the provincial administrative structure in the second half of the nineteenth century, see Mariia Nikolaeva Todorova, "Midhat Paşa's Governorship of the Danube Province," in *Decision Making and Change in the Ottoman Empire*, ed. Caesar E. Farah (Kirksville, MO: Thomas Jefferson University Press, 1993); Petrov, "Tanzimat for the Countryside."

administration with which he desired to make himself acquainted"[55] prior to submitting his plans for the provincial administration reform of 1864; however, we cannot assume that either *Tanzimat* in general, or the main framework for the administrative reforms had their origins in such trips and direct borrowings from other countries.[56] Furthermore, the Ottoman Empire's ability to incorporate local notables as part of its provincial rule—through a single government of state officials and local elite—pre-dated the mid-nineteenth century.

In his analysis of the provincial notables prior to the *Tanzimat* era, Adanir notes the following for the seventeenth century:

> The replacement of feudal forms of revenue distribution went hand-in-hand with the spread of ... tax-farming techniques that had previously been in use only on some larger estates. [... In this system tax was] levied not on a household basis [... but was] calculated for each commune as an annual lump sum. ... On the whole, the new regime had the effect of de-emphasizing differences in social status, religious affiliation and the urban or rural character of one's residence. The relationship between the state and the taxpayer became more fluid, and the land, the basic means of production in an agrarian society, became increasingly mobile, capable of being bought and sold.[57]

This transformation coincided with population decline in the countryside and local notables' ascendancy to power at the provincial level.[58] As the population decline of the seventeenth century was reversed in the Balkans in the course of the

---

[55]   Ali Haydar Midhat, *The Life of Midhat Pasha: A Record of His Services, Political Reforms, Banishment, and Judicial Murder* (London: J. Murray, 1903), 34–5.

[56]   Studies of Midhat Pasha's governorships show his sensitivity to the local socioeconomic and political structure in introducing the reforms elsewhere as well: Nejat Göyünç, "Midhat Paşa'nın Niş Valiliği Hakkında Notlar ve Belgeler," *İstanbul Üniversitesi Edebiyat Fakültesi Tarih Enstitüsü Dergisi*, 12 (1982), 279–316. Butrus Abu-Manneh, "The Genesis of Midhat Pasha's Governorship in Syria 1878–1880," in *The Syrian Land: Processes of Integration and Fragmentation in Bilad Al-Sham from the 18th to the 20th Century*, eds Thomas Philipp and Birgit Schäbler (Stuttgart: Franz Steiner Verlag, 1998).

[57]   Adanir, "Semi-Autonomous Provincial Forces," 166–7. The practice of communal levy continued until the last quarter of the nineteenth century.

[58]   Suraiya Faroqhi, "Crisis and Change, 1590–1699," in *An Economic and Social History of the Ottoman Empire*: vol. 2, *1600–1914*, eds Halil İnalcık and Donald Quataert (New York: Cambridge University Press, 1994), 442–52; Suraiya Faroqhi, "Rural Life," in *The Later Ottoman Empire*, 383–5; Jane Hathaway, "Egypt in the Seventeenth Century," in *Modern Egypt*, 38–9.

eighteenth century,[59] the financial pressure applied by tax farmers and notables to the peasants increased, at times leading to significant conflicts between the local power-holders and the imperial administration.[60]

"These power-holders ... nominally owed their positions to appointments on the part of the central government, and the execution of all too powerful *a'yan* was a frequent occurrence. Yet many magnate families for generations remained in the area where they once had become established."[61] As the prominence of these families increased so did their relations with other local families in the region. This eventually led to a many-tiered elite network in which the high-ranking imperial power-holders would exert their influence at the frontiers of their influence zone through lesser elites.[62]

When the highest tier of *a'yans* gradually lost their power vis-à-vis the imperial administration by the end of the eighteenth century, the lower tiers remained active and powerful and benefited from cooperation with the Ottoman administration.[63] In the eighteenth and nineteenth centuries, the power of local notables was primarily a function of two interdependent factors: their role as a part of the Ottoman state by getting involved with the tax collection practices; and their role as prominent figures of provincial communities as they became money lenders to peasants in need. Increased mobility of land in the nineteenth century meant accumulation of usufruct—and eventually ownership rights—on land in the hands of these notables.[64] This transformation of Ottoman "social integration"[65] was closely linked to the crisis of the "traditional social formation"[66] in the Empire that became apparent in the eighteenth century.

---

[59]   Bruce McGowan, "The Age of the Ayans, 1699–1812," in *Economic and Social History of the Ottoman Empire*, vol. 2, 652–3.

[60]   Ibid., 658–72; Adanir, "Semi-Autonomous Provincial Forces," 170–85; Zens, "The *Ayanlık* and Pasvanoğlu Osman Paşa," 44–98.

[61]   Faroqhi, "Coping with the Central State," 366–7.

[62]   Meeker, *A Nation of Empire*, 185–226. Meeker gives a four-tiered stratification consisting of the imperial elite, regional elite, greater local elites, and lesser local elites (see particularly his Table 2 on pages 224–5). Cf. Zens, "The *Ayanlık* and Pasvanoğlu Osman Paşa," 38–9; Khoury, "The Ottoman Center versus Provincial Power-Holders," 153–5; McGowan, "The Age of the Ayans," 662–3.

[63]   Meeker, *A Nation of Empire*, 210–26.

[64]   McGowan, "The Age of the Ayans," 662; Faroqhi, "Crisis and Change," 448; Faroqhi, "Rural Life," 381–5. Cf. Zens, "The *Ayanlık* and Pasvanoğlu Osman Paşa," 22–4.

[65]   My use is consistent with "System Integration and Social Integration," in *A Dictionary of Sociology*, eds John Scott and Gordon Marshall (New York: Oxford University Press, 2005).

[66]   I borrow this term from Jürgen Habermas, *Legitimation Crisis* (Boston, MA: Beacon Press, 1975), 19. Interestingly, the imperial reform decrees in the *Tanzimat* period often

Because these transformations mostly had to do with the way people related to means of production, particularly land, the institutional readjustment of the "system integration" in the nineteenth century focused on them as well—such as the transformation of tax collection methods, measures taken to prevent arbitrary confiscation of individuals' properties, and the Land Code of 1858.[67]

Crisis in a social system occur when "the consensual foundations of normative structures are so much impaired that the society becomes anomic. Crisis states assume the form of a disintegration of social institutions."[68] The Ottoman social formation responded to the crisis with an institutional reconfiguration during the long nineteenth century. These revisions to the institutional structure focused on legitimating the imperial order, which was done through a series of reforms that led to establishing particular limits on the power of the state. This process began prior to the *Tanzimat* era (1839–71) and continued into the early twentieth century. Among the more significant reforms was the establishment of local councils as provincial extensions of a newly emerging modern state that increasingly relied on economic exchange as the dominant steering medium and sought to complement the functioning of the self-regulative market commerce with civil law.

---

referred to the everlasting validity of a traditional order. A contemporary observer of the 1839 imperial decree of Gulhane—announcing the beginning of what came to be known as *Tanzimat* reforms—noted that the decree "starts by imputing the decline of the state principally to the transgression of the old laws, and then proceeds to adopt new regulations in the state, and then ends by praising the restoration of old manners and customs, as the sole means of salvation." James Porter and G.G. de Hochepied Larpent, *Turkey: Its History and Progress*, 2 vols (London: Hurst & Blackett, 1854), 2: 24. İslamoğlu, in her analysis of the Land Code of 1858, which introduced the "singular claim of ownership by the titleholder," points out how "drafters of the Code shunned all talk of a revolutionary change in property rights but were adamant in pointing to the fact that their task had been simply one of compiling and codifying old regulations and not introducing any new ones." Huricihan İslamoğlu, "Property as a Contested Domain: A Reevaluation of the Ottoman Land Code of 1858," in *New Perspectives on Property and Land in the Middle East*, ed. Roger Owen (Cambridge, MA: Harvard University Press, 2000), 26, 34.

[67]   I am not claiming that *all* of the nineteenth-century reforms associated with the *Tanzimat* era had to do with means of production. However, an analysis of some of these reforms indicates that the long nineteenth century corresponded to the crisis of the traditional social formation, the institutional restructuring related to that crisis, and the early phases of liberal-capitalist social formation. Mehmet Safa Saraçoğlu, "Letters from Vidin: A Study of Ottoman Governmentality and Politics of Local Administration, 1864–1877" (PhD dissertation: Ohio State University, 2007), 15–97.

[68]   Habermas, *Legitimation Crisis*, 2.

Local Councils as Spaces of Negotiation

Local councils were not unprecedented prior to the 1864 provincial regulation. Tax collection councils (*muhasıllık meclisi*) established two decades prior to the administrative councils *can be* considered as predecessors to the latter. These provincial councils helped with the institutional transformation of the long nineteenth century in three significant ways. First, they provided an essential framework to which different institutions of the new administrative model could be linked.[69] Second, they helped with the establishment of the reforms at the provinces and also disseminated the "textually mediated organization" of the modern Ottoman state.[70] This process was closely related to the growth of "a public sphere of state administration."[71] Third, they served as a means to institutionalize participation of the local notables in the administrative processes of the Ottoman state—a method which *may* render the application of reforms less problematic. Overall, these councils constituted a significant component of "a single government of state officials and local elites."[72]

Two closely related provincial regulations in 1864 and 1871 organized the structure and the procedures of the nineteenth-century Ottoman provincial administration in a rather systematic fashion. On the one hand, local notables were included in this framework as members of different provincial councils. On the other hand, the imperial administration sought to limit their influence by limiting the time local notables could serve on these councils to two years. This reflects the intentions of the state to establish a certain level of integration between the imperial administration and local populace, as much as to protect local administrative and judicial practices from being influenced by local politics.

Despite the imperial center's intentions, certain local notables in Vidin seem to have secured a prolonged presence on these councils. The provincial regulations of 1864 and 1871 did limit the time that members could serve to two years, yet did not ban reelection. Provincial yearbooks and other local correspondence referring to active council members indicate that many members managed to remain active in the institutional complex centered on the county administrative and judicial councils in Vidin through reelection. By serving on one council

---

[69] These included a variety of financial and scribal units of provincial administration that organized the economic, administrative, and judicial affairs of the county—such as the early forms of state-owned loan institutions, a survey committee, a commercial court, etc.

[70] Anthony Giddens, *The Nation-State and Violence: Volume Two of a Contemporary Critique of Historical Materialism* (Cambridge: Polity Press, in association with Basil Blackwell, 1985), 179.

[71] Ibid.

[72] Meeker, *A Nation of Empire*, 210.

for consecutive terms or by switching from the administrative council to council of appeals and crime, certain local notables established an organic link between the administrative and judicial public spheres of the modern Ottoman state in Vidin.[73] Thereby, the judicio-administrative sphere in Vidin reflected the power-politics among these local notables as its institutions became domains of negotiation. This sphere, with its institutions regulating the way local inhabitants related to means of production, provided a way for the local notables to respond to the legitimation crisis of the traditional social formation. It served as a space for the notables to continue their influence in the age of the modern state.

The local notables not only had a chance to exert their influence in the judicio-administrative sphere of the county but also—as part of a single government of state officials and local elites—did not feel the need to conceal this from the "imperial gaze" of the Ottoman Empire. Publication of these members' names in the pages of provincial yearbooks year after year indicate that both the provincial and the imperial centers were aware of their long-term influence within the administrative space despite specific regulations designed to prevent such sustained authority. Together with an official chronology of the empire, the timetable for the prayers, and a list of titles among the administrative ranks, the names of these notables became a part of the textually mediated organization of the Ottoman state presented in these yearbooks. Despite some minor errors, provincial yearbooks help us understand further details regarding the provincial administration. The names of people in different offices indicate that the judicio-administrative sphere was not limited to the administrative council and the council of appeals and crime. Several of those who served in these two more prominent offices of the judicio-administrative sphere served in other offices as well—such as the municipal council or the commercial court. When we take all these names into account, what emerges is a relatively consistent presence of a group of local notables in this sphere. These notables may not have been significant enough to be well known at the imperial level; the archives in Istanbul do not seem to have a lot of information about them, aside from some petitions that were sent either directly from Vidin or via the provincial capital in Ruse. This does not change the fact that they were rather prominent at the local level, and understanding how they operated within the judicio-administrative sphere is essential for contextualizing the correspondence from the provinces regarding the local populations' response to the transformations in the nineteenth century.

---

[73]   See n. 52 above.

It is mostly through the reports of these councils that the imperial administration became aware of what was happening in the provinces. And it is these councils that the local populace mostly consulted in order to resolve issues regarding property and taxation.[74] To a certain extent, these councils translated provincial life to the imperial center and explained the imperial perspective to the locals. Some members' long-term presence in this broader judicio-administrative sphere points to the significance of this local institutional complex and how it served as a space where notables could exert their influence.

Consider, for example, two significant members of this sphere: Ma'ruf Ağazade Ahmed Bey[75] and Sevastaki Ivanov Gunzovyanov (or Sevastaki Ağa as he was known as part of the Ottoman administrative framework). In the course of ten years that provincial yearbooks were published between 1868 and 1877, Ahmed Bey's name is listed as a member of the judicio-administrative sphere for a total of nine years and Sevastaki Ağa for six years. Other provincial correspondence and newspapers reveal that both were significant members of this sphere earlier.[76] While Sevastaki Ağa, coming from a notable family of Vlach descent from the village of Gumzovo[77] (approximately 9 miles northeast of Vidin), appears to have lost his prominence after Ottoman rule in Vidin County *de facto* ended in 1878,[78] Ahmed Bey remained active in the local administrative sphere even after 1878. Akhmed Beg Marufov, as he came to be known as part of the Bulgarian administration, was a member of Vidin's municipal council and among the donors of a large sum to the municipality

---

[74]   I do not wish to presume that these offices were the only places that property disputes were resolved. In addition to the *shar'i* court that dealt with inheritance cases there might be other socially accepted but unofficial venues for dispute resolution that were not recorded by the institutions of the judicio-administrative sphere: Agmon, *Family and Court*, 68–97. Property cases regarding foreigners in the Ottoman Empire had to use the council of appeals and crime after 1870: Sir Travers Twiss, *On Consular Jurisdiction in the Levant and the Status of Foreigners in the Ottoman Law Courts (Read at the Eighth Annual Conference of the Association for the Reform and Codification of the Law of Nations Held in the Hall of the National Council at Berne)* (London: William Clowes and Sons Ltd, 1880), 12ff. For a good account of the judicial transformation see Avi Rubin, "Ottoman Modernity: The Nizamiye Courts in the Late Nineteenth Century" (PhD dissertation: Harvard University, 2006).

[75]   The suffix "-zade" translates as "son of." Thus Ma'ruf Ağazade would mean "son of Ma'ruf Ağa."

[76]   Milena Christova Stefanova, *Kniga za Bulgarskite Chorbadzii* (Sofia: Univ. Izdat. Sv. Kliment Ohridski, 1998), 152 (Sevastaki Ağa's name is listed as a local notable in 1856); Saraçoğlu, "Some Aspects," 246–50.

[77]   Genadi Vulchev, *Vidni Vlasi ot Vidinskiya Krai* (Vidin: SD Ekspres, 2006), 148.

[78]   Ibid., 156–7.

in 1883.[79] Although he was affiliated with the Ottoman administration, and a "Turkish Muslim," he was appointed by the Russian imperial commissar, Duke (Kniaz) Dondukov-Korsakov, to the Constituent Assembly in Veliko Turnovo in 1879.[80] Akhmed Beg Marufov, together with Sevastaki Ağa's nephew by marriage, Ilia T. Tsanov[81]—(aka Hacı İliya Efendi), who served as a council member for several years in the Ottoman administration)—were among the 229 intellectuals who drafted the Turnovo Constitution that served Bulgaria from 1879 to 1947.[82]

Perhaps what is more interesting is the fact that Ma'ruf Ağazade Ahmed Bey and Sevastaki Ivanov Gunzovyanov were descendants of former *gospodars* Ma'ruf Ağa and Ivan Ganzov who, with other *gospodars*, wrote a letter thanking the imperial administration for giving them inheritable treasury certificates in exchange for land that was formerly under their control.[83] The "end" of the *gospodarlik* regime did not necessarily prevent these two families from using the new administrative structure as a space to continue their influence. While a contemporary Bucharest-based newspaper, *Svoboda* (*Freedom*), labeled Sevastaki Ağa "Turcophilic"[84] in an anonymous article that called for a regime change to eliminate both Christian and Muslim members of the old administration, Ahmed Bey's continued career suggests that the call was not heeded completely. Sevastaki Ağa must have ceased claiming a space for himself for more complex reasons; after all, other members of the Ottoman administration continued serving the Bulgarian administration.[85]

The council members were clearly aware of their powers. The elected members of these councils were not paid a salary, yet being at the center of these institutions rendered them significant members of the judicio-administrative sphere. In this position, they engaged in strategic negotiations of power with the rest of the members of this sphere and with the community in general. This was not a system where one person (such as Sevastaki Ağa or the appointed sub-governor) consistently dominated other Vidiners. Arguing for such domination, I believe, would not necessarily contribute to understanding how this complex power operated at the local level, interweaving the institutional

---

[79]   Vidin State Archives, f. 17 K, op. 1, l. 30 ▨▨▨.

[80]   Genadi Vulchev, *Vidinskite Rodove*, vol. 1 (Vidin: n.p., 2001), 73.

[81]   Ibid., 32, 158.

[82]   Ibid., 622.

[83]   BOA İ.DH. 13733 (15 February 1851).

[84]   *Svoboda*, 8 January 1872.

[85]   Such as Tseko Vanchov, who represented Vidin in the Second General National Assembly (*Obiknoveno Narodno Subranie*) of the newly established Bulgaria in 1881: Genadi Vulchev, *Deputatite ot Vidinski Oblast* (Vidin: n.p., 2003), 624.

structure and the agents utilizing that structure. Local administration was a highly politicized process at this time of institutional restructuring, and documents produced or edited by the offices of this textually mediated judicio-administrative sphere reflected the political nature of this process. One thing seems to be certain, however: the local notables were not left out of this transformation. They adapted and survived through the formation of the modern state in the Ottoman Empire into the Bulgarian kingdom.

Index